PHARAOHS AND MORTALS

EGYPTIAN ART
IN THE MIDDLE KINGDOM

Frontispiece: King Senusret III, Cat. no. 28

PHARAOHS AND MORTALS

EGYPTIAN ART
IN THE MIDDLE KINGDOM

Catalogue by Janine Bourriau,
Keeper of Antiquities,
Fitzwilliam Museum,
with a contribution
by Stephen Quirke

Exhibition organised by
the Fitzwilliam Museum
Cambridge 19 April to 26 June
Liverpool 18 July to 4 September
1988

Cambridge University Press

Cambridge
New York New Rochelle
Melbourne Sydney

Fitzwilliam Museum

Cambridge

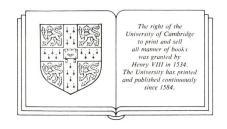

Published by the Press Syndicate of the University of Cambridge
The Pitt Building, Trumpington Street, Cambridge CB2 1RP
32 East 57th Street, New York, NY 10022, USA
10 Stamford Road, Oakleigh, Melbourne 3166, Australia

First published 1988

British Library cataloguing in publication data
Bourriau, Janine
Pharaohs and mortals: Egyptian art in the Middle
Kingdom: exhibition organized by the Fitzwilliam
Museum, Cambridge 19 April to 26 June, Liverpool
18 July to 4 September 1988. –
(Fitzwilliam Museum publications).
1. Art, Egyptian – Exhibition
I. Title II. Quirke, Stephen III. Fitzwilliam
Museum IV. Series
709'.32'074   n5350

Library of Congress cataloguing in publication data
Bourriau, Janine.
Pharaohs and mortals: Egyptian art in the Middle Kingdom/
catalogue by Janine Bourriau; with a contribution by Stephen
Quirke.
p. cm. – (Fitzwilliam Museum, publications)
"Exhibition organised by the Fitzwilliam Museum, Cambridge 19
April to 26 June, Liverpool, 18 July to 4 September 1988."
Includes index.
ISBN 0 521 35319 X. ISBN 0 521 35846 9 (pbk)

1. Art, Egyptian – Exhibitions. 2. Art, Ancient – Egypt –
Exhibitions. 3. Egypt – Civilization – To 332 B.C. – Exhibitions.
I. Quirke, Stephen. II. Fitzwilliam Museum. III. Title.
IV. Series.
N5336.G7C3634 1988
709'.32'07402659 – dc19   87-30908

ISBN 0 521 35319 X hard covers
ISBN 0 521 35846 9 paperback

Filmset and printed by BAS Printers Limited,
Over Wallop, Hampshire

CONTENTS

FOREWORD

For most of us Egyptian art means the monuments of the New Kingdom (1550–1070 BC) which still dominate the landscape: the temples of Karnak and Luxor, the Valley of the Kings, and the tombs of the nobles at Qurnah. The buildings and sculptures of the Middle Kingdom (2023–1650 BC) were conceived on a less massive scale, and they have not survived so well into our own time; but in quality of design and execution they frequently surpass the achievements of later artists. The elegance of the gold pectoral from Eton and the brutal power of the colossal head of Senusret III in Cambridge were not to be matched. Since it is through objects, rather than through standing monuments, that Middle Kingdom art has survived, we can hope to indicate its range in this exhibition.

Our purpose is to illustrate the distinctive style of the epoch in all the arts: in sculpture, painting on wood, jewellery, calligraphy, literature, ceramics and metalwork. It is perhaps surprising that no previous exhibition on this theme has been mounted. It would not have been possible now to draw together such a wealth of material without the generous collaboration of the many lenders.

Almost every major collection of Egyptian antiquities in the United Kingdom, both public and private, has contributed objects. Our profound thanks are due to all of them: the Bolton Museum and Art Gallery; the Bristol Art Gallery and Museum; the Museum of Archaeology and Anthropology, Cambridge; the Oriental Museum, University of Durham; the Royal Museum of Scotland, Edinburgh; the Myers Museum, Eton College; the Burrell Collection, Glasgow; the Liverpool Museum and Department of Egyptology, the University of Liverpool; the British Museum; the Petrie Collection, University College, London; the Manchester Museum; Norwich Castle Museum; the Ashmolean Museum, Oxford; a private collection in East Anglia. One of the lenders, the Liverpool Museum, has joined with us in offering the exhibition to the public. We are delighted that it will be shown there after its inauguration in Cambridge.

Cambridge in 1988 seems a propitious place and time to inaugurate an exhibition on this theme, for several reasons. Principal among them is the choice and scope of the Fitzwilliam's own collection of Middle Kingdom art, which contains two of the acknowledged masterpieces of royal sculpture of Dynasty XII: the granite head of King Senusret III, Cat. no. 28; and the shelly limestone head of Amenemhat III, Cat. no. 31. Such sculptures have too often been treated as magnificent aberrations outside the normal conventions of Egyptian art. One of our aims is to place them in a context, to allow them to be seen alongside earlier and later royal sculpture, such as the superb reliefs of Senusret I from the Petrie collection or those of Nebhepetre Montuhotep from the British Museum, and alongside the sculptures produced to honour individual men and women of the Middle Kingdom. Another stimulus has been the recent research in many different branches of Egyptology which is forcing scholars to reconsider many of the inherited certainties conditioning our interpretation of the history and culture of the time.

Above all, the exhibition has been made possible by generosity, both the generosity of the lenders and, no less essential to our enterprise, that of our sponsors, Edward Billington & Son Ltd; Jack Ogden Ltd; and the Hon. Lady Hastings.

We gratefully acknowledge a loan from the Marc Fitch Fund to meet the cost of colour printing of the catalogue. The Cambridge University Press has borne the costs of printing and distribution. Public support has come in the form of Treasury indemnity to cover the major part of the insurance costs of loans.

MICHAEL JAFFÉ

INTRODUCTION

The art of the Middle Kingdom (2023–1650 BC) early attracted the attention of scholars and connoisseurs, and Henry Wallis summed up its charm for the first generation of Egyptologists as a combination of skill in execution and refinement of taste. He chose the head of King Amenemhat III, Cat. no. 31, to encapsulate the style of the epoch (*Burlington Fine Arts Club*, 1895, p. ix).

Between 1890 and 1914 all the important Middle Kingdom sites shown on the map, p. 167, were excavated, and at the end of those twenty-four years the framework defining the history, art and archaeology of the period seemed fixed and immutable. Just as one ceases to notice the features of an acquaintance as the eye becomes dulled by familiarity, so scholars did not remark the inconsistencies and the lack of precision in dating even the most characteristic products of the age. The first full account of the period as a whole is contained in W. C. Hayes's first volume of *The Scepter of Egypt*, published in 1953 as a 'background to the study of the Egyptian Antiquities in the Metropolitan Museum of Art in New York'. Hayes drew on a magnificent and comprehensive col-

31

lection of Egyptian art, but by 1953 very few studies had been published which undertook a reappraisal of what was already known by 1914. What Hayes provided was a synthesis of the state of knowledge at the end of the first two and a half decades of excavation, together with tantalising glimpses of more recent discoveries as yet unpublished.

Thirty-five years further on from Hayes, much of what he said still appears valid but needs testing against a vastly increased body of knowledge. Almost all of this derives from specialist studies of particular regions, for example Dendera (Fischer), Abydos (Kemp, Snape), Thebes (Arnold) and Elephantine (Habachi, Edel), or of particular classes of object, for example scarabs, stelae, coffins, statuary and pottery. It is noticeable that only the work of Habachi, Edel and Arnold is based on the results of new excavations; the rest depends upon study of objects whose original find-spots are unknown or on minute analysis of the records from the prime period of excavation in the late nineteenth to early twentieth century.

From these studies a few themes emerge which contrast sharply with the traditional views of Middle Kingdom art and society. The first and most far-reaching question is whether or not Egypt was a cultural unity throughout the period, as had been assumed by almost all the early excavators. In my view, apart from a relatively brief period of just over 100 years in the late XIIth Dynasty, Upper, Lower and Middle Egypt need to be considered independently. It follows from this that comparisons between sites in different regions may be misleading, and that a grave of Dynasty XI at Qau will contain different objects from one of the same date at Sidmant: see comment on Cat. no. 131. The Delta is even today almost completely unknown apart from preliminary reports from Tell Dab'a in the East. This Middle Kingdom town was taken over by a foreign community in the late XIIIth Dynasty so may in any case hardly present a typical picture.

Another theme is the way in which society functioned, where power resided and how the King's authority was delegated to run the state. It is clear that the last of these changed dramatically more than once, and our appreciation of this dynamic contrasts with the static view of the Middle Kingdom held by earlier scholars. One reason for this is that the XIIIth Dynasty is now generally thought of as belonging to the Middle Kingdom, whereas formerly it was placed in the following Second Intermediate Period. Much of the evidence for the way in which society was organised has come from study of the monuments of private individuals, and particularly stelae such as Cat. no. 49. The people of the Middle Kingdom, or rather the literate elite who held offices in the state, left their names everywhere, on statues, in tombs, in rock inscriptions and on their personal possessions as well as in their official records. The potential of this rich documentation is only being realised now that it is being collected together and published by scholars such as Franke, Simpson, Malaise and Vernus. However, it is already providing evidence to challenge the accepted chronology of the period, see below p. 4. Since it provides a series of dated monuments by means of a network of family relationships with occasional references to contemporary Kings, e.g. Cat. no. 45, the potential

value for the art historian is immense.

The idea of holding this exhibition grew naturally out of a desire to re-examine objects in the Fitzwilliam's collection in the light of these new studies. Through the generosity of the lenders it has been possible to enlarge its scope so as to present to the public many beautiful and relatively unknown objects, and to explore the many different ways in which the culture of the time was expressed.

The exhibition contains only 260 items, so can make no claim to survey the whole range of Middle Kingdom art, but certain aspects have been chosen for emphasis. The glory of the Middle Kingdom is its sculpture and this is a major theme. Within it we can observe the contrast between sculptures made for the King and those produced for private persons, the use of different materials and the changes which occurred in the course of time. The first section of the catalogue is devoted to Sculpture with three chronological subdivisions. The next section, written by Dr Stephen Quirke, is devoted to Writing and Literature. The Middle Kingdom was as creative in this sphere as in that of the visual arts, and in a culture where, it has been argued, representational art grew out of writing, the two remain inextricably bound together.

49

2

The next two sections, Funerary Art and Art and Magic, aim to set objects within the contexts for which they were made. Many aspects of Egyptian culture are alien, and some frankly repugnant, to a society like ours where the supernatural world has no role in the commerce of daily living. Explanations of the concepts involved may or may not help but should not be allowed to come between an object and the observer's appreciation of it. The final section includes the whole range of the Decorative Arts, from ceramics to metalwork. Here the aim has been to illustrate the craftsmanship and inventiveness in both materials and design that so characterise the Middle Kingdom.

A few comments on the format of the individual entries may be helpful. The chronology used for the Middle Kingdom is discussed and set out in the section following this introduction and has been written by Stephen Quirke. For sculpture in the round a standard set of measurements of the face is given. The length of the face is measured from the wigband to the chin, and the width is taken at the widest part, which is usually, but not invariably, at the eyes. The normal position for the ears is for the ear hole to be level with the outer corner of the eye. The first part of each entry provides a description of the object, then after details of provenance, source, museum number and measurements, a commentary is given. The line drawings have been printed at a scale of 1:1 except for Cat. nos. 119, 122a, 186–7, which are at a scale of 1:2, and Cat. nos. 176a, e, 178a, b, and the lotus pendant from Cat. no. 154, which have been enlarged to 2:1. In the case of inscribed objects all the names of private persons and any titles or epithets which occur have been included in an index on pp. 164–6. It is hoped that this index, in conjunction with the photographs, will satisfy the needs of scholars until facsimile drawings and full philological commentary are eventually published.

Some of the painted wooden objects in the exhibition are extremely fragile and cannot be sent to the showing in Liverpool. These, all Fitzwilliam Museum objects, are the coffins, Cat. nos. 68, 70, 72, the mask, Cat. no. 69, and the tomb models, Cat. nos. 92–5. It is hoped that similar objects from the Liverpool collections will replace them and it has already been agreed that the outer coffin of Userhet, which is in the Department of Egyptology of the University of Liverpool, will replace his inner coffin, Cat. no. 72. For this reason the outer coffin has been included in the catalogue as Cat. no. 71.

One of the greatest pleasures the preparation of this catalogue has given me is the opportunity to visit again my colleagues in other museums. They have been unstintingly generous of their time and expert knowledge and their encouragement has supported me throughout. I should like to thank the following for their help: Mrs Barbara Adams, Miss Carol Andrews, Mr Michael Balance, Miss Mary Cra'ster, Dr Rosalie David, Mr Vivian Davies, Dr Elizabeth Goring, Miss Barbara Green, Miss Rosalind Hall, Mr John Hayman, Mr Harry James, Mr Paul Quarrie, Mr John Ruffle, Professor Peter Shore, Mr Stephen Spurr, Dr Jennifer Stewart, Dr Angela Thomas, Mr James Thompson, Dr Helen Whitehouse and Miss Patricia Winker. Many people have generously supplied me with information from work unpublished or in press, namely Dr Dorothea Arnold, Miss Diana Magee, Dr Jaromír Málek, Dr G. T. Martin, Dr Geraldine Pinch, Dr Stephen Quirke, Dr Stephen Snape and Dr Donald Spanel. The title of the exhibition was suggested by an English translation of a series of essays on Egyptian history by Professor Torgny Säve-Söderbergh published in 1963. I am most grateful to him for allowing me to use it.

I owe particular debts to four people: Dr Piotr Bienkowski of the Liverpool Museum, whose enthusiasm has been instrumental in arranging a showing of the exhibition in Liverpool; Dr Stephen Quirke, who wrote the sections on Writing and Literature and Chronology, and supplied background information on names and titles; Mr Peter French, who helped throughout in the checking and correcting of the manuscript; and Mr Aidan Dodson, who helped in innumerable ways in the preparation of the text.

My colleagues in the Fitzwilliam have contributed to the catalogue in many ways: the Director, Professor Michael Jaffé, has provided continuous support for the project; Miss Julie Dawson, Mr Robert Bourne and Mr Matthew Buckley have cleaned and restored many of the Fitzwilliam's objects; Miss Bridget Piper has photographed many items specially for the catalogue; Mr Andrew Norman and Mr Andrew Morris have contributed photographs, including those from the Myers Museum, Eton. I am especially grateful to Miss Imogen Isern and Miss Pery Burge, who typed the manuscript.

All the line drawings are the work of Mr Andrew Boyce and the map was drawn by Mr Michael Clifford.

I am also particularly grateful to Mr William Davies and Miss Lynn Chatterton who supervised production of the catalogue, and to its sub-editor, Dr Rosemary Morris, and designer, Mrs Margaret Downing, all of Cambridge University Press.

J.D.B.

CHRONOLOGY

In reckoning time across years, the Egyptians had no fixed starting point in the manner of our eras BC–AD, but instead dated events by the year of the current King's reign. In theory, then, a complete list of reign-lengths, allowing for gaps and overlaps, should provide a timetable for the full three thousand years of pharaonic history. Although no single text contains an unbroken series, ancient Kinglists do survive from Egyptian and Greek sources. The most valuable of these lists is the fragmentary papyrus known as the Turin Canon, dating to the Ramesside period (thirteenth century BC). It records the exact length of each reign, down to the nearest day, and in its present condition covers all the Kings from the mythical period when gods ruled on earth to the end of the Second Intermediate period (first half of the sixteenth century BC). The traditions recorded in the Kinglists by and large confirm the evidence of contemporary sources for each period, and the resulting internal framework is pegged at intermittent points to absolute dates calculated from Egyptian records of astronomical observations. Thanks to the astonishing continuity of pharaonic culture, and through its links with other kingdoms, the chronology of ancient Egypt acts as a touchstone for the history of the entire ancient Near East.

At the heart of the Middle Kingdom stands the XIIth Dynasty, the most stable royal line ever to rule Egypt. In at least three cases the King took his heir to the throne as coregent during the last few years of the reign, to consolidate the dynasty at the vulnerable transfer of power. From this secure base, its eight monarchs cover a span of two centuries. The internal sequence and absolute dates of the period have been regarded as among the most secure in the pre-classical world. Lengths of reigns were established from the Turin Canon with the corroboration of contemporary inscriptions, while papyri from the temple of Senusret II at Lahun included notes on observations of the moon and the star Sirius, from which absolute dates could be reckoned and allotted to a particular King's reign. During the past decade, the scholarly consensus on this standard chronology has given way to uncertainty. The new debate revolves around the reigns of Senusret II and his son and successor, Senusret III. According to the previous interpretation of the Lahun papyri, Senusret III cannot have ruled for less than thirty-six years. An accountancy text in one of the papyri reveals that year 19 of one King in the late XIIth Dynasty was followed by year 1 of the next King. Since Senusret III was thought to have reigned thirty-six years, and since we have records of a year

46 of Amenemhat III, the year 19 and year 1 could only refer to Senusret II and Senusret III respectively, in the scheme of the standard chronology. The accepted arrangement of the Turin Canon fragments supports this view; the loose fragment placed in line with the spaces for Senusret II and Senusret III would allot them 19 and 30 + x years.

Up to this point there is no difficulty, but serious problems arise when we try to accommodate contemporary hieroglyphic inscriptions. In year 14 of Senusret III, an expedition sent to quarry stone in the Eastern Desert included three 'overseers of gangs of quarrymen', by name Sehetepibra, Montuhotep and Khetywah; the third of these is attested again in an expedition of year 2 of Amenemhat III, while the first two (or men of the same name and title) took part in an expedition in year 3 of Amenemhat III. If the standard chronology is retained, the texts would show the same men in the same positions returning to the quarries after an interval of twenty-five years (year 14 Senusret III to years 2/3 Amenemhat III). The same difficulty with the standard chronology recurs at Abydos, where the temple of Osiris was embellished by a team under the direction of the treasurer Iykhernofret and his assistant Sisatet; the stelae left by members of the team date to year 19 of Senusret III and year 1 of Amenemhat III. Since no text speaks of separate building work at Abydos under Amenemhat III, it is difficult not to conclude that his year 1 followed immediately upon year 19 of his father, Senusret III. A third problem for the traditional chronology arises with the career of a military official, Khusobek; a stela from Abydos tells us that the 'commander of the town regiment' Khusobek was born in year 27 of Amenemhat II, while a graffito at the Second Cataract, the frontier, dates Khusobek 'commander of the sovereign's troops' to year 9 of Amenemhat III. If the two texts refer to the same person, and we keep to the dates of the traditional chronology, then Khusobek would be in active service at the Second Cataract at the age of 69. This is not impossible, but it does seem impractical in terms of military patrolling. The most reasonable interpretation of the hieroglyphic sources taken together would place year 19 of Senusret III immediately before year 1 of Amenemhat III. Accordingly the Lahun account papyrus of year 19 to year 1 would refer respectively to Senusret III and Amenemhat III, and not to Senusret II and III. As additional strong support for the new interpretation, it can be noted that no contemporary text records a date higher than year 7 for Senusret II, and year 19 for Senusret III.

4

If we wish to argue that Senusret III ruled for nineteen years, instead of thirty-six, we must account for the astronomical data in the Lahun papyri and the evidence of the Turin Canon, since those two pillars established the former standard chronology. The contemporary material from Lahun does not seem to present insurmountable obstacles to the new dates. The exact dating from astronomical calculations can accommodate parallel series of possible solutions in cases where the papyrus itself omits to mention the name of the reigning King. The most recent re-examination of the papyri which contain astronomical observations has come down in favour of the new chronology with a short reign for Senusret III. To obtain the correct concordances between astronomical dates and the regnal years of unnamed Kings in the papyri, future research will depend as much on identifying and following the careers of officals in the texts as on the ambivalent astronomical information. Whereas the Lahun papyri can be reconciled with the revised chronology, it is not yet possible to explain the figures given in the Turin Canon. Even if the fragment for the length of reigns of Senusret II and III is misplaced, the explicit total of 213 years for the XIIth Dynasty does not allow for shorter reigns for the two Kings. In defence of the new chronology, it can only be said that the Turin Canon was compiled some six hundred years after the death of Senusret III, and at that distance in time it is conceivable that errors may have crept into the Kinglist tradition.

Below, the former standard chronology is laid out beside the revised dates for the XIIth Dynasty. It would be rash in the present uncertainty to be didactic in selecting one set of dates against the other, and this exhibition follows the revised chronology in order to explore its challenge to the previous consensus, rather than to impose it as the correct history. If the new dates are finally accepted, it will be necessary to find a satisfactory explanation for the duration of the dynasty as preserved in the Turin Canon. Another stumbling-block may prove to be an accounts text from Kahun in which year 26 of a late XIIth Dynasty King appears to postdate a year 33 (Griffith, *Kahun Papyri*, pl. xxi, lines 1–14), an order of dates which would contradict the revised chronology.

Although the problem of chronology introduces an uneasy note of doubt into Middle Kingdom studies, it is worth setting this into context. The likely margin of error, at thirty years, cannot be considered daunting when the period in question stands at a remove of forty centuries from our own time. In both versions of the chronology for the Middle Kingdom, the XIIth Dynasty determines the dates for the preceding and following periods. The XIIIth Dynasty is a particularly confused age, in which about fifty Kings came and went on the throne in the space of perhaps little over a century. In the middle of the XIIIth Dynasty some political stability was restored with a 'sub-dynasty' of three brothers, Neferhotep I, Sihathor and Sobekhotep IV. By an indirect connection to Mesopotamian chronology, Neferhotep I can be dated with some certainty to c. 1730–1720 BC, and this agrees with the scattered evidence for the Kings between the end of the XIIth Dynasty and his reign. Curiously the frequent change of King seems to have affected neither the cultural continuity nor the ideology of kingship, and the XIIIth Dynasty slavishly shadows its more glorious predecessors of the XIIth Dynasty.

King/Period	Standard chronology	Revised chronology
Dynasty XI	2040–1991	2023–1963
Dynasty XII	1991–1783	1963–1787
Amenemhat I	1991–1962	1963–1934
Senusret I	1971–1926	1943–1899
Amenemhat II	1929–1892	1901–1867
Senusret II	1897–1878	1869–1862
Senusret III	1878–1841	1862–1844
Amenemhat III	1844–1797	1843–1798
Amenemhat IV	1799–1787	1797–1790
Sobeknefru	1787–1783	1789–1787
Dynasty XIII	1783–1650 (?)	1786–1650 (?)

R. A. Parker, *The Calendars of Ancient Egypt* (Chicago, 1950), passim; R. A. Parker in *Studies in Honour of George R. Hughes* (Chicago, 1976), pp. 177–89; R. Krauss, *Sothis- und Monddaten* (Hildesheim, 1985), passim; J. von Beckerath in *GM* 83 (1984), pp. 13–15; W. K. Simpson, 'Sesostris II and Sesostris III' in *LÄ*, v, 899–906; K. A. Kitchen in *Orientalia* 36 (1967), pp. 39–54.

GENERAL ABBREVIATIONS

D: diameter
H: height
L: length
W: width

JOURNALS AND OTHER PUBLICATIONS

Aldred, *Middle Kingdom Art*: C. Aldred, *Middle Kingdom Art in Ancient Egypt* (London, 1950).

Aldred, *Jewels of the Pharaohs*: C. Aldred, *Jewels of the Pharaohs* (London, 1971).

Andrews, *Jewellery*: Carol A. R. Andrews, *Catalogue of Egyptian Antiquities in the British Museum. Jewellery*, I: *From the Earliest Times to the Seventeenth Dynasty* (London, 1981).

Arnold, *Mentuhotep*: D. Arnold, *Der Tempel des Königs Mentuhotep von Deir el-Bahari*, I–II (Mainz, 1974).

Arnold, *Temple*: D. Arnold, *The Temple of Mentuhotep at Deir el-Bahari* (New York, 1979).

ASAE: *Annales du Serivce des Antiquités de l'Egypte* (Cairo, 1900ff).

Aryton *et al.*, *Abydos III*: E. R. Ayrton, C. T. Currelly and A. E. P. Weigall, *Abydos III* (London, 1904).

Barta, *Selbstzeugnis eines altägyptischen Künstlers*: W. Barta, *Das Selbstzeugnis eines altägyptischen Künstlers* (Munich, 1970).

von Beckerath, *Zweiten Zwischenzeit*: J. von Beckerath, *Untersuchungen zur politischen Geschichte der zweiten Zwischenzeit in Ägypten* (Glückstadt and New York, 1965).

BIFAO: *Bulletin de l'Institut Français d'Archéologie Orientale du Caire* (Cairo, 1901ff).

Blackman, *Meir*, I–VI: A. M. Blackman, *The Rock Tombs of Meir*, I–VI (London, 1914–1953).

BMMA: *Bulletin of the Metropolitan Museum of Art* (New York, 1905ff).

BMQ: *British Museum Quarterly* (London, 1926–1973).

Boston Bulletin: *Bulletin of the Museum of Fine Arts* (Boston, 1903ff).

Bourriau, *Three Middle Kingdom Sculptures*: J. Bourriau, 'Three Middle Kingdom Sculptures in the Fitzwilliam Museum, Cambridge', *Fourth International Congress of Egyptologists: Abstracts of Papers* (Munich, 1987), 26–7.

Bourriau, *Pottery*: J. Bourriau, *Umm el-Ga'ab: Pottery from the Nile Valley before the Arab Conquest* (Cambridge, 1981).

Breasted, Jr, *Servant Statues*: J. H. Breasted, Jr. *Egyptian Servant Statues* (Washington, 1948).

British Museum, *Hieroglyphic Texts*, II: British Museum, *Hieroglyphic Texts from Egyptian Stelae etc. in the British Museum*, Part II (London, 1912).

British Museum, *Hieroglyphic Texts*, IV: British Museum, *Hieroglyphic Texts from Egyptian Stelae etc. in the British Museum*, Part IV (London, 1912).

British Museum, *Sculpture Guide*: British Museum, *Guide to the Egyptian Galleries in the British Museum (Sculpture)* (London, 1909).

Budge, *Catalogue*: E. A. Wallis Budge, *A Catalogue of the Egyptian Collection in the Fitzwilliam Museum, Cambridge* (Cambridge, 1893).

Burlington Fine Arts Club, 1895: Burlington Fine Arts Club, *Exhibition of the Art of Ancient Egypt* (London, 1895).

Burlington Fine Arts Club, 1922: Burlington Fine Arts Club, *Ancient Egyptian Art* (London, 1922).

Carnarvon and Carter, *Five Years*: The Earl of Carnarvon and Howard Carter, *Five Years' Explorations at Thebes* (Oxford, 1912).

Chassinat and Palanque, *Assiout*: E. Chassinat and C. Palanque, *Une Campagne de Fouilles dans la Nécropole d'Assiout* (Cairo, 1911).

David, *Pyramid Builders*: A. R. David, *The Pyramid Builders of Ancient Egypt* (London, 1986).

de Garis Davies, *Antefoker*: N. de Garis Davies, *The Tomb of Antefoker and his Wife Senet* (London, 1920).

Davies, *A Royal Statue Reattributed*: W. V. Davies, *A Royal Statue Reattributed*, British Museum Occasional Papers no. 28 (London, 1981).

Downes, *Esna*: D. Downes, *The Excavations at Esna, 1905–1906* (Warminster, 1974).

Dunham Essays: *Studies in Ancient Egypt, the Aegean and the Sudan. Essays in Honor of Dows Dunham*, ed. W. K. Simpson and W. M. Davis (Boston, 1981).

Egypt's Golden Age: *Egypt's Golden Age: The Art of Living in the New Kingdom 1558–1085 BC* (Museum of Fine Arts, Boston, 1982).

Emery, Smith and Millard, *Buhen*, I: W. Emery, H. S. Smith and A. Millard, *The Fortress of Buhen. The Archaeological Report* (London, 1979).

Engelbach, *Harageh*: R. Engelbach, *Harageh* (London, 1923).

Erman, *Literature*: A. Erman, *The Literature of the Ancient Egyptians*, translated by A. M. Blackman (London, 1927. Reprinted New York, 1977).

Evers, *Staat aus dem Stein*, I, II: H. Evers, *Staat aus dem Stein*, I–II (Munich, 1929).

Faulkner, *Dictionary*: R. O. Faulkner, *A Concise Dictionary of Middle Egyptian* (Oxford, 1962).

Fechheimer, *Kleinplastik*: H. Fechheimer, *Kleinplastik der Ägypter* (Berlin, 1922).

Firth and Gunn, *Teti Pyramid Cemeteries*: C. M. Firth and B. Gunn, *The Teti Pyramid Cemeteries* (Cairo, 1926).

Fischer, *Dendera*: H. G. Fischer, *Dendera in the Third Millennium B.C.* (New York, 1968).

Fischer, *Turtles*: H. G. Fischer, *Ancient Egyptian Representations of Turtles* (New York, 1968).

Franke, *Personendaten*: D. Franke, *Personendaten aus dem Mittleren Reich* (Wiesbaden, 1984).

Gardiner, *Grammar*: A. H. Gardiner, *Egyptian Grammar* (Oxford, 1957).

Gardiner, *Onomastica*, I, II: A. H. Gardiner, *Ancient Egyptian Onomastica*, I–II (Oxford, 1947).

Garstang, *Burial Customs*: J. Garstang, *The Burial Customs of Ancient Egypt* (London, 1907).

Garstang, *El Arábah*: J. Garstang, *El-Arábah* (London, 1901).

GM: *Göttinger Miszellen* (Göttingen, 1972ff).

Ll. Griffith, *Kahun Papyri*, I, II: F. Ll. Griffith, *Hieratic Papyri from Kahun and Gurob*, I–II (London, 1897–1898).

Habachi, *Heqaib*: L. Habachi, *The Sanctuary of Heqaib, Elephantine IV* (Mainz, 1985).

Hayes, *Scepter*, I, II: W. C. Hayes, *The Scepter of Egypt*, I–II (Metropolitan Museum of Art, New York, 1953–1959).

ILN: *The Illustrated London News* (London, 1842ff).

JARCE: *Journal of the American Research Center in Egypt* (Boston, 1962ff).

JEA: *Journal of Egyptian Archaeology* (London, 1914ff).

JNES: *Journal of Near Eastern Studies* (Chicago, 1942ff).

Kaczmarczyk and Hedges, *Faience*: A. Kaczmarczyk and R. E. M. Hedges, *Ancient Egyptian Faience* (Warminster, 1983).

Kemp and Merrillees, *Minoan Pottery*: B. J. Kemp and R. S. Merrillees, *Minoan Pottery in Second Millennium Egypt* (Mainz, 1980).

Klebs, *Reliefs*: L. Klebs, *Die Reliefs und Malereien des Mittleren Reiches* (Heidelberg, 1922).

Kühnert-Eggebrecht, *Die Axt*: E. Kühnert-Eggebrecht, *Die Axt als Waffe und Werkzeug im alten Ägypten* (Berlin, 1969).

LAAA: *Liverpool Annals of Archaeology and Anthropology* (Liverpool, 1908–1948).

LÄ: W. Helck, E. Otto and W. Westendorf, *Lexikon der Ägyptologie* (Wiesbaden, 1972–1987).

Lichtheim, *Literature*, I: M. Lichtheim, *Ancient Egyptian Literature*, I: *The Old and Middle Kingdoms* (Berkeley and Los Angeles, 1975).

Lilyquist, *Mirrors*: C. Lilyquist, *Ancient Egyptian Mirrors from the Earliest Times through the Middle Kingdom* (Munich, 1979).

Lucas, *Industries*: A. Lucas, rev. J. R. Harris, *Ancient Egyptian Materials and Industries*, 4th edn (London, 1962).

McConnell, *Treasures of Eton*: J. McConnell, *The Treasures of Eton* (London, 1976).

Mace and Winlock, *Senebtisi*: A. Mace and H. E. Winlock, *The Tomb of Senebtisi at Lisht* (New York, 1916).

Martin, *Seals*: G. T. Martin, *Egyptian Administrative and Private-Name Seals* (Oxford, 1971).

Mélanges Vercoutter: F. Geus and F. Thill (eds), *Mélanges offerts à Jean Vercoutter* (Paris, 1985).

MDAIK: *Mitteilungen des Deutschen Archäologischen Instituts. Abteilung – Kairo* (Augsburg, Wiesbaden and Mainz, 1930ff).

Mogensen, *Glyptothèque Ny Carlsberg*: M. Mogensen, *La Glyptothèque Ny Carlsberg. La collection égyptienne* (Copenhagen, 1930).

MMJ: *The Metropolitan Museum Journal* (New York, 1968ff).

Murray, *Splendour*: M. A. Murray, *The Splendour that was Egypt* (London, 1949).

Naville, *Deir el-Bahari*, I, II, III: E. Naville, *The XI Dynasty Temple at Deir el-Bahari*, Parts I–III (London, 1907–1913).

Newberry, *Beni Hasan*, I, II: P. E. Newberry, *Beni Hasan*, Parts I, II (London, 1893, 1894).

Page, *Egyptian Sculpture*: A. Page, *Egyptian Sculpture from the Petrie Collection* (Warminster, 1976).

Peet, *Cemeteries of Abydos* II: T. E. Peet, *The Cemeteries of Abydos*, II (London, 1914).

Petrie, *Dendereh*: W. M. Flinders Petrie, *Dendereh* (London, 1900).

Petrie, *Diospolis Parva*: W. M. Flinders Petrie, *Diospolis Parva* (London, 1901).

Petrie, *Gizeh and Rifeh*: W. M. Flinders Petrie, *Gizeh and Rifeh* (London, 1907).

Petrie, *Illahun*: W. M. Flinders Petrie, *Illahun, Kahun and Gurob* (London, 1891).

Petrie, *Kahun*: W. M. Flinders Petrie, *Kahun, Gurob and Hawara* (London, 1890).

Petrie et al., *Labyrinth*: W. M. Flinders Petrie, G. A. Wainwright and E. Mackay, *The Labyrinth, Gerzeh and Mazghuneh* (London, 1912).

Petrie et al., *Lahun*, II: W. M. Flinders Petrie, G. Brunton and M. A. Murray, *Lahun*, II (London, 1923).

Petrie and Brunton, *Sedment*, I–II: W. M. Flinders Petrie and G. Brunton, *Sedment*, I–II (London, 1924).

Petrie, *Tombs of the Courtiers*: W. M. Flinders Petrie, *The Tombs of the Courtiers and Oxyrhynkhos* (London, 1925).

Petrie, *Tools and Weapons*: W. M. Flinders Petrie, *Tools and Weapons* (London, 1917).

PSBA: *Proceedings of the Society for Biblical Archaeology* (London, 1879–1918).

Quibell, *El Kab*: J. E. Quibell, *El Kab* (London, 1898).

Quibell, *The Ramesseum*: J. E. Quibell, *The Ramesseum*, bound with R. Paget and A. Pirie, *The Tomb of Ptah-hetep* (London, 1898).

Ranke, *Personennamen*: H. Ranke, *Die ägyptischen Personennamen*, I–III (Glückstadt, 1935–1977).

Reisner, *Ships and Boats*: G. A. Reisner, *Models of Ships and Boats* (Cairo, 1913).

RdE: *Revue d'Egyptologie* (Paris, 1933ff).

SAK: *Studien zur altägyptischen Kultur* (Hamburg, 1973ff).

Saleh and Sourouzian, *Cairo Museum*: M. Saleh and H. Sourouzian, *The Egyptian Museum, Cairo* (Mainz, 1987).

Schneider, *Shabtis*: H. D. Schneider, *Shabtis*, I–III (Leiden, 1977).

Simpson, *Terrace*: W. K. Simpson, *The Terrace of the Great God at Abydos: The Offering Chapels of Dynasties 12 and 13* (New Haven and Philadelphia, 1974).

Smith et al., *Buhen*, II: H. S. Smith et al., *The Fortress of Buhen: The Inscriptions* (London, 1976).

Smith, *Art and Architecture*: W. Stevenson Smith, *The Art and Architecture of Ancient Egypt* (Harmondsworth, 1958).

Spanel, *Boat Models*: D. Spanel, 'Ancient Egyptian Boat Models of the Herakleopolitan Period and Eleventh Dynasty' (in press).

Steindorff, *Magical Knives*: G. Steindorff, 'The Magical Knives of Ancient Egypt', *Journal of the Walters Art Gallery* 9 (1946), pp. 41–51, 106–7.

Top. Bibl., I–VII: B. Porter and R. L. B. Moss (eds), *Topographical Bibliography of Ancient Egyptian Hieroglyphic Texts, Reliefs and Paintings*, I–VII (Oxford, 1927ff).

Tufnell, *Scarab Seals* II: O. Tufnell, *Studies on Scarab Seals*, II: *Scarab Seals and their Contribution to History in the Early Second Millennium B.C.* (Warminster, 1984).

Vandier, *La Statuaire Egyptienne*: J. Vandier, *Manuel d'Archéologie Egyptienne*, III: *Les Grandes Epoques: La Statuaire* (Paris, 1958).

Vernus, *Le Surnom*: P. Vernus, *Le Surnom au Moyen Empire* (Rome, 1986).

Wallis, *Ceramic Art 1898*: H. Wallis, *Egyptian Ceramic Art: The Macgregor Collection* (London, 1898).

Wallis, *Ceramic Art 1900*: H. Wallis, *Ancient Egyptian Ceramic Art* (London, 1900).

Ward, *Scarab Seals*, I: W. A. Ward, *Studies on Scarab Seals*, I: *Pre-12th Dynasty Scarab Amulets* (Warminster, 1978).

Wildung, *L'Age d'Or*: D. Wildung, *L'Age d'Or de l'Egypte*, translation of *Sesostris und Amenemhet: Ägypten im Mittleren Reich* (Fribourg, 1984).

Wilkinson, *Egyptian Jewellery*: A. Wilkinson, *Ancient Egyptian Jewellery* (London, 1971).

ZÄS: *Zeitschrift für ägyptische Sprache und Altertumskunde* (Leipzig and Berlin 1863ff).

CONCORDANCE OF MUSEUM NUMBERS AND CATALOGUE NUMBERS

E.489.1954	149c	N.501	19
E.498.1954	168b	N.1984	52
E.500a–e.1954	168a		
E.501.1954	169		
E.616.1954	180c		

Museum collections concordance

E.489.1954	149c
E.498.1954	168b
E.500a–e.1954	168a
E.501.1954	169
E.616.1954	180c
E.626.1954	175a
E.641.1954	81
E.671–5.1954	170a
E.676–80.1954	167
E.683–4.1954	170a
E.686–7.1954	170b
E.689.1954	170b
E.36.1955	176e
E.64.1955	164b
E.72.1955	122b
E.16.1969	21
E.5.1979	166a
E.6.1979	166b
E.10.1979	166c
E.426.1982	104a
E.60.1984	114
E.2.1986	104b
EGA.607.1943	181a
EGA.1728.1943	173b
EGA.1729.1943	173c
EGA.1945.1943	176b
EGA.2416.1943	129a
EGA.2418.1943	129b
EGA.2420.1943	129c
EGA.2424.1943	129d
EGA.2431.1943	129e
EGA.2433.1943	129f
EGA.2442.1943	129g
EGA.2450.1943	129h
EGA.2452.1943	129i
EGA.2478.1943	87b
EGA.3005.1943	30
EGA.3079.1943	89a
EGA.3080.1943	89b
EGA.3127.1943	5
EGA.3143.1943	2
EGA.3298.1943	44
EGA.3994a.1943	73a
EGA.3994b.1943	73b
EGA.4591a.1943	128d
EGA.4591b.1943	128e
EGA.4698.1943	161
EGA.6502.1943	34
EGA.82.1949	29
EGA.226c.1949	176c
E.FG.42a	128b
E.FG.42b	128c
E.S.11	147c
E.SC.41	182c
E.SC.170	182b
E.SC.180	183a
E.W.66a	67a
E.W.66b	67b
E.W.82	66

Oriental Museum, University of Durham

H.2259	143

N.501	19
N.1984	52

Royal Museum of Scotland, Edinburgh

1911.260	97
1911.284	121
1991.338	87a
1914.1079	159
1921.893	102
1923.350	16
1952.158	51
1952.197	17
1959.24	18
1965.6	56

Myers Museum, Eton College

1	90
7	23
10	35
17	22
36.15	24
634	127
832	156
2199	123

Burrell Collection, Glasgow

13/242	54

Liverpool Museum, National Museums on Merseyside

49.56	36
55.82.114	74
1966.178	55
1977.110.2	99

Department of Egyptology, University of Liverpool

E.30	48
E.160	108
E.512	71
E.7081	115

British Museum, London

EA.579	20
EA.969	58
EA.1348	45
EA.1450 (1907 10–15 460)	3
EA.1450 (1907 10–15 497)	4
EA.2572	140
EA.2736	186
EA.3077	154
EA.10060	59
EA.10182/1	60
EA.10549	61
EA.10676/24	64
EA.10752/3	62
EA.21578	139a
EA.21579	139b
EA.35004	111
EA.49343	83

EA.54678	138
EA.57375	190
EA.58080	47
EA.58240	134
EA.65268	171a
EA.65429	53
EA.65440	27
EA.69519	38

Petrie Collection, University College, London

6482	157
8711	46
14363	32
14786	11
16027	77
16069	98
16126	76
16229	174
16657	14
16741	109
18232	131
18356	137
18744	88b
18758	126
19625	33
21660	136a
21662	136b
27975	88a
30072	191
32036	65
32037	63

Manchester Museum, University of Manchester

169	125
189	185
206	184
268	116
6135	43

Norwich Castle Museum

37.21(1)	91

Ashmolean Museum, Oxford

E.1971	9
E.2149	146
E.3275	106a
E.3297	113
E.3299	106b
E.3738	80
E.E.472	163
1922.212	96
1971.950	124

Private Collection, Cambridgeshire

	118

Private Collection

	179

DYNASTY XI–EARLY DYNASTY XII: NEBHEPETRE MONTUHOTEP TO SENUSRET II, 2023–1862 BC

The reign of Nebhepetre Montuhotep of Dynasty XI represents a turning point in Egyptian history, which was recognised by contemporaries and successor Kings just as much as it is now by scholars. His statues and monuments were never defaced or usurped by later Kings and he was venerated, like Amenhotep I who ruled at the beginning of the New Kingdom, as the initiator of a new and powerful line of kings. When Montuhotep came to the throne and, in the Egyptian fashion, immediately commanded work to start on his tomb and mortuary temple, Cat. nos. 3–7, he controlled Thebes and the area immediately around it, equivalent to modern Luxor and the province of Qena. The rest of Egypt was controlled by local princes like Sennedjsui of Dendera, Cat. no. 1, and Mesehti of Asyut, Cat. no. 23. At Heracleopolis, just south of the Faiyum in Lower Egypt, was the capital of a rival dynasty, each of whose Kings claimed, as did Montuhotep himself, to be 'the Lord of the Two Lands, King of Upper and Lower Egypt'. By 2004 BC, nineteen years

8

after he became King, Montuhotep had conquered the North, defeated the Heracleopolitans and taken Memphis and become in reality King of Upper and Lower Egypt. He commemorated this by including the epithet 'Uniter of the Two Lands' in his titles for the rest of his reign. The impact of

the unification on the art of the King's reign was profound because Montuhotep found in the necropolis of Memphis, between Giza and Saqqara, the great line of pyramids and temples built for the Kings of the Old Kingdom. He took into his service men trained in the traditions of the Memphite workshops, men like Intefnakht who describes on his stela (Barta, *Selbstzeugnis eines altägyptischen Künstlers*, pp. 128–9) how he first served the Heracleopolitan Kings and was then brought to Thebes where he served Montuhotep as overseer of sculptors (*gnwtyw*), craftsmen (*hmww*) and casters of metal (*mstw*). The skills of such a man were thought of as akin to those of a priest or sorcerer because he made images which he could imbue with life and power. When his skills were devoted to preparing the buildings to celebrate the King's mortuary cult, upon the efficiency of which the survival of the order of the world depended, then he must have commanded immense authority, setting him above the rivalries of Dynasties. After the unification Montuhotep rebuilt his great mortuary temple at Thebes to a more grandiose design, incorporating into it elements of architecture and decoration (see Cat. no. 7), taken from the royal temples of the Old Kingdom. The style as well as the content of the relief in the latest part of the temple, the sanctuary (Cat. nos. 5–6) differs remarkably from the earliest, Cat. nos. 3–4. It is altogether less mannered, cut less deep but showing a subtle contouring of the surface. This late style evolves into the relief of the reign of Senusret I (Cat. no. 11), invigorated by a further, more brutal, confrontation with the Old Kingdom monuments of Memphis.

Amenemhat I, father of Senusret I, moved the royal residence north, to a new site, called appropriately *Itj-Tawy*, 'Seizer of the Two Lands' (close to modern Lisht 40 miles south of Cairo). There he built his pyramid and mortuary temple, which were completed by his son, Senusret I, after Amenemhat's premature death by assassination, see Cat. no. 60. The builders of the pyramid of Amenemhat I demolished royal buildings at Giza and Saqqara to provide rubble fill for its interior, but ironically, during the process of destruction both the style and the decorative scheme of the older relief were taken over by the royal artists. The same artists worked on the mortuary complex of Senusret I, built a few miles to the south of that of Amenemhat I, and as one might expect much of the relief is very similar. The Koptos relief, Cat. no. 11, dates from later in the reign and shows the mature style evolved during Senusret's massive building programme and as the previous generation of master sculptors was replaced by a new one. The stela (R. O. Faulkner in *JEA* 38 (1952), pp. 3–5, pl. 1) of one such man, Shen, tells us how he moved from Lisht to work for the King at Abydos and, en passant, that his son was also a sculptor (*gnwty*). Shen exemplifies a pattern of life which we may assume all the master craftsmen of the King followed – *viz* an introduction into the royal workshops as a boy through a relative or patron and a long apprenticeship learning to copy the methods and style of the masters, until finally sent out by the King to work on a series of building projects. Firstly this process explains a basic homogeneity of style we can observe in the buildings and statuary of a particular reign, no matter where they are situated in Egypt. Without it, our attempts to analyse royal monuments or date private ones by analogy to royal styles would be futile. The question of whether the style of royal monuments did vary by following the artistic traditions of different localities still remains and is discussed below pp. 37–9. Secondly the training process explains the attachment of the work of the early part of a reign to the artistic traditions of a King's predecessor. This makes true innovations, when they occur, for example in royal sculpture in the round in the reign of Senusret III, all the more startling and radical. We can be sure, too, that changes when they appear as suddenly as this were willed by the King, since only he had the authority to break with the past and so speed up the natural rate of change determined by the replacement of one generation of craftsmen, approximately every twenty to twenty-five years, with another.

Relief and sculpture on private monuments at all times shows a time lag, before the changes we observe first on royal monuments appear. The length of the gap depends on many factors, and at the beginning of the Middle Kingdom we can identify some of them. Geography was one factor. Permanent royal workshops we may presume to have existed in Upper Egypt at Thebes and Abydos, the sacred necropolis, burial place of Osiris and place of pilgrimage; in Lower Egypt at Lisht, the new capital; and, we may presume, at Memphis. Temporary royal workshops were set up for individual projects, and we can estimate how long they existed, and thus how they might have affected private sculpture from the locality, only if there is independent evidence in the building itself, or in the administrative record of the length of time the project took. We can contrast the situation of Dendera, relatively close to Thebes and where Nebhepetre Montuhotep, Nebtawy-re Montuhotep and Senusret I all built shrines to Hathor, with Asyut and Beni Hasan, remote from the centres of royal power, ruled by local families and with strong artistic traditions of their own going back to the First Intermediate Period.

Another vital factor was access to royal patronage. A man usually achieved this by being attached to the King's service in the Residence or elsewhere (Cat. no. 21), or to a cult important to the King, as was the priest Senusret, son of Ip, Cat. no. 19. What royal patronage could mean, the story of Sinuhe, placed in the reign of Senusret I and the most popular and certainly the most entertaining story to come down to us from the Middle Kingdom (see below p. 75) tells us: 'A stone pyramid was built for me in the midst of the pyramids.

The masons who build tombs constructed it. A master draughtsman designed it. A master sculptor carved in it. The overseers of construction in the necropolis busied themselves with it. All the equipment that is placed in a tomb shaft was supplied. Mortuary priests were given me. A funerary domain was made for me. It had fields and a garden in the right place, as is done for a Companion of the first rank' (Lichtheim, *Literature*, 1, p. 233). The king allowed the most favoured ones a site for their tombs close to his own funerary monument and a place for a statue in his mortuary temple. He supplied materials (stone and precious metals were mined and distributed under royal control) and the craftsmen to work them. As is to be expected, the resulting private monuments copy the style of contemporary royal monuments, while adapting the architecture and iconography for private use.

25

Lesser figures within the orbit of these great men shared in the benefits of their patrons and so the artistic influences spread outwards from the centre.

The reign of Senusret I, which was long (forty-five years) and marked by an extensive building programme all over Egypt, was also crucial in spreading what has been called the court style. From south to north, remains of his buildings have been found at Elephantine, El Kab, Hierakonpolis, El Tod, Armant, Karnak, Koptos (see Cat. no. 11), Dendera, Abydos, Memphis, Heliopolis and Bubastis, and also in the Faiyum. Nevertheless, the artistic resources of the country were rich enough for the same period to see splendid monuments erected for provincial governors, called nomarchs, at El Bersheh, Meir, Beni Hasn, Asyut and elsewhere. During the First Intermediate Period, when no single ruler controlled Egypt, each province evolved its own style (see Cat. nos. 23, 90), and those traditions continued through the XIth and early XIIth Dynasties, idiosyncratic and self-contained. The statuary which has survived from these provincial centres shows a preference for the use of wood (Cat. nos. 23, 25, 27), perhaps because hard stones or the skill to carve them in the round (the limestone relief of the rock-built tombs of the nomarchs, though variable, can show the highest skill) were not available without access to the royal workshops.

It is not surprising that the innovations in private sculpture, for example the block statue, Cat. nos. 21–2, and the pose showing a seated man wrapped in a cloak, Cat. no. 19, and the practice of dedicating a statue or stela to receive offerings in temple or private shrine appear first within the sphere of the court style. Nevertheless the provincial centres produced their finest work at this period, due perhaps to the increased resources of a strong and unified country. Their workshops produced not only sculpture but also coffins (see Cat. nos. 67, 68, 70–3), ceramics (Cat. nos. 130, 132), and jewellery, but they did not survive long after the political changes of the late XIIth Dynasty. The local power of the nomarchs was destroyed, and as a result local craftsmen lost their patrons. The late XIIth–XIIIth Dynasty successors of the major and minor officials who had been buried at Beni Hasan in the early Middle Kingdom, for example, left their monuments at the sacred site of Abydos or in the vast cemeteries growing up around the mortuary establishments of Kings, in the Faiyum, at Lisht, Dahshur and Thebes.

1 RELIEFS FROM THE TOMB OF SENNEDJSUI
Dynasty IX, c. 2134–2040 BC.

Two fragments from a stela, (a) and (b), which join, and one from an architrave (c) from a tomb, carved in deep sunk relief in limestone. The stela shows the steward Sennedjsui leaning on a staff facing the two much smaller figures of his daughters, Hetepi and Bebi. They offer him cylinder jars of scented ointment, sealed and tied with string, see Cat. no. 149. The architrave fragment (c) comes from a procession of sons and daughters bringing food offerings. This fragment shows Sennedjsui's fourth son, Khui, offering the symbolic haunch of meat, and a daughter holding a tray of cakes. Above their heads runs part of the autobiographical

1a

inscription of Sennedjsui, written from right to left. Each figure is identified in a line of vertical hieroglyphs, whose signs face the same direction as the figures. The women wear long wigs with straight lappets, the men full shoulder-length wigs. All faces share the same mannered style with large features crammed into a tiny face, with a minimum of interior modelling. Brows are straight, eyes enormous and heavily outlined, inner canthi (tear ducts) marked despite the small scale, noses prominent with a profile continuous with the forehead, and lips shown as two strips fitted into a triangular groove between nose and chin. The ears are set low, their outer rim represented as a simple oval loop. Both men and women wear bead collars, and the men a short kilt with a triangular fold in the front.

From Dendera, mastaba of Sennedjsui. (a), (b) Bolton 56.98.37; (c) Bolton 56.98.36. (a), (b) H: 32.8 cm. W: 94.0 cm. (c) H: 37.5 W: 37.0.

These reliefs represent just one of the schools of sculpture which grew up in the provinces during the period immediately before the unification of Egypt in Dynasty XI at the beginning of the Middle Kingdom. Local craftsmen evolved their own distinctive styles in response to the demand of powerful local rulers for funerary monuments to commemorate themselves and their families, cf. also Cat. no. 23. Senned-

1c

1b

jsui belonged to one such provincial dynasty and tells us in his inscription how he rewarded the builders of his tomb with bread, beer, grain, copper, clothing, oil and honey. His name means 'Brother of the common people' and he goes on to claim that he provided the security which allowed every citizen to go safely about his business, the gardeners to gather their leeks and the foresters to grow their sycamore trees. His claims may be no more than the formulae of conventional piety, however, since neither his title nor those of his son suggest great power. Dendera itself, 35 miles north of Thebes, was rather a backwater, its prestige arising mainly from the local cult of the goddess Hathor, whom Hetepi served as a priestess.

The Bolton reliefs show the Dendera sculptural style at the end of its evolution from the Old Kingdom, when it was barely a generation away from being overtaken by a new one. This was introduced by the artists serving the Theban princes who became rulers of Upper and Lower Egypt in later Dynasty XI. The reliefs still contain archaisms, attaching them to the art of the Old Kingdom, both in general composition and in details of pose, costume and inscriptions. The impact on private sculpture of the new artistic stimulus at Dendera may be judged by comparing these reliefs with the dyad of Mentuhotep and Nefermesut, Cat. no. 9, from the same site, or the stela of Mentuhotep from Abydos, Cat. no. 10.

Petrie, *Dendereh*, pl. x; Fischer, *Dendera*, pp. 154–65, figs. 31, 33c.

2 KING NEBHEPETRE MONTUHOTEP WEARING FEATHER CROWN

Dynasty XI, early in reign of Nebhepetre Montuhotep, 2023–2004 BC.

Fragment of fine limestone sunk relief showing the head and part of the feather crown of the King. The fragment probably comes from a seated figure, because of the position of the handle of a flail held against the left shoulder. The features compare closely with Cat. no. 4. The eyebrow, which is carved in relief, is exceptionally long, running the whole width from forehead to crown. It is almost straight, making a slight dip at the outer corner of the eye in order to run parallel with the cosmetic line. The eye itself is unnaturally large and wide and outlined with a relief band ending in a long fish-

tailed cosmetic line. There is a pronounced 'beak' to mark the inside tear duct, the eyeball is round and the pupil painted black. There is considerable modelling under the eye. The ears have the overall shape of those of Cat. no. 4, but show differences of detail, such as the question-mark shape of the outer rim. The short broad nose, the thick protruding lips of almost equal size and shape, and the round chin, are common to all three reliefs, Cat. nos. 2–4. The King wears a bead collar of five strands. The generally rounded surfaces of the relief are especially noticeable at the base of the neck and behind the ears.

2

Gift of R. G. Gayer-Anderson. Fitzwilliam EGA.3143.1943. H: 12.2 cm. W: 17.1 cm. Depth of relief 0.25 cm.

We do not know where or when between 1910 and 1944, when he lived in Egypt, Gayer-Anderson acquired this relief, but we can place it with reasonable confidence among the early relief sculptures of the reign of King Nebhepetre Montuhotep. The deep, crisp cutting and the mannered yet elegant style are unmistakable. Sunk relief in this style is known to occur at the mortuary temple of the King at Deir el-Bahri, in the shrines of the King's six concubines (see Cat. nos. 3–4), and in the corridor leading to the offering chamber of his Queen Neferu. However, none of the fragments from these monuments published to date shows the king wearing this distinctive crown. It is composed of a double plume of feathers fitted on to a helmet base and has the unique particularity that the feathers overlap the front edge of the helmet. The same headdress, but without this feature, is worn by the god Amun in the scenes in the sanctuary of the temple, but these were carved later in the reign in a completely different style, see Cat. no. 5. Early in his reign Nebhepetre Montuhotep built a small chapel at Dendera in honour of the goddess Hathor, and enough of it has survived for its decorative scheme to be reconstructed by Labib Habachi. The King does appear there wearing this crown, among others, but there is no gap in the scenes, which are mostly executed in raised relief, which could be filled with a figure of the King holding the flail, probably seated, and wearing the feather crown. The only other reliefs in which he wears this crown are on sandstone blocks from a shrine at Elephantine at Aswan, executed in a significantly different style, and several graffiti on Konosso island, close to Philae. However, little remains to us of the monuments of this King. Many buildings have disappeared altogether or are represented for us by a few blocks recovered by chance from their re-use in later buildings. We know he built at Karnak, Abydos and Gebelein, as well as Dendera and Elephantine, but very little of the decorative scheme of these buildings remains.

Even if we cannot assign this fragment to a particular royal monument, it is evidence nevertheless that early in his reign Nebhepetre was adopting for his own use a version of a divine crown. This crown was in origin an attribute of the god Min, who at this time was being assimilated at Thebes with the minor deity, Amun. The innovations in royal iconography of this reign are another illustration of the changes in ideas accompanying the increase in the King's authority which culminated in the reunification of Upper and Lower Egypt.

Cf. L. Habachi in *MDAIK* 19 (1963), pp. 16–52; for Amun in the Sanctuary see Arnold, *Mentuhotep*, II, p. 33, pl. 43.

3 THE ROYAL CONCUBINE, KEMSIT

Dynasty XI, early in reign of Nebhepetre Montuhotep, 2023–2004 BC.

Limestone fragment of high raised relief, with most of the original paint preserved, showing a seated woman holding a jar of scented ointment to her nose. The hand of a servant pouring liquid into a pottery drinking cup is visible in front of her and above is a line of hieroglyphs which reads 'for thy *ka*, gifts and offerings'. The background colour of the relief is pale grey, and of the figure deep pink, and the plaster or pigment has been applied thickly, sometimes obliterating the fine detail of the carving. Kemsit wears her natural hair, which is painted black, short, and tightly curled. Her ear, like other areas of the prominent relief, has suffered damage. Her brow is carved in relief and generally, but not slavishly, follows the contour of the eye. This is large, wide open and outlined in relief which ends in a long thin cosmetic line. The inner canthus is emphasised, marked by a sharp downward curve at the inner corner of the eye (cf. Cat. nos. 2, 4). The pupil, brow, band around the eye and cosmetic line were originally black. The nose is short and broad, the deep curve defining the nostril obscured by paint. The mouth characteristically (cf. Cat. nos. 2, 4) shows upper and lower lips of equal size and shape. They are straight and full, defined by an incised line, and meet in a deep groove at the corner of the mouth. The chin is small and the cheeks are plump with the jawline only faintly suggested. Her arms are well rounded, with a marked indentation for the elbow, and the fingers and thumb exceptionally long and thin. There are traces of a deep reddish brown pigment on hands and arm of the servant and the thumbnail is painted white. Kemsit wears a shawl, painted white over finely incised cross-hatching which may indicate the weave of the linen. The ends of the

shawl lying on her shoulders, simplified into two elongated triangles, have been painted green like the rest of her dress. This is probably a mistake by the painter. The dress itself is the usual tunic, ending under the breasts with narrow straps over the shoulders, but it is shown here in elaborate detail. Both the band under the breasts and the straps are decorated, and this is indicated by vertical and horizontal incisions respectively. The dress itself, by comparison with other examples, appears to have two layers, an overskirt decorated with a feather motif on top of a plain pleated tunic which appears below her knees. Each feather of the decoration is outlined and, in the upper part of the overskirt, the internal markings of each one are incised, only to be obscured later by the painter. Her jewellery consists of bracelets (green) and a collar of six rows of beads.

From the shrine of Kemsit, temple of Nebhepetre Montuhotep at Deir el-Bahri, Thebes. Gift of the Egypt Exploration Fund. British Museum EA. 1450 (1907 10–15 460). H: 37.5 cm. W: 35.4 cm.

The great temple of Montuhotep went through at least three major changes of design, and this fragment belongs to the earliest stage of the building. When Montuhotep brought Upper and Lower Egypt under his sole authority, c. 2004 BC, he took the name, *Sma-tawy*, 'Uniter of the Two Lands', into his titulary. The resulting change in his inscriptions, together with a meticulous study of the architecture, have helped Dieter Arnold to identify the different phases of the building. The tombs and associated cult shrines of six concubines of the King were part of the original plan. This fragment comes from the east wall of the shrine of one of them, called Kemsit, and shows her seated receiving offerings from a servant, if the extremely provisional restoration by Naville, the original excavator, is accepted (Naville, *Deir el-Bahari* II, pl. xx). Part of it is certainly incorrect; the fragment of an ostrich feather shown above Kemsit's head belongs to the feather fan behind the King and is not part of her headdress. Fragments of relief from the shrines, from the stone sarcophagi of these women and from the tomb of a Queen called Neferu, whose monument also belongs to the early phase of the building, are now scattered world wide in Museums and private collections. Until they are reunited in a thorough study we can only make isolated observations on the extraordinary quality and subject matter of the reliefs (see also Cat. no. 4).

The fine texture of the limestone has helped to create the sharp edges and rounded surfaces which characterise this early relief style. By cutting so deep (0.5 cm) in both raised and sunk relief (cf. Cat. no. 4) the sculptor has given himself space for overlapping layers of relief, each carrying an immense amount of surface detail. The technical virtuosity of the sculptor was not shared by the painter who followed him, and there are marks of his carelessness everywhere. Much of the sculptural detail, of the feather pattern on the dress for example, is simply obliterated, nor are the transitions from one plane to another respected, for example in the painting of the arms.

The subject matter of the relief from the shrines of the concubines is unique for their period, in that the figure of the King is introduced into scenes adapted from the repertoire

3

used for private tombs. It is likely that figures of the King, not much larger than Kemsit herself, were carved in registers on either side of her seated figure. She sits in a pose little changed from one popular in Old Kingdom tombs, holding an ointment jar, of a similarly old-fashioned shape, up to her nose. She carries no special mark of the King's favour. The only unusual element in her dress is her shawl; in other respects she is dressed like an ordinary woman. The colour and ornamentation of her dress may seem exceptional, but this is not so. What is exceptional is the loving reproduction in the carving of every element in the design. Elsewhere this is often carried out in paint alone, which frequently does not

survive, so leaving us with a false impression that the ubiquitous dress for women was a tunic with shoulder straps, made of plain linen. Kemsit is sometimes shown with her skin painted black, but this does not imply, as Naville thought, that she was African. For Egyptians black was the colour of the soil: the 'Black Land' was Egypt itself. Black symbolised fertility and rebirth, so it was an appropriate colour for the dead seeking their own renewal in the Next World. Funerary masks and coffins often have black faces, see Cat. no. 72. In Kemsit's robbed tomb two mummies were found lying on two feet of accumulated debris. Naville identified one of them, for no good reason, as Kemsit herself, stating the skull was of negroid type. Unfortunately this cannot now be verified because this mummy is not in the British Museum as he states (W. V. Davies, personal communication).

Naville, *Deir el-Bahari*, I, pp. 50–1, pl. XVII, c; II, pl. XX; *Top Bibl.*, I², Part I, p. 385; for the temple generally, Arnold, *Mentuhotep*, I, passim; Arnold, *Temple*, pp. 39–45. For Kemsit's dress, cf. Hayes, *Scepter*, I, fig. 174.

4 KING NEBHEPETRE MONTUHOTEP AND KEMSIT

Dynasty XI, before the unification, 2023–2004 BC.

Fine limestone fragment of sunk relief with much of the original paint preserved, showing Montuhotep and Kemsit. The dominant colour of the relief is yellow and the body of the King shows traces of deep pinkish red over a thin layer

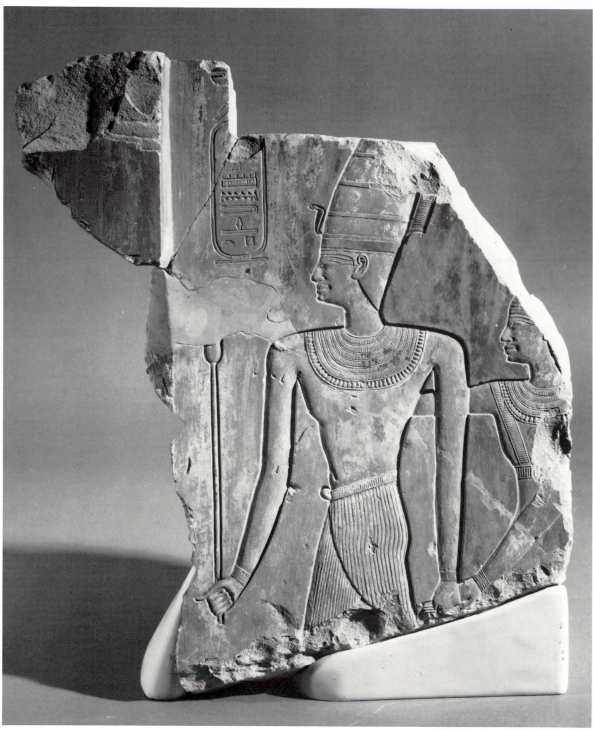

4

of fine white plaster. The same colour was used for his crown and bracelets. His bead collar was originally blue and Kemsit's hair, black. They hold each other by the hand and her right arm enfolds him. The dress and the modelling of the head of Kemsit closely follow that of Cat. no. 3, though the work is certainly not by the same hand. The shape of the eyebrow is straighter and thinner on this relief and she does not wear a shawl over her back. She is shown only slightly smaller than the King, her nose being level with his shoulder. The King, whose name, in a cartouche, is carved in front of him, wears an extraordinary crown, unique not only to him but to representations of him in the early relief style of his reign. It is the crown of Upper Egypt, with a uraeus-snake in front and two feathers at the back, shown overlapping each other. The features of the face are identical to those of Kemsit, with the same strong curves around the nose, at the corner of the mouth and defining the chin. The ear is long and oval, very much as shown in Cat. no. 2, with a well-defined outer rim, a flattened lobe and a zigzag ridge representing the inner ear. The cosmetic line, closer to Cat. no. 2 than Cat. no. 3, widens at the end in a fish tail. The King wears an enormous bead collar with seven strands and holds a lotus-bud sceptre. His short, pleated kilt is painted white. His arms are long and rounded and, like the smooth torso, show little musculature.

From the shrine of Kemsit (?), temple of Nebhepetre Montuhotep at Deir el-Bahri, Thebes. Gift of the Egypt Exploration Fund. British Museum EA. 1450 (1907 10–15 497). H: 56.0 cm. W: 46.5 cm.

This relief, though published by Naville, is not assigned specifically to the shrine of Kemsit. Scenes like this one, also sunk in relief, belong to two of the other shrines and we can assume that all the shrines shared a similar if not identical scheme of decoration. The scale of the scene, as much as its subject matter, is striking. The King appears as a husband, not at all like a King in the Egyptian manner. Only his regalia (and it is significant that on this relief, executed before the unification, he wears only the crown of Upper Egypt) and the inscriptions provide his rank. He is not even the most prominent figure in the overall decorative scheme – that is undoubtedly Kemsit herself.

Naville, *Deir el-Bahari*, I pl. XII, a (part only); *Top. Bibl.*, II², p. 389.

5 KING NEBHEPETRE MONTUHOTEP

Dynasty XI, late in the King's reign, 1997–1982 BC.

Fragment of painted limestone raised relief showing the sign of life, the *ankh* sign, being presented to the King's nose. The relief is relatively low, about half the height of Cat. nos. 3–4. The face and the crown are painted reddish brown, the *ankh* sign white. The King wears a uraeus-snake, painted yellow, on his brow, with the crown of Lower Egypt. His eyebrow, executed in relief, curves naturally over the eye, then straightens out to run parallel with the cosmetic line, which widens out very slightly at its end. The eye itself is widest at the centre, not towards the inner corner as in Cat. no. 2, and instead of slanting downwards it is set straight. The inner

5

canthus is strongly marked but not exaggerated. The ear is small in proportion to the eye and, while simplified, is naturally shaped with an indentation in the outer rim before the rounded ear lobe. The curve around the nostril is just visible before the fragment breaks off.

Probably from the sanctuary of the temple of Nebhepetre Montuhotep at Deir el-Bahri. Gift of R. G. Gayer-Anderson. Fitzwilliam EGA.3127.1943. H: 7.3 cm. W: 18.7 cm.

Hundreds of fragments of raised relief, now scattered world wide, originally came from the rock-cut sanctuary of the temple. They have been meticulously studied, and the scenes as far as possible reconstructed, by Dieter Arnold, so we can with some confidence suggest that this fragment comes from there. Arnold himself questions whether this fragment may have come from the shrines of the concubines, but in my view this is not at all likely. The relief, so different from Cat. no. 3, is lower, the cutting is softer and the features rendered in a more naturalistic fashion, in terms of their proportions as well as their shape.

This work (see also Cat. nos. 6–7) was part of the last building phase of the temple and was carried out after the unification. It shows the impact of the Memphite style, with its unbroken traditions going back to the building of pyramids and temples for the Kings of the Old Kingdom in the necropolis of Memphis between Giza and Saqqara.

The purpose of the sanctuary, the holiest part of the temple, was to celebrate the King's relationship to the gods. He is shown being embraced by them, offered life (as in this relief) by them, and seated on his throne accompanied by them; in return he presents offerings and carries out rituals, like the *Sed* festival (see also Cat. no. 11) before them. The sanctuary was also the centre of the King's mortuary cult and originally contained a large granite altar for offerings.

Arnold, *Mentuhotep*, II, pl. 38, no. 3792.

6 A GODDESS

Dynasty XI, late in reign of Nebhepetre Montuhotep, 1997–1982 BC.

Fragment of painted limestone raised relief showing the face and part of the wig and shoulders of a female figure.

Her face is painted yellow, her wig black and her shoulder strap white. The treatment of the facial features lies between Cat. nos. 3 and 5 but is closer to the latter. The relief brow is a long, uninterrrupted, gently curved line, which does not initially follow the profile of the eye but finishes up parallel to the cosmetic line. The eye itself slants downwards, with the usual exaggerated peak on the inside to mark the tear duct. The eye is not outlined in relief but the eyeball is rounded and the pupil painted black. The relief cosmetic line is long and widens out to the width of the eyebrow. The ear is much larger in proportion to the eye than Cat. no. 5, but is similar in outline. The inner ear is represented very simply by a kidney-shaped groove. A chip has destroyed the profile of the nose but the usual emphatic curve around the nostril is visible. The mouth, while of the same character as Cat. nos. 2, 3, 4, is carved in a less mannered style. It is a natural part of the face rather than applied to it. The lips are outlined with an incised line and the lower lip is slightly fuller than the upper one. The modelling of the surface is slight, though the chin is distinctly rounded. The woman wears a long wig with straight side lappets and the straps of her tunic are just visible.

6

Probably from the sanctuary of the temple of Nebhepetre Montuhotep at Deir el-Bahri. Gift of C. Ricketts and C. Shannon. Fitzwilliam E.21.1937. H: 8.2 cm. W: 27.0 cm.

The identification of the woman on this relief as a goddess depends on the attribution of it by Arnold (see Cat. no. 5) to the sanctuary, since only the King, gods and goddesses are represented there. The style of the relief seems consistent with this view, taking into account the fact that the sculptor of this relief was less skilled than others who worked on the decoration of the temple and whose work is represented in this exhibition. It has been suggested that the object in front of the goddess is part of a figure of the King, his arm perhaps. This is unlikely, since goddesses were represented as of equal stature to the King in the sanctuary relief.

Ricketts and Shannon formed their antiquities collection in London, between 1880 and 1937, and attended most of the important auction sales, but they left no information on the source of this particular relief.

Arnold, *Mentuhotep*, II, pl. 44, no. 5065.

7 A RAID ON A DUCK'S NEST Illustrated in colour on pl. I, 1.

Dynasty XI, late in reign of Nebhepetre Montuhotep, 1997–1982 BC.

Block of painted limestone raised relief showing a jackal(?) stealing a duckling from its nest in a thicket of papyrus. The scale of the relief is very large, approximately life-size, except for the stems of papyrus, which stand up like small trees. The papyrus and the water are painted blue, the ducklings reddish-brown, the jackal(?) pinkish-brown and the background yellow. The surface shows patching with fine plaster in several places before the paint was applied and there are traces of the underlying guide outlines executed in black. At the top of the block the feet, tail and wing tips of the parent bird, flapping its outspread wings in a vain attempt to distract the predator, are visible. Behind it is a papyrus stem, painted directly on to the block in contrast to the other three stems and the over-sized papyrus umbel upon which the nest sits, which are all carved in raised relief. This device allows the sculptor more space within the depth of the shallow relief to overlap the elements in his design. The ducklings are shown sitting on top of the nest, not inside it, and both chicks are shown rising up (the one in the centre slightly more), flapping their helpless, immature wings in agitation. The duckling about to be dragged off by the jackal(?) is a much older bird, with a tail, developed wings and a long neck. Its eye is closed, as if it were already dead. The jackal(?) is shown with its jaws firmly clenched around the neck, the muscles of its own neck tensed to pull the body down from the nest and scramble away.

From the south wall of the ambulatory of the temple of Nebhepetre Montuhotep at Deir el-Bahri, Thebes. Gift of the Egypt Exploration Fund. Fitzwilliam E.5.1906. H: 35.4 cm. W: 54.6 cm.

Naville reports that fragments of scenes of the King hunting in the desert and in the papyrus marshes of the river were found and that all belonged to the decoration of the ambulatory. The fragments published in his report, which do not include this one, show reliefs of similar scale and style. The ambulatory was a covered colonnade, three pillars deep on its south side, with a square hall in the centre. It was lit from channels left at intervals high in the side walls. The decorative scheme was taken over from the temples built in the Old Kingdom, for example by Userkaf and Neuserre of Dynasty V, in the necropolis of Memphis. It was only after Montuhotep had unified Upper and Lower Egypt that Memphis became accessible to artists working for him; equally, it was only then that artists trained in Memphis were able to enter his service (see above, p. 10). Therefore this relief is likely to belong to the later part of his reign, a supposition strengthened by the architectural study of the building, which suggests that this decoration was carried out at the same time as the Sanctuary reliefs, Cat. nos. 5, 6. The identification of the animal raiding the duck's nest is uncertain. Various authorities have called it a fox, an ichneumon and a jackal.

Top Bibl., II², p. 397 and bibliography there cited; for a comparable relief of Userkaf, Smith, *Art and Architecture*, pl. 47; for jackal(?), Blackman, *Meir*, II, p. 20, pl. XXXII, 1.

8 KING NEBHEPETRE MONTUHOTEP Illustrated p. 10.

Dynasty XI, 2023–1982 BC.

Quartzite head of a King wearing *nemes* head cloth and with the uraeus-snake on his brow. Length of face: 6.4 cm.

7

Width of face: 6.0 cm. Length of eye: 2.4 cm. Length of ear: 3.8 cm. The *nemes* carries a pattern of broad single stripes which continues down the side lappets. It is flat across the top of the head with a slight peak at the side fold and there are broad tabs in front of the ears. The uraeus-snake rises from the bottom of the band (the frontlet) which holds the *nemes* in place. The hood is tall and wide and the snake's body twists nine times as it passes over the top of the head. The band of the *nemes* comes down low on the forehead. The brows are prominently carved in high relief and are long and almost completely straight, curving slightly downwards at their outer ends. In contrast the eyes are set at a slant, exaggerated by the pronounced 'beak' of the inner canthi. The eyes are very wide (1.1 cm at their maximum) and outlined with a relief band which extends into a short, distinctly 'fish-tail' cosmetic line. The eyeballs are rounded and the pupils painted black. The ears, set a little high (if the norm is taken to be that the earhole is level with the outer corner of the eye), are long and oval and show no inner detail. The nose, as so often, has been chipped, so that the original profile is lost, but the nostrils are broad and defined by a strong curve. The mouth shows a definite upward curve of the lower lip, on the verge of becoming a smile. Both lips are thick and straight with a deep groove at the corners of the mouth. The chin is round, and plump in keeping with the fleshy cheeks. The face presents a broad, full, oval shape, with the modelling concentrated in a band down the centre. This shows the muscles around mouth, nose and cheeks pulling the features upwards into an expression of beneficent dignity.

Gift of Mrs L. C. R. Phillips. Bristol H5038. H: 12.2 cm. W: 11.9 cm.

We do not know where this fine sculpture came from, but it seems likely that it was made in the royal workshops at Thebes. The hardness and coarser texture of quartzite preclude the gem-like precision visible on the early limestone reliefs, Cat. nos. 2–4, but the sculpture does show, in three dimensions, exactly the same treatment of the facial features. This is especially obvious in the details of the disporportionately large eyes, and in the heavy brows. The head also has much in common with a head of the King in the Metropolitan Museum of Art in New York, found in the forecourt of the temple at Deir el-Bahri. This was made, along with all the other statues for the temple, during the final stage of the building and shows clearly that royal sculptures in the round did not follow the same stages of development we can observe in the relief style of the temple. The mannered treatment of the eyes and brows, with a straight, heavy brow set over slanting, wide eyes, a short fish-tail cosmetic line and 'beak' shaped inner canthi, is common to all the temple statues. There is another quartzite head of similar dimensions (the maximum difference is 0.5 cm) in the Royal Museum of Scotland in Edinburgh. The style is exactly the same but the cutting is coarser, making it appear even more mannered, and the uraeus has a longer tail.

19

The *nemes* with uraeus was worn exclusively by Kings, Queens and Gods, and occurs first worn by the King in Dynasty III, approximately one thousand years before this head was carved. The *nemes* itself was a simple headcloth of striped linen worn to protect the hair or wig from dust (cf. Cat. no. 90), but is conventionally shown in this stylised form, with two ends brought forward from behind the ears to form side lappets and the other two pulled in to a pigtail at the back of the neck. The cobra worn on the diadem which holds the headcloth in place was the insignia of divine kingship. The uraeus-snake was personified as a goddess, called the 'Great One' or 'Great of Magic', who fought for the king against his enemies. A uraeus possibly once worn by King Senusret II was found in 1920 by Guy Brunton in the offering chamber outside the King's burial chamber. It is made of gold, inlaid with carnelian, lapis lazuli and turquoise. The body is hollow with two hooks fixed inside where it was sewn on to the cloth. It is a compelling object and suggests that the appearance of the uraeus provided by this and other sculptures, Cat. nos. 5, 28, 31, is altogether too bland. The uraeus has often suffered damage, especially to the prominent hood of the cobra. The Lahun uraeus would have reared up over 6 cm high on the forehead, its body arching forward to strike, with head of lapis and eyes of garnet ringed with gold. 'Let the fear of him be as the fear of thee', from a hymn to the crown of Lower Egypt in the Pyramid Texts.

L. V. Grinsell, *Guide Catalogue to the Collections from Ancient Egypt* (Bristol, 1972), fig. 16, p. 34; C. Aldred in *MMJ* 3 (1970), pp. 7–8, figs. 7, 8; head in New York, *ibid*, p. 4, figs. 3–4; Arnold, *Temple*, pp. 45–8, pl. 24; head in Edinburgh, Aldred, *op. cit*, fig. 6; *nemes*, H. Winlock in *BMMA* 60 (November 1916), pp. 240–1; uraeus from Lahun, Petrie *et al.*, *Lahun*, II, p. 12, pl. xxv; Saleh and Sourouzian, *Cairo Museum*, no. 108; hymn, Erman, *Literature*, p. 10.

9

9 MONTUHOTEP AND NEFERMESUT

Dynasty XI, 2023–1963 BC.

Painted limestone dyad of Montuhotep and his wife Nefermesut shown seated on a rectangular block. The head of Montuhotep is missing and the base is repaired. An inscription painted in black on each side of the block consists of the funerary offering formula on behalf of Montuhotep (right side) and Nefermesut (left side). Montuhotep sits with his right hand clenched on a roll of cloth, see Cat. no. 19, and his left lying flat on his knee. His torso is strongly modelled: clavicle, pectoral muscles, nipples, the median line from navel to sternum, backbone and shoulder muscles are shown in detail. The bone and musculature of the arms and legs are shown; note the unusual attention given to the knees and ankles, with the same anatomical precision. The shoulders and biceps are heavily muscled in contrast to the slender waist. Hands and feet have elongated fingers and toes with the nails individually carved. Montuhotep wears the short kilt with central tab, painted white, and his body is painted a deep reddish-brown. Nefermesut wears a long wig with rectangular lappets painted black with a deep central parting, which reaches the top of her breasts. Length of face: 2.7 cm. Width of face: 3.7 cm. Length of eye: 1.0 cm. Length of ear: 1.5 cm. The heavy brows, executed in relief, are straight over the eyeball, then change direction sharply in order to finish parallel with the cosmetic line. The eyes are set at a slant, with pronounced inner canthi, and outlined in relief. There is a long (0.6 cm) fish-tailed cosmetic line. The eyeball is painted white and the pupil black. The ears are set a little high (cf. Cat. no. 8) and little detail beyond the outer rim and the large round ear lobe is shown. The nose is long and wide, the nostrils strongly defined and the philtrum marked. The full lower lip and the deep grooves at the corner of the mouth and at the wings of the nostrils suggest a smile. The lips are outlined with an incised line. The chin is small and square. The cheeks are full, defined by a deep naso-labial furrow. Breasts, stomach, knees and legs are subtly suggested under the clinging tunic, and hands, feet and ankles are treated like those of Montuhotep. Nefermesut wears the usual tunic with broad shoulder straps, bracelets and anklets and probably a bead collar. Traces of blue pigment remain at the base of her neck.

From Dendera. Gift of the Egypt Exploration Fund. Ashmolean E.1971. H: 31.0 cm. W: 23.0 cm.

This small dyad of fine quality was found by Petrie in the inner offering chamber of the tomb of Nefermesut and Montuhotep at Dendera in 1898. Montuhotep is given no title in the inscription, but he must have been an important local man to merit such a substantial tomb and to command the work of a sculptor of skill. Although executed on a much smaller scale, the figures can be compared with the statue of one of the concubines of Nebhepetre Montuhotep found in her shrine at Deir el-Bahri, and with a group of sculptures of the reigns of Senusret I and Amenemhat I from Aswan. The male torso is given a strongly bipartite character, and is short in relation to the heavy, broad shoulders. It is interesting to see this distinctive style of the early XIIth Dynasty established already in Dynasty XI. Dendera was close to Thebes and early in his reign Nebhepetre Montuhotep built a shrine to Hathor there, so we can presume that its craftsmen already felt the impact of the new style at this time. Confirmation comes from comparing this sculpture with the reliefs, barely a generation older, from the tomb of Sennedjsui, also from Dendera. Some elements of the latter's extraordinary mannerism survive – for example, the elaborate detail of wigs and jewellery and the elongated limbs. Nevertheless, the sculpture owes much more to influences emanating from the capital at Thebes than it does to inheritance of the traditions of local sculptors.

Petrie, *Dendereh*, pp. 21, 26, 65, pls. XV, XXI; cf. Evers, *Staat aus dem Stein*, I, pl. 11; Habachi, *Heqaib*, pls. 17, 19, 189.

10 MONTUHOTEP AND HIS FAMILY
Dynasty XI, 2023–1963 BC.

Limestone slab stela from Abydos. The composition divides into three sections: the autobiographical inscription of the priest Montuhotep, in four lines of large hieroglyphs reading from left to right; below them the four seated figures of Montuhotep, his wife Sent, his father Neferpert and mother Hathoremhat before a table of offerings; finally, to the left of them, the three registers of offering bringers. The first register shows three women: two sisters, Renesankh and Nebetet,

and a nurse, Rehutet; the second shows a son, Neferpert, followed by a daughter, Hathoremhat, and two servants, Ita and Idi; the third shows a daughter, Renesankh, and three servants, Sent, Shema and Neferpert.

The female figures in the procession, whether family or servants, are dressed alike in close-fitting tunics tied under the breasts and they wear long, full-bottomed wigs. Montuhotep's son, Neferpert, wears the short kilt with triangular front apron, in contrast to the servant Shema who wears a simple kilt. Neferpert, as his father's son, was responsible for setting up and maintaining his father's funerary cult, and this duty is symbolised by the haunch of an ox which he offers. With this exception, only the servants carry offerings in the procession. It is significant that the nurse, Rehutet, is grouped in this respect with the family, not the servants. The offerings consist of scented oil, a mirror, two basins and a pot carried in a string bag, a duck, a small gazelle (?) and a tray of cakes. The gazelle, a desert animal, is brought by Shema, whose name means 'nomad'.

The four seated figures share the same physiognomy: the brow is lightly modelled and follows the contour of the eye, the eyes are wide with inner canthi marked, the wing of the broad nose is emphasised by a curve, the mouth is straight with a full and prominent lower lip. They all wear broad collars, and Neferpert the short kilt with a central tab, see Cat. no. 25. No indications of the women's dress are given, but since they would not be represented naked, we must assume an oversight by the sculptor, which also explains the absence of Hathoremhat's hand on her husband's shoulder.

The front chair legs, however, are deliberately omitted, preference being given by the artist to representing the legs of Neferpert. The men wear shoulder-length wigs covering their ears.

10

Fitzwilliam E.9.1922. H: 42.0 cm. W: 77.8 cm.

The most prominent object on the stela is the table of offerings set in the centre of the slab. It is covered with a row of round, flat loaves placed on edge, and a carefully disposed arrangement of food – sealed beer jars, a duck and an ox head and haunch. Both sets of figures on the stela look towards the table. On the right, large scale, two generations of the dead are seated, passive, waiting for the offerings which will ensure their immortality; on the left, the living walk in procession – the family and servants whose duty it is to ensure the offerings continue. The table is the point at which the worlds of the dead and the living connect. The living visit the tomb chapel to recite the funerary formula in front of the stela and to leave offerings on the table. The autobiographical inscription addresses them directly: 'O ye who live and are upon the earth and who shall pass by this tomb, who love life and hate death, say ye, "May Osiris, head of the Westerners, glorify Montuhotep"'. Even without the recitations, the existence of the stela itself ensured the perpetuation of offerings, because the inscriptions and figures had, it was believed, their own independent life.

The relation of text and image in Egyptian relief was an intimate one, necessarily so, since the hieroglyphic script itself is a series of images. The figures on the stela are in a sense enlarged pictograms to be 'read' after the personal names and titles given in the script. Thus it is unremarkable that Neferpert and Hathoremhat, the parents of Montuhotep, are shown in their youthful prime, as he is himself. The different scales used for different parts of the text and the varied orientation of the hieroglyphs help us to understand the various elements which make up the monument. Horizontally written hieroglyphs are read from the direction the signs face – thus the autobiographical inscription in the largest hieroglyphs is written from left to right in the first four lines. It is no accident that the four largest figures below this inscription face the same way. They are identified by inscriptions made up of signs, at a slightly smaller scale, grouped carefully in an inverted L-shape around their heads. The sculptor, however, did not have enough space for the name of Montuhotep's mother-in-law, so that was inserted in the space between the bodies of Montuhotep and Sent. Again the names are to be read so that the seated figures serve as determinatives, that is non-phonetic signs indicating the sense of the word. The signs identifying the processional figures are smaller and face the opposite direction, i.e. read from right to left. The change in direction thus reinforces the division between the figures on either side of the offering table. The figures and text of the procession are so much smaller in scale that two registers can be fitted into the space of one, reinforcing the image of the wealth and status of the commemorated dead which the procession itself helps to create.

Montuhotep certainly intended to leave such an image behind him – he boasts in his inscription that he was one whose (own) counsel replaced for him a mother at home, a father making the family fortune: 'although I was become an orphan, I acquired cattle and got oxen . . . I built a house and excavated a garden pool.' If we take the inscription literally, and it is sufficiently unusual for us to have no reason not to do so, Montuhotep was orphaned young and honours his long-dead parents on his stela. His father has no title to show he held any administrative or religious office, although his father's father was a 'sealer of the god'.

Everyone whose name appeared on the stela shared potentially in the offerings which it depicted, so it was important to get as many names included as possible. In addition to the people depicted, some are mentioned only by name: Montuhotep's mother-in-law Hepi, his father's father Renesankh and his mother's mother Benernit. These filiations, on some stelae going back four or five generations, are one of the most useful documentary sources for the social history of the Middle Kingdom.

Petrie, *Tombs of the Courtiers*, pp. 10, 19, pls. XXII, XXIII.

11 JUBILEE RELIEF OF SENUSRET I
1914–1899 BC.

Limestone sunk relief showing King Senusret I running between boundary stones, symbolising the limits of his kingdom. The rite was part of the ceremony of the *Sed* festival and possibly refers to the one held in Senusret's thirty-first regal year. The King runs before the god Min (not shown) and in front of him are two of his five names: his throne name, Kheperkare (the *Ka* of Re comes into being) and his Horus name, Ankh-mesut (Life of Births). The line of vertical text below the names reads 'hastening by boat to Min, the great god who is in the midst of his city'. Behind the King the text reads 'the protection of life is around his Lord'. Senusret wears the red crown of Lower Egypt, with the uraeus-snake on his brow, and the bull's tail hangs from his waist to indicate his kingship. In addition he wears a short pleated kilt with central tab, on ornamental belt and a necklace of graduated spheroid beads. He holds in his hands an oar and another object, which may be part of a boat's steering mechanism. Both of these are traditionally held by the King during his ceremonial run, but also refer to the 'hastening by boat' which captions the scene. The relief is cut deep, especially around the body of the King where it measures 0.8 cm, and this allows the sculptor scope for subtle and detailed modelling. The brow is carved in a relief band, first following the contour of the eye, then becoming straight. The eye is outlined in relief and the eyeball sculpted and painted. The eye is oval and long with a pronounced inner canthus and a cosmetic line in relief which runs parallel with the straight section of the brow. The ears are naturalistically carved with the inner ear shown in detail. The nose is small and straight, the nostril carved out and the line made by the muscle at the wing of the nostril shown clearly. The lips are straight, full and outlined with a deep notch at the corners. There is a faint suggestion of fleshiness around the chin and jawline.

The muscles of the limbs are shown in detail, even to the tiny crease where the arms join the trunk. The bulge of muscle above the elbow, where the tensed right arm holds the oar, is contrasted with the more relaxed, smoother contours of the left arm. The stretched muscles of the legs, thighs and knees, and the right foot lifting off the ground in the

11

action of running, are shown in detail and in contrast to the
torso, which is only lightly modelled except for the navel
groove.

From Koptos. Gift of the Egypt Exploration Fund. University
College 14786. H: 111.0 cm. W: 92.2 cm.

This superb relief was found in three pieces by Flinders
Petrie, face down in the foundations of the Ptolemaic temple
of Min at Koptos. It was, until Petrie cleaned it, covered with
a thin layer of fine plaster in preparation for painting. The
plaster protected the surface and also serves as a reminder

to us of the original intentions of the relief's makers. They
aimed at the effect of Cat. nos. 3–4 and perhaps, in this case
too, paint would have obscured much of the subtle modelling.

The scene itself occurs on royal monuments from
Dynasty III to Roman times, a period of over two and a half
thousand years, since it depicts one of the most significant
and mysterious of the rites of kingship. The *Sed* festival normally took place when the King had reigned for thirty years,
and we know that Senusret celebrated one in his thirty-first
year. For this reason the relief may be dated between that

year and the end of his forty-five year reign. The *Sed* festival included a re-enactment of the rites of coronation, and one of the most important of these was the ceremonial run. It reaffirmed both the extent and power of the King's authority and the physical strength he needed to match it. It seems likely that the run was an actual not a symbolic event. The buildings around the Step Pyramid of King Djoser (c. 2620–2600 BC) of Dynasty III include a large open court with stones set in it, which is thought to be the site of the run or an exact copy for the King's use in the Afterlife. Min, the paramount deity of Koptos, was closely involved with the *Sed* festival, so the subject is appropriate to his temple. Senusret I was a prodigious builder and blocks from his monuments are found on sites from the Delta to Aswan. Central government records and the autobiographies of his officials tell us how some of the work was organised, and as a result there is probably more evidence from a variety of sources for this reign than for any other in the Middle Kingdom.

The style of the relief, as well as its subject, accord with a date after the first ten years of his reign, during which he shared the throne with his father. The few relief blocks which survive from this time show that the fine but flat relief style of Amenemhat I's reign (cf. Cat. nos. 6–7) still continued. The contrast with this vigorous work is remarkable. This relief succeeds in placing the violent action of the King's run within the harmonious, unchanging framework of the King's relationship to the gods. The carefully spaced, intricately worked hieroglyphs set around Senusret's body are one of the ways in which this is achieved.

W. M. Flinders Petrie, *Koptos* (London, 1896), p. 11, pl. IX, 2; H. M. Stewart, *Egyptian Stelae, Reliefs and Paintings from the Petrie Collection*, Part 2 (Warminster, 1979), no. 56, pl. 39; *Top. Bibl.*, V, p. 125 and bibliography there cited; R. Freed in *Dunham Essays*, p. 76; for Senusret I's reign, Simpson in *LÄ*, V, 890–9.

12 RELIEFS FROM THE PYRAMID COMPLEX OF SENUSRET II

1869–1862 BC.

Three fragments of painted limestone. (a) Fragment from a list of funerary offerings, comprising an inventory arranged in columns in sunk relief, with two heaps of offerings in raised relief below it. Much of the original colour remains. The hieroglyphs and numbers in the list are green, as are the lines dividing up and differentiating the columns. The pile of offerings on the right side consists of a bundle of vegetables, possibly leeks, with green stems and red roots; a row of cakes or loaves, yellow with a red crust; a trussed duck, and an unmistakable bundle of spring onions. The pile of offerings on the left consists of a large lotus with a yellow flower and green outer leaves and stem, a joint of meat and a conical loaf or cake, also yellow with a red crust. The spaces between the offerings are painted green. The scale of the relief is small, each square measuring 3.3 cm high by 4.1 cm wide. (b) Fragment in raised relief consisting of part of: an upper register; a border of yellow stars; a row of three jabiru storks, the word *baw*, meaning 'spirits', in the hieroglyphic script. The bodies,

plumage and heads of the birds are painted green, their wattles, eyes and beaks, red. The birds are more than 4.2 cm high, so the fragment comes from a larger-scale inscription than (a). (c) Fragment in raised relief from an inscription containing a single hieroglyph, read *wah*, meaning 'endure', and representing a swab made from a hank of fibre. The size of the sign is similar to that of fragment (b), and the right side shows the original edge of a block.

From the Lahun pyramid complex of Senusret II. From the shrine on the north side of the subsidiary pyramid. Fitzwilliam E.52.1914, E.158.1914, E.53.1914. (a) H: 14.3 cm. W: 16.8 cm. (b) H: 11.9 cm. W: 9.5 cm. (c) H: 4.7 cm. W: 3.6 cm.

12a, b, c

Flinders Petrie excavated the subsidiary pyramid at Lahun and its shrine in 1888 and 1914. He assigned both to an otherwise unknown queen of Senusret II on the basis of a fragment of inscription published only in a line drawing. No plan of the shrine was made and only the fragments of relief, now mostly in Cambridge, survive from it, together with an altar in black granite and fragments of a diorite statue which is unpublished. The reliefs belong, as one would expect, to funerary inscriptions, but the fragments are so small that no single item in the offering list, for example, can be reconstructed. The quality of the carving and the brilliant colour, especially the unexpected use of green, provide a tantalising glimpse of what must have been an exquisite building. Fragment (b) is also interesting in demonstrating how the Egyptian artists used strictly parallel overlapping lines to show three birds in a row moving forward. It was essential to make clear the number of birds represented, since three of anything represent a plurality. The birds are saddlebill storks, natives of sub-Saharan Africa and no longer to be found in Egypt itself.

Petrie *et al.*, *Lahun*, II, pl. XVII, 14, 36. Fragment (c) is unpublished. For the hieroglyphs, see Gardiner, *Grammar*, G 29–30, V 29, pp. 470, 525; for the birds, P. F. Houlihan, *The Birds of Ancient Egypt* (Warminster, 1986), pp. 23–5, 147.

13 RELIEF FROM THE PYRAMID COMPLEX OF SENUSRET II

1869–1862 BC.

Fragment of painted limestone relief. Part of three vertical columns of a hieroglyphic inscription in raised relief. The central column contains the word *hmwt*, meaning 'crafts-

13

men', written with a sign representing the stone-mason's drill. The dividing lines are painted green, the two uppermost signs on the left blue and the handle and stem of the drill and the face and body of the seated man, reddish-brown. The scale of the inscription is very large, the drill sign being 16.5 cm in height.

From Lahun, from the mortuary temple of Senusret II. Fitzwilliam E.55.1914. H: 33.0 cm. W: 31.4 cm.

When Flinders Petrie began excavating the pyramid complex of Senusret II in 1888, he found it devastated by the workmen who had used it as a stone quarry. The destruction may have begun as early as Dynasty XVIII, and is well attested from the reign of Ramesses II (1290–1224 BC). Petrie found the ground covered to a depth of some feet with limestone chips. 'On turning over all this stuff we recovered many pieces of sculpture' (Petrie, *Illahun*, p. 4). So many were found that only some were published. This fragment was not among them, but it seems likely to have come from the mortuary temple attached to the King's pyramid since only this building produced inscriptions of the same kind and of a comparable size.

The large scale has allowed the sculptor to introduce considerable detail into each sign. The seated man determinative (i.e. a sign without phonetic value but indicating the general sense of the word) shows modelling of the muscles of the arms, and the face has a distinctive physiognomy which echoes that of the King himself (see Petrie *et al.*, *Lahun*, II, pl. XVIII, top left). The elements of the stone-mason's drill – the handle, the stones bound to the shaft and the drill bits – are all shown distinctly. The word *hmt*, 'craft', is one of the words used to describe the work of a sculptor and the same hieroglyph, the bow drill, survives in the word more commonly used in the New Kingdom for a sculptor, *s'ankh* – one who makes to live. These two ideas of a sculptor as

a craftsman, in kind no different from a carpenter, and as a creator, under the special protection of the creator god Ptah, were not considered mutually exclusive by the Egyptians as we might consider them to be.

Cf. Petrie *et al.*, *Lahun*, II, pl. XIX, top right. For *hmwt*, Faulkner, *Dictionary*, p. 170; Gardiner, *Grammar*, U 24–5, pp. 518–19; Barta, *Selbstzeugnis eines altägyptischen Künstlers*, pp. 63–4.

14 A QUEEN

Early Dynasty XII, 1963–1862 BC.

From a standing statue of black granite broken off at the waist. Length of face: 5.4 cm. Width of face: 6.0 cm. Length of eye: 1.8 cm. Length of ear: 3.7 cm. The Queen wears the so-called Hathor wig and bears a uraeus-snake on her brow. Her coiffure is made up of two layers of hair; the top layer, whose strands are indicated by incised wavy lines, is drawn into two wide bunches and brought round to hang in two fat curls over her chest. The under layer, characterised by straight incised lines, hangs down her back and may represent her natural hair. The uraeus-snake, a cobra, rises from the outer edge of her wig and reaches the top of her head, its body twisting twice on its course. Her eyebrows are arched and their curve joins the line of her nose, and with the strong modelling of the cheek-bone forms deep, almost circular sockets for the eyes, cf. Cat. no. 17. These are set straight and are wide (0.7 cm) in relation to their length. The inner canthi are clearly shown, but not the eyeballs or upper lids. The ear is very broad as well as long, and only the outer rim and lobe are indicated. The area between the nostrils and chin

14

25

is bruised but the lips appear to be slightly protruding and straight. Apart from the emphatic cheek-bones, the face shows little modelling, as does the body. Breasts and slim waist are shown and a wide, shallow depression between the breasts suggests the breast bone. Her dress, a close-fitting tunic with broad shoulder straps covering the breasts, is indicated by incised lines. The shoulders are exceptionally narrow, especially seen in contrast to the broad wig. The back pillar, which thickens as it descends, begins at the base of the wig. It is 5.0 cm wide at the top, 6.1 cm wide at its broken base, between 1.2 and 2.2 cm deep, and 7.8 cm high.

University College 16657. H: 22.0 cm. W: 13.9 cm.

Few statues of Queens have survived from the Middle Kingdom. This sculpture may be from a standing statue as no bend is visible in the left arm. The date depends on comparisons with the two statues in Cairo inscribed for Nefert, Queen of Senusret II (1869–1862 BC), although Sourouzian has suggested a slightly earlier date, in the reign of Amenemhat I or Senusret I. The form of the uraeus is similar to that worn by the Queen (R. Engelbach, in *ASAE*, 28 (1928), pl. IV, B). A significant difference is the absence of a cosmetic line, although this no longer appears consistently on statues of the King himself. Her hairstyle, the so-called Hathor wig, is worn by royalty and commoners alike, see Cat. no. 37. In the Middle Kingdom it first occurs slightly earlier, worn by women shown on a statue of Senusret-ankh (reign of Senusret I) in the Metropolitan Museum of Art in New York. The association of the hairstyle with Hathor may be a later development, when, instead of being the universal fashion of the day, the hairstyle had become confined to representations of Queens or goddesses. The facial characteristics, extremely broad face, round cheeks, curved brows and wide straight mouth, in addition to the absence of a cosmetic line and the position of the uraeus, may be compared with a statuette in Copenhagen, identified as Senusret II.

Page, *Egyptian Sculpture*, no. 24; Petrie, *Exhibition Handbook*, 1915, p. 31, no. 428; H. Sourouzian in *MDAIK* 37 (1981), p. 449, pl. 71a; cf. Evers, *Staat aus dem Stein*, pls. 69, 72–5; Vandier, *La Statuaire Egyptienne*, pp. 222–4, 257–8; for hairstyle, Mace and Winlock, *Senebtisi*, p. 45, n. 2.

15 A WOMAN

Early Dynasty XII, 1963–1862 BC.

Upper part of statuette of a woman. Obsidian. Length of face: 2.1 cm. Width of face: 2.4 cm. Length of eye: 0.8 cm. Length of ear: 1.2 cm. The woman wears a long wig with side lappets, the individual strands of hair represented by incised lines. The brows curve naturally following the contour of the eye and the eyes themselves are set straight and wide apart. The upper lid is outlined. The ears are broad (0.6 cm) as well as long, and set exceptionally low so that the hollow of the ear is level with the nostrils. The outer rim, lobe and anti-helix are shown. The nose and mouth have both been damaged, but the nose appears to have been short and wide and the mouth blunt, summarily indicated with incised lines. The chin is small, round and receding. The shoulders are narrow, almost completely covered by the wig

lappets, and the breasts are round and high. The edge of the back pillar, 2.9 cm wide, is visible at the botton of the back hair.

Gift of the Reverend G. S. Bird. Fitzwilliam E.63.1926. H: 6.1 cm. W: 4.8 cm.

G. S. Bird was the grandson of Samuel Shepheard, who founded Shepheard's Hotel in Cairo in the 1870s, and this statuette once belonged in his collection. Shepheard's was on the itinerary of every British traveller to Cairo and eventually became so identified with the British in Egypt that it became a target for the nationalists and was burnt down in 1952.

15

The bruise in the centre of the wigband was first identified as the remains of a uraeus (see Cat. no. 14) by F. W. Green, Honorary Keeper of Egyptian Antiquities, and the statuette was thereafter described as that of a Queen. Examination under the microscope suggests that the bruise is accidental, since the second horizontal line of the wig goes across it and there is no trace of the body or tail of the snake. Obsidian is a natural glass produced by volcanic action and breaks into conchoidal fractures like manufactured glass. It was used in Egypt from Predynastic times but mainly for beads, scarabs and the pupils of inlaid eyes (Cat. no. 73). Its use was most widespread during the Middle Kingdom, but sculptures in obsidian are nevertheless exceedingly rare. There is a small head in the Gulbenkian collection in Lisbon, attributed to Senusret III, and a fragment of the face from a statuette of a woman, which provides a close stylistic parallel, in the Metropolitan Museum in New York. An early analysis of obsidian objects from Egypt suggested that most of them were made from stone mined in Abyssinia, but more recent work shows that Lake Van, near the Black Sea, is another possible source.

For obsidian, Lucas, *Industries*, pp. 415–16; J. R. Cann and C. Renfrew in *Proceedings of the Prehistoric Society*, NS 30 (1964), pp. 111–31; head of Senusret III, Vandier, *La Statuaire Egyptienne*, pl. LXVI, 7; face fragment in New York, *BMMA Supplement* (January 1911), p. 24, fig. 17.

1

2

3

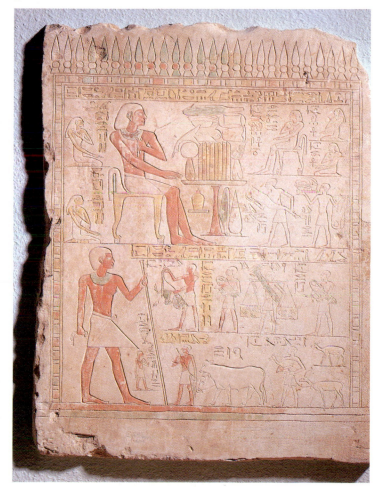

4

PLATE I
1. A raid on a duck's nest, Cat. no. 7
2. Model granary with scene of men playing a board game, Cat. no. 91
3. Stela of Montuhotep, Cat. no. 36
4. Stela of Amenemhat Nebuy, Cat. no. 39

1

2

3

4

1

2

4

3

PLATE II
1. King Amenemhat III, Cat. no. 31
2. King Senusret III, Cat. no. 29
3. A King's Singer, Cat. no. 37
4. The soldier Khnemu, Cat. no. 42

PLATE III
1. Mesehti of Asyut, Cat. no. 23
2. Servant girl, Cat. no. 90
3. Inner Coffin of Userhet, Cat. no. 72
4. Coffin of Nakht, Cat. no. 70

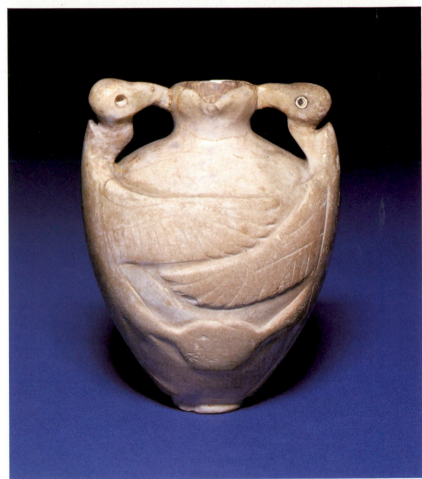

PLATE IV
1. Scarab ring of King Amenemhat III, Cat. no. 179
2. Gold pectoral, Cat. no. 156
3. Electrum pendant and gold hair pin, Cat. no. 158
4. Vulture flask, Cat. no. 142

16 HEAD OF A WOMAN
Reign of Senusret I, 1943–1899 BC

Face and part of the wig from a life-size statue of a woman. Diorite. Length of face: 9.9 cm. Width of face: 9.2 cm. Length of eye: 3.3 cm. The woman probably wears the Hathor wig (see Cat. no. 14). Her brows are naturalistically shaped but follow a straight line in relation to the eyes, which are wide and set at a slant in her face. They protrude slightly, the inner canthi are marked, and the lower lids deeply cut. The nose is long and straight with well defined, rounded nostrils which are hollowed out. The philtrum is similarly emphatic, and the full lower lip curves upwards in a smile. The chin is square. There are deep grooves at the corner of the mouth and around the wings of the nose, and a sharp ridge along the top of the cheeks.

16

Gift of W. L. Ferguson. Royal Museum of Scotland 1923.350. H: 17.8 cm. W: 11.7 cm.

The large scale of this sculpture is surprising. There are very few private sculptures of the Middle Kingdom which approach life-size. The quality of the workmanship and the treatment of the face, especially eyes, brow, nose and cheeks, recall the fine statue of the Lady Sennuwy in the Boston Museum of Fine Arts, which is also close to life-size and like this one shows no cosmetic line. Sennuwy's husband, the nomarch Hepzefa, served King Senusret I. The appeal of this anonymous woman's face is in her smile, which gently pushes upwards and outwards all her facial contours. Its gentle idealisation recalls the face of the funerary statues made for Senusret I's mortuary chapel at Lisht. What Vandier calls 'L'architecture du visage' is very similar – a broad, square face with prominent cheek bones level with the wings of the nostrils, wide open eyes with pronounced inner canthi, square chin, and deep creases running out from the wings of the nostrils.

Cf. Smith, *Art and Architecture*, p. 102, pls. 65(B), 66, Evers, *Staat aus dem Stein*, I, pl. 29.

17 HEAD OF A MAN
Early Dynasty XII, from reign of Senusret I onwards, 1943–1862 BC

Head of a man, broken away at neck. Quartzite. Length of face: 3.9 cm. Width of face: 4.7 cm. Length of eye: 1.6 cm. Length of ear: 2.2 cm. The man wears a shoulder-length wig, which probably ended in the front in rounded lappets. The rounded brows follow the contours of the eyes, and with the nose and cheek-bones form circular eye sockets. The eyes themselves are wide, measuring 0.5 cm; inner canthi are evident but not exaggerated. The fold of the upper lid is shown and the modelling of the flesh under the eye is remarkably subtle. The ears, which are set low, show the same attention to detail, the anti-helix and tragus as well as the outer rim being shown. The nose is short, with large nostrils emphasised by deep grooves. The mouth is wide with thin lips, the philtrum clearly present. The face is exceptionally broad, being in fact wider than it is long. The chin beard, which was probably not much longer when complete, may represent natural hair rather than an artificial beard, since no strap attaching it to the ears is visible.

Gift of K. M. Mylne. Royal Museum of Scotland 1952.197. H: 9.6 cm. W: 9.3 cm.

The beautiful colour and subtle modelling of this extremely hard stone is typical of the best sculpture of Dynasty XII. Attention is focused on the eyes, the seat of life. The reconstruction of the wig remains uncertain. The bottom is

17

just visible at the back, proving it was shoulder length, but the side view suggests it had long side lappets. The absence of a cosmetic line, (cf. Cat. no. 11), is unusual but not unprecedented. The statue of Sennuwy in Boston, already referred to in relation to Cat. no. 16, is firmly dated to the reign of Senusret I and has no line. It may have been retained longer on royal than on private sculpture, since it seems invariable on the former until the reign of Senusret II.

C. Aldred, *The Egyptians* (London, 1961), p. 251, pl. 32; for wig, cf. Vandier, *La Statuaire Egyptienne*, pl. LXXXIV, 5; pl. LXXXVIII, 3; for facial type, cf. Senusret I from Lisht, Evers, *Staat aus dem Stein*, pl. 29, and wooden statuette of the same date, *ibid.*, pl. 46.

18 STATUE OF KHUSOBEK
Early Dynasty XII, 1963–1862 BC.

Seated statue in black diorite. Length of face: 3.6 cm. Width of face: 3.7 cm. Length of eye: 1.4 cm. Length of ear: 2.1 cm. Khusobek wears a bag wig (*khat* in Egyptian). The eyes were originally inlaid and damage occurred to the brows and the eye socket rims when this was removed. The outer rim and the inner elevation of the ear are shown. The nose is long, its profile flattened by wear, and the nostrils are wide. The philtrum is marked and there are traces of an incised line around the lips. These are full and straight with a pronounced hollow at each corner. There is a small chin beard, 0.7 cm long with wavy vertical incisions to represent the hair. The overall impression is of a broad, triangular face delineated by high, prominent cheek-bones and beard. The surface of the torso is divided in front by a vertical groove extending from navel to pectoral muscles, and at the back by the backbone. Pectoral muscles, rib cage, shoulder muscles and navel are shown, and so are the biceps of the upper arms. The lower arms and legs are more summarily treated, emphasising bone rather than musculature. The fingers and toes, with their nails shown, are long and splayed. The right hand, gripping a handkerchief (see Cat. no. 19), rests on the knee. Two lines of a crudely incised inscription are scratched on the cube base, in front of the feet and alongside the left foot.

Royal Museum of Scotland 1959.24. H: 38.1 cm. W: 12.6 cm.

The pronounced median line of both front and back of the torso and the heavy, well-muscled shoulders and upper arms are typical of the private and royal sculptures of early Dynasty XII. The dignity and authority of the figure is such that the empty eye-sockets, mutilated by the clumsy removal of inlays, shock us. Inlaid eyes are rare in private stone statues though common in wooden statues of the early Middle Kingdom.

The cult of the crocodile god, Sobek, was especially popular in the Middle Kingdom, as witnessed by the many people who honoured him in their personal names. Khusobek means 'Sobek protects [him]' and following the usual practice of honorific transposition the god's name is written first. The inscription is clumsily scratched in irregularly spaced hieroglyphs and part of it is now illegible. It contrasts poorly

18

with the fine quality of the sculpture itself and it is possible that the statue was taken over by Khusobek, having originally been made for someone else.

Davies, *A Royal Statue Reattributed*, p. 20, n. 92; cf. statues of Sarenput I and Hapy from Elephantine, both dated to reign of Senusret I, Habachi, *Heqaib*, nos. 3, 4, pp. 31–3, pls. 17, 19.

19 THE OVERSEER OF PRIESTS, SENUSRET SON OF IP
Early Dynasty XII, from reign of Amenemhat II onwards, 1901–1862 BC.

Inscribed statuette of a seated man in black basalt. Length of face: 2.1 cm. Width of face: 2.1 cm. Length of eye: 0.9 cm. Length of ear: 1.5 cm. Senusret, son of Ip, sits wrapped in a cloak which reaches his ankles, his arms crossed, right over left, on his chest, and his right hand holding a handkerchief. He wears a full shoulder-length wig with pointed lappets, and a rectangular back pillar reaches from the base of his seat to the bottom of the wig.

Senusret has an impressive list of titles. He was priest or overseer of priests in five shrines or temples dedicated to Wadjet, Hathor, Anubis, Min and Khnum, and mayor of the town called the Horizon of King Senusret. His brows, distinctly rounded and following the outline of the eye, are carved in raised relief, and the eyes themselves show the upper lid and a sculpted pupil. The eye sockets are deep and carry the suggestion of bags under the eyes. The outer rim of the ear is shown, and the inner ear suggested by a raised crescent of stone. The nose is long and straight with a pointed tip. The mouth has a thin upper and full lower lip with deep notches at the corners. The chin is round and marked with a small indentation. The body and limbs show little modelling, but the nails on fingers and toes are meticulously shown. The statuette is inscribed on both sides of the base and down the back pillar.

19

Probably from Lisht. Ex Northumberland collection. Oriental Museum, University of Durham N.501. H: 21.3 cm. W: 7.8 cm.

The proportions of the face, which is as broad as it is long, the relief brows and the thick, straight lower lip all suggest a date in the early xiith Dynasty. The inscriptions suggest that he was mayor of the town which grew up to serve the pyramid complex of King Senusret I (see Cat. no. 11) at Lisht. Of the five cults which he served, those of Hathor of Atfih (a town about twenty miles south of Lisht) and of Anubis were celebrated in the King's mortuary temple within the pyramid complex, and the three others, those of the gods Min, Khnum and Wadjet, were probably attached to shrines in the region immediately south of Lisht. This circumstantial evidence strongly suggests that Senusret's statuette was originally set up in the royal mortuary temple at Lisht and not long, judging by its style, after the King's death. The seated pose showing the dead man totally wrapped in a close-fitting cloak recalls the small mummiform figures on model boats (Cat. no. 79). According to Vandier, the cloak itself first appears on private statuary in the round in the middle of the Dynasty, and during the reign of Amenemhat II on the stelae analysed by Malaise. For the absence of a cosmetic line, see note on Cat. no. 17. The object held in the right hand is identified as a small roll of cloth – a handkerchief; it is more clearly shown here than on Cat. no. 18. This object, which occurs on Egyptian sculptures in the round and in relief from Dynasty iv down to the Graeco-Roman period, has been much discussed but is now generally agreed to be a roll of linen.

S. Birch, *Catalogue of the Collection of Egyptian Antiquities at Alnwick Castle* (London, 1880), pp. 6off.; F. Gomáa in *SAK* 11 (1984), pp. 107–12, pls. 2–3. For wig and facial type, cf. statue of Sarenput II in Habachi, *Heqaib*, no. 13, p. 42, pls. 32–3, and for the roll of cloth, H. Fischer in *MMJ* 10 (1975), pp. 143–55; for cloak, see Malaise in Mélanges Vercoutter, p. 221, n. 24.

20 STELA OF THE SCULPTOR, USERWER

Early Dynasty xii, 1963–1862 BC.

Rectangular limestone stela carved in sunk relief. The composition divides horizontally into three unequal parts. The first and longest section consists of five lines of large well-spaced hieroglyphs setting out in conventional phrases the request for offerings for Userwer and an appeal to passers-by to recite the offering formula at his tomb. The two bottom registers are of equal size. The first shows on the right, Userwer and his wife, Sitdepetneter, being presented with offerings by another wife, Sitenameny, and on the left, his parents, Senkhonsu and Sitnebniwt, receiving the symbolic offering of the leg of an ox from Userwer's son, Seneferwuser. In the bottom register is a row of five daughters, from right to left, Sitwadja, Sitseri, Iymery, Ankhyt and Sitnebniwt, preceded by a son, Horuser, and followed perhaps by Userwer himself and a brother, Nebniwt. The signs in the principal inscription and the figures and their captions at the bottom face to the left, so these registers are to be read from left to

20

right. The middle register divides in the centre, where the two figures making offerings stand back to back, and the captions are arranged accordingly, i.e. the signs face the direction in which the figure to which they refer is looking. The men are all dressed alike in a shoulder-length curled wig, knee-length wrapover kilt with front pleat, bracelets and a bead collar. The women's dress is also undifferentiated, consisting of tunics reaching from under their breasts to the ankles, with narrow shoulder straps, long full-bottomed wigs, bead collars, bracelets and anklets. The three most prominent women, those in the middle register, all have mirrors in cases, beside them or under their chairs.

The special interest of this otherwise conventional monument lies in the fact that the owner was a sulptor (*gnwty* is the word used), and that it is unfinished and shows every stage in its making. First the thick framing lines were applied defining the base lines of the registers and the lines of the inscription. Then grid squares 5 mm × 5 mm were applied over the areas which were to carry human figures. Both sets of lines were applied in red, the thicker ones probably freehand and the grid by dipping string into the pigment, stretching it across the surface and snapping it hard to transfer a straight line on to the stone. The figures were then drawn in full in black on to the grid, the outline cut out and, in the final stage, interior detail sculpted. All the inscriptions were added after the black line drawings were made but before the figures were cut out.

British Museum EA. 579. H: 55.0 cm. W: 47.5 cm.

The various stages of completeness of the stela demonstrate that it was worked from top right to bottom left, thus following the principal orientation of the figures and inscriptions. It was also executed by a team of craftsmen of differing abilities. The black ink drawings show great confidence of line and an ability to introduce uncluttered detail into a small-scale drawing. Not all these details are reproduced by the stone-cutter: the cosmetic line, for example, clearly present in the ink drawings, disappears in the finished figures. Since the presence or absence of a cosmetic line is chronologically significant, this is an important omission. The quality of the stone-cutting itself shows the presence of at least two hands. The figures and objects in the central register show careful cutting with considerable interior modelling of the sunk relief. The same is true of the first two figures in the bottom row, but thereafter the cutting line deteriorates rapidly and flat incision replaces modelling. One may imagine that the stela was needed in a hurry with six figures remaining to be cut and it was handed on to be completed by a novice who progressively lost his nerve, giving up altogether on the fourth figure. A similar, but less gross, disparity exists in the execution of the hieroglyphic inscriptions. Following the usual conventions the signs become smaller in the lower two registers, but the spacing and arrangement of the signs also becomes very clumsy. Note especially the *sat* group suspended alone in front of the sixth figure in the bottom register.

Which of the various functions illustrated on this stela were actually performed by Userwer we no not know. The precise meaning of *gnwty*, and the way it may have differed from the word *hmww* 'craftsman' when applied to a sculptor (Cat. no. 13), are not yet known. A relatively lowly status for Userwer and his family may perhaps be inferred from the fact that he is the only person who bears a title. I have assumed throughout that the pronoun 'his' attached to a kinship term refers to Userwer. The seventh figure in the bottom register is called 'his father, Userwer', so I have assumed that the 'his' here refers to Userwer's son Horuser who heads the procession of daughters. This lack of clarity is typical of the family relationships given on Middle Kingdom stelae. They are an immensely important source for social historians but unless the precise filiation is provided, as in 'Userwer born of Sitnebniwt', we are often at a loss to understand the nuances of relationships within an extended family – in this case covering four generations. Userwer's two wives are another example. Both carry the usual designation for wife, *hmt.f*, but we may surmise that Sitdepetneter shown embracing Userwer in front of the table of offerings is dead, having died before her husband, while his widow Sitenameny stands before them, taking on the responsibility for the funerary cult of both her husband and his first wife. There is little unequivocal evidence to suggest that men commonly had more than one wife in the Middle Kingdom, but conversely there seems to have been no legal or social barrier against it. Where filiation is provided on a stela it is more usual for the mother's rather than the father's name to be given, and this is typical of the whole Middle Kingdom. It is interesting also to note the passing on of personal names within the family: one of Userwer's daughters bore her grandmother's name; another, her great-grandmother's name.

The date of the stela can be established from the general character of the inscription, the inclusion of certain phrases in the formula, and the precise form of some of the hieroglyphic signs. In contrast to Cat. no. 10 the main text is conventionally funerary, not autobiographical, and given Userwer's profession this is to be regretted, but it is an indication of a date in the early XIIth rather than XIth Dynasty. The phrase *n-ka-n-imakh*, 'for the *ka* of the revered one', the writing of 'Lord of Busiris', the epithet of Osiris, and the form of the book roll sign in the bottom register all indicate a date early in Dynasty XII before the reign of Senusret III. The narrow shoulder straps of the women's tunics are also characteristic of this period.

British Museum, *Hieroglyphic Texts*, II, p. 7, pl. XV; K. R. Lepsius, *Auswahl der wichtigsten Urkunden des aegyptischen Alterthums* (Leipzig, 1842), pl. XXI; Lilyquist, *Mirrors*, p. 48, n. 547; for women's dress, Malaise in *Mélanges Vercoutter*, p. 220.

21 BLOCK STATUE OF A GENERAL
Reigns of Amenemhat I to Senusret I, 1963–1899 BC.

Fragment of front of a block statue in hornblende gneiss. The back has been sawn away in modern times. The pose is that of a man seated with his legs drawn up in front of his body, his elbows resting on his knees, his arms crossed and his hands resting flat on his upper arms. The legs are bare. The bones and musculature of the knee and lower leg are precisely, even pedantically, defined. Between the legs are two vertical lines of hieroglyphic inscription naming 'the general and seal bearer of the King, Montu . . .'.

Probably from Thebes. Fitzwilliam E16.1969. H: 40.0 cm. W: 20.5 cm. D: 12.8 cm.

The provenance of the fragment is unknown, but we may surmise that the man for whom it was made came from the Theban area. He is described as one revered before Montu, who was, before the ascendency of Amun, the most important god of Thebes. Montu was also part of his name (the rest is lost) and it was commn practice to incorporate the name of the local god into one's personal name. In Munich there is a block statue in the same material of a man called Nes-Montu, also a seal bearer of the King and a general whom we know from other monuments to have lived in the reigns of Amenemhat I and Senusret I. The coincidence of two of the titles (although Nes-montu has the epithet 'great' added to his title of general), part of the name, the material and the singular pose strongly suggest that both statues are of

21

trated); cf. Firth and Gunn, *Teti Pyramid Cemeteries*, pl. 41; for Munich statue, D. Wildung in *MDAIK* 37 (1981), pp. 503–7.

22 THE STEWARD ANUY, SON OF SITHATHOR

Reigns of Amenemhat II to Senusret II, 1901–1862 BC.

Granite block statuette of the steward, Anuy, squatting with folded arms resting on his knees. Length of face: 1.9 cm. Width of face: 2.4 cm. Length of eye: 0.9 cm. Length of ear: 1.6 cm. Anuy is entirely enveloped in a long cloak, the hem of which is just discernible at the ankles. He wears a wide shoulder-length wig, which meets the parent block directly in front but is slightly undercut at the back. The brows are lightly cut and follow the contour of the eye. The eyes themselves are wide, with the inner canthi marked, but they narrow sharply towards the outer edge. The upper lid is marked. The ears are remarkably asymmetrical, the right set noticeably higher than the left, and little detail is suggested beyond the outer rim and the lobe. The nose is long with a sharp tip and both lips are straight and thick and slightly pouting. The face is broad with rounded cheeks and the chin is small. There is no neck, the head appearing to grow out of the block with only a minimal gap between them. The contours of the body under the garment are just visible, helped in side view by the contrast between the polished and unpolished areas of the stone. The top of the block where the hands are shown palm downwards in relief has been left rough and unfinished, making an unnaturally sharp edge where the elbows rest on the knees. In contrast the feet emerge sturdy and broad from

the same man. Even if this is not accepted, the Munich statue provides a parallel close enough to justify the date suggested. The material of the Fitzwilliam statue fragment was identified by Dr Colin Forbes of the Sidgwick Natural History Museum, Cambridge.

The block statue was an innovation of Dynasty XII, incorporating the functions of a funerary stela and those of a statue. It evolved out of the increasing demand for statues of private individuals to be set up in tomb chapels and mortuary temples. The squatting pose reproduces the natural seated position of everyday life – chairs, then as now in Egypt, were used for more formal occasions. The bare legs add to the air of informality. The owner appears to be entirely naked, but he almost certainly wore a short kilt of which all trace is lost because the back is missing. The statue was intended to be seen only from the front and the sculptor has taken advantage of this to use the legs as a frame for the inscription. Nevertheless by emphasising their bones and musculature he has created a strongly three-dimensional sculpture, which expresses the energy and strength of the human body rather than the block of stone from which it emerges.

Bourriau, *Three Middle Kingdom Sculptures* (in press); *Christie's Sale Catalogue*, 10 June 1969, lot no. 131 (illus-

22

the cloak, and the lower legs provide a vertical frame for the one-line inscription.

Eton College, Myers Museum 17. H: 17.7 cm. W: 8.2 cm.

The sculptor of this small monument obviously had difficulty carving the inscription in the hard granite. The signs are scratched and poorly spaced. In the development of Middle Kingdom block statues, this type, with only the feet exposed, occurs between Cat. no. 21, where the legs are three dimensional, and those examples in which the figure is completely enveloped in its cloak. The earliest dated example of the group to which the Eton statue belongs is the statue of Sihathor in the British Museum, of the reign of Amenemhat II. In support of this date, Anuy's statuette shows none of the facial traits of the late XIIth Dynasty, though it must be said that the definition of the features is not strong. Again one senses that this sculptor at least was not able to overcome his intractable material.

Burlington Fine Arts Club, 1895, p. 11, no. 68.

23 MESEHTI OF ASYUT Illustrated in colour on pl. III, 1.

Reign of Nebhepetre Montuhotep, 2023–1982 BC.

Wooden statuette of a striding man on its original base, made in four parts with joins at the shoulders and the front of the right foot. Length of face: 5.0 cm. Width of face: 5.5 cm. Length of eye: 1.9 cm. Length of ear: 3.2 cm. The knots in the wood, originally covered with a thick layer of fine plaster and pigment, are now very evident. The shaven head is remarkably flat and broad. The sculptured brows, originally painted black, are thick and blunt-ended and do not follow the contour of the eye. The eye itself, painted flat inside a deeply cut-out socket, is very wide and round. It is outlined in black; the eyeball is painted white and the pupil black. There is a faint trace of a cosmetic line on the left eye. The enormous ears curve outwards from the skull, and only the outer rim, in stylised outline, is shown. The nose is long and straight with rounded nostrils and the lips are thick, widening in the centre, with deep grooves at the corner of the mouth. The chin is small and round.

In contrast to the face, which has lost definition with the loss of its paint, the body is strongly modelled. A deep navel notch extends upwards to the breasts which are emphasised by strong curves and separately made nipples. The waist is narrow but the stomach swells out gently and is evidently constrained by the belt of the kilt. The muscles at the back of the neck are shown, but none elsewhere on the torso. The muscles and bones of the arms are merely suggested, but the fingers of the extended hand are long with white-painted nails. The toe nails were also originally painted white. There are faint traces of a necklace, clearest at the back. The end tie of the wrapover kilt projects and is made of a separate piece of wood. A square notch has been cut in the right side of the front pleat of the kilt, presumably to take the handle of the short sceptre once held in the right hand. However, due to warping of the wood, the notch does not now line up exactly with the hole in the clenched right hand. The figure is supported by tenons on the underside of the feet

23

which slot into the base. The feet were originally covered with a thick layer of coarse plaster which may have been intended to secure them to the base.

From Asyut, tomb of Mesehti. Eton College, Myers Museum 7. H: 62.8 cm. W: 14.8 cm.

The statuette is at present uninscribed, but there may once have been a painted inscription on the base. Its attribution to the tomb of Mesehti is given unequivocally by the catalogue of the Myers collection at Eton, and it was published as such in 1895. Newberry certainly believed the attribution and for this reason presented Eton in 1936 with a staff, also supposedly from the tomb, which he bought at the Macgregor sale in 1922, see Cat. no. 24. There is one piece of independent evidence. The tomb was not excavated; it was discovered and robbed by local villagers in 1893, although a large model boat from the tomb had been acquired by the Cairo Museum as early as 1875. In 1893 some of the robbers' finds were bought for the Cairo Museum, including two famous models of troops of soldiers. In describing these, Grébaut, an official of the Museum writing before 1900, mentions that at least one of the larger wooden figures from the tomb had been bought by an Englishman and was now in a private collection. Myers kept a diary which is also in Eton, but one volume is missing, the one recording a visit to Egypt between June 1893 and March 1894.

The style of the statue supports the attribution. The troop of model Egyptian soldiers from the tomb shows very similar treatment of the torso and the painted features of the face. The flat skull and the stylised treatment of the ear with its angular outer rim may be compared with Cat. no. 25, also probably from Asyut. A smaller (43 cm high) wooden statuette, also uninscribed, which is now in Copenhagen, has been attributed to the tomb of Mesehti, although the most recent publication simply states that it is thought to have come from Asyut. It is in a rather different style, showing a man wearing a short kilt and short curled wig and having inlaid eyes. It is certainly of the same date as the Eton statuette (incorrectly dated to Dynasty XII–XIII by Mogensen), and there are several examples from Asyut of statuettes of the same man made in quite different styles.

Exactly when Mesehti lived is not certain; he may have been living at the time of the unification of Egypt under Nebhepetre Montuhotep, to judge by the style of his coffin, which compares with that of one of the King's concubines. He was a seal bearer of the King and overseer of the priests of Wepwawet, the chief god of Asyut, and he lived at a time when local princes controlled their own schools of craftsmen, who produced individual and often outstanding work under their patronage. The characteristic preference for wood rather than stone may be due to the inaccessibility of stone quarries to men whose power, though great, was confined to their own locality. A small alabaster sculpture attributed to Mesehti in Cairo is crude and unskilled by comparison with the wooden objects from the tomb.

Burlington Fine Arts Club, 1895, p. 37, no. 8; see also M. E. Grébaut, *Le Musée Egyptien*, I (Cairo, 1890–1900), p. 32; for statuette in Copenhagen, Mogensen, *Glyptothèque Ny Carlsberg*, p. 16, pl. XIV, A62; for date, E. Brovarski in *Dunham Essays*, p. 24, n. 75; Spanel, *Boat Models*, n. 20; model soldiers, Saleh and Sourouzian, *Cairo Museum*, nos. 72–3.

24 STAFF OF MESEHTI OF ASYUT
Reign of Nebhepetre Montuhotep, 2023–1982 BC.

A wooden staff said to be of olive wood, rounded off at both ends. It is undecorated, there are signs of wear at both ends, and the whole surface is polished from frequent handling.

From Asyut, tomb of Mesehti. Gift of Percy Newberry. Eton College, Myers Museum 36.15. H: 99.3 cm.

The staff was acquired by the Reverend William Macgregor with this provenance, between the 1880s, when he began collecting, and 1922, when his vast collection of Egyptian antiquities was sold at Sotheby's in a sale of 1800 lots lasting nine days. It was purchased by Newberry, who catalogued the collection for Sotheby's, and presented by him to Eton to accompany the statue of Mesehti, Cat. no. 23, during Henley Week in 1936. The staff shows clear signs of use – it was Mesehti's staff of office, or at least one of them – and its fine condition suggests it may have been protected by being placed inside the coffin (cf. Chassinat and Palanque, *Assiout*, fig. 3).

The Macgregor Collection, Sotheby's Sale Catalogue, June–July 1922, lot no. 637; see H. Fischer in *MMJ* 13 (1978), p. 15.

25 A STRIDING MAN
Early Dynasty XII, 1963–1892 BC.

Statuette of a striding man on its original base. Carved, except for the toes of the right foot, from a single piece of tamarisk wood (identified by the Jodrell laboratory, Kew Gardens). Length of face: 3.0 cm. Width of face: 3.2 cm. Length of eye: 1.0 cm. Length of ear: 1.8 cm. He wears a skull cap or close-cropped natural hair, and the top of his head is unnaturally flat. The eyebrows are long and straight and painted black; a painted cosmetic line encircles each eye. The eyes themselves are inlaid with alabaster and obsidian; the pupil of the right eye is missing. The ears are large in relation to the small triangular face, and shown in some detail, but the ear lobe is not differentiated. The nose is short with a pronounced central ridge, and the mouth is straight and turned slightly downwards. The chin is small and rounded. The torso is treated in some detail: the clavicle has a pronounced central notch, the breasts are prominent with rolls of fat underneath them and the navel is very wide. There is a subtle but unmistakable suggestion of plumpness in the outward curve of the stomach above the kilt. In contrast the arms, back and buttocks emphasise only bone and muscle, though there is another neat roll of fat on the back of the neck. He wears a long wrapover skirt and his right hand is tucked into the flap. The whole figure is tilted back slightly to suit the forward walking pose. The base is covered with a red pigment, but apart from the eyes and brows there is no trace of paint elsewhere.

Probably from Asyut. Gift of the Friends of the Fitzwilliam Museum. Fitzwilliam E.3.1922. H: 40 cm (including 4 cm base). W: 9.0 cm.

F. W. Green, Honorary Keeper of Egyptian Antiquities, bought the statuette at the sale of the Macgregor Collection in 1922 for £6 for the Friends of the Fitzwilliam. No provenance or date is given in the catalogue. Nevertheless the distinctive treatment of the torso, combined with the pose of the right hand holding the kilt flap, seem peculiar to a group of wooden sculptures excavated by Chassinat and Palanque in Asyut in 1903. The closest parallel is the magnificent life-size statue of Nakht, now in the Louvre. In his publication Chassinat makes it clear that both before and after his work, objects exactly similar to those he was finding appeared on the art market. There is a possibility worth mentioning, but, I suspect, beyond final proof, that the Fitzwilliam statuette is from the tomb of Nakht itself. There are discrepancies between the text descriptions, compiled by Chassinat several years later from Palanque's notes, and the statuettes illustrated in the plates.

'Un léger embonpoint' (the phrase is Chassinat's) is characteristic of depictions of the tomb owner in relief and sculpture

24

left foot. Length of face: 3.2 cm. Width of face: 3.6 cm. Length of eye: 1.4 cm. The body, including the head, and the base are painted reddish-brown, the kilt is white and brows, eyes, mouth and edge of the hair are outlined in black. All the paint is applied over a thin layer of fine white plaster. Itefib is shown with his natural hair covering his ears, and the individual curls are separately incised in the wood. His brows are modelled and the eyes are exceptionally large and wide (0.6 cm). They are set at a slant and their outline is incised and painted black. The eyeball is white and the pupil black, and a painted cosmetic line extends from the outer corner to the hair. The nose is a long, solid wedge in the face and the mouth wide and thin, the lower lip protruding slightly. The chin is small and square and a thin black painted line, representing a trimmed natural beard, runs around it and reaches the ear lobes. The body, especially below the waist, is disproportionately small and slender in relation to

25

in the round throughout the Middle Kingdom. Plumpness was, as it still is in Egypt today, a sign of wealth, status and good health. In this case the artist has taken care to see that an impression of vigour is in no way impaired by it. The mannered style is a reminder that this statue also represents one of the provincial schools of sculpture which evolved during the preceding First Intermediate Period.

Bourriau, *Three Middle Kingdom Sculptures* (in press); cf. Chassinat and Palanque, *Assiout*, pls. VI–VII, XI; C. Desroches-Noblecourt and J. Vercoutter (eds.), *Un Siècle de Fouilles Françaises en Égypte* (Paris, 1981), no. 106.

26 THE GENERAL ITEFIB

Early Dynasty XII, 1963–1862 BC.

Wooden statuette of a striding man on the original base, carved in four pieces, with joins at shoulders and front of

26

the head. The neck is short and fat and there is a suggestion of plumpness around the waist. Front and back of the torso are divided by the navel groove and the backbone respectively. The principal muscles and bones of arms and legs are represented and hands and feet carefully shown, with particular attention to toe and finger nails which are painted white. Itefib wears a short pleated kilt with a central tab, and his name and title with an abbreviated form of the funerary formula have been carved on the base.

Ex Rustafjaell collection. Bequest of E. Towry-Whyte. Fitzwilliam E.219.1932. H (including base): 35.9 cm. W: 8.8 cm.

In this sculpture all attention is focused on the head, which appears to jut forward following the forward movement of the body; compare Cat. no. 27. The statuette would originally have been provided with two staffs, a long one for the left hand and a short one held horizontally in the right hand. These were symbols of his authority. Itefib's title, also shared by Cat. no. 21, is commonly and conveniently translated as 'general', but this may be a little misleading, cf. Cat. no. 61. The title can mean simply someone in charge of a group of soldiers or a gang of workmen. This may be the case here, since Itefib has no other titles or indications of high rank. Small-scale wooden sculptures such as this and Cat. nos. 25, 27 were placed inside the tomb, sometimes beside or inside the coffin, to provide an additional home for the deceased's spirit or *ka*.

The statuette was purchased by Towry-Whyte at the Rustafjaell sale.

Sotheby's Sale Catalogue, January 1913, lot no. 711A.

27 NAKHTNETER FROM BENI HASAN

Reigns of Amenemhat II to Senusret II, 1901–1862 BC.

Wooden statuette of a striding man, made in seven pieces with joins at shoulders, left elbow, front of both feet and toes of left foot. Length of face: 2.5 cm. Width of face: 2.6 cm. Length of eye: 0.8 cm. Length of ear: 1.1 cm. The statuette, including the kilt, is covered with a thin layer of plaster and painted reddish-brown. The original base, into which the tangs projecting from the feet once fitted, is now lost. Although the skull is painted brown, the outline of the natural hair, with tabs in front of the ears, is given in black, suggesting perhaps that the head was not shaved. The brows, carved thin and straight, are emphasised by a painted black line which is less curved than the sculptured line. The rim of the eye is deeply incised, with a pronounced inner canthus and a cosmetic line 0.3 cm long. The eyes are large, wide open, with black painted pupils. The ears are shown in full and naturalistically proportioned detail. The nose is long and straight, with an emphatic curve around the nostrils. The philtrum is marked and the lips protrude, the lower lip being fuller than the upper. The bunched muscles at the corner of the mouth push the mouth upwards into a smiling expression. The chin is square and juts forwards. The cheeks show extensive modelling, suggesting the underlying bony structure of the face.

The treatment of the body is mannered, unlike that of the

27

head. The ridge of the clavicle is pronounced, but far below its natural position. The breasts are carved, with nipples painted black, and a deep vertical groove runs from them to the navel. Backbone and shoulder muscles are shown, but there is a suggestion of fleshiness in the line running under the breasts and the faint bulge about the kilt. The muscles and bones of the shoulder and forearm, and (exceptionally) of knee, calf and ankle, are carefully shown, and there is individual shaping of the toes. The thumbs on both hands are large and well shaped. Nakhtneter wears a very short pleated kilt, and originally carried a long staff and a short sceptre.

From Beni Hasan, tomb 720. Ex Kennard collection. British Museum EA. 65440. H: 14.0 cm. W: 6.2 cm.

The statuette was found by Garstang in a tomb at Beni Hasan, identified as the burial place of Nakhtneter by the remains of his inscribed but unpublished coffin. The crudely cut sticks representing his staff and sceptre are visible on the plate in the Sotheby's sale catalogue of the Kennard collection. The pottery suggests the burial belongs in the mid-XIIth Dynasty. Despite its curious proportions – the head is much too large for the body – the sculpture conveys a lively energy, due to the vigorous modelling of the eyes and mouth. The presence of the painted cosmetic line is noteworthy. It was no longer universal, by the reign of Senusret II, but it may have remained longer among the more conservative craftsmen in the provinces. The line may also have faded with time on both stone and wooden statues, if it was painted and not carved. A similar comment may be applied to the apparently shaven heads of some statues, Cat. nos. 23, 25 and even Cat. nos. 53 and 56. The skull may originally have been painted black to represent the natural hair.

Garstang, *Burial Customs*, pp. 137–8; *BMQ* 17 (1952), no. 4, pp. 71–2, pl. xxviia; *Sotheby's Sale Catalogues*, July 1912, lot no. 500, pl. ix; July 1950, lot no. 198.

LATE DYNASTY XII: SENUSRET III TO SOBEKNEFRU, 1862–1787 BC

The sculptures of Senusret III and his son Amenemhat III present us with something totally new, the combination of individual portrait and royal icon. The royal features were faithfully reproduced and, as their reigns progressed, showed signs of ageing and in the case of Senusret III a deepening

28

expression of sorrow and disdain. We can study the physiognomy of these Kings, assured that we are looking at individual men, not an idealised image of kingship. We can see the family resemblance and observe the burden of being Pharaoh etching its way into their faces.

However, this is Middle Kingdom Egypt, not Renaissance Europe, and our instinctive response to the humanity of the portraits may distort our view. Relatively few complete statues have come down to us compared with the number of heads which survive, over 100 of Senusret III alone. In

itself this encourages us to underestimate the magisterial quality of this sculpture in favour of its humanity. The body of the King remains totally idealised, strong and vigorous; no sign of age is permitted to touch the royal limbs. Even the sleek plumpness of the middle-aged official (see Cat. no. 35) is never applied to the King. The traditional poses and iconography continue; although there are innovations which we do not fully understand, and explorations of old images, such as the lion sphinx, they all express facets of the same ancient idea, the awesome divinity of Pharaoh. The concept is fundamentally unchanged in the late xiith Dynasty, but it is amplified and celebrated in both art and literature:

Hail to you, Khakaure [Senusret III], our Horus, Divine of Form!
Land's protector who widens its borders,
Who smites foreign countries with his crown.
Who holds the Two Lands in his arms' embrace.

(Lichtheim, *Literature*, I, p. 198)

This is an excerpt from a cycle of hymns to Senusret III composed to be sung, it is suggested, before statues of the King in the temple at Lahun.

For whom and for what purpose were these royal statues made? The quarrying of the stone, the making and distribution of statues, colossal as well as life-size, took much time and many resources, but was considered an important and necessary function of kingship. Most were made for a particular architectural setting, which has usually been destroyed by time and by the ruthless quarrying of their buildings by successor Kings, see Cat. nos. 12–13. The setting was usually a temple, either a mortuary temple celebrating the King's own or a predecessor's cult, or the temple of a god. In either case the statue would have been seen regularly only by priests admitted to these holy places. Nevertheless we may presume that the installation of a royal statue was an occasion of rejoicing and for reasserting the power of the King in a particular locality, and that thereafter it became a focal point of piety.

In this context we can understand that the way in which the King was represented, down to the smallest detail, was enormously significant. Kings usurped the statues of predecessors, but it was often not enough to change the name; headdress and sometimes features had to be recut to suit the contemporary image. If these details were so significant to the Kings who commanded them to be made, it justifies the seemingly pedantic attention given to them by art historians. We count the stripes in the *nemes* headcloth and the number of coils in the body of the uraeus, not only because they vary from one reign to the next, and even within a reign, but because we know that all such changes were consciously wrought.

Much ink has been spilt on trying to arrange the portraits of Senusret III and Amenemhat III into stylistic groups, using criteria such as this. The five sculptures of these Kings in the exhibition do not allow us to survey the whole problem, but they do suggest some comments upon it. The starting point for grouping the portraits has been to analyse those statues whose provenance is known, in order to identify the style of local schools to which unprovenanced sculptures can be attributed. Vandier, the most authoritative proponent of this method, attempts to isolate products of Thebes from those of Faiyum/Memphis and the Delta. The interpretation based on Vandier's work which emerges in most general accounts hardly does justice to his painstaking and acute analysis when it speaks of the 'realism' of the Theban school as opposed to the 'idealisation' of the Memphite school, heir of the traditions of the Old Kingdom. This generalisation gains support from the contrast we have already observed between the early and later sculpture of Nebhepetre Montuhotep, representing 'brutal realism' (Cat. nos. 2, 4) and bland idealisation (Cat. no. 5), respectively.

Of our five sculptures, none is inscribed and only one, the head of Amenemhat III from Aswan, Cat. no. 31, is provenanced, and I think it unlikely to have been made there. This highlights three of the difficulties which undermine the whole structure. The number of inscribed and provenanced pieces is very small, and of these some must be eliminated because we know (in the case of the sphinxes brought to the Delta by Ramesses II) or may infer that they were not made where they were found. Furthermore the identification of

uninscribed heads as representing one King rather than the other is not universally agreed. The head now attributed to Senusret III, Cat. no. 29, was assigned by Gayer-Anderson to Amenemhat III. To confuse the matter even further, statues proved to be from the same site do not invariably exhibit a homogeneous style, and we know that the King sent his master sculptors out to different places to supervise work for him. Since 1958, when Vandier's study appeared, no-one has attempted a comprehensive reappraisal of the problem with full illustration of the many pieces still inadequately published. Until this is done the attribution of individual sculptures to a particular school on stylistic grounds alone is in my view unwise.

The sculptures in the exhibition illustrate three characteristics of the royal portraits which have perhaps been underestimated. First, the differences which resulted from the use of stones of varying hardness and colour (see Cat. no. 32); second, the differing interpretation of their models by sculptors of greater or lesser skill; and finally, the relationship between the portraits of the two Kings. The first two characteristics, choice of material and skill in manipulating it, are

32

linked. The Middle Kingdom saw a well-organised exploitation of the Eastern and Western deserts in the search for new and beautiful stones for buildings, statuary and stone vessels and ornaments. The preference for hard stones – quartzite, granite and diorite – for statues is remarkable, but the sculptor was not always complete master of his material and an uncertain chisel has sometimes led to arguments over attribution.

If one surveys the two reigns as Aldred has done (*MMJ* 3 (1970), pp. 14–24), it is possible to observe a change of pace between the reign of Senusret III and that of Amenemhat III. This may simply be due to the fact that (following the chronology used here) Senusret reigned nineteen years and Amenemhat forty-six years. The creativity of Senusret III's reign is extraordinary, evinced by a series of portraits showing him from youth to old age, executed in the hardest stones with consummate skill. As one might expect, the early portraits of Amenemhat III show some of the features of his father's image carried over by artists who had not yet adjusted to the new one. Once that phase is passed, however, Amenemhat III's portrait does not evolve as dramatically as that of his father, but becomes fixed halfway through his reign. There are no portraits of Amenemhat III as an old man. Perhaps it is as a result of this decline in inventiveness that mannerisms begin to appear, and these originally slight exaggerations become amplified in the sculptures of the Kings of Dynasty XIII into a new formalism.

If we are entitled to apply the word 'portrait' to royal sculptures of Senusret III and Amenemhat III can we also apply it to the statuary of private individuals of the late XIIth Dynasty? In my view, with some exceptions the answer must be 'no'. The statuette of a plump middle-aged official, Cat. no. 35, is one of the exceptions, and perhaps it is no accident that it is made of wood. We do not know its provenance, but it may have been made at one of the provincial workshops which, though disappearing fast, still produced some of their finest work in the reign of Senusret III. Most of the private hard-stone sculpture of the period shows the unmistakable cast of the royal visage. Eyes were the most important part of the face, the last element to be finished and the first to be attacked by an enemy wishing to destroy the efficacy of a statue; thus it is the heavy-lidded, protuberant eyes of Senusret III which look out from the faces of private sculptures. In addition, a thin-lipped, downward-curving mouth, high cheek bones and pouches under the eyes, an amalgam of the features of both Kings, becomes the convention of the time.

Senusret III precipitated a profound reorganisation in the government of Egypt which had the effect of reducing the power of the local families who controlled the provinces (nomes) into which Egypt was divided. During the First Intermediate period these nomarchs, as they were called, became entirely autonomous with private armies of their own, see Cat. no. 23. However, during the XIth and early XIIth Dynasties, as the monarchy grew in strength and confidence, the power of the nomarchs became increasingly incompatible with the centralised government based in the royal Residence

35

and run by officials appointed by the King. The military campaigns, quarry expeditions and extensive building programme of XIth and XIIth Dynasty Kings drew resources of men and materials to the Residence and so the balance of power inevitably began to shift towards the King. We can observe the results of the change in various ways. A poem composed originally, we may guess, for a local nomarch or mayor, now appears in a cycle of hymns addressed to Senusret III:

How great is the lord of his city:
he is a canal that restrains the river's flood water!
How great is the lord of his city:
he is a cool room that lets a man sleep till dawn!
How great is the lord of his city:
he is a walled rampart of copper of Sinai!

(Lichtheim, *Literature*, I, p. 199)

The King was now being looked to for the protection and patronage that had once come from the 'lord of the city', and this protection extended into the Afterlife. None of the relationships or obligations of daily life ended with death; they continued once the dangers of the transition between this life and the next were overcome. The King's protection was therefore as important after death as it had been in life, but in order to benefit from it it was necessary to be buried as close to the royal tomb as was permitted. This period saw an enormous expansion of the cemeteries around the mortuary complexes of XIIth Dynasty Kings, at Lisht, Dahshur, Hawara and Lahun. For example, we can very clearly observe at the North Cemetery at Lisht the change between early XIIth and late XIIth–XIIIth Dynasties. The cemetery was begun during the long reign of Amenemhat I, the first King of Dynasty XII, and the most important of his officials and members of the royal family had tombs within or close to the royal pyramid and mortuary temple complex. Outside the perimeter wall a cemetery of more humble shaft tombs grew up. In the late XIIth Dynasty, to judge by the pottery, there was a great increase in the use of the cemetery. The original shafts were re-used and many more were dug, sometimes within the precincts of the large tombs of the great men of Amenemhat's reign. From the relatively few inscriptions which survive we can see that the cemetery had been taken over by minor officials and their social equals, people of much lower status than those who had built the large tombs of the earlier reign. These latter people, the viziers and treasurers of the King, had moved away to be buried close to the King they served (Senusret III was buried at Dahshur, Amenemhat II built pyramids at Dahshur and Hawara), leaving Lisht to be overwhelmed by eager newcomers. They benefited from the continuing practice of the royal cult and the prestige of the proximity of the great King.

Opportunities for burial, or at least commemoration, in a sanctified place, close to a royal mortuary temple for example, were open to more people than ever before. This is reflected in changes in the rites and equipment for burial as well as simply in the number and status of those being buried (see below p. 86). Montuhotep, Cat. no. 36, for example, was a simple priest and no other member of his family bore any title. Statues were increasingly deposited in temples, near the doors and in the outer courts, so that the deceased might 'dwell near the god', in the same way that he wished to be sheltered by his lord, the King. His spirit could also benefit in a tangible way from a share of the temple offerings. The most popular site of all for commemorations was the 'Terrace of the Great God' at Abydos, the Great God being Osiris, primeval King of Egypt and ruler of the dead. His tomb was thought to be in the cemetery of the Kings of Egypt's First Dynasty; more particularly it was identified with the tomb of King Djer, see Cat. no. 48. Many people were actually buried at Abydos, mostly local people (see Cat. no. 40), but thousands more set up statues, offering tables and stelae in small offering chapels. These might be families, like that of Amenemhat Nebuy, or groups of people drawn together by work (see Cat. no. 49), down to the most modest who could not afford a carved hieroglyphic stela but were commemorated in ink on crudely carved pieces of limestone, see Cat. no. 41. The practice grew and grew from the late XIIth Dynasty onwards until by the end of the Middle Kingdom, the 'Terrace of the Great God' may have looked something like the cemetery of Père Lachaise in Paris, with streets upon

50 as it was found

streets of chapels of different sizes and shapes, smaller ones squeezed in beside or in front of the more imposing ones. The buildings were of mud brick, sometimes with doorways and columns of stone, with stelae free-standing or set into the walls. The stelae and other objects in the chapels were dedicated over a period of time. Perhaps few people actually made the pilgrimage to Abydos, to take part in the festivals of Osiris and to watch the progress of the god's decorated image in his gilded barque surrounded by protecting deities. They may have hoped to carry it out after death as a sanctified spirit, see Cat. no. 79. Many more people passing up or down river in the course of their duties (see Cat. no. 61) called at Abydos to arrange for a commemoration to be left for them, their families, patrons or protégés.

The composition and texts of the late xiith–xiiith Dynasty stelae from Abydos, while displaying an immense variety – hardly surprising since they cover a period of over 200 years – show a distinct evolution from the stelae of the early Middle Kingdom. Autobiographical texts are rare, being replaced by religious ones and by endless offering formulae and hymns to the gods. The number of people represented on them, or commemorated in name only in genealogies or simple lists of names, greatly increased. A comparison between the xith Dynasty stela of Montuhotep (Cat. no. 10) and the stela of Amenemhat Nebuy (Cat. no. 39) shows what has happened. The procession of offering-bringers takes up approximately one-third of the composition of the former, but in the later stela it has taken over the whole design, and the number of people included in the dedication, i.e. all those passively seated and not carrying offerings in the procession, has risen from four to seven.

28 KING SENUSRET III, 1862–1844 BC
Illustrated in colour on frontispiece.

Head from a colossal statue of a king in pink granite. Length of face: 19.8 cm. Width of face: 21.1 cm. Length of eye: 5.5 cm. Length of ear: 11.5 cm. The king wears a *nemes* headcloth and carries a uraeus-snake on his brow, see Cat. no. 8. The *nemes* has a triple stripe, one broad followed by two narrow bands, and the uraeus-snake, which rises from the top of the frontlet, winds in a single horizontal loop to the top of the head. The heavy brow-ridge frames deep eye-sockets and on its surface, hardly visible, the eyebrows are incised in outline and cross-hatched. The upper lid, 1.0 cm broad at its widest point, is a complete semicircle covering one third of the eyeball. The tear ducts (canthi) at the inner and outer corners of the eye are both marked. The lower lid is deeply cut and follows a natural curve around the eye. The eyes themselves are set straight and protrude like balls from their deep sockets. Both ears are damaged, and only the tip of the outer rim and the enormous ear lobes remain. The nose is also lost, but we can say that it was 5.7 cm wide at its base and that channels were cut for both nostrils. The philtrum is marked, but the shape of the upper lip is irrecoverable, although it was clearly thinner than the full pouting lower lip. The mouth is set in an uncompromising downward curve, accentuated by two short shallow lines at the corners.

28

The chin, emphasised by a triangular groove under the mouth, is square and juts forward to the level of the mouth. The contours of the face are reproduced with such subtlety that they may be lost to the eye because of the variegated colour of the stone, and only by touch can they be discovered. The strongest modelling is reserved for the cheek- and jaw-bones. The line of the cheek-bone is visible from the ear hole to a point on the outer edge of the eye-socket level with the wing of the nostril. Here the cheek-bone appears to protrude through the flesh in a sharp peak. The line of the jaw is even stronger, providing the base line for the forward thrust of the head. It is above all in the modelling of the muscles and the flesh of the face that the sculptor shows his consummate skill and mastery of this most intractable of materials, pink granite. The flesh of the cheeks seems to fall away from the peak of the cheek-bone. The pouches under the eyes are suggested by indentations which run from the inner and outer corners but do not join. The inner groove is deeper and wider and is almost parallel to one running out from the wing of the nostril. The bunching of muscles around the upper lip and corners of the mouth is masterly and, together with the eyes, gives the face its unmistakable character.

Gift of F. W. Green. Fitzwilliam E.37.1930. H: 32.3 cm. W: 34.0 cm.

There can be no doubt that this head provides us with a portrait of Senusret III, nor that the anonymous sculptor was one of Egypt's greatest artists. The question it raises is why the King was represented in this realistic fashion, with the signs of age and discontent visible on his face. The scale of the change can be measured by comparison with the relief of Senusret I, Cat. no. 11, or the head of Nebhepetre Montuhotep, Cat. no. 8. These are not individuals but embodiments

41

of divine kingship, who are represented in a style which in both general and particular fits into an evolutionary sequence, so that it is difficult, sometimes impossible, to isolate features which derive from the actual physical appearance of the King. The eye of Montuhotep, for instance, takes on a different shape as the relief style of his reign evolves – compare Cat. nos. 2, 4, 5. In contrast to this, from the beginning of his reign Senusret III decided that his facial features should be rendered realistically and include blemishes such as pouches under the eyes and an incipient double chin (Aldred in *MMJ* 3 (1970), figs. 21, 22). Enough statues survive to allow us to observe the process of ageing through changes in the royal portrait, and inevitably to read into them changes in thought and feeling. The expression of this portrait, embittered and resigned but uncompromisingly autocratic, contrasts with the unquestioning arrogance of power visible in his young face.

The traditional chronology allots thirty-five years to his reign, but Simpson has recently argued for reducing it to nineteen years (see above p. 4), which is the highest date recorded on contemporary monuments. If this is so, it would help to explain the extraordinary character and consistency of the sculptures of the King, since it would place his entire reign within the working lifetime of a single sculptor. Once the King, and it could only have been he, had decided to have himself depicted in this way, the traditional procedure would have been followed of having portrait sculptures prepared for various special occasions, such as jubilees and the completion of building projects. They would have been made by the chief royal sculptor, or under his supervision, and distributed throughout Egypt. The accuracy and subtlety of the modelling of the face may seem to confirm that the sculptor's aim was total realism, but what he achieves is a sublime expression of a human being wielding superhuman power. This is surely what is behind the change, a new way of expressing an unchanging view of divine kingship. Senusret III loses nothing of his authority in allowing himself to be shown with a less idealised face than his predecessors. It is worth remembering that the 'realism' of his reign was never applied to the royal body, which is invariably shown vigorous and young, although the head, as here, may bear the marks of middle age.

The head was given to the Fitzwilliam Museum in 1930 by F. W. Green, then Honorary Keeper of the Egyptian Collection. It had been given to Green in 1869, perhaps as a christening present, by his aunt, Mrs Thurburn, who lived in Alexandria. This lady became interested in Egyptian archaeology and was responsible for directing Green's enthusiasm in that direction. I owe this information to F. W. Green's son, Major F. Green.

C. Winter, *The Fitzwilliam Museum* (London, 1958), no. 4; Wildung, *L'Age d'Or*, p. 204, fig. 178; J. R. Harris, *Egyptian Art* (London, 1966), pp. 36–7, pl. 17.

29 KING SENUSRET III, 1862–1844 BC
Illustrated in colour on pl. II, 2.

Fragment of a head from an over life-size statue of a King in basalt. Most of the right side of the face survives. Length of eye: approximately 4.9 cm. The King wears the *nemes* headcloth and uraeus-snake, see Cat. no. 8. The *nemes* carries a series of single narrow stripes, deeply incised and spaced

29

at roughly four per 2.5 cm. The uraeus-snake rises from the top of the frontlet; its head and body are broken off. A tab of the *nemes* is visible in front of the right ear. The brow is naturally rounded and there are two short vertical lines incised in the centre of the forehead above the bridge of the nose. The surface of the right eye is badly bruised, so that only the lower lid can be clearly discerned, but both the inner canthi are marked and the beginning of the upper lid is visible. The eyes are set level in the face. The lower lid of the right eye is deeply cut, like Cat. no. 28, projecting 0.3 cm from the surface and curving naturally around the eye. It is emphasised by a line incised underneath it. The nose is broad, with rounded nostrils defined by a deeply incised line; in profile, though chipped at the base, it shows a strong curve. The philtrum is marked and there is a corresponding groove in the upper lip. The latter is flat and angular in contrast to the rounded lower lip. Both straighten out towards the corner of the mouth, which is emphasised, as in Cat. no. 28, by a short downward line. The modelling of the facial contours is softer than in Cat. no. 28. The cheek-bone stands out less strongly and the cheeks are fuller, but in both cases the almost parallel, diagonal lines from the inner corner of the eye and the wings of the nostril are shown, as is the bunch of muscles gathered at the corner of the mouth. They seem almost ready to lift the mouth into a smile.

Bequest of R. G. Gayer-Anderson. Fitzwilliam E.82.1949. H: 21.1 cm. W: 17.5 cm.

The identification of this fine sculpture as Senusret III depends on analysis of facial features and comparison with recognised (though uninscribed) portraits of the King, such as Cat. no. 28, and the relatively few inscribed statues which survive. The naturalistic modelling of the features, especially the eyes and mouth, rules out any Kings in the Dynasty except Senusret III or Amenemhat III, Cat. nos. 28, 31. The convex curve of the nose dissociates it from Amenemhat's portraits. The most telling features are the vertical wrinkles on the forehead and the shape of the mouth. Similar vertical wrinkles are found on at least two inscribed statues of Senusret III from Deir el-Bahri, Thebes, respectively in Cairo, Temp. no. 18/4/22/4, and the British Museum, EA. 686. The shape of the mouth compares with that of the inscribed sphinx in the Metropolitan Museum, New York, and that of the granite head from Karnak, now in the Luxor Museum. Unfortunately the profile of the nose survives on none of the inscribed statues of Senusret III, but the spring of the nose remains on a head in the Metropolitan Museum, 66.99.5, identified by Aldred as Senusret III. It is clearly strongly arched, as it is here. The only portrait which shows the nose complete is the tiny head in obsidian in the Gulbenkian Museum in Lisbon. The different scales of the two sculptures make detailed comparisons unwise; however, the shape of the nose, a prominent triangular wedge, perhaps made more angular than natural by the small scale and the hard material, is compatible with the profile on this fragment. The odd feature of the Fitzwilliam sculpture is the narrow stripes on the *nemes* headcloth. The only parallel is an unpublished fragment in the Metropolitan Museum, 1978.204, assigned to a Queen's statue of early Dynasty XII.

Bourriau, *Three Middle Kingdom Sculptures* (in press). For comparisons in general, C. Aldred in *MMJ* 3 (1970), figs. 21–7; Cairo, Temp. no. 18/4/22/4, Wildung, *L'Age d'Or*, fig. 177; British Museum EA 686; Aldred, *Middle Kingdom Art*, pl. 51 (lines not visible in the photograph); Gulbenkian head, Vandier, *La Statuaire Egyptienne*, pl. LXVI, 7.

30 KING SENUSRET III, 1862–1844 BC

Fragment of the face of a colossal statue in pink granite. Most of the right side of the face remains, but the surfaces of the eye and mouth are bruised and the tips of the nose and chin are missing. All that remains of the right eye is the lower lid, which is deeply cut, with the inner canthus marked. The nose is 5.5 cm wide at the base (compare 5.7 cm of Cat. no. 28), with a strongly arched profile and prominent nostrils. The philtrum is marked and there is a corresponding groove in the upper lip. The character of the mouth can be 'read' through the bruising, despite some possible recutting of the upper lip. This is angular and strongly wedge-shaped, the lower one rounded and slightly pouting. The contours of the facial muscles and flesh are suggested, but the modelling is not strong. Nevertheless the high cheek-bone, hollows of the cheek and under the eye, the curl around the nostril and the bunch of muscle at the corner of the mouth, all familiar from Cat. no. 28, are present.

Gift of R. G. Gayer-Anderson. Fitzwilliam EGA.3005.1943. H: 20.3 cm. W: 15.0 cm.

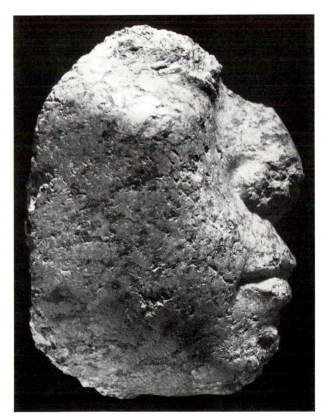

30

43

The colossal scale and the material of this fragment provide good evidence that it comes from a royal statue, since over life-size private sculptures in pink granite are unknown in the Middle Kingdom. The shape of nose and mouth, compared with Cat. nos. 28, 29, suggests it comes from a head of King Senusret III. However, it was cut with a much less confident hand than these sculptures. Compare the line around the nostrils with the corresponding line on Cat. no. 29, and the indentations suggesting the holes of the nostrils with the deep channels cut in Cat. no. 28. It is the colour and the texture of the stone which dominate, not the features themselves.

31 KING AMENEMHAT III, 1843–1798 BC
Illustrated in colour on pl. II, 1.

Head and shoulders of a statuette of a King in a dark shelly limestone. Length of face: 4.5 cm. Width of face: 5.2 cm. Length of eye: 1.4 cm. Length of ear: 3.75 cm. The King wears the *nemes* headcloth with a triple stripe, one broad and two narrow, and carries the uraeus-snake on his brow. While small chips are missing from the chin, uraeus and nose, and

from the edges of the *nemes*, the head is otherwise complete, having been broken from the body at the base of the neck and retaining parts of both shoulders. The uraeus-snake rises from the bottom of the frontlet and twists in a single horizontal s so that its tail reaches the top of the head on an imaginary line drawn across the head from the side wings of the *nemes*. The brows are so lightly modelled as almost to disappear. The eye-sockets are correspondingly shallow and the eyes long, oval and set straight in the face. The upper and lower lid are carved in relief, the upper one being slightly heavier. It closes over an eyeball which is much flatter than that of Senusret III, Cat. no. 28, and appears to look downwards. The enormous ears are made even more obtrusive by being set low, at right angles to the face against the wings of the *nemes*. Only the outer rim of the ear is shown and the lobes, which are slightly indented, are pushed forward. The nose is short and wide and its profile, miraculously preserved, shows a small, straight wedge. The philtrum is marked by a deeply carved channel and the v indent in the upper lip corresponds to a notch in the lower one. The lower lip is full but straight; the upper lip seems to turn up at the corners of the mouth, but this is an illusion produced by the deep

31

44

cutting of the corner groove. The chin, emphasised by a semi-circular groove under the mouth, is round and slightly protruding. The modelling of the facial contours, exploiting this relatively soft stone, is very sensitive. A fine line runs from the inner corner of the eye to meet the prominent cheek-bone, and two short creases almost parallel to it run from the wings of the nostrils and the corner of the mouth. The cheeks are flat and there are pouches under the eyes. The underlying bone structure shows a strong, square face, but the painstaking surface modelling suggests the vulnerability of flesh about to fall into the creases of middle age.

From Aswan. Bequest of Oscar Raphael. Fitzwilliam E.2.1946. H: 11.6 cm. W: 14.3 cm.

Thanks to the careful research of Rosalind Hall, the provenance of this magnificent sculpture has recently come to light. The head was brought by Oscar Raphael for £265 at the 1917 Sotheby's sale of antiquities belonging to Lord Grenfell. It was already known that Grenfell obtained the head in Egypt between 1882 and 1892, when he was Commander-in-Chief of the British garrison in Egypt and formed his first Egyptian collection. We now have evidence to suggest that the head, part of a 'sitting figure of the usual type', came from one of the tombs he excavated at Qubbet el-Hawa on the west bank at Aswan in 1886. As often happens with new discoveries, this one poses as many questions as it answers. How did a small statuette of a King come to be placed in a private tomb? Was the statuette made in Aswan as well as found there? It is virtually certain that the statuette was not originally placed in the tomb but got there by accident, in the course of tomb robbery, ancient or modern. Grenfell states that the tomb had been robbed, and there is a parallel in a small royal head, identified as of Senusret III, now in the Metropolitan Museum (see above p. 42), found at Lisht in the shaft of a private tomb. It had got there, the excavators surmised, in the course of the looting and demolition of the mortuary temple nearby. Similarly, this statuette was probably originally set up in one of the many shrines on Elephantine Island, which are known to have contained statues of xiith and xiiith Dynasty Kings. The material of which the statuette was made is a rare stone, a dark fossiliferous limestone for which no ancient quarry has yet been found, though a modern source occurs at Giza (Lucas, *Industries*, p. 414). The preferred material for statuary made at Aswan was the local hard stones, such as granite, so the material as much as the quality suggest an origin elsewhere, probably in the royal workshops at the capital.

A curiosity of the head is the position of the uraeus. It rises from the bottom of the frontlet, not from the top, or just above or below it, like the uraeus on every other head of the King. This may be a feature retained from the portraiture of Amenemhat's father, Senusret III (see British Museum EA 686 – above p. 43). The same artists must, at least at the beginning of the new reign, have served both Kings. Other characteristics of the portraiture were retained, such as the vertical wrinkles above the nose which appear incongruously on a statuette of Amenemhat as a young man. (Aldred in *MMJ* 3 (1970), p. 48, n. 80). The Fitzwilliam head is closest to a fragment in the Metropolitan Museum,

29.100.150, of which the face is complete but only a small portion of the *nemes* survives. The style, material and dimensions are close enough to suggest the two sculptures came from the same workshop. Unfortunately the New York piece has no provenance. When studied together, however, they suggest how a degree of stylisation, in the treatment of the upper eyelid for example, was already beginning to intrude into the realistic style of royal portraits.

C. Ricketts in *JEA* 4 (1917), pp. 211–12, pls. xxxix, xl; *Burlington Fine Arts Club*, 1895, p. 17, no. 16, pl. x, 51; *Burlington Fine Arts Club*, 1922, p. 77, no. 19, pl. v; Aldred, *Middle Kingdom Art*, pl. 69; A. Weigall, *Ancient Egyptian Works of Art* (London, 1924), p. 97; Fechheimer, *Kleinplastik*, pp. 22–3; J. R. Harris, *Egyptian Art* (London, 1966), pp. 36–7, pl. 18; C. Winter, *The Fitzwilliam Museum* (London, 1958), no. 5; *Treasures of the Fitzwilliam* (Cambridge, Pevensey Press, no date), p. 11, no. 4; R. Hall in *Apollo* (London, August 1984), pp. 124–5, 127, fig. 9; R. Hall in *The Egyptian Bulletin*, no. 15 (London, December 1985), pp. 20–3; for shape of uraeus cf. R. Engelbach in *ASAE* 28 (1928), pl. iv, D2.

32 HEAD OF AMENEMHAT III, 1843–1798 BC Illustrated on p. 38.

Head from a diorite statuette of a King wearing the *nemes* headcloth and carrying the uraeus-snake on his brow. Length of face: 7.2 cm. Width of face: 8.0 cm. Length of eye: 2.1 cm. Length of ear: 4.6 cm. The headcloth carries a pattern of repeated triple stripes, one broad and two narrow. The head and hood of the cobra are badly damaged, but it is clear that the snake rises from the top of the frontlet and coils three times vertically before reaching the top of the head. The brow ridge is more strongly modelled than on Cat. no. 31, but the eye-sockets are relatively shallow, with the result that the eyeball protrudes in the manner of Cat. no. 28. The heavy upper lid covers almost half the surface of the eyeball, reducing it to a long, narrow slit. The lower lid projects and there is a line underneath it. The ears are set higher than on Cat. no. 31 but are shown in a similar way, with prominent outer rim, interior chiselled out with a slight contour to suggest the inner ear, and very large round lobes, projecting forward. The King is not wearing ear-studs, as Anthea Page suggests. The shape of the nose, which is both chipped and worn, is almost completely lost, but what remains of the profile at the bridge seems to conform to Cat. no. 31. The mouth has also suffered, particularly from abrasion of the upper lip, but the deep notches at the corners are clear, each with a tiny groove directed downward, and so is the fullness of the lower lip. There is a horizontal indentation under the mouth, emphasising the round chin. The modelling of the muscle and bone of the face is hard to pick up by eye because of the colour of the stone, but there are distinct pouches under the eyes, high cheek-bones and a slight swelling of muscle at the corners of the mouth. The cheeks are flat and there is a deep hollow between the high point of the cheek and the nose.

Gift of Amelia Edwards. University College 14363. H: 16.9 cm. W: 18.8 cm.

This portrait of Amenemhat III in diorite differs markedly from Cat. no. 31 in shelly limestone, and this can be largely explained by the differing hardness of the stones. The relatively soft limestone permits subtle modelling and crisp cutting, while the granular texture and mottled colour of the diorite handicap skilful work. The sculptor of this head never quite dominates his material, but it is easy to underestimate him because much of the modelling, especially around the eyes, escapes the notice of an observer distracted by the variegated colour of the stone.

A fairer comparison is between this head and the seated statue inscribed for Amenemhat III in the Hermitage Museum (no. 729), which is of roughly the same size and made of porphyritic diorite. Both sculptures confirm that the portrait of the King was beginning to become fixed, perhaps through the proliferation of copies, resulting inevitably in the stylised over-emphasis of certain features. The apparent reduction of the eyelids to two bands of relief, the narrow eye and the slight peak at the corners of the *nemes* are examples of this stylisation, which carries over into private sculpture and into the royal sculpture of the succeeding Dynasty.

Page, *Egyptian Sculpture*, no. 31, with bibliography there cited; Vandier, *La Statuaire Egyptienne*, p. 201; Evers, *Staat aus dem Stein*, ii, p. 113; cf. N. Landau and I. Lapis, *Egyptian Antiquities in the Hermitage* (Leningrad, 1974), pls. 21–2; for shape of uraeus, cf. R. Engelbach in *ASAE* 28 (1928), pl. iv, D1.

33

33 A MAN FROM BUHEN

Late Dynasty XII, 1862–1787 BC.

Face from a quartzite statuette of a man. Length of face: 5.0 cm. Width of face: 4.8 cm. Length of eye: 1.7 cm. The edge of a wig or the frontlet of a headcloth is visible at the top of the fragment. The brow and the ridge of the cheek-bone define the eye-socket, in the manner of Cat. no. 17. Within the shallow socket the eye is shaped schematically, with heavy upper lids over long narrow eyes set wide apart. The eyes are asymmetrical, the right one narrower than the left, and outlined with irregular incised lines. They appear to look downwards. A small chip off the base of the nose distorts the profile, making it appear sharper than it is, but the nose is small and wide (2.1 cm at base), with a straight profile. The philtrum is marked; the lips are thin and unshaped but set in the gentle upward curve which gives the face its sweet expression. The chin, following the strong jawline, is square. The underlying shape of the face is very simply expressed, in the pronounced ridge of the cheek-bone which runs from the nostril all the way to the break at the side of the face, and in the bunch of muscles on either side of the mouth.

From Buhen, from the debris in square H9. Gift of the Egypt Exploration Society. University College 19625. H: 8.7 cm. W: 5.9 cm.

It is interesting to compare the material and technique of this fragment with Cat. no. 17, also a male head in quartzite. The stone of the Buhen piece is coarser, and it is perhaps for this reason that the sculptor has (successfully) sought to achieve his effect with a few strong contours and no detailed modelling. The result is very appealing.

Its simplicity may also be due to the fact that it was probably carved at Buhen in Nubia and is therefore the product of a sculptor working far from the main artistic centres. We can assume that it comes from a statue originally dedicated in the temple belonging to the fort, and there is corroborative evidence of local manufacture at the site in the form of the tools and debris associated with stone working. The fortress was built during the reign of Senusret I and occupied continuously until the end of the XIIIth Dynasty. The find-spot of the sculpture does not help to date it within this period but on stylistic grounds a date late in Dynasty XII after the reign of Amenemhat III seems likely. The face clearly shows traits introduced into the repertoire from royal portraits of Senusret III and his son Amenemhat III – the heavy upper lid and protruding eye from the former, the nose and square jaw from the latter. The possibility remains, because the head covering is lost, that this fragment actually comes from a royal statue. In my view this is unlikely since the features do not consistently copy the portrait of either Amenemhat or Senusret but show a mixture of traits, nor do they clearly suggest the physiognomy of any XIIIth Dynasty King.

Page, *Egyptian Sculpture*, no. 28; Emery, Smith and Millard, *Buhen*, I, pp. 98, 150, pl. 104 (find-spot corrected from that given by Page).

34 HEAD OF AN UNKNOWN MAN

Late Dynasty XII, 1862–1787 BC.

Head from a quartzite statuette of a man. Broken away at the back of the head and at the neck. Length of face: 5.6 cm. Width of face: 6.0 cm. Length of eye: 2.2 cm. The front section of the wig is preserved from the right ear to the centre of the left eye. The treatment of eyes and brow is similar to that of Cat. no. 33, in that a shallow eye-socket has been excavated leaving a low ridge which provides the contour of brow and cheek. The eyes are incised, set straight but asymmetrical – the left higher than the right. A deep groove has been cut between the brow and upper lid, and the latter is very wide, 0.4 cm at its maximum. The eyeball protrudes and appears to look upwards. The shape of the nose is lost, but it was 1.6 cm wide at its base. The mouth is badly bruised but the thin upper lip and full, pouting lower lip seem clear. There is a deep horizontal furrow under the mouth and the chin is round but prominent. The left side of the face is distinctly less weathered than the right, showing sensitive modelling of cheek and jaw, and muscles around the mouth. The head appears to be thrusting itself forward on its long neck, but the angle may be distorted by the nature of the break. There is a narrow horizontal groove at the back, level with the top of the neck, which may indicate where the top of a rectangular back pillar once existed.

Gift of R. G. Gayer-Anderson. Fitzwilliam EGA.6502.1943. H: 11.4 cm. W: 6.1 cm.

34

This head of an anonymous individual is not a portrait, for it copies too slavishly the idiosyncratic features of the portraits of Senusret III. It shows how the realism of the royal sculptures created a new formalism in private sculpture. The dominant facial characteristics of the King reappear, simplified and transmuted by the hands of lesser artists.

Cf. Quartzite head in Boston Museum of Fine Arts, Wildung, *L'Age d'Or*, p. 218, fig. 193.

35 A MIDDLE-AGED OFFICIAL Illustrated on p. 39.

Late Dynasty XII, 1862–1787 BC.

Upper part of a wooden statuette of a striding man, made in four parts with joins at shoulders, right elbow and waist. Length of face: 2.3 cm. Width of face: 2.1 cm. Length of eye: 1.0 cm. Length of ear: 1.5 cm. The whole face and body is covered with a thin layer of reddish-brown pigment through which the grain of the wood is visible. Eyes and brows are picked out in black and white. The eminences and depressions of the skull are naturalistically rendered with great subtlety. The brows are strongly curved over wide open eyes framed in black with an emphatic upper lid and inner and outer canthi marked. The iris is white and the pupil black. The ears are shown in exceptional detail. The outer rim, elevation of the inner ear, tragus and lobe are all quite distinct. The nose is long and straight with the interior of the nostrils marked in black. The mouth is slightly pursed, suggested by tiny downward-leading notches at the corners. The lips are thin and straight and the chin is square. The lines of aging on the face and its underlying bony structure are shown with consummate skill. The forehead carries two horizontal wrinkles and there are two vertical lines over the nose. The hollows under the eyes emphasise the cheek-bones, and a diagonal line runs out from the wings of the nostrils. The torso is fleshy, with prominent breasts and nipples, and the only bone visible is the backbone. In contrast the musculature of the arms is shown in detail, and the fingers are exceptionally long with nails painted white. A faint line at the back shows that the statuette originally wore a high-waisted kilt, painted white.

Eton College, Myers Museum 10. H: 9.9 cm. W: 5.9 cm.

The quality of this tiny sculpture is outstanding and shows the artist's complete mastery of his medium. He has exploited the grain of the wood and even used a knot in it to emphasise the left nipple. The realistic detail of face and figure is also exceptional, but recalls Cat. no. 27. The face is that of an individual despite the conventional pose. The statuette would originally have held a long staff in the right hand and a short sceptre in the left. The small scale and the medium suggest it was originally placed inside or beside a coffin. The high-waisted kilt, of which just the faintest trace remains, is attested by Vandier on sculptures from the reign of Senusret III and this is confirmed by the group sculpture of Ukhhotep of Meir with his wives and daughters, now in Boston.

Burlington Fine Arts Club, 1895, p. 38, no. 25, pl. XXIII, 188; McConnell, *Treasures of Eton*, fig. 118; Fechheimer, *Kleinplastik*, p. 33; for kilt, Vandier, *La Statuaire Egyptienne*, p. 257; *Boston Bulletin* 72 (1974), no. 368, pp. 100–4.

36 STELA OF MONTUHOTEP Illustrated in colour on pl. I, 3.

Late Dynasty XII, from reign of Amenemhat III onwards, 1843–1787 BC.

Round-topped limestone stela carved in sunk relief for the

36 [also in colour on back cover]

priest, Montuhotep. Much of the original colour remains. The bodies of the male figures were once painted reddish-brown, as were the pottery, the supports of the tables of offerings and the meat upon the tables. The border of the stela was decorated with alternating squares of red and blue, and traces of blue remain in the hieroglyphs. The lunette carries two eyes, like those painted on coffins (see Cat. no. 68), and a *shen* sign – a circle symbolising the eternal circuit of the sun – with the names of Re, the sun god, and Osiris, King of the dead, in opposition to each other, in the corners. They may represent the rising and the setting sun, East and West. In the two lines of the funerary formula, carved in large, well-spaced signs, Osiris, Lord of Ankh-Tawy, is called upon on behalf of Montuhotep, born of Henut. The first and most important register of the stela shows Montuhotep sniffing a lotus flower while seated on a chair with lion legs, before a large table of offerings on which are symmetrically arranged an ox head and leg, bread, fruit and vegetables. Under the table are two large wine jars, one still sealed, one tipped invitingly towards Montuhotep. A drinking cup on a tall stand is beside him, ready to hand. The composition of the next two registers is similar but every element is roughly half the size. In the second register Montuhotep reappears

seated opposite his father, also Montuhotep, and in the bottom his daughter Henut and her husband (?) Kememu are being presented with offerings by another priest, Renefsenebu.

Ex collection of Cononel L. H. Hanbury. Liverpool Museum 49.56. H: 45.6 cm. W: 30.0 cm.

This fine stela presents us with several puzzles. The style of the carving and the choice of personal names suggest the xıth or early xııth Dynasties, but the phrases of the formula, the design of the lunette and the shape of the wine jars all point to a date towards the end of the xııth Dynasty. The provenance is unknown, and while the appeal to Osiris Lord of Ankh-Tawy suggests Abydos, where this epithet of the god is most common on stelae of the late Middle Kingdom, the name Montuhotep suggests connections with the Theban cult of the god Montu. The stela was shown to Budge at the British Museum in 1886, and Budge's notes, simply a description and a translation, are on file in Liverpool Museum.

The stela commemorates a family group: four men and four women are mentioned (of whom four men and one woman are represented), and all except Renefsenebu appear to be related to each other. The relationships are not quite clear (was Dedetnub, the mother of 'his daughter' Henut, the wife of Montuhotep?), and this may be because the stela was not intended to stand alone but in a chapel with other monuments of the same family, see Cat. no. 39. The only title which occurs is *wab* – meaning 'priest' – and this suggests a family of modest status. It was nevertheless able to command the services of a sculptor of great, if idiosyncratic, skill. The mannered detail of the musculature of the legs, echoed in the treatment of the chair legs, the extraordinary ears, in which the lobe appears like a pendant earring, the relief outline to the eye, the heavy modelling around nose and mouth and the attenuated limbs are remarkable. Another striking detail is the care taken to show, in the case of every seated figure, how the far foot overlaps the base of the pot-stand which holds a drinking cup. This is intended to make it clear that the cup stands beside the chair on the far side, while at the same time making the cup fully visible and incorporated into the design of the register as a whole. The date of the stela is confirmed by one in Florence dated to the reign of Amenemhat III by the presence of the King's name in the lunette. The Florence stela, although in poorer condition, shares some of the stylistic peculiarities of this one – the elongated limbs and the exaggerated ear lobes – as well as the overall design and writing of the funerary formula. I am grateful to Amy de Jola, who is preparing a catalogue of the stelae in Liverpool, for bringing this parallel to my attention after study of the internal evidence had itself suggested such a date.

For the formula, J. Bennett in *JEA* 27 (1941), pp. 77–82; for the lunette, H. W. Müller in *MDAIK* 4 (1933), p. 197; for the jars, Do. Arnold in *MDAIK* 38 (1982), Abb. 5; for Osiris of Ankh-Tawy, J. Spiegel, *Die Götter von Abydos* (Wiesbaden, 1973), pp. 16–23; J. Malék and D. N. E. Magee in *Bulletin de la Société d'Egyptologie de Genève*, 9–10 (1984–5), pp. 178–9; for Florence stela, S. Bosticco, *Le Stele Egiziane dall'antico al Nuovo Regno*, pp. 36–7, fig. 36.

37 A KING'S SINGER Illustrated in colour on
pl. II, 3.

Late Dynasty XII, 1862–1787 BC.

Greywacke statuette of a woman, inscribed down the rectangular back pillar. There is a diagonal break from the top of the right thigh to the tip of the left hand. Length of face: 1.9 cm. Width of face: 2.3 cm. Length of eye: 0.8 cm. Length of ear: 1.7 cm. The woman stands with her arms at her sides and, we may assume, her feet together in the immemorial, passive pose traditionally given to women. The inscription provides the beginning of the funerary formula and her title of royal singer. The name which follows is illegible. She wears the Hathor wig (see Cat. no. 14) and a close-fitting tunic with broad shoulder straps which cover the breasts. Her facial features are shallowly cut; the brow follows the line of the upper lid and joins the ridge of the nose; the narrow eyes are set straight and wide apart and there is rudimentary shaping of the pupil. The ears are enormous, almost as long as the face between brow and chin, and 0.75 cm wide. They are treated similarly to those on the head of Amenemhat III, Cat. no. 31, especially as regards the prominent lobes. The profile of the nose has been worn down, but it is very broad, as broad in fact as the mouth. The lips are straight and of equal width, and the chin is small and round. There are deep grooves under the lower lip, around the nostrils and at the corners of the mouth, and shallow depressions under the eyes, but there is no modelling of the cheeks. The contours of the body, by contrast, are shown with great sensitivity. The navel groove is deep, extends almost to the sternum, and emphasises the subtle curves of stomach, waist and thigh. The arms are long and rounded, without anatomical detail, and the fingers of the outstretched hand are also elongated.

Bequest of E. Towry-Whyte. Fitzwilliam E.67.1932. H: 15.0 cm. W: 5.1 cm.

In the manuscript catalogue of his collection Towry-Whyte records buying this statuette from a dealer called Lincoln in 1898 for 7s. 6d. The funerary formula written on the back pillar contains the name of Osiris written with the hieroglyph representing a palanquin, a form which does not occur before the reign of Senusret III. The treatment of the ears and of the eyes, which are narrow and wide apart with heavy upper lids, supports a late XIIth Dynasty date.

Her title, 'singer', is a common one, and we may imagine that the royal palace, like every large household, had its group of musicians and singers. Her singing may have been closer to chanting, to the accompaniment of harps, Cat. no. 96, and clapping, Cat. no. 101.

Writing of name of Osiris, see C. J. C. Bennett in *JEA* 27 (1941), p. 78.

38 HEAD OF A WOMAN

Late Dynasty XII, 1862–1787 BC.

Head from a granite statuette of a woman. Length of face: 2.3 cm. Width of face: 2.7 cm. Length of eye: 1.1 cm. Length of ear: 1.1 cm. The woman wears the Hathor wig (see Cat. no. 14), the two side bunches of which are visible around and below the ears, and the back hair can be seen above the break, viewed from the back. The brow ridge and the cheekbone delimit the eye-socket, in the manner of Cat. no. 33. There is a groove between the brow and the upper lid, and both lids are outlined. The upper lid is wider than the lower. The eyes are set straight and wide apart and appear exceptionally long and narrow, an impression created by the heavy upper lid. The eyeball itself protrudes. The outer rim of the

37

38

ear is shown, and the lobes are large and round and project forward. The inner ear is simply chiselled out. The nose is small and straight with wide nostrils. The mouth has thin, well-defined but straight lips and the chin is small and square. The modelling of the face, carved on such a small scale in a very hard stone, is minimal. The diagonal line of the cheek-bone, and furrows at each corner of mouth and nostrils, are visible.

British Museum EA. 69519. H: 5.2 cm. W: 5.7 cm.

The hairstyle identifies this head as belonging to a woman, and the treatment of the eyes (see Cat. no. 37) and cheek-bone suggest a date late in the XIIth Dynasty.

Bourriau, ed. in *JEA* 71 (1985), p. 162, pl. XVII, no. 173.

39 STELA OF AMENEMHAT NEBUY
Illustrated in colour on pl. I, 4.

Late Dynasty XII, from reign of Amenemhat III onwards, 1843–1787 BC.

Rectangular limestone stela carved in sunk relief for Amenemhat Nebuy, steward of the temple estates. Large figures of Amenemhat dominate both registers of the stela and, unlike all the other figures, they are deeply cut to allow detailed interior modelling of face and body. His body is painted reddish-brown, his bead collar green and his chair yellow (wood?) with a green back (rush matting?). Behind Amenemhat in the top register are the two seated figures of his mother Nefert and the lady of the house, Seneb, who is presumably his wife. On the other side of a gigantic table of offerings sits his brother, Sankh, also deceased, and behind him another brother, Renefankh, and a sister, Rehutankh. Below them stand two house servants: one is an Asiatic with the ordinary Egyptian name of Renefseneb, who offers Amenemhat the symbol of perpetual food offerings – the fore-leg of an ox – while the other, Senusret, effortlessly carries two enormous loads of meat. The text heading the second register reads, 'inspecting the abundant produce [of his lands]', and so Amenemhat stands, holding his staff of office, before a procession of men. These include another Asiatic servant, bringing geese and ducks, a herdsman bringing oxen and a man leading a family of gazelle. Nebsumenu, the Asiatic who brings the ducks, carries them in baskets on a yoke, and the sculptor has sought to clarify the image by showing in the traditional way both the outline of the baskets and the ducks inside them. Perhaps as an afterthought the figure of Amenemhat's young half-brother, Sirenenutet, is slipped into the space behind the former's staff. He wears the side lock of youth and, like all the seated figures on the stela, holds his far hand against his chest in a gesture of reverence. Much of the colour still remains. The flat, round loaves of bread piled on edge on the offering-table are painted yellow, the cos lettuce at the top of the offerings and the upright one below are green, and the support of the table is red–brown.

From Abydos, Cemetery E.295. Gift of the Egyptian Research Account. Fitzwilliam E.207.1900. H: 82.7 cm. W: 66.5 cm.

Garstang, the excavator of this stela, assumed that it came from a tomb chapel, but he was writing in 1900, before the

enormous number of purely commemorative chapels at Abydos was known and their nature understood. There is no supporting evidence to associate it with a burial. There is a companion stela in the Fitzwilliam (E.273.1900), found with this one and held in reserve because the surface is badly rubbed. It is clearly by the hand of the same sculptor and commemorates the same family, but in it the two brothers, Amenemhat Nebuy and Sankh, are of equal size and share the stela with their parents, Senusret and Nefert. Amenemhat Nebuy is also called simply 'Nebuy', i.e. his first, more formal name, associating him with the great Kings of the XIIth Dynasty named Amenemhat, was dropped in favour of his personal name, which was presumably the one by which he was known in the family. Within the Middle Kingdom double naming is a practice which becomes most common in the late XIIth and XIIIth Dynasties. The choice of names, how they are written, and the context in which one or both were used, have a lot to tell us. It is significant that on this stela, on which Amenemhat Nebuy is the dominant figure, both names appear, but on the stela where he shares equal status with his brother and parents only one is used, and that his personal name.

Two of the four servants on the stela are called 'Asiatics' but carry ordinary Egyptian names. The term is applied widely in Egyptian records to people from the Eastern desert, Sinai or the Syro-Palestine region. Asiatics turn up frequently in administrative records as well as on stelae (see Cat. no. 48) and in a variety of occupations, often skilled ones. Sometimes their own names are recorded, more often the Egyptian names they were given. It used to be thought that these families were brought to Egypt under duress, as prisoners of war or as trade goods, like Joseph, who was sold to Ismaelite traders for twenty pieces of silver. An alternative which now seems likely is that they were voluntary immigrants looking for an easier life in the richest country of the Near East. The current excavations at Tell el Dab'a, a town in the Eastern Delta, have shown that a substantial community from Syria–Palestine gradually established itself there during the XIIth Dynasty. It seems most likely that from this or similar ports of entry newcomers filtered down into the valley and were quickly absorbed into Egyptian society, so that they can appear, as on this stela, with nothing but the appellation 'Asiatic' to distinguish them from the rest of the household.

The two brothers Amenemhat and Sankh held related titles: one was 'steward of the temple lands' and the other 'overseer of estate workers', illustrating yet again how occupations became linked with certain families. The phrases of the funerary formula and the epithet 'lady of the house' applied to Seneb suggest a date late in the XIIth Dynasty.

Garstang, *El Arábah*, pp. 33–4, pl. VI; Simpson, *Terrace*, ANOC 56; Franke, *Personendaten*, dossier 83; Vernus, *Le Surnom*, no. 18.

40 THE STELA OF THREE BROTHERS

Late Dynasty XII, from reign of Amenemhat III onwards, 1843–1787 BC.

Limestone stela carved in sunk relief commemorating

39

three brothers, Dedusobek Renseneb, Renefankh
Amenemhat and Montuhotep, all born of the lady of the
house, Meryt. A mummiform fourth figure, Minhotep born
of Memi, may be their father, but the relationship is not
expressed. The top of the stela is missing, but almost all the
text is present. It consists of eight horizontal lines of the conventional 'Appeal to the Living' to recite the funerary formula
before Osiris and the other gods in the Sacred Land so that
the brothers might share in the festival offerings made to the
gods. Two of the brothers sit opposite each other before the

51

40

to 'steward of the divine offerings of the Abydos Temple'. The other two brothers were respectively 'steward, accountant of ships' and 'district councillor'. The fourth man, Minhotep, was a simple steward and this may imply a lower rank. The double naming popular in the late Middle Kingdom occurs here, and the phrases of the formulae as well as the epithet, lady of the house, also suggest a late xIIth Dynasty date.

We can perhaps detect the beginning of the so-called chess-board style of some xIIIth Dynasty stelae (see Cat. no. 49) in the boxing-in of the two figures in the bottom register behind their lines of vertical inscription. The mummiform figure is introduced sporadically on stelae from the reign of Amenemhat III and recalls both the development of the anthropoid coffin and the introduction of shabti figures (see Cat. nos. 80–3) at this time.

Garstang, *El Arábah*, pp. 6, 32, pl. IV; Franke, *Personendaten*, dossier 84; Cairo stela, H. O. Lange and H. Schäfer, *Grab und Denksteine des Mittleren Reichs im Museum von Kairo* (Berlin, 1902), I, p. 348, no. 20336; IV, pl. XXV, no. 20336.

41 STELA IN HIERATIC
Late Dynasty XII, 1862–1787 BC.

Roughly shaped piece of limestone, smoothed on one side to receive the text. A black round-topped frame encloses vertical columns of hieratic, giving the words of the common prayer for food in the Afterlife and invoking Osiris, god of the dead. The names and titles of the beneficiaries are as follows: the steward Sobekhotep Seneberau, born of Itete; the steward Senusret; the lady of the house Kesenet; her daughter, Sitsobek; Kemes, born of Qedment (?); Renefseneb, born of Itete; Sobekhotep, born of Sithathor; Atu, born of Nakhti; . . . (illegible); his father, Sobekhotep (?); the lady of the house Itete, born of Duahetepi.

From Abydos. Gift of the British School of Archaeology in Egypt. Fitzwilliam E.60.1926. H: 27.5 cm. W: 18.2 cm.

This makeshift stela comes from one of the numerous Middle Kingdom tomb-chapels in the northern part of the necropolis of Abydos. Those who set up the monument evidently could not or would not pay for a sculptor to make a carved inscription for them. Instead they left as their memorial this simple stone with its painted hieratic text. The low cost involved, and the number of people commemorated, would suggest that these people stood at the outer limits of the social groups that could afford 'monuments of eternity'. Other features confirm their relatively low status, notably the titles. Only two of the men hold designations of their official role in life, and that is merely the generalised 'steward' or estate manager. Again, only two women in the list of names receive social identification, in both cases 'lady of the house', probably signifying that they are each wife of a master over a household. The first steward, at the head of the list, bears two names, as happens most frequently in the late xIIth and xIIIth Dynasties. A similar date is indicated by the use of the phrase 'lady of the house', not attested on stelae before the reign of Senusret III. It is during this period that less wealthy

table of offerings, and the two lines of text above their heads, which contain their names and titles, are orientated so that the signs are directed towards the face of the appropriate figure. All three are dressed alike in a short kilt with triangular front pleat, and a bead collar. They wear short chin beards and shoulder-length wigs. The fourth figure, Minhotep, appears as a standing mummy, or more probably a mummy within an anthropoid coffin, see Cat. no. 72. He wears the sacred beard and the long wig with side lappets. The inscription in the second register is arranged in vertical columns, but it divides in the middle, the two left columns referring to Minhotep and the three right ones to Montuhotep.

From Abydos, Cemetery E.181. Gift of the Egyptian Research Account. Fitzwilliam E.51.1901. H: 86.2 cm. W: 53.6 cm.

This stela may, like Cat. no. 39, have come from an offering chapel rather than a tomb, since no other objects are known from E.181. However, it seems likely that the brothers belonged to a family who lived in Abydos, so were certainly buried there. Another stela of Renefankh Amenemhat exists in the Cairo Museum and on it his title, 'steward of divine offerings', i.e. temple lands (see also Cat. no. 39), is amplified

41

Egyptians begin to enter the record in our sources, as compared with the early Middle Kingdom, age of the provincial governors of Middle Egypt.

Among the men, two are born of Itete, who could be the lady of the house Itete at the end of the text. The only other relationships specified are a mother and daughter, and a father and child. Although the connection between all these people may be tenuous, it is tempting to regard them as members of one family, who have been included on the monument of the two most successful men, the stewards. Since there is no reference to masters or mistresses, their status was above that of the serving classes. They also make no mention of an easily identifiable local deity, which might have given the home town of the family. Sobek, crocodile god of the river margin, and the goddess Hathor do both occur, but their cult-places are known from several different towns throughout Egypt.

The identification of a group from the lowest fringe of officialdom adds significantly to our knowledge of ancient Egyptian society, because the sources for pharaonic history tend to record only the rulers and their immediate personal servants. Here we see individuals from among the elusive middle ranks between literate official and illiterate farmer. Though the stela presents little of artistic merit, by surviving it fulfils its function no less adequately than the more refined products of royal sculptors. Even this simplest form of the funerary prayer would in the Egyptian view secure an eternal supply of food and drink in the hereafter.

Petrie, *Tombs of the Courtiers*, p. 11, pl. xxix, no. 1 (top left).

DYNASTY XIII, 1786–1650 BC

The exhibition contains only three royal sculptures of Dynasty XIII, in contrast to fourteen private ones, and this is not unrepresentative of the period. A mass of documentation on the organisation of the state survives from this time, enabling us to reconstruct the succession to the major offices of government and in some cases (see Cat. no. 49) the careers of individual men. Our knowledge of the Kings whom these officials served is, in comparison, pitifully small. Only a few are represented by more than a handful of monuments, and the positions of many of these Kings in the sequence, and the lengths of their reigns, are uncertain. The approximately 130 years of the Dynasty witnessed a series of short reigns interrupted only by the more stable rule of the Kings from Sobekhotep III to Sobekhotep IV, c. 1744–1720 BC, but the stability of the country was maintained by the close-knit bureaucracy of central government.

The effect of this gradual but ultimately calamitous diminution of royal power on the art of the period is clearly seen in the private sculpture of the time. It is not yet possible to chart the evolution in royal sculpture in the round or in relief, since full publication of the most important monuments has yet to be done. The list provided by W. V. Davies shows how little we know of sculpture in the round (Davies, *A Royal Statue Reattributed,* passim). The three pieces in the exhibition all belong to the late XIIIth Dynasty. The two statuettes, Cat. nos. 53–4, show that an undemanding, mannered idealism had replaced the extraordinary individuality of the late XIIth Dynasty royal portraits. The stela of Wepwawetemsaf, Cat. no. 58, shows the beginnings of something new. Its stylistic and textual affinities link it firmly to the succeeding XVIIth Dynasty. The apparent gap between Dynasties XIII and XVII is due to the numbering of the dynasties which we derive ultimately from Manetho, who lived from 323 to 245 BC. It probably does not correspond to historical reality, and the XVIIth Dynasty Kings were in fact the successors of the XIIIth Dynasty in Upper Egypt, based in Thebes. The continuity between Dynasties XIII and XVII is apparent in many aspects of the culture of Dynasty XVII. A much more profound cultural break occurs in the early New Kingdom, but the new culture is not fully established until the reign of Tuthmosis III (1479–1425 BC). There is no break of comparable importance between the end of the XIIIth Dynasty and the succeeding XVIIth Dynasty.

Private sculpture in the round and in relief shows two apparently contradictory trends. On one hand, the number of sculptures dedicated in temples, shrines and private chapels continued to proliferate, but on the other, their size and quality diminished. The technical ability to handle and carve hard stones, and above all to design and cut hieroglyphic inscriptions, shows a clear decline. We do not know what happened, but it is difficult not to associate it with

53

This is speculation, but the results are evident to the eye. While fine sculptures were still made, many statues were taken from stock and inscriptions crudely cut to order, e.g. Cat. no. 42. Extra inscriptions, designed to add yet more names to those commemorated, were squeezed in in barely legible signs after a stela was finished, e.g. Cat. no. 49. The stylistic trends visible in the late XIIth Dynasty continue but become increasingly exaggerated: the emphatic pectoral muscles become a straight line almost parallel with the line of the high-waisted kilt, a self-satisfied plumpness grows into a protruding stomach, and the facial features become characterless or fixed in a rigid mode from which much of the vigour of the original models, the royal portraits of the late XIIth Dynasty, has dissipated. The insecurity of the age appears in the increasing number of military titles (see Cat. nos. 42, 45) and the tendency, illustrated by the group stelae, for lesser men to place themselves under the protection of more powerful ones. Family stelae like Renseneb's, Cat. no. 50, are

50

the simultaneous decline in the power and resources of the King. As the establishment of a strong unified monarchy produced an immediate and visible effect on the art of the XIth Dynasty, so the reverse happens in Dynasty XIII. The centralised bureaucracy continued to function unimpaired, at least for roughly the first half of the Dynasty, which suggests that it was the enfeeblement of the King himself which was the crucial factor in the decline. Loss of expertise implies that the organisation of the royal workshops was breaking down. Perhaps for a while they simply contracted, so that fewer skilled artists were available, and fewer still travelled beyond the Residence, since fewer royal building projects were undertaken. With the decline in royal patronage more artists turned to work for private individuals, but outside the environment of the royal workshops, where training and supervision were less rigorous, so that standards fell rapidly.

not of course new, but the commemoration of a group of people whose common bond, as far as we can see, was their occupation, e.g. Cat. nos. 45, 49 is an innovation of the time.

54

42 THE SOLDIER KHNEMU Illustrated in colour on pl. II, 4.

Reign of Amenemhat III to early Dynasty XIII, 1843–c. 1730 BC.

Statuette of a standing man in basalt, broken off at the base of the kilt, inscribed down the front and back. Length of face: 2.4 cm. Width of face: 2.5 cm. Length of eye: 0.8 cm. Length of ear: 1.7 cm. The vertical inscription on the front names the soldier Khnemu, son of Nemtyemhat, and the back pillar inscription contains the offering formula, appealing to 'Ptah–Sokar–Osiris, Lord of the *Shetayet*'. Khnemu wears a heavy, shoulder-length wig tucked behind the ears so that the sides fall forward in triangular points on to the chest. The ringlets, bound together in pairs, of which the wig is composed are carefully shown. The line of the brows, which follows the shape of the eyes, is lightly incised, cf. Cat. no. 28. The eyes themselves are set straight, the eyeballs protrude, half covered by the heavy upper lid, and the outer canthi are marked. The ears are set high, the lobe being level with the eyebrow, and they are wide as well as long, with a prominent outer rim and large lobes projecting forward. The inner ear is not shown, cf. Cat. no. 31. The nose is long with a straight profile and wide nostrils, strongly emphasised at the wings. The straight lips are compressed in a downward curve, almost a grimace, and the square chin projects forward. The cheek-bones are high, the cheeks flat. The musculature of torso and arms, both back and front, is reproduced in great detail, emphasising the large muscles of the shoulders and upper arms. There is a shallow groove from navel to sternum which meets the strong, conjoined pectoral muscles, cf. Cat. no. 53. The nipples are outlined and the rib cage and stomach muscles are faintly indicated. The torso is disproportionately narrow in relation to the breadth of the heavily muscled arms, and the hands, similarly over-large, have elongated fingers and thumbs. Khnemu wears a long kilt, from waist to (probably) ankles, tied at the waist with a triangular pleat in front. The back pillar, which starts from the base of his wig, is rectangular, becoming wider and thicker between top (2.0 cm × 0.9 cm) and bottom (2.3 cm × 1.3 cm). Compared with the sensitive modelling of the face the inscription is crudely done. The signs are hammered, bruising rather than cutting the hard stone, and in the area between the thumbs the signs are consequently hard to identify.

Possibly from Atawla, near Asyut. Gift of the Friends of the Fitzwilliam Museum. Fitzwilliam E.500.1932. H: 18.6 cm. W: 7.0 cm.

Khnemu was a soldier like Userhet, whose anthropoid coffin is also in the exhibition, see Cat. no. 72. The title means no more than a private soldier, but it is clear that both these men had the resources to command a fine-quality burial, and in Khnemu's case to arrange that a votive statue be placed in his local temple. It is difficult to date the statue precisely, since the criteria for dating private sculptures in the round or in relief do not change significantly between the late XIIth Dynasty, the reign of Amenemhat III (1843–1798 BC), and the first part of Dynasty XIII. This continuity can be observed in every aspect of Egyptian culture, see below p. 128. The features of the face relate strongly to the royal portraits of

42

Senusret III (eyes, mouth, incised outline of brows) and Amenemhat III (ears, nose, square face); the pose with both hands held flat against the kilt does not occur before the reign of Senusret III; finally the mannered, though immensely skilful, treatment of the torso suggests a slightly later date, i.e. in Dynasty XIII.

The provenance is unknown, since the sculpture was bought for the museum by F. W. Green, probably on the London art market in 1932, but it may tentatively be inferred from the name of Khnemu's father, Nemtyemhat, which means, '[the god] Nemty is the foremost'. Nemty was a falcon god, patron of travellers (the god's name is written with an ideogram of a falcon standing in a boat), and in Dynasty XIII a temple dedicated to him existed at Atawla, five miles south of Asyut. The presumption is that the name of Khnemu's father honoured Nemty because he was the family's local god, and so Khnemu is likely to have placed a statuette in his shrine. His cult was not widespread, like that of Khnum or Ptah–Sokar–Osiris, the other gods mentioned in the inscriptions, so this may make the suggestion more likely. The inscriptions are poorly executed, a characteristic of many private statues of the period, and the explanation may be that the pieces were not made to order but taken from the sculptor's stock and inscribed, often by a less competent stone-cutter, as they were needed.

Annual Report of the Friends of the Fitzwilliam 24 (1932), p. 3, fig. 1; M. Harrison, ed., *Three Little Books about Sculpture* (Arts Council, 1983), p. 29, no. 21; for reading Nemtyemhat, see O. Berlev in *JEA* 58 (1972), p. 3, and below Cat. no. 74; for provenance, Gardiner, *Onomastica*, II, p. 72* ff. and Simpson, *Terrace*, p. 4, n. 27; for the *Shetayet*, I. E. S. Edwards in *Egyptological Studies in Honor of Richard A. Parker* (Hanover and London, 1986), p. 33, n. 40.

43 SHESMUHOTEP, OVERSEER OF THE INTERIOR OF THE PALACE

Reign of Amenemhat IV to early Dynasty XIII, 1797–c. 1730 BC.

Diorite statuette of a man sitting cross-legged with his feet tucked under him, holding his left hand against his chest and wearing a long cloak. Length of face: 1.7 cm. Width of face: 2.1 cm. Length of eye: 0.85 cm. Length of ear: 1.2 cm. The statuette has a tall (2.7 cm), rectangular base, and is inscribed vertically and horizontally on the left arm and horizontally across the front of the legs. The inscription is the conventional formula requesting offerings, and it names Shesmuhotep, overseer of the Interior [of the Palace], and describes him as praised of Anubis, Lord of Life. Shesmuhotep wears a wig, or his natural hair, its strands radiating outwards from the top of his head and reaching his shoulders. The brows are straight and lightly modelled and the eyes extremely narrow, the upper and lower lids represented by bands of stone leaving no space between for the eyeball. The upper lid is considerably longer and wider than the lower. The ears are set very low, the outer rim is shown, and a raised band represents the inner ear. The lobe is flat and pushed forward. The nose is short and sharp, though a chip missing from the tip exaggerates this feature. The mouth has little shape, beyond a distinct downward curve, and the upper lip is remarkably long and thin in relation to the lower one. The chin is square, and there is little modelling of the structure of the face apart from the prominent cheek-bones. The curves of the body are almost entirely hidden by the all-enveloping cloak, which exposes only the right shoulder and arm. The toes of both feet are represented underneath the crossed knees.

From Haraga, tomb 606. Gift of the British School of

43

Archaeology in Egypt. Manchester 6135. H: 13.5 cm. W: 6.5 cm.

This modest statuette was found with the remains of a male burial, an (unpublished) inscribed coffin and an uninscribed offering table, in a shaft tomb in Cemetery E at Haraga, close to Lahun. It is likely that the statuette and the table do not come from the burial at all, but were originally set into a simple brick-built rectangular superstructure on top of the shaft. The deep plinth of the statuette supports the idea that it was part of an ensemble, since it would have raised it above the height of the offering table. The statuette's purpose, like that of the stelae in the cemetery which were installed in the same manner, was to attract the attention of passers-by, who would recite the formula and so perpetuate the offerings for Shesmuhotep.

The excavator, Reginald Engelbach, dated it to Dynasty XI, because he dated Cemetery E, where 606 was situated, earlier than Cemetery A; the latter he placed between the reigns of Senusret II and Amenemhat III on the basis of inscriptions found on objects. His dating of Cemetery E was tentative, he admits the pottery 'was not characteristic', and there is no supporting evidence from the statuette itself to confirm such an early date. The style and the inscriptions all point to a date in late XIIth to early XIIIth Dynasties, which is the period to which, to judge by the pottery, most of the burials at Haraga belong. The physiognomy, though blurred by the sculptor's uninspired carving, relates to the late XIIth

Dynasty royal portraits, but the narrow slits which the eyes have become suggest a later date. All attention is focused on the head, as with a block statue, and the informal seated pose is one that became increasingly fashionable in the late Middle Kingdom. Confirmation of date comes from the signs in the *htp di nsw* funerary formula, which are arranged in a sequence which only becomes common late in Dynasty XII. The earliest dated example is of the reign of Amenemhat IV (1797–1790 BC) on a stela of the vizier Senusretankh in Florence. Shesmuhotep's title is surprisingly vague, since the usual practice of the time was to append qualifying phrases to previously unspecific titles, but it shows that he was an official of some importance of the royal palace. His name, meaning '[the God] Shesmu is content', is rare, only one other example being known.

Engelbach, *Harageh*, pp. 13, 29, pl. XIX, 1; Ranke, *Personennamen*, II, p. 391; for funerary formula, D. Franke in *SAK* 10 (1983), p. 163, n. 8.

44 HEAD OF A MAN
Dynasty XIII, 1786–1650 BC.

Head of a man from a diorite statuette, broken off below the chin. Length of face: 2.7 cm. Width of face: 3.1 cm. Length of eye: 1.1 cm. Length of ear: 1.7 cm. The man wears a broad wig or headcloth with striations running parallel to his forehead; it tucks in behind his ears and presumably fell to his shoulders. The brows are lightly modelled and the eye-sockets shallow. Within them the eyes are long and oval, with pronounced but rounded inner canthi and narrow ridges representing the upper eyelids. They are set straight, but one is slightly higher than the other and the eyeballs are flat. The ears are very stylised and the lobe, unusually, is barely differentiated from the outer rim. The inner ear is represented simply by a ridge parallel to the rim. The nose is long and straight, with a deeply incised curl defining the nostrils. The philtrum is marked on the upper lip, and the full lower lip curves upwards in a smile. Like the eyes, the mouth is asym-

metrical, the left side being higher than the right. There are deep grooves at the corner of the mouth, which is only a little wider than the base of the nose. The cheek-bones are prominent but set low, thus enlarging the eye-sockets.

Gift of R. G. Gayer-Anderson. Fitzwilliam EGA.3298.1943. H: 4.6 cm. W: 6.1 cm.

While this small head still carries features held over from the late XIIth Dynasty royal portraits, the narrow eyes and small smiling mouth belong in Dynasty XIII. Vandier has argued that the head covering, which is of a type common throughout the Middle Kingdom, may be a striped kerchief worn over a wig, shaved head or natural hair, like a private person's version of the royal *nemes* headcloth.

Cf. B. V. Bothmer in *Brooklyn Museum Annual* 10 (1968/1969), p. 78, fig. 1; Vandier, *La Statuaire Egyptienne*, p. 252.

45 STELA OF SIHATHOR AND SENEBSENI
Dynasty XIII, reign of Ibia, c. 1715–1704 BC.

Round-topped limestone stela carved in raised and sunk relief. The figures of Sihathor and Senebseni and the table of offerings which they share are carved in raised relief, the rest of the stela being in sunk relief. The lunette carries two vertical columns of inscription framing two eyes and a *shen* sign, see Cat. no. 36. The columns carry the name and titles of the 'royal seal bearer and overseer of the compound', Ibia on the right and on the left those of the [King] 'the Good God, Lord of the Two Lands, Ibia, given life'. The main body of the stela is almost entirely given over to the text, which consists of a mere one and a half lines of the funerary formula for the benefit of Sihathor, 'commander of the crew of the ruler' and his wife Senebseni, 'hand-maiden among the first of the King', and a list of thirty-three names and titles. Only the first eight of the people named have a relationship with Sihathor: his parents, Senusret Wesi (father) and Khonsu (mother), four brothers, a son and a daughter. The abbreviated offering scene in the lower right corner shows Sihathor wearing the now fashionable long wrapover kilt knotted under the breast, and a bag wig. Details of face and form are incised without modelling, but there is one unusual detail. Sihathor is shown in the act of walking forward, his right foot lifting off the ground and the knee bent. Senebseni wears the usual tunic dress with straps and the long wig. The hands are shown, following convention, in identical fashion, so that on each hand the thumb and all the fingers are visible.

From Thebes. British Museum EA. 1348. H: 54.5 cm. W: 38.0 cm.

This stela was found at Thebes by local people in 1900, when it was first copied by Percy Newberry, but its Theban provenance could have been surmised from the inscriptions alone. The funerary formula invokes Amun, Lord of the Thrones of the two Lands, the most common epithet of Amun worshipped in the temple of Karnak, and many of the people listed on the stela have titles connected with his cult and personal names incorporating his name. The other titles on the stela are connected with the palace: Sihathor himself was one of the King's senior military officers, his father, son and

44

45

several brothers bore the title, *Sab r Nekhen* which apparently applied to men who served on commissions for the King, perhaps specifically in Southern Upper Egypt and Nubia, see Cat. no. 62. Two men called Dedamen, a grandfather and grandson, but not apparently related to Sihathor, were each 'chief of tens of Upper Egypt', a similarly unspecific title perhaps held by people on commissions for the departments of state. The most important official on the stela is the Ibia named in the lunette. His relationship to Sihathor is not stated, and it seems most likely that he is being honoured as Sihathor's superior. Ibia was 'overseer of the compound' (*hnrt*), one of the most important departments of the central administration, since it was the headquarters of the organisa- tion which controlled the labour owed to the state by every- one, though often carried out by substitutes, see Cat. no. 83. This corvée labour, as we might call it, represented one of the greatest resources of royal power.

The King himself, also called Ibia, a common name of the period, has left behind little evidence of his lordship of the Two Lands. The Ramesside Kinglist, now in Turin, assigns him just under eleven years, but apart from scarabs, cylinder seals and a bead, this modest private stela is the only monu- ment to bear his name. From it we may deduce that the centre of royal power had now shifted south to Thebes, and that although the King still controlled a complex bureaucracy, close-knit by family ties, his authority was becoming confined in practice to Upper Egypt and Nubia. It is interesting to note that the overseer of the compound Ibia is otherwise known from a statue dedicated in the shrines on the island of Elephantine at Aswan.

Since the stela is precisely datable to a King's reign, in this case one which lasted for just over a decade, it provides a reference point for the changes in style and writing of private stelae in the latter part of the XIIIth Dynasty. The most strik- ing characteristic is the contraction of the funerary formula and offering scene and the corresponding increase in the number of people commemorated. The actual phrases and forms of signs used do not, on the other hand, show signifi- cant change from those current in the late XIIth Dynasty.

British Museum, *Hieroglyphic Texts*, IV, pl. XXVII; L. Habachi in *SAK* 11 (1984), pp. 120–1, n. 23–5; P. Newberry in *PSBA* 25 (1903), p. 130ff.; M. Malaise in *SAK* 5 (1977), p. 198; Vernus, *Le Surnom*, no. 211; E. W. Budge, *A History of Egypt*, Vol. 3 (London, 1902), pp. 104–5; British Museum, *A Guide to the Egyptian Galleries (Sculpture)* (London, 1909), pp. 80–1. For the official Ibia, see Franke, *Personendaten*, dos- sier 61, 62. For King Ibia, see von Beckerath, *Zweiten Zwis- chenzeit*, pp. 59, 250–1.

46 STATUETTE OF A MAN

Dynasty XIII, 1786–1650 BC.

Upper part of a standing greywacke statuette of a man. Length of face: 3.5 cm. Width of face: 4.2 cm. Length of eye: 1.2 cm. Length of ear: 2.7 cm. The man wears a shoulder- length wig or head cover, see Cat. no. 44. The brows are lightly modelled but outlined with an incised line (cf. Cat. no. 42), and the eye-socket is very shallow. The narrow,

46

naturalistically shaped eyes are also outlined with a deep line which is prolonged at both inner and outer corners. The pupils are incised and the upper lid defined by another incised line. The ears are shown in detail, with outer rim, tragus, elevation of inner ear and lobe. The nose is badly worn, but the nostrils are wide and emphasised by a deep groove around the wings. The mouth also shows signs of wear, but the lips appear to be thick and straight and slightly pursed. The chin is square, but now slightly chipped. The pouches under the eyes are subtly defined, as are the hollows at the corners of the mouth. There is an incised line at the base of the long cylindrical neck, from the centre of which a shallow groove descends to the breasts. These are outlined by a strongly mod- elled ridge which runs from one armpit to the other. The nip- ples are incised. The muscles of the shoulders and upper arms are faintly suggested. Just visible above the break are the knot-tie (on the right) and upper fringed edge of the long wrapover kilt. There is a rectangular back pillar starting underneath the wig, 3.3 cm wide and 1.2 cm deep.

Ex Wellcome collection, A400,020. University College 8711. H: 14.1 cm. W: 11.0 cm.

The high-waisted kilt which the man wears becomes pop- ular from the late XIIth Dynasty onwards (see Cat. nos. 45, 51), and is often shown, as here, in conjunction with the fleshiness of an affluent middle age. The strong line joining both sets of pectoral muscles eventually becomes a fixed convention, appearing as a simple line and without the subtle modelling this statuette shows.

Page, *Egyptian Sculpture*, no. 47.

47 DEDUNUB, SON OF SENEBET

Dynasty XIII, 1786–1650 BC.

Basalt statuette of a man standing with his left foot advanced and his left hand held against his chest. He stands on a high base against a tall rectangular back pillar which is inscribed with his name and that of his mother. Length of face: 2.5 cm. Width of face: 2.5 cm. Length of eye: 0.7 cm. Length of ear: 1.4 cm. Dedunub is shaven headed. His brows curve gently over the eyes, which are cut in shallow sockets. The eyes are wide, 0.3 cm, but taper dramatically so that the outer edge almost reaches the ear lobe. The upper lid is represented by a narrow ridge and the pupils are modelled. The ears are set high, so that the lobe is level with the outer edge

47

of the eye, and they are extremely wide, 0.9 cm, as well as long. Only the outer rim is shown, the interior being simply hollowed out. The nose is long with broad nostrils and the philtrum is marked. The mouth, which is very wide, projects slightly, and the corners turn downwards into a grimace. The cheek-bones are high and, with the line of the brow, serve to define the edge of the eye-socket. The body musculature is hinted at in the narrow shoulders, pectoral muscles and muscles of the elbow and upper arm. The suggestion of thinness does not suit the conventional representation of a protruding stomach under the long kilt. The arms are exceptionally long, especially the left one, with long thin fingers on which the nails are indicated, albeit crudely. The feet are immensely broad, with long, splayed toes. Dedunub wears the long fringed wrapover kilt (cf. Cat. nos. 46, 52), tied on the right. The folds of the rectangular piece of cloth which formed the kilt are shown in unusual detail. The vertical and horizontal folds appear, and the latter show alternate raised and sunken ridges reproducing the natural character of the folds made when the material was kept in storage. The back pillar starts below the shoulder and is consistently 1.9 cm wide, but the depth varies from 1.0 to 1.5 cm following the contours of the body. The inscription is cut in clear, but crudely shaped and poorly spaced hieroglyphs.

From Khizam, near Thebes. British Museum EA. 58080. H: 24.7 cm. W: 5.5 cm.

Although Dedunub wears the long kilt denoting a person of some status, a minor official at least, the absence of any title and the crude writing of his inscription suggests he aspired to a greater position in the Next World than he had enjoyed in this one. The provenance comes from the dealer through whom this and several other small statuettes of the same date were acquired by the British Museum in 1925. The modelling is minimal, the essentials of the head and body being picked out to conform with contemporary fashion, producing a figure without individuality but with a vigorous charm.

48 STELA OF AMENYSENEB, PRIEST OF ABYDOS

Dynasty XIII, reign of Khendjer, c. 1760–1755 BC.

Limestone stela carved on both sides in sunk relief, with a large *ankh* sign (meaning life) in the centre. The upper right and lower left corners are missing. The owner of the stela is Amenyseneb, controller of the *phyle* (see Cat. no. 63), the monthly rota of priests in a temple. One side of the stela shows Amenyseneb, his mother Nebetit, his two sisters Nebukhusy and Renseneb, and Sankhenptah, a doorkeeper of the temple, and his wife Titiu. The relationships of the other men and women on the stela to this group are not clear, in some cases because they were never stated and in other cases because of the fragmentary state of the monument. A large figure of Amenyseneb stands in an attitude of worship on either side of the *ankh* sign. He wears a long, full, transparent, high-waisted skirt on top of a short kilt. His limbs and face are painted red and his necklace, green. There are traces of green in the hieroglyphs and on the necklaces of the other figures.

48

48 [reverse]

The other side of the stela shows scenes illustrating the growing and preparation of the food requested in the conventional funerary formula, which lists 'offerings of bread and beer, meat and fowl'. The bottom register shows sowing, and probably ploughing; the second, oxen pulling a sledge full of produce; the third, harvesting of grain and threshing by oxen; the fourth, grinding flour and making beer and bread; the fifth, butchering an ox; the sixth, roasting a duck and stewing meat. All the men and women carrying out these tasks are identified by name, and sometimes title. Some are specialists like the brewer, the Asiatic, Irsi, and the baker, Wepwaweteni; then there are two priests, Wenemu and Amenhotep, and two more Asiatics, Sobekiry and Senebnebit.

From Abydos, Garstang excavations of 1907, loci 304, 360. University of Liverpool Department of Egyptology, E.30. H: 51.0 cm. W: 35.0 cm.

All the men who are given titles on this stela served as priests at Abydos or in the temple of Onuris at nearby This. On two other stelae now in the Louvre, one of which carries the cartouche of King Khendjer, the same Amenyseneb describes how he restored the temple of Osiris at Abydos. During the same brief reign of Khendjer the Osiris 'Bed', now in the Cairo Museum, a basalt figure of the mummified god–king lying on a lion bed, was placed in the tomb of King Djer at Abydos, because it was believed to be the grave of Osiris himself. In view of this strong association with Abydos, the presence there of three large stelae all belonging to Amenyseneb is not surprising. The stela in Liverpool was found in several pieces in different loci within the surface debris, so has no definite associations. It is however carved on both sides, so one may suppose it originally stood in the centre of an offering chapel.

At the end of every month the outgoing *phyle* of priests (see Cat. no. 63), made a solemn declaration to the incoming one that the temple was in working order. The Syndics of the Fitzwilliam Museum in making their earliest reports to the University in the 1860s used a similar formula.

The presence of the priests Wenemu, Sianhur and Amenhotep in the 'daily life' scenes on the stela shows their responsibility for the continuity of the food offerings for Amenyseneb. However, it is not likely that they would have taken part in cooking or agricultural work, since they belonged to the official classes, who set themselves apart from manual labour. The composition looks forward to the scenes of agricultural life in New Kingdom tombs where, similarly, the deceased, in his finest pleated linen garments, can be shown pushing the plough in the Next World.

K. Kitchen in *JEA* 47 (1961), pp. 10–18, pls. II, III; *id* in *JEA* 48 (1962), p. 159; Franke, *Personendaten*, dossier 125; cf. Simpson, *Terrace*, ANOC 58, pl. 80; for the 'Osiris Bed' of Khendjer, A. Leahy in *Orientalia* 46 (1977), pp. 424–34.

49 STELA OF TITY AND HIS STAFF

Mid Dynasty XIII, 1740–1720 BC.

Rectangular limestone stela with cavetto cornice and thick frame, carved entirely in sunk relief. Much of the original colour remains. Reddish-brown pigment was carelessly applied to the heads and bodies of the male figures and to the objects on the offering tables. The cornice is painted in bands of green and red and the frame is black. The heads of the figures and the two chairs are painted black and the men's kilts are white. There are traces of blue in the hieroglyphic signs. The two lines of funerary formulae at the top name 'the overseer of sealers, who accompanies the King, Tity', and the man himself is shown in the top register, receiving offerings and holding a flywhisk as symbol of his superior status. The 'keeper of a chamber and cupbearer' Khenmes stands before Tity, and behind him sits Khentkhetyhotep, who holds the same office. The remaining people represented are grouped in twos and set either side of a small offering table in six subdivisions of the three registers. Reading from left to right, they are: the 'carrier of the Presence', Ptahwer; the 'scribe of the House of Life', Keku; the 'cupbearers', Sobekherheb, Nebirut, unnamed man, Renseneb and Renseneb (sic); the 'scribe of the front (of the Palace)', Renseneb; the 'cupbearers and keepers of chambers', Sobekhotep and Ameny; the house servant Sobekhotep and his sister Sitsobek. The figures are crudely carved, and exactly alike in dress and pose except for the single female figure. They were carved before the inscriptions, which have had to be squeezed in around them in a very inelegant fashion.

From Abydos. Gift of the Reverend G. Peacock. Fitzwilliam E.1.1840. H: 61.4 cm. W: 37.6 cm.

This stela commemorates a group of people who worked together in the palace of the King. The palace was at the same time a household unit and the centre of the bureaucracy which ruled the country, so that the personal servants of the King were, *ipso facto*, powerful officials of the state. The most important man on the stela, Tity, was a high official in the treasury, who accompanied the King when he left the palace. The others are scribes of various kinds, or servants concerned especially with the provisioning of the palace. The link between them seems to be that all had duties which took them into the living quarters of the palace, and some, for example Ptahwer, who was responsible for documents handed out by the King, presumably had access to the King himself.

In view of the close association with the palace the poor quality of the stela is at first glance surprising. However we can presume it was commissioned not by Tity himself, but by one or more of the other officials of much lower status who are shown on it. Khenmes, since he is shown in the position of chief dedicant, seems a likely choice although other monuments of his, as opposed to monuments where he occurs as a member of a group, are superior in quality. In the case of Tity, who is named on five stelae, there is an even more striking difference in quality between those where he is the sole beneficiary (Cairo 20556; Louvre C 199; Aswan 1118) and those where he occurs in a group of people (Fitzwilliam E.1.1840; Vienna 143). The reason is, I think, obvious. The first group of stelae are the ones he commissioned himself with all the resources of one of the most powerful men in the kingdom; on the second group his name appears merely as a mark of respect, or perhaps as a result of his having given permission for the stela to be made. A

49

parallel is the appearance of the name of the royal sealbearer Ibia on Cat. no. 45.

Budge, *Catalogue*, no. 76; for other monuments of the people named, Franke, *Personendaten*, dossiers 241, 287, 362, 364, 460, 473, 570, 583, 586, 725, 732; Simpson, *Terrace*, ANOC 50, 54; Habachi, *Heqaib*, pls. 129, 131b, 211b, c; for name Khentkhetyhotep, P. Vernus in *RdE* 22 (1970), pp. 155–69.

50 A FAMILY FROM QAW EL KEBÎR
Illustrated on p. 54

Dynasty XIII, 1786–1650 BC.

Round-topped limestone stela carved in sunk relief, with two standards of the jackal god Wepwawet in the lunette. The figures in the first two registers show traces of the original paint, the men's bodies and faces being painted reddish-brown and those of the women, yellow. The stela begins with two lines of the conventional funerary formula for the *ka* of the 'carrier of lands', Iy, son of Keki. In the first register Iy is shown seated on a chair (everyone else on the stela squats on the ground with one knee raised) in front of the table of offerings. His wife Atu, his sons, Ibi and Sneferu, and his daughter Keki face him. In the second register are his parents, Ibi and Keki, two priests, Id and Neh, who may be brothers of Iy, using information from other stelae, and a woman, Tity. The third register contains the figures of five more women whose relationship to the rest of the family is not stated.

From Abydos, Garstang excavations of 1907, locus 321. Bolton 10.20.11. H: 50.7 cm. W: 34.0 cm.

This stela came from an offering chapel, and the excavator's unpublished notes show that it consisted of a solid five-foot square brick-built structure with a courtyard on the west and an enclosure wall around it (see p. 40). Four stelae were set into niches, one in each face of the structure. The other three are now in Cairo (Simpson, *Terrace*, pl. 29), another having been found by Garstang and the other two, identified by Simpson by the names and titles on them, coming to Cairo in the original dispersal of stelae from Abydos in the mid-nineteenth century. The four stelae fall by style and subject matter into two pairs, the Bolton stela and Cairo Ent. no. 39069, and Cairo Cat. 20087 and 20100. The link between them is the names of Iy and his father Ibi, which occur on Cairo Cat. 20087. The latter pair of stelae are larger, more carefully cut monuments, and the chief person honoured on them is the high steward Nemtyemweskhet, a palace official second only to the treasurer. Tity, honoured on stela Cat. no. 49, held a rank just below him. Nemtyemweskhet was far above Iy in the social scale. Iy's title, 'carrier of lands', means the scribal assistant responsible for documents concerning local building or agricultural work. What brought them, their families and retainers together to share an offering chapel in Abydos may have been a common origin in the tenth nome of Upper Egypt, whose capital was at Qaw el Kebîr. The personal names, Iy, Ib and Nemtyemweskhet, all have associations with that region. Nemtyemeweskhet also deposited a model stone sarcophagus in the offering chapel, which contained a wooden coffin, Cat. no. 74, and a 'gilded figure' whose present location is unknown.

The family stela of Iy contrasts with the stela of Tity, which represents a group of people linked by occupation rather than relationship. On Iy's stela fifteen people are named, and, unusually, fifteen are represented, nine of whom are women, in contrast to the one woman on the stela of Tity. A peculiarity is that no filiations except that of Iy himself are given and the title of Ib, his father, 'scribe of the necropolis workers', and the identification of Id and Neh as brothers of Iy derive

from the other stelae. The reason for this is that the Bolton stela was intended to be read with its companion piece, now in Cairo, and the information on the family was spread between them. Both stelae are generally similar in composition, but the differences are sufficient to show that they are not by the same hand. The Bolton stela shows a careful and clear arrangement of the text, the signs of each name orientated to suit the direction faced by the figure they refer to – with the single exception of the figure of Id in the middle register.

V. A. Donohue, *The Egyptian Collection* (Bolton, 1967), no. 25; Franke, *Personendaten*, dossiers 17, 51, 52, 165, 675; Simpson, *Terrace*, pp. 4, 18, 23, pl. 29.

51 STATUETTE OF MESEHI

Dynasty XIII, 1786–1650 BC.

Greywacke statuette of a man standing with left foot advanced, inscribed down the back pillar and on the base in front of the right foot. Length of face: 3.1 cm. Width of

51

65

face: 3.0 cm. Length of eye: 1.2 cm. Length of ear: 1.9 cm. Mesehi's name can be tentatively read only from the badly worn inscription on the base. The funerary formula on the back pillar invokes Ptah–Sokar–Osiris. Mesehi is shaven headed, his brows are straight and only faintly marked, the eyes long and narrow with heavy upper lids. The large ears project from the skull and are very lightly carved, only the outer rim being clearly shown. The nose is long and pointed with a sharp central ridge and broad nostrils. The philtrum is suggested but the long thin lips have little shape. The chin is square. While there is little modelling of the underlying structure of the face, the head is sensitively shaped. Almost no musculature of the body is shown: the impression, an intentional one, is of a smooth plumpness, cf. Cat. nos. 46, 47. The nipples are very prominent, there is the faintest suggestion of pectoral muscles, and the stomach protrudes under the kilt. The arms and legs show no modelling, except for a slight indication of elbows and ankles. Both fingers and toes are elongated. Mesehi wears a long, full wrapover kilt, tied under the breast on the right, made of a striped and fringed material. The rectangular back pillar extends from just above the top of the kilt down to the high pedestal base.

Royal Museum of Scotland 1952.158. H: 31.7 cm. W: 6.7 cm.

52 THE OBELISK STELA OF AMENEMHAT
Dynasty XIII, 1786–1650 BC.

Limestone obelisk carved on all four sides in sunk relief, in the manner of a funerary stela, and set into a square pedestal. The principal figure on the obelisk is the 'overseer of the storeroom of the chamber of fruits', Amenemhat, who is cited on all four sides and is the beneficiary of the offerings requested on two of them. On side one, Amenemhat is shown making offerings to the prince, Beb, son of the lady-in-waiting, Iureri. The funerary formula invokes Osiris, Wep-wawet, Min-Harnakht and all the gods of Abydos. After the formula comes a hymn to Osiris. The offering formula on side two is dedicated by Amenemhat to Henu, son of Benbu and Renefankh, and invokes the god Geb. A figure presumed to be Henu stands above the text on side two, Amenemhat occurs again on side three, and the god Min on side four. None of these figures is identified by an inscription. The figure of Min was shown with an erect phallus, but, as so often on Egyptian monuments, this has been hammered out. The prince Beb is shown seated on a chair, wearing a short pleated kilt and bead collar and sniffing a lotus. The other human figures are dressed alike, without wigs, each wearing a long full skirt tied at the waist and a bead collar. The carving both of the inscriptions and of the figures is flat, without any interior modelling. The writing of the signs is poor, with minimal distinction, for example, between the various signs representing birds, and the spacing of the text is uneven, so that there is little consistency of design between one side of the obelisk and the others.

From Abydos. Ex Northumberland collection. Oriental Museum, University of Durham N. 1984. Obelisk: H: 75.5 cm. W: 9.5 cm. Base: H: 12.5 cm. W: 21.0 cm.

This is an extremely rare example of a private monument in the form of an obelisk. Almost all Middle Kingdom obelisks are dedicated by Kings. The shape would appear to be almost fortuitous – simply a means of providing four stelae from a single piece of stone. The texts are clumsily arranged in horizontal lines, rather than in vertical ones, and no use is made of the apex of the obelisk. Nevertheless it is an interesting sculpture in its own right.

The most important person named is the King's son, Beb. This title did not necessarily mean the man was literally the King's son; his mother, we know, was a commoner. There is a tenuous connection between Beb and Henu, which may partly explain why they are both honoured by Amenemhat. Henu's father, Bembu, occurs on another stela from Abydos now in the Vatican Museum, and the family tree which can be reconstructed from it shows that Bembu and his wife Rene-fankh had another son, Nebsenet, who married a daughter of the King. This stela also carries part of a royal name ending in *hetep*, indicating a king in Dynasty XIII. Amenemhat himself has an extremely precise title, 'overseer of the storeroom, with access, of the chamber of fruits', of a kind common in the administrative records of that dynasty. In a large household or royal palace, which we may presume to be where Amenemhat worked, storerooms, where food was both stored and prepared, were divided into chambers, one for each commodity. It is possible that the phrase 'with access' meant that Amenemhat also had access to other parts of the palace. Henu and Bembu, father and son, both held the title of 'chief of tens of Upper Egypt' (see Cat. no. 45) which would have placed them considerably above Amenemhat in the social scale but would have attached them, like him, to the palace administration.

The reference in the text to 'all the gods who are in Abydos' demonstrates that the obelisk came from there. The cult of Min became increasingly popular in the XIIIth Dynasty, but this stela also shows another change taking place in the composition of private funerary monuments. Representations of gods and hymns to the gods are extremely rare on Middle Kingdom stelae before the late XIIth Dynasty. The change may have been encouraged by the increasing importance given to the pilgrimage to Abydos and the belief that even after death the devout could continue to participate in the festivals of the gods there by leaving a stela or a statue behind to receive offerings. As images and hymns to the gods became popular they replaced the autobiographies and appeals to the living on earlier stelae (see Cat. no. 10), and herald the entirely religious texts on the stelae of the New Kingdom.

Amenemhat describes himself as 'one who made his (Henu's) name live' in dedicating one side of the obelisk to him. Profound changes in the ideas and practice of funerary religion may have been taking place, but concepts fundamental to Egyptian culture were untouched. By reciting a name, or better still carving it in stone, one ensured that the possessor of that name lived on to enjoy the funerary offerings and the pleasures of the Afterlife.

S. Birch, *Catalogue of the Collection of Egyptian Antiquities at Alnwick Castle* (London, 1880), pp. 324–6, pl. VI; Sir E. Wallis Budge, *Cleopatra's Needles and other Egyptian Obelisks*

52

(London 1926), pp. 260–7; K. Martin, *Ein Garantsymbol des Lebens* (Hildesheim 1977), pp. 90–2, Abb. 9; for Bembu, Franke, *Personendaten*, dossier 230; Simpson, *Terrace*, pl. 65; for representations of Min on stelae, M. Malaise in *SAK* 9 (1981), pp. 259–83; D. Franke in *JEA* 71 (1985), pp. 175–6.

53 KING MERYANKHRE MONTUHOTEP

Late Dynasty XIII, c. 1680 BC.

Greywacke statuette of the King, striding with his left leg advanced. There is a diagonal break from below the left calf to below the right knee. The back pillar is inscribed with the King's nomen (personal name) and prenomen (throne name). Length of face: 2.1 cm. Width of face: 2.2 cm. Length of eye: 0.9 cm. Length of ear: 1.5 cm. The King wears the *nemes* headcloth and uraeus-snake on his brow, see Cat. no. 8. The headcloth carries a single broad stripe, contracting to narrow irregular bands on the side lappets, each of which also shows a vertical seam down its inside edge. The frontlet band is exceptionally wide, with ill-defined tabs in front of the ears. The uraeus, whose head is lost, rises from the top of the band. Its body winds in two contiguous, horizontal coils immediately behind the hood of the cobra and the tail then continues straight to the top of the head, to a point level with the side fold of the *nemes*. At the back, the cloth is gathered into a long queue which reaches to the bottom of the King's shoulders, where it meets the top of the rectangular back pillar. The brows are rounded, over narrow eyes set at a slant with heavy upper lids. The ears are oval, with an incised line defining the outer rim. The nose is short and broad with a straight profile, and the small mouth, no wider than the base of the nose, has pursed lips. The chin is round and receding and the cheeks are full. Considerable attention is given to the musculature of the body and limbs. The navel notch is deep, and prolonged as far as the sternum. The lower pectoral muscles are prominent and joined, and the abdominal muscles are shown slightly contracted to emphasise the curve of the stomach and the narrow waist. The biceps and the muscles of the upper arms are faintly suggested but the bones and muscles of the legs are strongly marked. The muscles of knee and thigh are shown in unusual detail and subtlety, and the shin-bone of the forward left leg is very prominent. The calf muscles are also shown in detail. The King wears the short pleated kilt with central waisted tab, and both hands grip a roll of cloth, see Cat. no. 19. The rectangular pillar is wider at the base (4.4 cm) than at the top (2.4 cm). The inscription was cut with a blunt-ended tool, as is evident on close inspection; furthermore, the outlines of the cartouches and other features betray the stone-cutter's shaky hand and the signs are inexpertly aligned. Neverthe-

67

less, it is more carefully executed than many private inscriptions of the time.

Probably from the Karnak cachette. Ex Northumberland collection. British Museum EA. 65429. H: 22.5 cm. W: 6.8 cm.

The exact place of this obscure King within the XIIIth Dynasty is not known, nor is his name identifiable without reservation in the Turin list of Kings. The only other object which carries his name is a headless statuette of similar style, also from the Karnak cachette. Oral tradition has it that the Duke of Northumberland acquired the statuette during his visit to Egypt, which coincided with the discovery of the hoard of statues in the cachette at Karnak in 1903–4. Meryankhre belongs to the last few years of the dynasty and is probably not far in time from Wepwawetemsaf, see Cat. no. 58. This would place his reign during the period when

the authority of the King was confined to the Southern Kingdom, Upper Egypt, with its capital at Thebes.

The work shows little individuality but considerable skill, especially in the modelling of the torso and limbs. The tripartite division of the torso occurs on other royal sculptures of XIIIth Dynasty Kings, most clearly on the colossal statues in Cairo of Semenkhkare Mermesha (c. 1750 BC). These also show the same detailed reproduction of the bone and musculature of the legs, but in a highly mannered style. Some details of the face and headcloth also belong to the common stock of royal statues: the narrow, heavy-lidded eyes under natural-looking brows, the small pursed mouth no wider than the base of the nose (cf. statuette of Khendjer in Cairo), the shape of the uraeus, the steep profile of the headcloth from forehead to back of head, and the vertical seam on the inside edge of the side lappets.

Davies, *A Royal Statue Reattributed*, p. 11, n. 1, p. 28, no. 40 and bibliography there cited; cf. for Semenkhkare, Evers, *Staat aus dem Stein*, pl. 148; for Khendjer, Vandier, *La Statuaire Egyptienne*, pl. LXXI, 3–4.

54 STATUETTE OF A KING
Late Dynasty XIII, c. 1680–1650 BC.

Upper part of seated greywacke statuette of a King, broken off at waist and elbows. Length of face: 2.0 cm. Width of face: 2.4 cm. Length of eye: 0.9 cm. Length of ear: 1.6 cm. The King wears the *nemes* headcloth and carries the uraeus-snake on his brow. The *nemes* carries a single broad stripe, deeply cut over the head and side wings, and a narrower, more shallow stripe on the side lappets; compare the carelessly executed lines on the lappets of Cat. no. 53. There are prominent peaks to mark the side folds of the *nemes* and clearly defined tabs in front of the ears. The uraeus-snake rises from the frontlet (forehead band); the head and most of the hood have broken away. The body winds first horizontally in two side coils which lay originally underneath the hood and head, then it winds once vertically and the tail reaches the top of the head, level with the side folds of the head cloth. The treatment of the eyes and ears is very similar to Cat. no. 53. The eyes are slanting and narrow (0.2 cm wide at maximum) under naturalistically rounded brows, with heavy upper lids. They are lightly incised and asymmetrical. The ears are schematic, only the outer rim being shown, and they are set low, so that the lobe is level with the base of the nose. The nose is small and straight with wide nostrils. There is a shallow groove at the wings of the nostrils. The lips are thin and straight, the overall shape of the mouth recalling Cat. no. 53, and there are deep notches at the corners. The chin is square and slightly receding. Again as in Cat. no. 53, the muscles and bone of the torso and upper arms are shown in detail. The navel, pectoral muscles, nipples (outlined by an incised line), sternum, rib cage and stomach muscles are all represented, though identifiable to touch rather than eye. There is the same tripartite division of the torso made by the elongation of the navel furrow and the joining of the line under the breasts.

Burrell Collection 13/242. H: 10.5 cm. W: 7.2 cm.

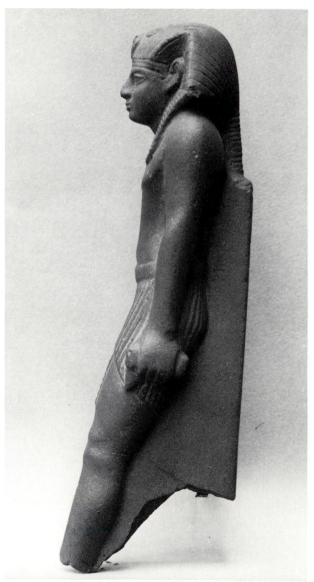

53 [also illustrated on p. 54]

54

Apart from the representation of the uraeus-snake, the similarity between this statuette and Cat. no. 53 is striking. The form of the uraeus can be paralleled on other royal sculptures of Dynasty XIII–XVII and its diagnostic features are the low position of the hood which intrudes into the frontlet; the symmetrical arrangement of the large side coils placed either side of the hood, cf. British Museum EA. 871; and the tip of the snake's body, which reaches the top of the head, cf. Cat. no. 53. However, a precise attribution, in the present state of our knowledge of the royal iconography of the XIIIth Dynasty, is not possible. Too few of the twenty statues attributable to the Kings of the Dynasty by inscriptions, and complete enough to provide dating criteria for this statuette, have been published with good photographs. Nevertheless the material, proportions and overall size of the two statuettes, as well as the features of the face, especially nose, mouth and eyes, are close enough to suggest that if they belong to different Kings they are not far apart in date.

Cf. Davies, *A Royal Statue Reattributed*, passim.

55 THE ROYAL HERALD, ANKHENMER OF ASYUT

Late Dynasty XIII, 1720–1650 BC.

Statuette of a striding man, in basalt. Inscribed in two lines of vertical inscription down the back pillar. Broken off at the ankles. Length of face: 2.3 cm. Width of face: 2.3 cm. Length

of eye: 0.8 cm. Length of ear: 1.1 cm. The inscription names the prince, mayor, royal acquaintance and herald of the King, Ankhenmer, and the appeal to the living names the god Wepwawet of Asyut, as follows: 'every priest and every *wab* priest who enters the temple of Wepwawet Lord of Asyut and sees this statue . . .'. Ankhenmer wears a wide shoulder-length wig or headcloth, which falls straight on to his shoulders. his rounded brows are modelled in relief, defining with cheek-bone and nose a deeply excavated eye-socket in the manner of Cat. no. 17. The eyes are small, almond shaped and asymmetrical, the right set at a distinct slant. The ears are outlined and set low, with a shallow depression representing the inner ear. The nose is short and very broad, the nostrils emphasised by a groove around the wings. The philtrum is marked and the mouth, its length equal to the width of the nose, has straight lips, the fuller lower lip pouting slightly. The chin is small and square. The structure of the face is clearly defined by the high cheek-bones above full cheeks, the strong chin, and grooves around the nose and at the corners of the mouth. Great attention is given to reproducing the bone and musculature of torso and limbs, albeit within the mannered tradition of the time. The torso is therefore strongly tripartite, the extended navel furrow almost meeting the strongly emphasised and joined pectoral muscles. The enlarged nipples are executed in relief. The notch at the base of the neck and the clavicle are shown and the rib cage suggested. The musculature of the shoulder and

55

arm, shown in front and at the back, is very pronounced, and the tension at the elbow resulting from the clenched fists is well observed. The bones of the knee and lower leg, and the muscles of calf and thigh, are equally painstakingly reproduced. Ankhenmer wears a short plain kilt with central tab and hold a roll of cloth in his right hand.

From Asyut. Liverpool Museum 1966.178. H: 25.5 cm. W: 9.4 cm.

The inscription presents difficulties because of the scribe's careless mistakes and because the text breaks off in the middle of the name. The reading of Ankhenmer is therefore extremely tentative. His titles are, however, clear enough, and they suggest a man of high rank who had access to the King and functioned on his behalf as a herald, i.e. a reporter of events. The inscription also explains the function of the statuette very clearly. It contains an appeal to every priest who enters the temple of Wepwawet of Asyut and sees the statue to recite the formula to provide offerings for Ankhenmer. We may assume further, not only that the statuette came from Asyut, but that it was made there. This provincial origin may explain the mistakes in the inscription and the lack of finish of the surface. Nevertheless it is a vigorous sculpture, very much in the style of the greywacke statuette of King Meryankhre Montuhotep, Cat. no. 53, but

it is superior in liveliness and strength of modelling.

Sotheby's Sale Catalogue, 13 June 1966, lot no. 113; for names formed with a god's name and *mr*, see P. Vernus in *BIFAO* 74 (1974), pp. 157–8.

56 A MAN BETWEEN TWO WOMEN
Late Dynasty XIII, 1720–1650 BC.

A small triad in black serpentine showing two women standing one on either side of a man. They each have a hand on his shoulder. Woman on man's left: Length of face: 1.3 cm. Width of face: 1.5 cm. Length of eye: 0.5 cm. Length of ear: 0.9 cm. Man: Length of face: 1.2 cm. Width of face: 1.5 cm. Length of eye: 0.6 cm. Woman on man's right: Length of face: 1.0 cm. Width of face: 1.2 cm. Length of eye: 0.5 cm. Length of ear: 1.0 cm. The man stands with his left foot forward and he wears a short curled wig or his natural hair. The modelling is simple, without subtlety and frequently asymmetrical. He holds a roll of cloth in each hand, a pose which goes back to the Old Kingdom, and wears a short pleated kilt with central waisted tab and a patterned belt. His eyes are narrow and heavy-lidded, the brows are rounded, the philtrum is marked and the thin mouth is slightly pursed, turning down at the corners. The torso shows

56

ate relationship to the man. They were probably his wife and mother.

The treatment of the man's torso, exaggerated though it is, relates closely to the style of the statuette of King Meryankhre Montuhotep, Cat. no. 53; for this reason, and because the fashion for triads seems to increase towards the end of the Dynasty, a late XIIIth Dynasty date is suggested. The short curled wig, popular in the early XIIth Dynasty, also came into fashion again at this time and continued into the early reigns of the XVIIIth Dynasty.

57 MOTHER AND SON
Late Dynasty XIII, 1720–1650 BC.

Diorite statue group of a mother and her young son. Woman: Length of face: 1.5 cm. Width of face: 1.6 cm. Length of eye: 0.9 cm. Length of ear: 0.9 cm. The two figures barely emerge from the large pebble out of which their images have been hammered. The tool marks of the pick are visible over the whole surface. Both figures stand with their feet together; the boy wears a side lock and has his left finger to his mouth in the pose conventionally adopted for children, and the woman embraces him in her right arm, which has to be unnaturally extended to accomplish this. She wears the so-called Hathor wig (see Cat. no. 14) and close-fitting tunic with wide shoulder straps. The modelling of face and body is rudimentary, but the features conform recognisably to the prevailing style. The eyes are narrow under a heavy upper

strong modelling of the deep navel furrow, the pectoral muscles and the slim waist, in contrast to the limbs which are no more than rounded columns of stone. The women share the same facial features with the addition of ears, which in the case of the woman on the left are set very high with prominent lobes. Their breasts are equally prominent, and navel and thighs are visible under their close-fitting garments. The considerably asymmetry is made more obvious by the small scale, and the different proportions of the faces and figures which result are striking. This is not intentional but due to poor design and/or execution by the sculptor.

Royal Museum of Scotland 1965.6. H: 13.6 cm. W: 8.9 cm.

This small monument is a three-dimensional version of the long lists of men and woman on XIIIth Dynasty group stelae, cf. Cat. no. 50. It is part of the proliferation of private commemorations in cemeteries and shrines which characterises the period. The quality of the monuments does not generally match the quantity, and this piece illustrates the sculptor's clumsy solution to the problem of carving three figures of equal size out of his block of serpentine. He has no space to represent each woman's second arm, so the man's arms are extended to match the women's outer arms, and the women's hands, deprived of any attachment to arms, are placed like epaulettes on the man's shoulders. It may not be technically accomplished, but the intention, the 'reading', of the sculpture, is made clear, that the two women stand in an affection-

57

lid, the ears are large and set low, the mouth is straight, the cheek-bones are high, the navel (unnaturally elongated) and breasts are prominent and the legs and thighs suggested under the tunic. The child is even more schematically shown; one ear is noticeably higher than the other and he is represented with the same heavy-lidded eyes and prominent navel as his mother.

From Haraga, tomb 162. Gift of the British School of Archaeology in Egypt. Fitzwilliam Museum E.3.1914. H: 12.1 cm. W: 9.2 cm.

A statuette from a tomb group is a rarity, and especially from one recorded well enough for us to be able to isolate the objects from a single burial. Tomb 162 was the grave of a woman in which traces of a coffin were found. Pottery, beads and another small statuette in the form of a man holding a bowl, Cat. no. 141, occurred with it. The most telling item for the dating of the group is a marl clay storage jar with a potmark; comparable vessels from the nearby site of Dahshur date this to the late XIIIth Dynasty.

As is often the case with small statuettes placed in graves, this one is not inscribed. The name would have been provided by the coffin and perhaps by other items in the burial which have not survived.

Engelbach, *Harageh*, p. 13, pl. XXV, 162; Vandier, *La Statuaire Egyptienne*, pp. 241–2, pl. XCII, 3; for pottery vessel, cf. Do. Arnold in *MDAIK* 38 (1982), Abb. 19, 7, pp. 62–4.

58 STELA OF KING WEPWAWETEMSAF
End of Dynasty XIII, c. 1650 BC.

Round-topped limestone stela carved in sunk relief showing the King, Sekhem-nefer-khaure Wepwawetemsaf, standing before the god Wepwawet-Re, Lord of Abydos. The lunette of the stela is entirely taken up by a crudely cut winged sun disk and cobras, spread over the four vertical columns which contain the name and epithets of the King. Below these are figures of the King and the god, separated by a line of text giving the name and epithet of the god. Both figures are of the same size, and lightly incised without interior modelling. The king wears a cap crown, bead collar, short kilt with triangular front fold, and a waist pendant terminating in cobras – part of the royal regalia. The god holds sceptres symbolising power and life. He is jackal-headed but also wears the long wig with straight side lappets. He wears a double bead collar and a short wrapover kilt, called a *shendyt* in Egyptian.

From Abydos. Ex Harris collection. British Museum EA. 969. H: 27.4 cm. W: 21.4 cm.

The stela is composed exclusively of images and texts of the King and his god, so we may assume it to have been dedicated by the King himself at Abydos. The poor quality of the monument is not surprising, since Wepwawetemsaf was undoubtedly a King with few resources, not known apart from this modest monument. His name has been recognised, without complete conviction, among the hieratic graffiti on the walls of the tomb of the nomarch Amenemhat at Beni Hasan. If this identification is correct, it suggests his authority was recognised also in that region of Middle Egypt.

Iconographically a development in the representation of the god can be seen between this stela and the stela of Amenemhat, Cat. no. 52. Instead of being a small figure at the top of the stela, the god's image is now much more prominent and commands equal space with the dedicant. The King's personal name, as opposed to the name he acquired at his accession, was Wepwawetemsaf, which means 'Wepwawet in his protection'. Wepwawet was presumably his personal god. Atlhough much simplified here, the epithets of the King and the arrangement of his titles under the protecting wings of the sun disk are characteristic of Middle Kingdom royal stelae. Nevertheless the stylistic affinities, in general and in detail, are with the stelae of the early Kings of the XVIIth Dynasty, such as Rahotep (British Museum EA. 283). The exact position of Wepwawetemsaf in the Dynasty is not known, but he is generally placed at its end. He wears a close-fitting cap or wig to which the uraeus-snake, symbol of royalty, is attached. This headdress is first attested worn by Sobekhotep II of Dynasty XIII, and continues to appear throughout Dynasty XVII to evolve in the New Kingdom into the famous blue crown. The character of the hieroglyphic signs also illustrates continuity with the succeeding XVIIth Dynasty. Figures of living creatures are mutilated, part of their bodies having been omitted or cut through, as in Cat. nos. 74, 83. This manner of writing is found on a range of funerary objects of Dynasties XIII–XVII from cemeteries in both Upper and Lower Egypt. The idea behind it, an old one in Egypt, seems to be to prevent the images of animals or reptiles from doing harm when the inscription containing them came to life, as it was believed to do with every recitation.

British Muesum, *Hieroglyphic Texts*, IV, p. 9, pl. 25; British Museum, *Sculpture Guide*, p. 81 (281); W. V. Davies in *JEA* 68 (1982), p. 72; M. Malaise in *SAK* 9 (1981), p. 282; von Beckerath, *Zweiten Zwischenzeit*, p. 69; stela of Rahotep, British Museum, *Hieroglyphic Texts*, IV, pl. XXIV.

58

WRITING AND LITERATURE

WRITING MATERIALS AND SCRIPTS

A scribe of the Middle Kingdom would not have looked very different from his colleagues of the Old and New Kingdoms, with the characteristic pack of palette, water-bowl and reed brushes that formed the sign for 'scribe' in the hieroglyphic script. The palette contained both the cakes of paint for writing and the reed brushes with which to write. At work the scribe would in fact paint rather than write in the modern sense. His 'ink' was the paint obtained with a wet brush from the cake of black or red pigment on his palette, and he kept his hand raised above the surface, like an artist at a canvas. His 'paper' was the wooden writing-board, like the old-fashioned slates of the primary school, or, for more permanent record, papyrus. A single sheet of papyrus was made from two rows of the split stems of a papyrus plant, laid out one row over the other, the second at right angles to the first. Several sheets could be glued together to form a long roll, the Egyptian equivalent of our book. When it was rolled up, the side with horizontal fibres parallel to the top of the roll (the so-called *recto*) would be vulnerable to straining and cracking if it were on the outside. Therefore the side with the fibres at 90° to the top of the roll (the side we call the *verso*) was left on the outside of the roll. It is for this reason that the *verso*, exposed and more vulnerable, was used last, while the *recto* served as the preferred first side. Although not strictly applicable in the same way, the terms *recto* and *verso* are used to refer to the 'front' and 'back' of single sheets of papyri as well as to full rolls.

The scripts of the Middle Kingdom also showed no radical departure from Old Kingdom practice. The basis of all scripts was the hieroglyphic, composed of images taken from the Egyptian environment according to the same canons of depiction that governed statuary and relief in art. Although the most familiar to a modern audience, the hieroglyphic script was the least widely used among the Egyptians themselves, being designed for the monuments of eternity rather than for daily use. Only a restricted number of scribes in priestly circles would have had access to the education necessary to write and read these texts, although most literate Egyptians would have had some grasp of the rudiments of the hieroglyphic script. Similarly restricted were the cursive hieroglyphs written not in stone but on papyrus with a brush, and also found on the inner face of wooden coffins of the early Middle Kingdom, Cat. no. 66. To distinguish the cursive hieroglyphs from the script of daily usage, it was written in

the opposite direction when on papyrus, i.e. from left to right instead of the Egyptian norm of right to left, Cat. no. 20. Texts in cursive hieroglyphs are of a magical, medical or religious character. The most common script in the Old, Middle and New Kingdoms was the form that hieroglyphs take when written quickly with a brush, a cursive script known to us by the Greek name hieratic, that is 'priestly', because at the time of Hellenic and Hellenistic civilisation after 600 BC the script was used only by priests. Hieratic in the Middle Kingdom varied from the formal, careful writing found in official legal documents, Cat. no. 63, to the virtually illegible scrawl of daily business texts or administrative orders copied for government files, Cat. no. 62. Every scribe would know hieratic, but it should be remembered that pharaonic Egypt, like pre-Victorian England, was a land of restricted literacy, in which the vast mass of the population could neither read nor write. The social division of writing, which separates those who live by writing from those who live by labour, is one we can recognise today and it was no less clearly observed by the Egyptians in their own society. Scribal apprentices were urged to pursue their studies and become scribes because this was the way to avoid the toil of manual labour: the *Satire of Trades*, known anciently as the *Instruction of Khety*, proclaims 'See, there is no profession without a boss, except for the scribe; he is the boss' (translation Lichtheim, *Literature*, I, p. 189). Writing was the key to a different world, of leisure and education, and of power. There was no military illiterate elite in the manner of medieval chivalry in Europe; every man in government service and every wealthy land-owner would read and write, and that alone sufficed to separate him from the world of service and labour.

Typically for ancient Egypt, the same attitudes governed life and death. Several 'Coffin Texts' pick up a theme from the Old Kingdom, according to which the deceased became the secretary of a major deity and so avoided working in the fields of the Hereafter. The same impulse led in the course of the xiith Dynasty to the introduction of the shabti figures, small-scale images of the deceased that were expected to answer for him in the land of the Dead should he be called to toil on state projects of agriculture or building works there, Cat. no. 83.

The scribal profession was not just restricted to a small number; it seems also to have been barred to women. By and large, women do not hold titles or positions in the central administration of state, and they never figure in an active role in the literary genre of 'instructions'. However, they were fully equal before the law and in economic dealings, and apparently took the role of managers in the important weaving industry. Women at the head of the richer households possessed their own personal name seals, indicating that they were fully involved in economic life. Within the literate elite, it is reasonable to suppose that women enjoyed economic, that is effective, independence, and had at least the opportunity of learning how to read and write, perhaps through their close relatives rather than in formal education. Their great disadvantage was their exclusion from public office up to the highest level, including the office of king. This barred them from receiving the considerable financial benefits of holding a title, and kept them in a secondary position throughout pharaonic history, albeit far superior to that of their closeted counterparts in the Graeco-Roman world.

LITERATURE

While scripts and materials saw great continuity from the Old to the Middle and through to the New Kingdom, the literature of the Middle Kingdom stands out for its creativity, and this was acknowledged by the Egyptians of later periods. Egypt stands so much at the beginnings of written traditions that any definition and subdivision of Middle Kingdom literature would risk arousing fierce debate. The surest approach is probably to begin with the definition of literature at its broadest as 'the self-conscious use of language'. That excludes administrative documents, medical prescriptions and magic spells, all of which aim at practical efficacy rather than aesthetic excellence of expression. The broad body of texts that remain as literature divides neatly into two groups on the basis of their intended application. The first group is made up of those texts intended to benefit their 'owner', that is the man responsible for having them written down; here

we may place the idealised 'autobiographies' of officials (Cat. no. 10), varying from lists of epithets to extended narrative, and the formal eulogies of kingship on royal stelae. Texts in this group are written on stone monuments in the appropriate script, hieroglyphic, but were recognised as literary works and sometimes copied onto papyri, leather or papyrus rolls, or wooden writing-boards. Much of the source material for our modern histories of pharaonic Egypt derives from this first group of literary texts. The second group consists of the works intended to benefit people more generally, either for instruction or for entertainment. Texts for instruction take either the form of straightforward 'instructions' (in Egyptian *sebayt*) or their mirror-image, the 'lament'. The instruction is cast as the advice of a father to his eldest son and heir (Cat. no. 60), and describes the best course of action to realise a happy and contented life. The lament takes the picture of perfect order and turns it on its head; by bewailing the misery and damage of chaos, it acts as an effusive paean to order itself. Both instructions and laments carry an attribution to a particular author and stand apart from the anonymous texts of entertainment. The latter are the narrative tales of wonder, which drew upon a tradition of oral story-telling now lost where it has not emerged in Egyptian or classical tradition. These tales are probably the most accessible of all Egyptian texts, and include the outstanding classic of pharaonic Egypt, composed during the Middle Kingdom, the *Tale of Sinuhe*.

Apart from texts written down for their 'owner' and texts addressed to people in general, there may be added as a third group the religious literary texts, written for wide circulation but applied in each instance to their one 'owner' of the moment. Funerary texts may be classed as literature where they take a more expansive form than the mechanical recipe of a simple spell. Hymns to the king, the royal crowns, and gods constitute an important but highly specialised stock of

59

self-conscious imagery, where the mingling of epithets and prose can be compared to the idealised 'autobiographies' of officials. While those memorials of officials and their royal counterparts belong on stone, and the texts of instruction and entertainment belong on papyrus, the hymns are at home on both media, being both individual and general in potential scope. One class of text which does not survive from the Middle Kingdom is the song, which is attested only in the specialised guise of the 'harpers' songs', Cat. no. 59. 'Harpers' songs' do not fall into any obvious category, owing as much to the tradition of 'laments' as to the funerary and religious literature. The failure of categorisation at this point serves as a useful reminder that these subdivisions form no more than an introduction to the treasures of Middle Kingdom literature. Their interpretation can come only from a reading of the texts themselves.

For later generations, the Middle Kingdom represented the classical model in both language and literature. Even the forms and spacing of hieroglyphic signs were admired and imitated for as long as the script survived. Partly this reverential attitude reflects the changes in the spoken language, which meant that already in the New Kingdom the vernacular bore little resemblance to the language of the monuments. The idiom of the XIIth Dynasty, Middle Egyptian, thereby acquired the distinction of antiquity, and was taught in schools much as Latin used to be taught in modern Europe. This does not diminish the sense of appreciation of the Middle Kingdom achievement in literature. The XIIth Dynasty can justly be recognised as an age in which Egypt produced its greatest flowering of literary genius, in works such as the *Instruction of Khety*, the *Song of the Harper*, Cat. no. 59, and the *Eloquent Peasant*. In the XIIth Dynasty new forms of text appear, notably the written tale and the 'lament', and to this period belong the oldest surviving literary manuscripts. Although we cannot date compositions more closely, a fact which undermines attempts to write political history out of literary works, we can be confident that the age of Middle Egyptian saw the most remarkable eruption of talent which laid the foundations of the written traditions that we take for granted.

59 THE SONG OF THE HARPER

Middle Kingdom composition as copied on a Ramesside papyrus of the thirteenth century BC. Papyrus roll with pages of hieratic in horizontal lines, written from right to left. The handwriting is a clear but dense example of that found in Ramesside literary papyri. The *recto* contains a series of songs, of which all but one are love-songs, the exception being the *Song of the Harper*; on the *verso* are two literary tales, the *Capture of Joppa* and the *Doomed Prince*. All of these date to the New Kingdom, except for the *Song of the Harper*, which is generally attributed to the Middle Kingdom on the basis of its contents and the royal name Intef in the heading. The song has survived only in this copy and in an incomplete version from the walls of an Amarna tomb (mid fourteenth century BC). The following is the complete text from the papyrus:

The song which is in the tomb-chapel of King Intef, justified, in front of the singer with the harp: He is happy, this good prince: Death is a kindly fate. A generation passes, another stays, since the time of the ancestors. The gods who were before rest in their tombs, blessed nobles too are buried in their tombs. (Yet) those who built tombs, their places are gone, what has become of them? I have heard the words of Imhotep and Hardedef, whose sayings are recited whole: what of their places? Their walls have crumbled, their places are gone, as though they had never been! None comes from there, to tell of their state, to tell of their needs, to calm our hearts, until we go where they have gone!

Hence rejoice in your heart! Forgetfulness profits you; follow your heart as long as you live! Put myrrh on your head, dress in fine linen, anoint yourself with oils fit for a god; heap up your joys, let your heart not sink! Follow your heart and your happiness, do your things on earth as your heart commands! When there comes to you that day of mourning, the Weary-hearted (i.e. Osiris) hears not their mourning; wailing saves no man from the pit.

Refrain: Make holiday! Do not weary of it!
Lo, none is allowed to take his goods with him,
Lo, none who departs comes back again.

British Museum EA. 10060 (= P. Harris 500) (*The Song of the Harper*, [translation of M. Lichtheim] is *recto* col. 6, 2–7, 2).

According to the heading given in the papyrus, the song formed part of the decoration in the mortuary complex of a King Intef; pharaohs of that name are known to have ruled in the XIth, XIIIth and XVIIth Dynasties. Although it is possible that a royal tomb of the XIIIth or XVIIth Dynasty might have contained such decoration, the XIth Dynasty royal necropolis at Thebes seems the most likely site of the original song. The XIth Dynasty rulers continued to be venerated under the XIIth and XIIIth Dynasties, so that this part of the tomb decoration may date to a period somewhat later than the XIth Dynasty itself. The composition may be dated to the early Middle Kingdom from parallels in an intriguing text of that date, the *Dispute of a Man with His Soul*. In that discourse on death, a man is portrayed longing for an end to life, while his soul urges him to enjoy it and not to trust in an Afterlife: in a central passage, the soul reminds the man that no cult of the dead can be guaranteed to last for ever, and says: 'Follow the feast day, forget worry!' The song addresses not a King but a 'prince', the Egyptian being the word for an official or nobleman. Since it was written in a royal tomb, it carried perhaps a general application to all courtiers, without attempting to refer to the god–king.

So much of our evidence for life in ancient Egypt comes from tombs that we can easily assign fixed and uncomplicated beliefs in an Afterlife to the people who built them. The literary texts, and first among them the *Song of the Harper*, force us to think again, by illustrating how keenly the Egyptians felt the uncertainty and inevitability of death. In direct contradiction of the prevailing custom of placing funerary equipment in the tomb, the song exclaims 'none is allowed to take his goods with him'. Doubt about an Afterlife hinges on the practical experience that 'none who departs comes back again'. The only sure immortality in the eyes of the singer is that attained by the author whose writings preserve his name on earth; the song refers to Imhotep, the wise minister of King Djoser who built the Step Pyramid at Saqqara in the IIIrd Dynasty, and to Hardedef, contemporary of the

Great Pyramids at Giza of the ivth Dynasty, because their collected sayings circulated still in the Middle Kingdom, whereas their tombs had disappeared. The starkness of tone compares with the 'laments' of Middle Kingdom literature, such as the bitter advice in the *Instruction of Amenemhat I*, Cat. no. 60. Notwithstanding the strength of this radical strain in the literary texts of the day, it should be understood that it did not replace more orthodox expression. The Middle Kingdom produced outstanding compositions in which traditional ideology was vigorously expounded, alongside its more disturbing new texts. It is significant that the very song that cast doubt on the usefulness of tombs was itself inscribed on the walls of a tomb. Fears and hopes existed side by side in the most concrete form, in an open admission of uncertainty which we may recognise as a universal human reaction to death.

J. Assmann, 'Harfnerlieder' in *LÄ*, ii, 972–82; Lichtheim, *Literature*, i, pp. 194–7.

60 THE INSTRUCTION OF KING AMENEMHAT I

Middle Kingdom composition, in a Ramesside copy (thirteenth century BC). First page from a roll containing Ramesside copies of Middle Kingdom literary texts; the hand is an excellent example of the calligraphy of xixth Dynasty

literary manuscripts. The upper margin of the roll contains correct forms of certain signs, and a correction has been entered above the second line of this page; these features indicate that the scribe was practising his hand on the famous compositions of the past, as a part of his further education. At the end of this *Instruction*, on another page of the roll, the text gives the name of the copyist as the apprentice scribe Inene, under his teacher Qageb; both served in the treasury under Seti II (c. 1214–1204 BC), and Inene is known from other literary papyri such as that containing the New Kingdom tale of the *Two Brothers*. On this roll, Inene copied the *Hymn to the Nile* of disputed date, and two xiith Dynasty masterpieces, the *Instruction of Amenemhat I* and the *Instruction of Khety*. The first page contains the first part of the *Instruction of Amenemhat I*, in which the King bitterly warns his son against confiding in the mortal men he rules:

Beware of subjects who are nobodies, of whose plotting one is not aware. Trust not a brother, know not a friend; make no intimates, it is worthless. When you lie down, guard your heart yourself, for no man has adherents on the day of woe.

British Museum EA. 10182 (=P. Sallier 2 [translation of M. Lichtheim]), frame 1.

The 'Instruction' was a set literary genre in which a man summed up the experience of a lifetime for the benefit specifically of his son and heir. In the *Instruction of Amenemhat I* that King addresses his son Senusret I in a 'revelation of

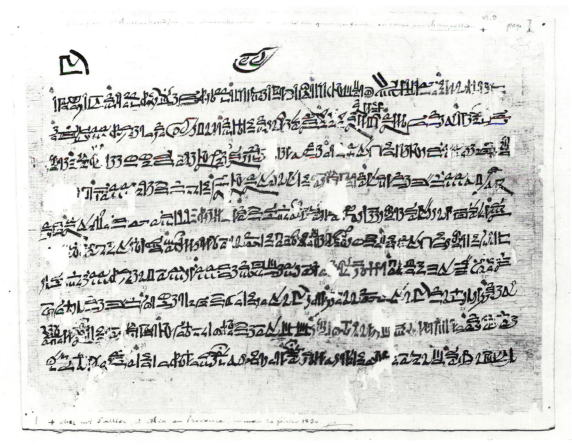

60

truth' after his death. The acrid cynicism of the text in its reflections on human nature comes as all the more startling for being in the mouth of the King. Amenemhat I is made to rail against the ingratitude of the subjects who had benefited from his years of beneficent rule and the prosperity they brought. The incident which causes the King the greatest anguish is recalled in the fulcral section of the text, which describes an assassination attempt on him in the palace during the night: 'as my heart began to follow sleep, weapons for my protection were turned against me, while I was like a snake of the desert'. This act of sedition contrasts with the picture of peace which the King claims as the achievement of his reign: 'none hungered in my years, none thirsted in them ... I had assigned everything to its place'. The text, which began with the caution 'trust not a brother, know not a friend', ends with an exhortation to Senusret I to reign as a good and pious King in the footsteps of his father.

In the absence of detailed political records for the xiith Dynasty, it is tempting to adduce direct historical information from this literary text, by taking at face value the date as the reign of Senusret I, and by accepting the assassination story as a true event. Both may be correct, but it should be observed that we can be sure of neither the date nor the authorship of the instruction. In a papyrus of the New Kingdom, possibly containing part of the lost *Instruction of Amennakht*, the *Instruction of Amenemhat I* is attributed without hesitation to a scribe called Khety in these words: 'it is he (Khety) who wrote the book of the *Instruction of Sehetepibra* (= Amenemhat I)'. This Khety is almost certainly the author of the *Instruction of Khety*, and the two works have a certain amount in common; both are written on this papyrus, and they were perhaps the two most popular Middle Kingdom texts in later times. We do not know whether the Middle Kingdom audience also attributed the *Instruction of Amenemhat I* to Khety, but there is little to be said against the idea. The power of the work derives not so much from its royal setting, even if this was intended to imply royal authorship, as from its remarkable use of the genre to express the duality of kingship. The mortality of Pharaoh comes to the fore in the stark realism of the assassination passage and the bitterness of the advice, while the divinity of the King takes precedence in the traditional praise of kingship. In assessing the lasting value of the text, recognised by the Egyptians themselves, we ought properly to set in the background the undecided political and historical interpretations and concentrate more fully on its literary character. This may provide an objective basis for establishing the date of the instruction and its relation to other masterpieces of the period.

In structure, the piece can be broken down into two balanced sections in a declamatory 'poetic' style, one on each side of the short central paragraph in straight narrative or 'prose' style. The first section contains the pessimistic and caustic reflection on the treachery of man, and leads into the vivid narrative account of the attempt on the King's life. The second 'poetic' section follows that narration with an idealised image of the perfect reign of the King, to sharpen the contrast between the good done by Amenemhat I and

the evil deed with which he has been repaid. The overriding theme of the composition is the dual nature of the King, who is both the god who declares 'no-one equalled me as a doer of deeds' and the vulnerable mortal who concedes almost plaintively 'I had not prepared for it, had not expected it, had not foreseen the failing of the servants'. The same duality that here finds literary form can be seen in the magnificent sculptures of the late xiith Dynasty Kings Senusret III and Amenemhat III (Cat. nos. 28, 31). They also testify to how the Egyptians strove to resolve the contradiction of Pharaoh, man and god.

Lichtheim, *Literature*, I, pp. 135–9; E. Blumenthal, 'Lehre Amenemhets I' in *LĀ*, III, 968–71; G. Posener, *Littérature et Politique* (Paris 1956), pp. 61–86; J. Foster in *JEA* 67 (1981), pp. 36–47, pls. IV–XI.

61 LETTER FROM A DISSATISFIED GENERAL

Late Dynasty XI, 2004–1963 BC.

A sheet of coarse papyrus, poorly preserved in the centre, and at the right hand margin of the *recto* reinforced by a narrow band. No earlier traces of writing are visible, indicating that the sheet was new when used for this text. Creases show where it was folded neatly into a small packet for delivery; on the blank space of the *verso* exposed after folding, the scribe wrote the names of the sender and addressee. The sheet bears nine columns of hieratic on the *recto* and two on the *verso*, written in the normal direction of right to left. The scribe used a thick reed brush applied in bold strokes; the handwriting suggests a date in the late xith Dynasty. The text is a letter

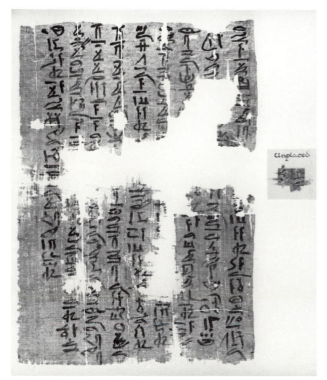

61

from a general, Nehesu, to a man called Kay, whose title is lost in the lacuna. An introductory greeting invokes Montu, the Theban falcon-headed deity, in favour of Kay, whom he then addresses as follows:

What of that letter to me from (the lady) Senet saying 'I have been brought no food'? [See, I sent x bushels (?)] to my household and ten bushels of barley to you. Did Kay's daughter . . .-senet and Kay's son Nefersesh fetch them from the cargo-ship? If they [did not,] then you fetch it (yourselves). Further: see, a delivery is made in full; what then of your [letting] yourself be turned against your daughter? You will have killed her by not giving that barley [to] my household. See well, I know the character of a father's wife; do you follow the wish of your wife in killing my household? Am I to be satisfied that I have given my household food, when I am told that there is no food? Send the cargo-ship. It has reached me. (Translation after T. G. H. James)

Possibly from Thebes. British Museum EA. 10549.

Interpreting the letter of a stranger can be difficult, because writers tend to take for granted the circumstances and personal relationships which connect them with the recipient. In this example, we can only guess at the tie between the general Nehesu and the man Kay, who seems to be acting as his agent or manager of his estates. Even Nehesu's title is ambiguous, because the word translated as 'general' could denote any commander of unskilled forces, from senior army officers to ordinary overseers of workgangs. Nevertheless, the cause for complaint is not hard to find; Nehesu is away from home, and has been told that one of his shipments has gone astray. The aggrieved party is a lady by the name of Senet, who seems to be Kay's own daughter. Nehesu here demands from Kay some account of his conduct, and holds him responsible for any misfortune. A clue to the affair lies in the declaration 'I know the character of a father's wife'; if the term means 'stepmother', Nehesu would be in effect accusing Kay's wife of plotting against her stepdaughter Senet, in the unhappy position of a Cinderella. The domestic discord strikingly recalls the letters of the same period from a mortuary priest called Heqanakht; those were sufficiently sinister to provide the plot of Agatha Christie's *Death Comes as the End*. Like Nehesu, Heqanakht was preoccupied with the treatment of a vulnerable member of his household, as well as with the proper distribution of food. The exaggerated language in the letters may reflect real economic hardship, since other texts of the XIth Dynasty refer to famines caused by low Nile inundations. However, the constant worry over provisioning also emerges in the ubiquitous prayer for offerings, spells to supply the deceased with food, Cat. no. 66, and the model granaries placed in tombs, Cat. no. 91. Taking up this theme, officials habitually claimed credit on their funerary stelae for feeding the hungry in their districts and estates, Cat. no. 25. In government service, official duties might take a man far from his family for extended periods, both inside Egypt and within the Egyptian-held territories in Nubia, Cat. no. 33. At such times the man's control of domestic affairs must have weakened and his worries increased.

T. G. H. James, *The Heqanakhte Papers* (New York, 1962), no. XVI on pp. 89ff., pls. 24–5.

62 A MILITARY DESPATCH FROM NUBIA
recto Year 3 of [Amenemhat III], 1841 BC; *verso* Dynasty XIII, 1786–1650 BC.

Third of six pages from a papyrus roll, badly damaged across the upper margin. The earlier text, on the *recto*, is a series of despatches from fortresses in Egyptian-controlled

62

Nubia. A later collection of magical spells, in a more rounded cursive hand of the xiiith Dynasty, occupies the whole of the *verso*. The scribe who wrote the despatches employed a rapid, extremely difficult hand, teeming with the compressed ligatures characteristic of the administrative documents of the late xiith Dynasty. The date 'year 3' recurs at several points on the *recto* and probably refers to the reign of Amenemhat III.

The despatch on the lower part of this page is typical of the series:

Another letter brought to him by the guard Ameny who is in Khesef-Medjau (Serra East), being a (communication) given by fortress to fortress.

It is a communication to the Master, may he live, prosper, be healthy, to the effect that the soldier of Nekhen, Senu's son, Reniqer and the soldier of Tjebu, Rensi's son Senusret's son, ditto (i.e. Senusret), came to report to this your servant in year 3, 4th month of spring, day 2, at the time of breakfast, on a mission from the officer of the town regiment, Khusobek's son Montuhotep's son, Khusobek ... (illegible), who is acting in lieu of the officer of the sovereign's crew in the garrison of Meha (a district of Nubia), saying:

'The patrol that went out to patrol the desert-edge near (?) the fortress of Khesef-Medjau in year 3, 3rd month of spring, last day, has returned to report to me, saying "We have found the track of thirty-two men and three donkeys ...".' (Translation after P. Smither)

From tomb 5, under the Ramesseum at Thebes. British Museum EA. 10752 (= P. Ramesseum C), frame 3.

This roll belongs to a group of papyri found in a wooden chest, together with magical and funerary objects (see p. 110). The chest lay at the bottom of a Middle Kingdom tomb-shaft. The other texts in the find are predominantly literary, magical and medical, and the despatches on this roll have survived only because the *verso* was subsequently used to record a collection of magical incantations. It is curious that official despatches came into the hands of a magical and medical practitioner, and it raises the intriguing question of how the government disposed of its old files.

The papyrus allows us to observe the way in which Egypt maintained her hold on Nubia. That land, as the Southern extension of the Nile Valley, had attracted the Pharaohs since the first days of unification in the Early Dynastic Period (from c. 3000 BC). In the Middle Kingdom, Senusret I conquered it and established a chain of fortresses, including Buhen (see Cat. no. 33) to control it. A series of military campaigns under Senusret III extended the area of Egyptian occupation to Semna at the Second Cataract, and in that reign the existing fortresses were expanded and additional ones founded in the new frontier area.

At Semna, Senusret III set up boundary stelae enjoining upon his successors the defence of the frontier and the checking of all northbound river traffic, to allow through only approved traders and envoys. The Semna Despatches on this papyrus demonstrate how this policy was enforced. Garrisons of Egyptians were sent to watch particular areas, such as the 'garrison of Meha' in our text. Patrols kept a close eye on all movement of men (and animals) and reported back to senior military commanders stationed in the principal fortresses. Those commanders might be served by a lieutenant, since

the 'officer of the town regiment' Khusobek acts in place of an unnamed higher-ranking officer, 'officer of the sovereign's crew', in this despatch. An account of all such reports and all decisions taken over movements of people was relayed by courier from one fortress to the next, until the message reached Thebes. The unidentified 'Master', recipient of the despatches, was a higher commander or official in the administration there, to judge from the honorific formulae used to address him. Even the most minor observations were reported to Thebes and copied there, testifying to a remarkable vigilance. Although this appears at first glance surprising and militarily unnecessary, there being no obvious threat from Nubia surviving in the archaeological record of the xiith Dynasty, the experience of Britain in the last century shows the problems that beset foreign armies controlling the Sudan from the Nile Valley. The names of Egyptian fortresses themselves declare the policy and concerns of Pharaoh, Serra East being Khesef-Medjau, 'He who repels the Medjay people/land'. The word Medjay denotes nomadic peoples of the Eastern desert, as distinct from Nehesy, 'Nubian', the settled inhabitants of villages in the river valley. Egyptian texts of the Middle Kingdom speak of the nomadic Medjay as an alien but co-operative group, and they may be identified in the archaeological record within Egypt itself as the 'Pan-Grave people' during the xiiith Dynasty. The control of immigration weakened at that time on both Asiatic and Nubian fronts, and at the end of the xiiith Dynasty the fortresses in the south were no longer manned by Pharaoh's troops. The visible adversaries of Egypt in the Second Intermediate Period in Nubia demonstrate how justified was the vigilance of Senusret III and the officials of the Semna despatches.

D. Spanel, *LÄ*, V, 844–7, 'Semna Papyri'; P. Smither in *JEA* 31 (1945), pp. 3–10, pls. II–VII; for military titles, O. Berlev in *RdE* 23 (1971), pp. 23–48.

63 THE WILL OF MERY, SON OF INTEF
Year 39 of Amenemhat III, 1805 BC.

Single sheet of papyrus, torn away at the lower margin and left side of the *recto*. The *recto* bears nine horizontal lines of hieratic, followed after a space by four more lines; the *verso* is blank except for a small rectangle of text giving the heading of the document: 'Deed of conveyance drawn up by the controller of the phyle, Intef's son, Mery, for his son, Mery's son Intef, called Iuseneb.'

The main text of the *recto* details the provisions made by Mery for his children:

I am giving my (office of) controller of the phyle to my son, Mery's son, Intef called Iuseneb, in exchange for (him being) my staff of old age, according as I am grown affirm; let him be appointed at once. As to the deed of conveyance which I drew up for his mother earlier, cancel it.

As for my estate which is in the region of Hut-. .., it is (to pass) to my children born to me by the daughter of the district councillor's bodyguard, Sobekemhat's daughter, Nebetnennisut, together with all that is in it.

After the space, the last few lines name the witnesses to the deed.

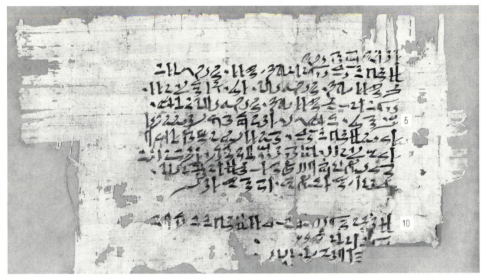

63

This copy is written neatly in the hieratic of the late XIIth Dynasty. Its clarity contrasts with the highly cursive forms found in administrative papyri (see Cat. no. 62), and suggests that this was the official or personal document, rather than some secondary copy or draft.

From Kahun. University College 32037 (=P. Kahun VII.1).

The document was found on its own among the houses of Kahun, the town founded by Senusret II beside his pyramid at the mouth of the Faiyum. Thanks to the dry conditions at the desert edge, where the town stands, the site has yielded the largest quantities of Middle Kingdom papyri yet discovered. The man who drew up the deed, Mery, held the title 'controller of the phyle', that is the priest responsible for the temple staff of a particular month; in Egyptian temples, staff were divided into four workgangs called 'phyles', each of which would supply the required manpower for one month three times a year, Cat. no. 19.

The titles of the witnesses are also priestly, and they were probably colleagues of Mery. Their common place of work may have been the mortuary temple of Senusret II, adjacent to the town. According to the extensive but fragmentary archive from that temple, it was dedicated to Anubis, jackal-headed god of mummification, and its staff were responsible for maintaining the pyramid temple and cult of Senusret II.

According to other sources of the Middle Kingdom and Second Intermediate Period, a priestly title carried with it a share in temple income, as well as servants and a supporting estate. This would explain why the cession of the title by Mery to his son Intef holds the principal place in the deed. In the text it can be seen how Mery in effect chooses his successor, although the phrase 'let him be appointed at once' implies that the actual appointment ceremony was formally conducted by others. Such a ceremony would permit the state to intervene where necessary, but a local priestly title would be less likely to attract the attention of central government than senior positions in the army or civil service. The inscriptions of rich governors in Middle Egypt during the early XIIth

Dynasty, such as those at Beni Hasan, explicitly state that, though the title of governor was 'inherited' from the father, the actual appointment was made by Pharaoh. The tension between the royal interest and the principle of succeeding to a father's office runs through Egyptian history, and surfaces in the Intermediate Periods of weaker central control. In return for obtaining his father's title, Intef must act as his 'staff of old age', an eloquent term to designate technically the financial supporter of an old man without income.

The deed contains clues that Mery's family had undergone certain changes. Earlier he had made a deed in favour of his son's mother, but he now cancels that deed and instead leaves his property to the children born to him by the lady Nebetnennisut. The wording implies that this lady is not the unnamed mother of his son Intef, but a second wife whom he married after separation from the first by death or divorce. The name Nebetnennisut means 'Lady of Nennisut', and is probably a reference to the goddess Hathor; Nennisut itself is a town about twelve miles south of Kahun (modern Ihnasya el-Medina, classical Heracleopolis) and probably the home-town of Nebetnennisut or her family. Her father was the military escort for visiting 'district councillors' sent by the central state to inspect local lands; she probably ranked in the same social class as the priest Mery whom she married. Through the legal affairs of one family, this document affords a concise glimpse of a busy town in the late XIIth Dynasty.

Ll. Griffith, *Kahun Papyri*, II, pl. XI, lines 10–27; A. Théodoridès, *Revue Internationale des Droits de l'Antiquité* 17 (1970), pp. 117–216; A. Théodoridès, *Revue Internationale des Droites de l'Antiquité* 19 (1972), pp. 129–48.

64 A SPELL FOR FOOD IN THE AFTERLIFE
Early Middle Kingdom, 2023–1862 BC.

One sheet from a roll of papyrus, now dark and cracked across its lower middle; the *recto* preserves ten columns of hieratic in a cramped hand of the XIth or early XIIth Dynasty. The scribe has kept each sign separate from its neighbours,

81

as in the texts on wooden coffins (e.g. Cat. no. 66), rather than joining groups of signs into cursive ligatures. The text, like those on the rest of the roll, belongs to the corpus of Middle Kingdom 'Coffin Texts', so called because they typically decorate the wooden coffins of the early Middle Kingdom. Like the 'Pyramid Texts' on the stone walls of VIth Dynasty pyramids, they were intended to secure a good life after death and formed the basis of the collections of spells on New Kingdom papyri known as the 'Book of the Dead'.

This spell reflects the preoccupation in life and death with the supply of food. The following extracts illustrate how the Egyptian sought to guarantee his place in the next world by merging with the deities and powers that prevailed there.

I am the great one, son of Nepri (the grain god) . . . lord of the nine portions in the fore of the Great Ennead, being the three loaves in Djedu, the three in On, the three in Hut-baut, foremost of the Field of Rushes.

Bread is given to me in the presence of Ptah, he opens my mouth; the four Ptahs, they open my mouth in the Council (of the Gods) in which Horus opened the mouth of Osiris.

The spell continues on the next sheet of the roll, where it is followed by a second version of the same spell.
British Museum EA. 10676 (=P. Gardiner 2), frame 24.
It is highly unusual to find spells from the corpus of 'Coffin Texts' on papyrus, which did not become the standard material for funerary texts until the New Kingdom. This roll

may have been a master copy for the use of priests or craftsmen. Possibly it was the actual ritual roll held by the lector–priest in the recitations at a funeral. The fastidious style of handwriting might be more appropriate to the practical textbook of a working priest, since personal collections of spells on later papyri are written in a much more cursive hand, see Cat. no. 62, *verso*.

At burial, the crucial rite for the deceased was the 'Opening of the Mouth', an ancient ceremony in which special implements were touched to the mouth of the mummified body, to reawaken its senses and thereby its ability to enjoy a full life after death. In the spell, the act of opening the mouth is performed by the creator-god Ptah of Memphis, taking as model the rite in the myth of Horus and his father Osiris, god of the dead. Without this passage, the rest of the spell, about the possession of food, would be meaningless, because the deceased would be unable to eat. In order to have food for eternity, the deceased lays claim throughout the spell to the status of a god, with access to provisions in the sacred cities of Djedu (Delta cult-centre of Osiris), On (the principal cult-centre of the sun-god Ra) and Hut-baut in the Field of Rushes. The last named was a region of the underworld comparable to the Elysian Fields of Greek mythology, and 'Books of the Dead' in the New Kingdom include pictures of the deceased contentedly at work harvesting there. Though different in approach, the spell carries the same intentions as the prayer for offerings which occurs on most funerary stelae.

64

Seeing the next life as a faithful reproduction of this one, the Egyptians understandably did their best never to want for food or drink there.

In contrast to the 'Pyramid Texts' in the Old Kingdom, 'Coffin Texts' were not restricted to the tomb of Pharaoh, but were copied widely for burials throughout the literate classes, see Cat. no. 66. The widening circle of eligibility has been called a form of 'democratisation', but, as with 'propaganda', our use of the word risks transplanting on to the ancient culture blunt and misplaced modern conceptions. The appearance of funerary texts on coffins probably has more to do with the emergence at the end of the Old Kingdom of schools of artists and craftsmen at the provincial capitals in Upper and Middle Egypt, see above p. oo. In earlier times hieroglyphic inscriptions had been restricted essentially to the stone monuments, royal and private, in the cemeteries of Memphis, the capital, and of Abydos. The First Intermediate Period brought an increase in the use of the hieroglyphic script coupled with the replacement of stone sarcophagi by wooden coffins which would be accessible to a wider social range for simple reasons of cost. It is thus not necessary to suppose that the nobles of the Old Kingdom entertained radically different aspirations from those of their Middle Kingdom successors, in their belief in a well-stocked Afterlife.

A. de Buck, *The Egyptian Coffin Texts*, III (Chicago, 1947), pp. 176–85, spell no. 215; translation in R. Faulkner, *The Ancient Egyptian Coffin Texts* (Warminster, 1973–8), I, pp. 171–2; M. Heerman van Voss, 'Sargtexte' in *LÄ*, v, 468–71.

65 A VETERINARY PAPYRUS

Late Dynasty XII, 1862–1787 BC.

Papyrus roll in broken condition, now consisting of one large piece and nine unplaced fragments. The *verso* is blank, while the *recto* contains vertical columns of a text written in cursive hieroglyphs from left to right across the roll. A horizontal margin above the columns encloses the heading for each separate section of the text. For most of the text the scribe used black, reserving red for passages that needed to be underlined or marked out from the words surrounding them.

Originally the roll bore a series of medical prescriptions, of which only one now survives in full (central section on the main piece). Unique among the records of ancient Egyptian medicine, these prescriptions refer to the treatment not of people but of animals. The syntax and presentation of each method of treatment do not differ from those of treatments in the great medical papyri of the same period.

First part of the second prescription on the main piece:

prescription for treatment of a bull suffering a cold fever (?). If I see [a bull suffering] a cold fever (?), its condition being that its eyes water, its temples are heavy, the roots of its teeth are reddened, and its neck is stretched out, one reads for it: it is to be placed on one of its sides, and it is to be sprinkled with cold water, and its eyes and its flanks and all its limbs are to be rubbed with bundles of reeds. (Translation after H. Grapow and W. Westendorf)

From Kahun. University College 32036. H: 14.5 cm. W: 59.0 cm (main piece).

The two best-preserved paragraphs in the series concern the treatment of sick bulls, but there is some uncertainty over the animals covered in the remainder of the roll. On the basis of words found in the smaller fragments, it has been thought that they dealt with diseases among dogs, geese and fishes, but the last of these seems especially improbable. Since we have no context for the word 'dog' in one fragment, it may be part of a phrase of indirect reference, perhaps a simile '[like] a dog'. Another word on the same fragment implies treatment of a bull. The two signs for goose and fish could be interpreted as writings of the names of diseases, such as perhaps *hetem* 'wasting (?)' for the goose-sign, and *shepet* 'blindness' for the fish. Therefore the whole roll could well have been devoted entirely to prescriptions for the treatment of bulls.

The use of cursive hieroglyphs, a select and more sacred script than ordinary hieratic, suggests that the roll came from the temple or from one of the specialised priests there. There is some confirmation for this in the other papyri found with or near the roll in one place within the town of Kahun. They include the cycle of hymns to Senusret III and an accounts text concerning priests and temple officials, as well as a state official, 'the accountant of cattle'. From the Lahun temple archive and the XIIIth Dynasty royal accounts ledger P. Boulaq 18, we know that bulls and oxen were offered to the gods at temples as gifts presented from people outside the temple (principally from the King himself) and that the temples maintained extensive cattle stalls. This explains why a temple would need an expert in so limited an area of veterinary practice, and also why we have no other veterinary documents from ancient Egypt. Normally, the welfare of livestock would be the concern of the herdsman, whose medical talent would be purely practical and so below the reach of the world of writing and texts. At the temple, the bulls offered would often come from herds outside the control of the temple staff, and

LV. 2. VETERINARY PAPYRUS.   PL VII

65

they might need specialist treatment after being presented to the god. Furthermore, meat was not widely available in ancient Egypt, and the palace and temples would deal in large livestock on a scale beyond the scope of the average farmer. Such features help to account for both the sacredness and the uniqueness of the Kahun veterinary papyrus.

H. Goedicke, 'Tiermedizin' in *LÄ* vi, 587–8; F. Ll. Griffith, *Kahun Papyri*, i, pp. 12–14, pl. vii; H. Grapow and W. Westendorf (eds.) *Grundriss der Medizin* (Berlin, 1958), iv¹, pp. 317–19; iv², pp. 237–40; v, pp. 546–9.

66 SPELLS FOR THE AFTERLIFE
Dynasty XI to early Dynasty XII, 2023–1867 BC.

Long, narrow fragment from the lower half of one side of a wooden coffin. The outer face bears plain decoration characteristic of the xith Dynasty and early xiith Dynasty, with simple pairs of columns separated by empty undecorated spaces. The few surviving signs probably contain part of the names of the deceased, a deity or a cult-place. On what would have been the inner face of the coffin, a continuous series of narrow columns contains a painted text which can be identified despite the lacunae as four spells from the Middle Kingdom corpus of funerary texts, or 'Coffin Texts'. The spells on this fragment belong to the same group as those on the spells papyrus of the early Middle Kingdom, Cat. no. 64. They testify again to the determination of the Egyptians to remain well supplied in the Afterlife, and not to become vulnerable to privations there.

The following extracts are taken from better-preserved examples of the spells found on this fragment.

First Spell (no. 203 in the modern collection of the Coffin Texts):

Thus says that one who cannot count: What will you live on in this land to which you have come that you may be a spirit?
I will live on the seven portions of bread: four loaves are in the House of Horus and three in the House of Thoth.
Who will bring it to you?
The nurse of the House of Horus and the stewardess of the Souls of On will bring it to me.
Where will you eat it?
Under the branches of the tree 'Praise-beauty' which supports the *hekenu*.

Third Spell (no. 574):

(Heading) Not to go upside-down so that a man may have power in his legs.

Fourth Spell (no. 210):

(Heading) Not to labour in the realm of the Dead.

From Asyut (?) Fitzwilliam e.w.82. H: 8.0 cm. W: 72.3 cm.

As frequently occurs in the Coffin Texts, the long spell no. 203 incorporates a conversation envisaged between the dead man or woman and a divine being that challenges the deceased to justify his or her claim to a place among the blessed dead. The questions allow us to determine the sex of the dead person, because the Egyptian language distinguishes between male and female in the singular second person pronoun, 'you'. In the fragment, the question 'What will you live on?' is addressed to a woman, establishing that the coffin from which it came was intended for the burial of a rich lady during the early Middle Kingdom. Spells in the Coffin Texts are rarely attested on more than a handful of different coffins, and even more rarely follow the same arrangement. Therefore it is interesting to find the same selection of spells in the same order on the coffin of Mesehti, xith Dynasty mayor of Asyut (Cairo coffin CG 28118): see Cat. no. 23. Although there is no hard evidence to prove it, it is possible that the same workshop produced both coffins, and perhaps at about the same time. The coffin fragment of the unknown lady was stored in the Museum with another fragment thought on internal evidence to be from Asyut, Cat. no. 67, and this slight circumstantial evidence strengthens the case for attributing the fragments to that city.

All four spells on the surviving fragment are intended to enable the deceased to overcome the weakness of death by first assimilating the powers of the gods, and then maintaining, through that strength, an orderly existence. The horror of losing order, tantamount to losing life itself, is expressed as the inversion of orderly conduct, for example 'walking upside-down' or 'eating faeces'. These phrases sum up the revulsion and fear inspired among the rich by the prospect of penury, among the powerful by the prospect of servitude. Such thoughts and fears of inverting order form part of a pattern of thinking also attested in the literary genre of the 'lament' (see above p. ooo).

For other versions of the spells, see A. de Buck, *The Egyptian Coffin Texts*, i–vii (Chicago, 1935–61), nos. 203, 204 and 574; translation from R. Faulkner, *The Ancient Egyptian Coffin Texts* (Warminster, 1973–8).

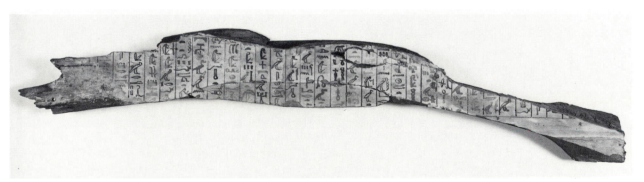

66

FUNERARY ART

The term 'funerary art' could be applied to almost any object in this exhibition, either because it was found in a grave or because it commemorates the dead. However, many of the objects found in tombs were not specially made for burial, as sections 4 and 5 of this catalogue demonstrate. This helps to offset the distortion which arises from the fact that many more Middle Kingdom cemeteries than towns or villages have been excavated.

Nevertheless, there existed all over Egypt workshops specialising in making the equipment for a 'goodly burial in the West'. There is evidence that contractors built tombs en bloc, and once space in one of these had been bought the most important piece of equipment was the coffin, see Cat. nos. 67–72, 74–5. This served the practical purpose of protecting the fragile body, but, equally importantly, also carried powerful spells to restore it to life and to revive the faculties destroyed by death and the processes of decay. Canopic jars, Cat. nos. 77–8, offered protection to the most vulnerable part of the body, the internal organs, and their significance in the rites of burial was in no way diminished by the fact that during the Middle Kingdom these organs were rarely actually removed from the body.

The other objects made for the burial were intended to ensure that, in his resurrected body, the deceased should enjoy a continuous supply of food and the company and support of his family and servants, see Cat. no. 91. The vision of the Next World as an extension of the familiar world of every day lies behind the elaborate preparations made to satisfy these two basic needs. The vision depended on confidence that this orderly and self-contained world could be perpetuated into eternity. The contrast between this view and the *Song of the Harper*, Cat. no. 59, is all the more remarkable. Nevertheless the vision included the possibility of failure. There is need for constant repetition of the basic offering formula promising 'bread and beer, oxen and fowl, alabaster and clothing, all things good and pure on which a god lives' (Gardiner, *Grammar*, pp. 170–3), and the gods are called upon to draw the deceased into their company and to prevent his final dissolution. Measures have to be taken to ensure the deceased enjoys his proper status in the Next World and is exempt from the duties of manual labour he finds so repugnant, see Cat. no. 83. Models are provided, both of the food offerings themselves and of servants in the act of preparing them or simply bringing them for their master's use, see

70

91

so to attribute to their place of origin unprovenanced coffins such as Cat. nos. 66–7. Nevertheless, the sequence of coffins at a single site, and so the evolution of the regional style, is often unclear, as exemplified by Beni Hasan, see Cat. no. 70. Coffins, being rich in texts and iconography, have been studied a great deal, but few of the other objects found with coffins have been sufficiently utilised to solve problems of chronology, see Cat. nos. 71–2.

We cannot confidently chart the process of change in the country as a whole throughout the Middle Kingdom until more regional studies have been completed, but perhaps a few general conclusions are suggested by the group of objects assembled here. In the late xIIth Dynasty there is a decline in the number of provincial cemeteries, and at the same time the decoration of coffins from the remaining centres becomes more standardised. Another definite change, not so far

Cat. no. 91. These can be animated by magic so that the deceased and his household have an endless supply of all that they need. In addition to models, real food and drink were placed in tombs, but we may presume that their efficiency was no greater than that of their modelled counterparts.

If the basic requirements for burial, i.e. protection of the body and provision for the deceased's material needs, were unchanged throughout the Middle Kingdom, can we observe from this exhibition any change in the objects chosen and/or their disposition in the tomb? If so, can these be related to the developments we have observed in the culture as a whole, and illustrated so far in sculpture and literature? So much of our information from Egypt comes from burials that we are driven, through lack of other source material, to analyse them for evidence of major cultural changes, whilst doing so with circumspection and never losing sight of the nature and limitations of this type of evidence.

We can see profound changes in burial practices during the Middle Kingdom, many of them derived from a changed view of the status of the dead first expressed at the end of the Old Kingdom. Magical spells and the objects and manual rites which accompanied them, which had formerly been reserved for the dead Pharaoh, were taken over by private individuals, see Cat. nos. 70, 72. The mere extension of the privilege of elaborate burial (as described in the Story of Sinuhe, see p. 11) to a larger group in society, and the resulting proliferation of rich provincial cemeteries, created the opportunity for great variety of practice.

This rich variety is one of the glories of the funerary art of the Middle Kingdom, but it also accounts for many of the problems it poses for scholars. Only within the last twenty years has the regional character of much of its output begun to be appreciated. Coffins, unlike small sculptures, are not easily transported and we can assume that most of them were made close to where they were found. In the xIth to early xIIth Dynasty there is a bewildering range of local styles, but following intensive work on coffin decoration and orthography by scholars such as Brovarski (for Bersha), Hayes (for Meir), Spanel (for Beni Hasan) and Magee (for Asyut) it is becoming easier to recognise a particular regional style and

72

67a, b

satisfactorily explained, is the apparently sudden cessation of the practice of placing elaborate wooden models of servants, e.g. Cat. nos. 90–5, in tombs. This happened after the reign of Senusret II (Petrie *et al.*, *Lahun*, II, p. 34). The change is not quite universal: models continue to appear at Beni Hasan, for example, and boat models continue into later reigns at several sites (see C. Lilyquist in *Serapis* 5 (1979), no. 1, p. 27). Nevertheless, in cemeteries in the Memphite–Faiyum region the presence or absence of models is indicative of a date before or after the reign of Senusret II.

At least in relation to one innovation of the late XIIth Dynasty, the writing of the shabti text on a funerary figurine, one may tentatively suggest how a practice spread outwards from the cemeteries in the region of the royal workshops, see Cat. no. 83. The creative impetus in funerary art, as in sculpture, seems to pass in the course of the XIIth Dynasty from the provinces to places where royal building activity was centred.

COFFINS AND MASKS

67 COFFIN FRAGMENTS FROM ASYUT

Early Dynasty XII, 1963–1862 BC.

Two fragments from the painted wooden coffin of the master physician, Wepwawetemhat. Both pieces come from the long side of a rectangular coffin, the longer piece (a) belonging above the shorter (b) with a gap between them. The orientation of the hieroglyphs suggests that the decoration of this side probably began with an eye panel (see Cat. no. 68) and continued with the funerary formula invoking the gods; the name of Geb, the earth god, can be recognised, arranged in three vertical columns. Then followed another panel with an offering scene, showing a miniature herdsman conducting an enormous bull, followed by a gazelle. Above the gazelle is the row of signs from which we can reconstruct Wepwawetemhat's name. Four more vertical columns of text intervene in which both the owner's name and his title occur, before the next panel which again shows a procession of offerings, a man leading a bull followed by two women, one of whom is named though too little remains for the name to be read.

67a (detail)

67a (detail)

The painting, carried out on a background of thick white plaster, is polychrome, the hieroglyphic signs alone showing black, red, green, yellow and blue–black colours. The dresses of the women are green, and the bull in the first panel shows an unusual attempt to use shading to suggest the mottled appearance of the animal's skin. The painter or painters worked confidently but fast; their finger marks are still visible on the body of the gazelle.

Probably from Asyut. Fitzwilliam E.W.66a, b. (a) H: 8.8 cm. W: 75.0 cm. (b) H: 6.0 cm. W: 72.0 cm.

These fragments were re-excavated from a cupboard in the

Upper Marlay Gallery of the Museum in 1957, and no record survives to explain how or when they came into the Museum. They were found in the gallery with Cat. no. 66, another fragment which may also come from an Asyut coffin, albeit a different one. This history is typical of the fate suffered by many of the antiquities from Asyut, see Cat. no. 23. The reasons for suggesting this provenance for these tantalising but beautiful fragments are two. Firstly the owner's name, Wepwawetemhat, is extremely rare outside the region of Asyut which was the cult-centre of the jackal god Wepwawet. Only much later, at the end of the Middle Kingdom (see Cat. no. 58), did Wepwawet become generally popular, and personal names invoking him therefore more widespread. Secondly, the unusual decorative scheme is entirely on the outside of the coffin, and this fact, together with the conventional funerary texts framing panels showing offering-bringers, the use of polychrome, and the individual shape and style of the hieroglyphic signs all find parallels among the coffins from Asyut. There is no exact parallel known to me, but many of the more than fifty Middle Kingdom coffins from the site are unpublished or unavailable in facsimile.

The title of the coffin's owner is particularly interesting and to be added to the small list of physicians known from ancient Egypt. Such a man would have owned and used the papyri found by Quibell in the Middle Kingdom shaft tomb under the Ramesseum, see below p. 000. His profession, to judge by the quality of his coffin, brought both considerable wealth and high status. It is hard, perhaps, to appreciate this quality from such small fragments, but the elegant detail of individual hieroglyphs, such as the lion and the swallow, shines out. Fine timber was scarce, the local tamarisk and acacia trees producing thin, narrow planks which had to be joined together with pegs, as here, to make up the desired breadth. The joins and knots in the wood were originally invisible, covered with a thick layer of fine stucco.

Cf. Chassinat and Palanque, *Assiout*, pl. XL, 2.

68 A COFFIN FROM BENI HASAN
Early Dynasty XII, 1963–1862 BC.

A rectangular wooden coffin and lid inscribed along the long sides and lid for a woman named Senuitef, also called, on the head and foot ends, Arthotepet. The hieroglyphs are blue on a yellow background, and are arranged so that all the long funerary inscriptions, on the lid and along the tops of the long sides, run from north to south, that is from head to foot of a body lying inside the coffin with its head behind the eye panel. These long inscriptions invoke Osiris, Lord of Abydos, on the eastern side, which also has the eye panel, and Anubis on the western side and the lid. The head and foot ends carry horizontal inscriptions invoking Isis and Nephthys respectively, and down each of the four sides are declarations that the deceased is revered before a particular deity. Starting from the eye panel the sequence of gods in the vertical inscriptions reads Imsti, Shu, Tefnut, Duamutef, Neit (at the foot), Hapy, Geb, Nut, Qebehsenuef and Selkis (at the head). The bottom of the coffin is missing, but what remains has been fitted together from at least 23 pieces of timber.

68

From Beni Hasan, tomb 65. Gift of E. Towry-Whyte. Fitzwilliam E.70.1903. H: 54.0 cm. L: 190.0 cm. W: 44.0 cm. All dimensions include lid.

The names on this coffin show no signs of alteration, so we may presume the owner bore two names, see Cat. no. 39. Alternatively, the possibility of an undertaker's mistake in assembling the coffin is not inconceivable: undertakers' assistants were almost certainly unable to read. The coffin follows the most common design found at Beni Hasan with the standard choice and arrangement of inscriptions, so we may further presume that several of the type were being made at the same time. The name Senuitef occurs on the coffin in several different versions, the hieroglyphs transposed or omitted following the dictates of balance or space, or through carelessness.

The rectangular coffin was thought of in two ways: as a dwelling for the spirit of the dead and as a protective casing for the wrapped body. The arrangement of the texts in long horizontal lines and short vertical ones is sometimes adapted for an anthropoid coffin, and then the analogy with the bindings of the wrappings of the mummy becomes very clear (Petrie, *Gizeh and Rifeh*, pl. XB). However, the arrangement as it appears on the rectangular box coffin also recalls the roof beams and column supports of a house, see Cat. no. 86.

The disposition and choice of deities invoked in 'column' inscriptions framing the panels, is of course, significant. The four corners of the coffin are guarded by the four sons of Horus, guardians of the dead, Imsti and Happy at the shoulders, Duamutef and Qebehsenuef at the feet, see also Cat. no. 77. The texts in the middle of the long sides invoke the cosmic deities of Earth (Geb), Air (Shu), Sky (Nut) and Dew (Tefnut). The centre-piece of the decoration, to which all the inscriptions are orientated, is the eye panel, the 'window' through which the dead look out on the world and receive offerings and, because it faces east, the life-restoring rays of the sun. The extraordinary eyes, outlined in black, with blue brows, cosmetic line and markings, are enlarged human eyes beneath which are markings taken from a falcon's head. These markings are one of the most powerful symbols in Egyptian religious iconography, and represent wholeness, goodness and healing. Their mythological origin goes back to the combat between the god Horus (identified with the falcon) and his rival Seth, murderer of Osiris, the father of Horus. During the fight, the eye of Horus was ripped out by Seth, but it was healed and restored to him by Thoth, god of knowledge. The 'Eye of Horus' thus became a symbol of health and, in the context of burial, of resurrection and restoration of the faculties of the body.

Garstang, *Burial Customs*, p. 214, pl. VII, 65; for construction of the coffins at Beni Hasan, *ibid*, pp. 164–6; on rectangular coffins, Hayes, *Scepter*, I, pp. 312–20.

69 MASK OF THE STEWARD THAY
Dynasty XI, 2023–1963 BC.

Funerary mask made up of alternating layers of plaster and linen, painted to represent an idealised human face. Only part of the wig remains, and the mask has broken off at its thinnest

69

section, under the chin. The wig, natural beard and moustache are painted black and the face is a greenish-white. The brows are black and straight; the eyes are very wide and outlined in black, with an elongated inner canthus, and carry a blue fish-tailed cosmetic line. The pupils of the eyes are black and there is a red spot at each corner. The ears, made entirely of plaster, are small and show just the outer rim. The nose is long and straight, and the mouth shows a full, slightly projecting lower lip. The philtrum is marked by a gap in the moustache on the upper lip.

From Beni Hasan, tomb 275. Gift of the Beni Hasan Excavation Committee. Fitzwilliam E.198.1903. H: 26.3 cm. W: 18.2 cm.

This mask was originally placed directly over the wrapped head of the corpse, and was held in place by long tabs front and back (which did not survive), these being in turn covered by further layers of wrapping. At Beni Hasan there was no evidence of mummification, defined as the removal of the internal organs and brain and the application of natron to the body. The bodies were simply wrapped tightly and carefully in layer after layer of linen. The mask was built up over, one may presume, a wooden or clay core. An initial thin layer of coarse plaster was laid down, followed by a layer made up of scraps of linen (different thicknesses of weave can be seen) pressed or stuck together. There followed three more layers of plaster and linen, ending with a final layer of very fine plaster which was painted.

The face is a stereotype which corresponds, especially in the treatment of the eyes, to the conventional physiognomy of the beginning of the Middle Kingdom, see Cat. no. 4. While this provides us with criteria for dating it to this period, we should allow for the fact that the style of funerary masks probably changed much more slowly than that of sculpture. Certain features such as the cosmetic line remained long after they had ceased to appear elsewhere. A reason for this which suggests itself is the influence of the iconography of the powerful icon of the 'Eye of Horus' (see Cat. no. 68), in which the cosmetic line was an indispensable element. The individuality of the mask lies in its representation of chin-beard and moustache, which corresponds, to judge by a head illustrated by Garstang (*Burial Customs*, fig. 177) to a copious reality. The name and title of Thay come from the inscriptions on his coffin. The objects in the burial, one of the few found intact, confirm the early date suggested by the style of the mask.

Garstang, *Burial Customs*, pp. 172–3, fig. 178; cf. Saleh and Sourouzian, *Cairo Museum*, no. 96; for date of model boat from the burial, Spanel, *Boat Models*, n. 25.

70 THE COFFIN OF NAKHT Illustrated on p. 85 and in colour on pl. III,4.

Dynasty XII, 1963–1787 BC.

A rectangular wooden coffin and lid inscribed for the Lady of the House, Nakht, and painted in polychrome with a series of monumental doorways. There are three of these on each of the long sides (including one below the Sacred Eyes) and one on each end. The blue-painted inscriptions follow the overall design and orientation of those of Cat. no. 68, but like that of Cat. no. 71, the lid carries three lines of text instead of one. In the centre of the lid is the funerary formula invoking Anubis, like that on Cat. no. 68, but above it is a spell invoking the sky goddess Nut like that on the lid of Userhet's coffin, Cat. no. 71.

The only other difference between the present coffin and Cat. no. 68 lies in the gods named in the vertical inscriptions. Starting from the eye panel they are: Imsti, Shu, Geb, Duamutef; on the foot panel, the Greater and Lesser Enneads (groups of nine gods); then Hapy, Tefnut, Nut, Qebehsenuef; on the head panel, the Great God Lord of Heaven and Selkis. Each of the four sides and the lid have been made up from at least three pieces of timber.

From Beni Hasan, tomb 23. Gift of the Beni Hasan Excavation Committee. Fitzwilliam E.68.1903. H: 54.5 cm. L: 185.5 cm. W: 43.8 cm. All dimensions include lid.

Both in decoration and in choice of texts this coffin closely parallels the outer coffin of Userhet from Beni Hasan, Cat. no. 71, and it would be difficult to believe that they are not close in date. The coffin of Nakht is not illustrated or discussed by Garstang, and he overlooks it as a parallel in discussing the texts on the coffin of Userhet. The only substantial difference lies in the decoration of the end panels, where Userhet's coffin carries figures of the goddesses Isis and Nephthys.

Brovarski and Hayes have both observed an evolution in the exterior decoration of rectangular coffins of the Middle Kingdom, from the plain box with a single line of horizontal text and an eye panel to the completely decorated exterior with an increasing number of panels framed by the vertical inscriptions. In broad terms this sequence seems to apply to the Beni Hasan coffins, in that this coffin seems later than Cat. no. 68. Difficulties arise, however, when we try to translate comparative dates into actual ones, and to decide where in Dynasty XII the Lady Nakht's coffin, and by analogy the coffins of Userhet, Cat. nos. 71, 72, belong. The reason is that much of the information needed to do this is missing from Garstang's report and is now irretrievably lost.

Few coffins provide independent evidence of their date (for example that the person named on them can be dated from other sources), and it is uncertain which other objects were found with them except in the case of the intact burials. Tomb 23, for instance, contained more than one burial. There are four entries in Garstang's list of names (*Burial Customs*, pl. VII), although there is no mention of inscribed material other than the coffin in his object list, but the pottery confirms that the tomb was in use from Dynasties XI to XII. We have, unfortunately, no evidence from the record to associate the coffin of Nakht with the earlier or later use of the shaft, and this is a particular loss because of the interest of the inscriptions on the lid. Nakht's title, Lady of the House, see above p. 00, the use of the phrase *n ka n* in the funerary formula, and the writing of *mwt* suggest the later date, consistent with the mid-XIIth Dynasty date (reign of Senusret III) suggested for the coffin of Userhet. The earliest version known of the spell invoking Nut occurs in the Pyramid Texts, and following the format of that version (intended for royal use), the deceased is identified with the god–king of the Dead, Osiris. The idea is not a new one and finds expression in different ways in the funerary art of the Middle Kingdom, but this simple invocation, in which the coffin lid is identified with the sky goddess, Nut, is one of the earliest texts in which the dead person is addressed directly as the god: 'O Osiris, the lady of the house, Nakht, your mother Nut has spread herself over you . . .'.

Garstang, *Burial Customs*, p. 212; Bourriau, *Pottery*, p. 64, no. 115; generally, Brovarski in *Dunham Essays*, p. 23, n. 70; p. 29, fig. 13; prayer invoking Nut, Hayes, *Scepter*, I, p. 314; K. Sethe, *Die altägyptischen Pyramidentexte*, II (Leipzig, 1910), p. 355, paragraphs 1607–8; Osiris epithet, Fischer in *ZÄS* 90 (1963), pp. 35–41; writing of *mwt*, D. Franke, *Altägyptische Verwandtschaftsbezeichnungen im Mittleren Reich* (Hamburg, 1983), p. 12, n. 2.

71 OUTER COFFIN OF USERHET

Mid-Dynasty XII, 1862–1844 BC.

A rectangular wooden coffin and lid inscribed for the soldier Userhet; painted in polychrome with a series of three monumental doorways down each long side and an eye panel on the eastern side. At each of the head and foot ends is a standing figure of a woman with her arms raised in worship, personifying the godess Isis and the goddess Nephthys respectively. Each wears the usual white linen tunic with narrow straps, black full-bottomed wig held by a band tied around her forehead, and a set of jewellery consisting of

anklets, broad collar and bracelets, painted green to suggest 'faience'. The inscriptions, painted in blue hieroglyphs, follow the design and orientation of those on the coffin Cat. no. 68, but on the lid are the same three lines of text found on Cat. no. 70. The vertical inscriptions also name the same gods in the same sequence as on the coffin of Nakht, except that at the head end the goddess Neith is invoked instead of the Great God, lord of Heaven. The construction of the coffin is similar to that of Cat. no. 68 and that of Nakht, Cat. no. 70, but the long sides are made up from only two pieces of timber and the four cross battens supporting the bottom still survive at the base of each vertical band of inscription.

From Beni Hasan, tomb 132. Department of Egyptology, University of Liverpool E.512. H: 65.0 cm. L: 193.8 cm. W: 46.1 cm. All dimensions include lid.

The elaborate linear and floral motifs of the panels along the sides of this coffin and that of Nakht, Cat. no. 70, have evolved a long way from their architectural origin in the recessed panelling of the mud brick palaces of Predynastic times. It is thought that this panelling was decorated with multicoloured reed matting which provided the source of many of the individual motifs. Monumental doorways decorated in this fashion became a feature of the earliest royal tombs, then of 'false door' stelae of the Old Kingdom and finally of coffins. At first glance the decorative scheme of the two coffins is very similar, but major differences become apparent when the individual panels are compared. The proportion of the height of the panel taken up by the actual door-

way, for instance, is one-half in the case of Nakht, but only one-fifth in the case of Userhet, and the choice of minor motifs is different. Much work needs to be done on analysing these decorative schemes, but eventually it may be possible to identify the handiwork of individual artists, as is being attempted with tomb painters.

There is no evidence to suggest that tomb 132 contained more than one burial, and in addition to the coffins Garstang mentions only pottery. As far as one can deduce from his extremely poor drawings this conforms well to a dating in the middle of Dynasty XII (about the reign of Senusret III). Hayes observes that the figures of the two goddesses at the head and foot ends are rare before Dynasty XIII, but the pottery certainly does not support such a late date and it is possible that the Isis/Nephthys motif is actually more common (Garstang, *Burial Customs*, p. 190), at least at Beni Hasan, than the few coffins illustrated in the publication suggest.

Garstang, *Burial Customs*, figs. 147, 180, pp. 173–4, 190–1; for the Isis/Nephthys motif, Hayes, *Scepter*, I, p. 318.

72 INNER COFFIN OF USERHET Illustrated in colour on pl. III,3.

Mid-Dynasty XII, 1862–1844 BC.

Anthropoid wooden coffin, covered with plaster and painted, inscribed for the soldier, Userhet, whose outer rectangular coffin is Cat. no. 71. The coffin is made in two parts, both modelled to the shape of a wrapped body prepared for nevertheless strongly sculptured. The brows, executed in relief, follow the line of the wigband; the painted eyes, white with black pupils, are very wide and large, with red spots at both outer and inner canthi. There is a long fish-tailed cosmetic line. The ears are set exceptionally low, and as well as being large, project forward so that they lie almost at right angles to the face. The nose is short and straight, and there is a deep philtrum with a corresponding notch in the upper lip. The lower lip is wide and full. The bone structure of the face is suggested by the muscles at the wings of the nostrils and at the corners of the mouth. On the chest is a painted replica of the funerary bead collar reduced to repeating bands of red, blue and green with a final string of green and blue petal beads.

From Beni Hasan, tomb 132. Gift of the Beni Hasan Excavation Committee. Fitzwilliam E.88.1903. H: 33.2 cm. L: 182.4 cm. W: 41.2 cm.

It is interesting to compare the face of this coffin with the funerary mask of Thay, also from Beni Hasan. Both are idealised human faces, but each echoes the contemporary sculptural style. The greater monumentality of Userhet's face owes much to the divine beard which he wears, further evidence of his identity with the god–king Osiris, which the text down the front also proclaims, see Cat. no. 70.

The starting point for the evolution of anthropoid coffins seems to be the appearance of the body wrapped in white linen for burial, with a funerary mask laid over the face and a collar of 'faience' beads laid on the chest. The earliest example so far known belongs to one of the concubines of King Nebhepetre Montuhotep and is made of cartonnage, like the mask of Thay. Many more may have existed and been too fragile to survive or have been mis-identified as masks only. Nevertheless a small group datable to Dynasties XII–XIII do exist, but since they come from many different sites, Rifeh, Lisht, Meir, Saqqara and Abydos as well as Thebes, it is not surprising that details of iconography and ornamentation show great variety, and it is difficult in the present state of our knowledge to put them into a single chronological sequence. Userhet's coffin is late in the sequence of Beni Hasan coffins and, as stated above, on the basis of the pottery from the tomb it should belong to mid-Dynasty XII in absolute terms.

Garstang, *Burial Customs*, pp. 173–4, 191, 217, figs. 180, 181.

73 PAIR OF EYES

Dynasties XII–XIII, 1963–1650 BC.

Pair of eyes, obsidian and limestone, originally inlaid in an anthropoid coffin or funerary mask. The eye has a convex polished surface into which the disk of obsidian has been fitted. The surface of the obsidian shows fine lines from grinding and polishing.

Gift of R. G. Gayer-Anderson. Fitzwilliam EGA.3994a, b.1943. Each eye: L: 7.4 cm. W: 2.5 cm.

The rounded surface and the size of the eyes indicate that they were used in an anthropoid coffin or mask, rather than in the eye panel of a rectangular coffin. The hardness of the material of which eyes are made means that they often

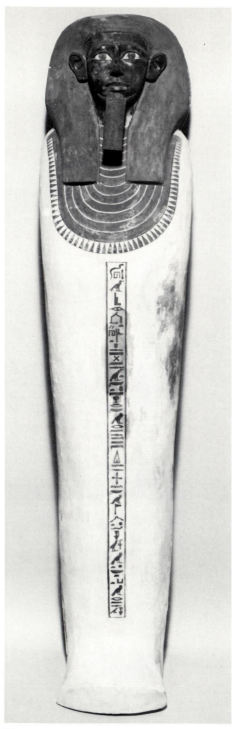

72

burial and wearing a funerary mask. The body is white, and the central band of vertical inscription, a repetition of the invocation to the sky goddess, Nut, on the lid of the outer coffin, is in blue hieroglyphs. The face is black and the wig, beard and eyebrows and cosmetic line are blue. The wig is the straight, full one with long side lappets, and attached to the chin is a long beard. The face is completely idealised but

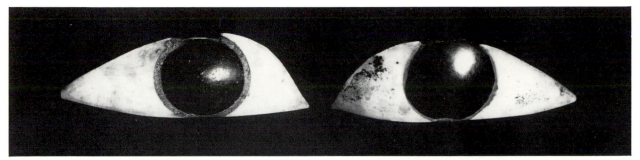

73a, b

survive after the vulnerable wood which held them has disintegrated. They may be all that remains in a disturbed tomb to suggest the original number or type of burials. In Lucas's classification of inlaid eyes, these belong in Class II.

See Lucas, *Industries*, pp. 107–14.

74 MODEL COFFIN OF NEMTYEMWESKHET
Dynasty XIII, 1786–1650 BC.

Miniature rectangular wooden coffin with vaulted lid and projecting end boards, inscribed in mutilated hieroglyphs (see Cat. no. 83) for the 'seal bearer of the King and high steward, Nemtyemweskhet'. The coffin and lid have each been constructed from four pieces of wood (the bottom of the coffin being missing). The wood was covered with a thick layer of fine plaster, painted yellow with the signs and eye panel applied in blue pigment. The only decoration consists of the tiny eye panel set within a rectangular frame. There is a band of horizontal inscription down the centre of the lid, one along each of the long sides, and one across each of the foot and head ends. Each long side is subdivided into three panels by

74

four columns of text invoking, among others, Geb, Osiris, Sokar, Ptah and Anubis. There are also two columns of text framing the panels at the head and foot. One of the texts at the head end is unusual in invoking the reigning King.

From Abydos, Garstang excavations of 1907, locus 321. Liverpool Museum 55.82.114. Box: H: 11.7 cm. L: 29.2 cm. W: 12.1 cm. Lid: H: 5.5 cm. L: 29.2 cm. W: 12.2 cm.

This miniature coffin contained what Garstang described as a 'gilt ushabti', perhaps similar to that of Wahneferhotep from Lisht, and was itself placed inside a model stone sarcophagus now in the collection of the Department of Egyptology, Liverpool University (information supplied by Stephen Snape). The sarcophagus was buried at the foot of a stela in an offering chapel at Abydos, which was shared between Nemtyemweskhet and the family of Renseneb (Cat. no. 50), and it is shown as it was found on p. 40. The coffin was more than a commemoration of Nemtyemweskhet: it was a dummy burial with a substitute body which enabled him to take part, after death, in the celebration of the mysteries of Osiris. As high steward he was one of the most powerful of royal servants, responsible for the provisioning of the King's residence, and so would have had, we may presume, a rich burial close to that of the King himself.

The shape of the coffin and the subject and arrangement of its inscriptions exactly copy full-sized coffins of the time. However, the signs have been carelessly painted and the texts abbreviated to fit the reduced space. The inscriptions themselves show the customary mutilation of bird, animal and human figures in which the lower half of the sign is omitted, see Cat. no. 83. No such mutilation occurs on the stelae of Nemtyemweskhet from the offering chapel because the signs on them were not close enough to pose a threat to his vulnerable body. The orientation and arrangement of the texts on the coffin show no great change from the XIIth Dynasty. The epithet 'Osiris' is applied to the deceased, but, as in the case of Nakht and Userhet, only in the inscription on the coffin lid. However, the texts themselves, the choice of deities invoked and their sequence in the vertical inscriptions around the coffin are different. The invocation to the reigning King in the inscriptions on the panel at the head of the coffin is particularly interesting. The full writing of the deceased's name is also confirmation of the reading *Nemty*, still disputed despite Berlev's observations, see Cat. no. 42.

There is at least one other example from Abydos of a similar dedication of a funerary statuette with a stela. It is from an earlier date in the Middle Kingdom and the statuette, although mummiform, was not placed in a miniature coffin.

Cf. statuette and miniature coffin of Wahneferhotep, Hayes, *Scepter*, I, fig. 229; Abydos statuette, H. Frankfort in *JEA* 14 (1928), pp. 239–40, pl. XXII, 3.

75 FUNERAL PROCESSION
Dynasties XII–XIII, 1963–1650 BC.

Fragment from the long side of a rectangular coffin, painted with a scene from the funeral procession. The procession may be reconstructed as follows: an ox; a man; two pairs of men, each pair made up of one dark- and one light-skinned man, carrying poles on their shoulders (possibly the supports for the sarcophagus); between them, a woman mourner, bending forward with her hair falling in front of her face, both hands held to her breast and her cheek stained with tears; three women following, all dressed like the mourner in white, close-fitting tunics with broad straps and wearing heavy wigs terminating in numerous, narrow plaits. They hold their hands to their breasts in a traditional gesture of grief. A column of text intervenes between each woman and the next and these contain spells promising food offerings, recited by various gods. Only a thin layer of plaster was applied before the coffin was painted and little of the original colour remains; however, the single figure of the mourner is complete and stands out clearly.

From Abydos, Cemetery E.281. Gift of the Egyptian Research Account. Fitzwilliam E.283a.1900. H: 39.3 cm. L: 116.5 cm.

Despite its poor condition this fragment affords us a glimpse of a Middle Kingdom funeral procession. This subject is rarely depicted on tomb walls, and no precise parallel for this arrangement and the pose of the chief mourner is known to me. Only part of the procession survives, but other fragments confirm that it once took up the whole of both long sides of the coffin. The coffin's scribe had some difficulty in fitting the vertical inscriptions in between the rows of mourners and offering-bringers, and the figures twice break through the lines framing the text. The vertical inscriptions bear no relation to the figures depicted in the panels (contra, Werbrouck, p. 99), some of whom are identified by name and are clearly servants, friends or relatives of the deceased.

The decoration is extremely unusual, but too many Middle Kingdom coffins remain unpublished for us to claim it as unique. An early Middle Kingdom coffin from Mi'alla shows mourners beside the deceased, who is laid out on a bier. It is hard to date the coffin precisely from its context. All the finds, with the exception of the coffin, are now in the collection of the Ashmolean Museum, and the excavator's marks on them indicate that the shaft tomb E.281 had at least two chambers. The objects consist of a mirror, an anhydrite vase and two small pottery dishes. None can be associated for certain with the coffin, or is closely datable in itself.

Garstang, *El Arábah*, pp. 8–9, 34, pls. X, XI; M. Werbrouck, *Les Pleureuses dans L'Egypte Ancienne* (Bruxelles, 1938), p. 99; for pose of woman mourner, cf. F. W. von Bissing in *Archiv für Orientforschung* 7 (1931–2), p. 160, pl. VII, 2d; Mi'alla coffin, P. Lacau, *Sarcophages antérieurs au Nouvel Empire*, I (Cairo, 1904), pl. VI, 28116.

76 FEMALE MOURNER
Dynasty XI, 2023–1963 BC.

Hollow pottery statuette of a woman with her hands raised to her head (pulling her hair?) in a traditional gesture of mourning. The statuette is made of a medium-textured straw-tempered Nile silt clay and the surface is covered with a thin white wash. It was thrown on the wheel in three parts; joins are visible below the chin and at the base of the neck. The chin and forehead were shaped by cutting, and the

75

breasts, arms, eyes, nose and ears were modelled by hand and applied to the surface, all before firing. A fringed (or torn?) garment which covers one breast but exposes the other is indicated by incised lines on front and back.

From Dendera. University College 16126. H: 24.0 cm. W: 11.7 cm.

This object is not a container, although it was made in a similar way. The three-dimensional elements are added to the surface but hardly succeed in more than suggesting a human shape. As in the case of fertility figures, only those elements necessary for its efficacy are shown, so nothing of

the body is represented below the breasts and arms. There is a companion statuette from the same tomb, now in Brussels, with the hands held up to the eyes. To judge by a set of four figures from Asyut, also in Brussels, there may originally have been two more. The closest parallel to the Dendera figures is from Arab el Borg, close to Asyut, but none of the small group of similar figures, all females, can be closely dated by associated material. They are plausibly assigned to the early Middle Kingdom by their technique of manufacture and the general character of the cemeteries in which they have been found. They belong, it seems, to the large class of funerary models depicting people or objects with a significant role in the ritual of the funeral itself.

Petrie, *Dendereh*, pp. 27, 65, pl. XXI, bottom left; cf. F. W. von Bissing in *Archiv für Orientforschung* 7 (1931–2), pp. 157–60, pl. VII; Museum of Fine Arts, Boston, *A Table of Offerings* (Boston, 1987), p. 8.

CANOPIC JARS

77 CANOPIC JAR AND LID

Late Dynasty XII, from reign of Amenemhat III onwards, 1843–1787 BC.

Limestone canopic jar and lid inscribed for the overseer of the storeroom, Iunefer. The lid is sculpted in the form of an idealised portrait of the deceased, like those shown on funerary statuettes or anthropoid coffins, see Cat. nos. 72, 79–83. The brow, cosmetic line, line around the eyes, and pupil are painted black. The face and neck show traces of yellow, and the wig was originally painted turquoise blue. The eyes are large and very wide, and both the inner and

76

77

the outer canthus are marked. The nose is short and straight, the lips are pursed, the philtrum is marked, but the mouth is small. The ears are set very low, and only the outer rim is shown. The cutting of the face is bold but schematic and the striations of the wig have been executed by a less certain hand. The shouldered jar itself is plain except for the three columns of hieroglyphic inscription which provide the usual Canopic jar text. This identifies the contents of the jar with Qebehsenuef, one of the four sons of Horus, and invokes the goddess Selkis for its protection. The hieroglyphs still bear traces of green pigment and there are remains of blackened resin on the inside.

From Hawara, tomb 57. University College 16027. Head: H: 10.4 cm. W: 15.2 cm. Jar: H: 20.8 cm. D: 19.0 cm.

A complete set of Canopic jars consisted of four jars, each intended to house one of the body's internal organs, viz. liver, lungs, intestines and stomach; each was associated with one of the sons of Horus, guardians of the dead, who also guarded the corners of the coffin. Each jar was also placed under the protection of a goddess, who is called upon in the text. The earliest Middle Kingdom Canopic jars are not inscribed, although the spell itself occurs in the Coffin Texts. Inscriptions start to appear on jars in the middle of Dynasty XII. The lids were either undecorated or, as here, carried a representation of the deceased. Canopic jars and the chest they were placed in were a regular part of wealthy Middle Kingdom burials, but they rarely show signs of actually having held the internal organs, since these were hardly ever removed from the body at this time, see above p. 85.

Two jars only were found in the plundered tomb from which this jar came, and the companion piece is in the Ny Carlsberg Glyptotek in Copenhagen. The tomb contained inscribed coffin fragments and a funerary statuette (cf. Cat. no. 81) naming two other people, so presumably originally held at least three burials. All the objects and the pottery are consistent with a date late in Dynasty XII, and the cemetery at Hawara was not begun until the reign of Amenemhat III,

when the King built a pyramid there.

Petrie *et al.*, *Labyrinth*, p. 36, pl. 31 (left, middle); V. Raisman and G. T. Martin, *Canopic Equipment in the Petrie Collection* (Warminster, 1984), p. 11, nos. 4–5, pls. 1, 17, 20 and bibliography there cited.

78 CANOPIC JAR LIDS
Dynasty XII, 1963–1787 BC.

Two practically identical lids (a, b) in the form of an idealised portrait of the deceased made in wood, covered with fine plaster and painted. The face and neck are yellow, brows, cosmetic line and wig are blue and the outlines of eyes and pupils are black. The brows are curved over large, wide open eyes with pronounced inner canthi, and the, by now, archaic fish-tailed cosmetic lines. Compared with contemporary sculpture the ears are small, and only the outer rim is shown. The nose is long and thin, somewhat distorted by a chip missing from the tip. The philtrum is marked on the upper lip and the mouth is wide with thin, well-shaped lips. The cheekbones are modelled, and the final impression is of a delicate, triangular face.

Bequest of Sir Robert Greg. Fitzwilliam E.26–7.1954. Average measurements: H: 12.5 cm. W: 9.7 cm.

These lids were purchased from a Cairo antiquities dealer in 1918, so their find-spot is unknown. They have also become dissociated from their original jars, which would have been of similar shape to Cat. no. 77 but could have been made of wood, stone or pottery. The jars with which they have been photographed do not belong with them and may not be ancient. It seems likely that they were made for a woman, since the skin is painted yellow and there is no beard, but we cannot be sure of this, see Cat. no. 77. Close parallels

78a, b

96

occur in two intact burials of Dynasty XII, Senebtisi at Lisht and the Tomb of the Two Brothers at Rifeh.

Stylistically the heads may be grouped with anthropoid coffins and funerary statuettes, which show the same aloof idealisation of a human face. The Canopic jar with its lid was, like them, identified by its form with the wrapped body of the mummy wearing a funerary mask.

Cf. Mace and Winlock, *Senebtisi*, pl. XXXIII; Petrie, *Gizeh and Rifeh*, pl. X D.

FUNERARY STATUETTES

79 FUNERARY STATUETTE FROM A MODEL BOAT

Early Dynasty XII, 1963–1862 BC.

Limestone statuette of a man shown seated on a cube-shaped throne, wearing a beard and a long wig with side lappets, his body completely wrapped as for burial. A great deal of detail has been introduced into the face, although the scale of the sculpture is very small. The brows were painted black and the eyes, very wide and set straight in the face, were outlined in black with black pupils. There is no trace of a cosmetic line. The ears, set low, are shown in detail, as regards both outer rim and inner ear. The chin is square below thin, slightly pouting lips and the face is extremely broad. The nose is short and straight. The contours of the body are merely suggested under the linen wrappings. A small hole has been drilled in the centre of the underside of the throne, for attachment of the statuette to the deck of a model boat.

Possibly from Abû Rawâsh. Gift of C. Ricketts and C. Shannon. Fitzwilliam E.24.1937. Statuette: H: 7.0 cm. W: 2.2 cm. Base: H: 2.1 cm. W: 3.4 cm.

The statuette still carries on the base a label marked Abû-Rawâsh, a site in the desert opposite Cairo, a few miles north of the Giza Pyramids. Few Middle Kingdom remains have been found there, and it is possible that the statuette came from the extensive early XIIth Dynasty cemeteries at Saqqara, further to the south. The date is suggested only by the fact that the practice of placing model boats in the tomb seems to have died out after the reign of Senusret II.

The deceased can appear in different guises in model boats, if he is present at all. Sometimes he is shown as a living man, sometimes as a mummy on a bier or inside a coffin, or as here, as a mummy seated on a throne. An example from Saqqara in the Cairo Museum shows a similar figure under a canopy with food offerings placed in front of him. These representations illustrate vividly the belief in the posthumous pilgrimage to Abydos. Probably few of the people commemorated at the sacred site visited it during their lives, but everyone wished in the Afterlife to be part of the company around Osiris, King of the Underworld. One way of achieving this was to become an Osiris, to become identified with the god by undergoing the process of mummification and to travel to Abydos to take part in the mysteries celebrating his

79

death and rebirth. Travel was of course by river, so the dead equipped themselves with boats to take them there, see also Cat. nos. 94–5.

Cf. Reisner, *Ships and Boats*, pp. 72–3, pl. XVII.

80 FUNERARY STATUETTE OF A YOUTH

Dynasty XII, 1963–1787 BC.

Egyptian faience statuette of a youth wearing the side lock and wrapped in a shroud. The figure is a bright turquoise blue with details painted in blue–black pigment. It stands on a small rectangular base also painted blue–black. The head is disproportionately large and the skull is flat and decorated with dots representing the shaved hair, cf. Cat. no. 114. The side lock, which hangs behind the right ear, is painted blue–black and the eyes and brows are outlined in black. The features are modelled schematically without individuality. The hands hold the all-enveloping garment tightly around the body, so that only the contours of shoulders, arms and buttocks are visible underneath. The garment, probably a shroud, is ornamented with the familiar lozenge pattern made up of flower petals.

From El Kab, tomb 1. Gift of the Egyptian Research Account. Ashmolean E.3738. H: 12.9 cm. W: 4.5 cm.

When Quibell published the results of his excavation in 1897 of a large XIIth Dynasty (his own dating) cemetery at El Kab, he followed the practice of the time and published only the more unusual objects with a sample of the rest. As a result this statuette is illustrated, but without any information as to the circumstances of the find or associated objects. His publication makes frustrating reading because it is clear that many burials were found, in which the whole group of grave offerings could be reconstructed. Nevertheless, three more objects from the tomb are known, since they were also

80

given to the Ashmolean Museum, and these are: a limestone statuette of three baboons, an adult and two babies, cf. Cat. no. 106a; a 'faience' bracelet and a model cucumber, also of 'faience'.

This statuette belongs to a rare class of Middle Kingdom funerary statuettes made of 'faience'. Only two others are known to me, and neither is published. One is in the Louvre; the other, in the Metropolitan Museum, is from Lisht. Both are simply inscribed with the name of the deceased and neither wears a side lock. The side lock was invariably worn by very young children of both sexes and by youths, like the youngest brother on the stela of Amenemhat Nebuy, Cat. no. 39. The garment may be identified as a shroud by its appearance on anthropoid coffins, which reproduce in a stylised way a mummy covered with a shroud and wearing a funerary mask. The pattern occurs frequently in the Middle Kingdom, usually ornamenting the dress of women. It was probably executed either by sewing alternating cylindrical and spheroid beads on to a cloth or leather backing, or by wearing a network of beads over a plain tunic. Scraps of cloth decorated in the former way have been found at Kerma in the Sudan.

Another uninscribed mummiform statuette, but in alabaster and in a different style, was found in a burial at El Kab,

close to the body of the tomb owner. Most large Middle Kingdom cemeteries produce a few such figures, mostly in hard stones (cf. Cat. nos. 81–2), but Beni Hasan tomb 65 (see Cat. no. 68) has produced another example in 'faience', though of a man wearing the dress of every day.

Quibell, *El Kab*, p. 18, pl. v, 1; Kemp and Merrillees, *Minoan Pottery*, p. 167; for shroud, cf. Petrie, *Gizeh and Rifeh*, pl. x B; E. Riefstahl, *Patterned Textiles in Pharaonic Egypt* (Brooklyn, 1944), pp. 11–12; for Louvre and Metropolitan Museum figures, Schneider, *Shabtis*, 1, pp. 179, 181; for Beni Hasan statuette, Garstang, *Burial Customs*, fig. 140.

81 FUNERARY STATUETTE OF INHORHOTEP

Late Dynasty XII, 1862–1787 BC.

Basalt statuette of a man wrapped in a shroud, wearing the full wig with rectangular side lappets. There is a vertical column of hieroglyphs down the centre of the body, giving, in garbled writing, the funerary formula and a name and title tentatively read as 'the soldier of the town regiment, Inhorhotep'. The man's hands are exposed, the left held flat against his chest in a gesture of reverence, the right holding the edges of his shroud together in the manner of the El Kab statuette, Cat. no. 80. Length of face: 1.8 cm. Width of face: 2.2 cm. Length of eye: 1.0 cm. Length of ear: 1.1 cm. The eyes are elongated, with a heavy upper lid, under lightly sculptured brows. The ears are extremely long and narrow, the outer rim is marked, and a kidney-shaped eminence represents the inner ear. The nose is short and broad, the mouth wide with thin lips, and the rounded chin projects out of the square face. A slight swelling marks the arms and buttocks under the shroud but otherwise the body's contours are not reproduced, apart from the feet which project to form the base.

Purchased in Luxor, so possibly from Thebes. Bequest of Sir Robert Greg. Fitzwilliam E.641.1954. H: 16.7 cm. W: 4.5 cm.

Like the 'faience' statuette, Cat. no. 80, this figure is not quite mummiform, since one hand is exposed clutching the shroud around the body, cf. also Cat. no. 19. Nevertheless, the wig and upright pose suggest the wrapped body of the dead. The inscription is cut in execrable hieroglyphs, quite at variance with the relatively skilled carving of the figure – but see comments on Khnemu, Cat. no. 42.

At the beginning of the Middle Kingdom, perhaps even slightly earlier, tiny figures modelled in wax, clay or wood, sometimes naked, sometimes fully mummiform and placed in miniature coffins, start to appear in burials. If they are inscribed they carry merely the name of the deceased with or without the funerary formula. They clearly indicate changes taking place in the funerary rites aimed at reviving the mummy so that the deceased might participate in the Afterlife. Iconographically they relate to the small figures on model boats (cf. Cat. no. 79), showing the glorified dead travelling in the Afterlife on pilgrimage to the great shrine of Osiris at Abydos. They may also have been used at the recitation of the shabti text (see Cat. no. 83), which first

81 and 82

deliberately or not, achieved monumentality on a small scale. The statuette compares closely with the anthropoid coffins of the XIIth Dynasty (see Cat. no. 72), and, in my view, developed out of them. There is some argument as to whether such figures as this and Cat. nos. 80–1 can be called shabtis. The earliest figures which carry the shabti text (cf. Cat. no. 83) are very similar in iconography, although there is no absolutely standard form at this time. Without an inscription we cannot be sure what precise function figures such as this one performed. It is consistent with what we know of the ancient Egyptians to assume a multiplicity of purposes. One of these might be to act out the age-old magic principle of substitution. The statuette could be a stand-in for the wrapped body of the deceased in funeral rites; for the deceased in the Afterlife if the real, more vulnerable body were destroyed; and in the offering cult, see miniature coffin Cat. no. 74.

In this case we can be sure that the figure was buried in the tomb, not placed in a shrine or offering chapel. Petrie excavated Diospolis Parva (Hu being the modern place name) in 1898–9, and he describes w38 as 'a rich [shaft] tomb entirely turned over by plunderers'. Consultation of his own and his wife's notebooks of the excavation have elicited considerably more information. The statuette was found among the remains of a single burial in the lower south chamber, which contained a coffin with 'the design of a false door and a chequer pattern in red and green' (Hilda Petrie) (cf. Cat. no. 70), ears from a plaster mask or coffin, and pottery (Petrie, *Diospolis Parva*, pls. XXXIII, 22, 30, XXXV, 122). These finds suggest a date in the second part of the XIIth Dynasty, which is important in confirming the period during which these mummiform figures begin to appear in graves. It corresponds to the time in which mummiform figures first appear on stelae (see Cat. no. 40), and follows the appearance of the first anthropoid coffins, see Cat. no. 72.

Petrie, *Diospolis Parva*, p. 43, pl. XXVI; for shabtis generally, see Schneider, *Shabtis*, I, passim.

appears at the same time among the spells written on the inside of coffins.

For Inhorhotep's title, see O. Berlev in *RdE* 23 (1971), pp. 23–48; D. Franke in *SAK* 10 (1983), pp. 167–8.

82 A FUNERARY STATUETTE FROM HU
Late Dynasty XII, 1862–1787 BC.

Uninscribed serpentine statuette of a man wearing the full long wig with side lappets. His body appears completely wrapped and virtually formless. There is only a slight swelling in front for his arms, and one at the back suggesting the buttocks. Length of face: 2.0 cm. Width of face: 2.4 cm. Length of eye: 0.6 cm. Length of ear: 1.3 cm. The brows are lightly marked and the eyes shallowly cut, being no more than ovals defined by an incised line. The nose is long and straight and the enormous ears, set high, show only their outer rim and lobe. The mouth is wide with thin, slightly pouting lips.

From Hu, tomb w38. Gift of the Egypt Exploration Fund. Fitzwilliam E.252.1899. H: 16.5 cm. W: 5.6 cm.

The shallow cutting of this hard stone scarcely seems to penetrate the surface of the material, but it has, whether

83 SHABTI OF RENSENEB
Dynasty XIII, 1786–1650 BC.

Limestone statuette of a man shown as a body wrapped for burial, wearing a mask with the full wig with side lappets and a beard. His arms are crossed on his chest and he carries in his left hand the *ankh* sign of life and in his right a *hes* vase, the hieroglyph meaning 'favour'. The wig, beard, *ankh* sign and *hes* vase are all coloured blue. Down the front of his body, arranged in eight horizontal lines of green-painted hieroglyphs, is the shabti text which includes his name, Renseneb, and title, 'the follower'. The brows are very wide (0.3 cm), curving only slightly over the eyes, modelled in relief, outlined in black and painted blue. The large eyes are set straight and show a fish-tailed cosmetic line which ends up parallel to the eyebrows. The eyes are outlined in black, the iris is white, the pupils black with a white spot in the centre to highlight them, and there are red spots at each corner of each eye. The nose is short and broad, the nostrils emphasised by a deeply cut outline. The mouth is wide with

83

could be watered and the crops grow. At the same time, no-one of the wealth or status of a tomb owner would have done manual labour, but would have designated substitutes from among his servants, see Cat. no. 45. It is interesting to note that this most menial type of labour is rarely depicted on tomb reliefs – instead it is the next stage, from the sowing of the seed onwards, that is represented. The idea that the structures of society were exactly and of necessity reproduced in the Next World, to impose order on an eternal Egypt made fertile by its everlasting Nile, is as old as the earliest religious writings we have from the Nile Valley. It may seem naive, even absurd, to us, but it represents the ancient substratum of belief upon which many of the complex rituals of burial were constructed.

This particular practice of writing the shabti text on a mummiform figure of the deceased seems to have evolved in the late XIIth Dynasty, at Lisht or at Dahshur, the cemetery around a pyramid built for Amenemhat III. The text was written in hieroglyphs, which were mutilated so that the birds, human beings and reptiles in the inscription should not harm the actual mummy whose form the figures imitated and with which it was identified. The practice spread to Abydos and continued throughout the XIIIth Dynasty, although it never became universal. The shabti text also continued to appear in other contexts, for example on small shrines containing mummiform figures, or on figures placed in miniature coffins in votive deposits, see Cat. no. 74. Plain mummiform figures, and those inscribed with name and title only, were in use over the same period (see Cat. nos. 80–2), indicating a variety of practice.

The shaft tomb in which the two shabtis of Renseneb were found originally contained at least five burials, one of which was found intact and may be dated by a scarab and stone vases to Dynasty XIII. The shabtis themselves were found in the shaft with a group of objects deriving from the plundered burials (minimum 2), in two chambers which lay roughly opposite each other. The objects are at least all compatible with a date in Dynasty XIII, and include a Tell el-Yahudiya juglet (BM EA 49344) and a hemispherical bowl (Fitzwilliam E.19.1910); see also Cat. no. 135b.

Peet, *Cemeteries of Abydos*, II, pp. 57–8, 113, pl. XIII, 3; Schneider, *Shabtis*, I, pp. 183–4; for shabtis at Lisht and Dahshur see *ibid*, pp. 182–3; Part III, fig. 6; D. Arnold and R. Stadelmann in *MDAIK* 33 (1977), pp. 16–17, pl. 4(a).

poorly defined lips, in contrast to the attention given to the eyes. The chin is square. The shape of the body under the wrappings is suggested only faintly at the back, and in the front at feet, arms and shoulders.

From Abydos, tomb B13. Gift of the Egypt Exploration Fund. British Museum EA. 49343. H: 22.6 cm. W: 6.8 cm.

The shabti text first appears on a mummiform statuette of the late XIIth Dynasty found at Lisht, although the text alone, in the oldest version known to us, first occurs amongst the spells on coffins of the early Middle Kingdom from Meir and Deir el-Bersha. The rubric of this early version states that the spell is to be recited over a wooden statue of the tomb owner, 'as he was on earth', and it is possible that Cat. nos. 23 and 25–7 were used for this rite. The spell is in the form of a legal contract, and sets out to provide the deceased with exemption from his duty to help maintain the irrigation system in the Afterlife, by appointing the shabti as his substitute. The spell undoubtedly reflects the practice of everyday life, in that each person bore responsibility for the upkeep of the canals, banks and ditches which alone allowed the annual flooding of the Nile to be controlled so that the fields

HEADREST

84 HEADREST
Dynasty XII, 1963–1787 BC.

Calcite headrest, made in three sections: neck support, stem and rectangular base.

Fitzwilliam E.9.1899. H: 23.0 cm. W: 23.9 cm.

Headrests were often placed inside the coffin, supporting the neck of the mummy. They were used in exactly the same way to support the head during sleep.

84

OFFERING TABLES

85 OFFERING TABLE OF NEFERPERT
Dynasty XI, 2023–1963 BC.

Limestone offering table inscribed for the seal bearer of the god Neferpert. In the centre, carved in high relief, is an enlarged *htp* sign, the hieroglyph which means an altar and which is composed of a tall loaf of bread sitting on a reed mat. The loaf element of the sign is, in its turn, carved in sunk relief with food offerings arranged as they traditionally appear on funerary reliefs, see Cat. no. 12c. First is the haunch of an ox, with ribs and a joint of meat; alongside it is a cucumber, and below it a duck; then come three round loaves, two sealed jars and an ox head. Below the offerings

85

and on either side are troughs for the water offering. They all interconnect so that any water ultimately runs down the central axis of the table. The hieroglyphic inscription consists of the common funerary formula repeated twice, invoking Osiris and Anubis respectively, and arranged so that the text begins and ends each time on the central axis and the hieroglyphs all face inwards towards the offerings.

From Abydos. Gift of the British School of Archaeology in Egypt. Fitzwilliam E.6.1922. H: 42.0 cm. W: 38.0 cm.

The offering table stood, like the stela, in the superstructure of the tomb, in a temple or offering chapel where it could be seen by the living. It carried all that was needed to maintain the offering cult of the dead: his name, the prayer for offerings and a depiction of the essential offerings of food and water.

The Fitzwilliam Museum received this table from Petrie's work at Abydos in 1922. It does not appear in his publication, since he included only a selection of those found. It is of the same date as Cat. no. 10 and the owner's name is the same as that of Montuhotep's father but this is insufficient evidence to associate them.

Cf. H. Fischer, *L'Ecriture et l'Art de l'Egypte ancienne* (Paris, 1986), pp. 121–2, figs. 47–8; C. Kuentz in *Bulletin du Centenaire. Supplément au BIFAO* (Cairo, 1981), pp. 243–55.

86 TRAY OF OFFERINGS AND SOUL HOUSE
First Intermediate period to Early Dynasty XI, 2134–2004 BC.

Combination of tray with models of food offerings, channel for the water offerings, and model house. Sculptured by hand in coarse, straw-tempered Nile silt clay. The offerings consist of two oxen, bound for butchering, a leg of meat, vegetables (cucumber and lettuce), loaves and a dish of figs. The offerings are set out in the courtyard of a house, which has an open portico supported by two pillars, a bench inside and another against the wall of the courtyard, and an outside staircase to the roof, on which there is a canopy.

Gift of the family of F. W. Green. Fitzwilliam E.15.1950. H: 10.7 cm. W: 28.0 cm. L: 41.0 cm.

Numerous examples of these crudely made pottery soul houses have been found at only one site, Rifeh, and from this evidence their evolution was worked out by Flinders Petrie. The starting point seems to have been a simplified uninscribed version of a stone offering table, in which model food offerings were shaped in clay and attached to a semicircular tray with a channel in front for the water offering. The appearance of these trays suggested the courtyard of a house, where food and water were commonly stored, and so the back of the tray began to imitate, at first simply and then more and more elaborately, the structure of a house. The trays were placed at the mouths of tomb shafts, without any superstructure over them. They would seem then to have had a dual purpose: to provide perpetual food offerings and, in default of a tomb chapel, also a dwelling in which the deceased's spirit could receive them.

Bourriau, *Pottery*, p. 118–19, no. 238; cf. Petrie, *Gizeh and Rifeh*, pp. 14–16; pl. xv, 106; Hayes, *Scepter*, I, pp. 255–6, fig. 161; C. Kuentz in *Bulletin du Centenaire. Supplément au BIFAO* (Cairo, 1981), pp. 243–55.

87 MODEL FOOD OFFERINGS

Late Dynasty XII to Dynasty XIII, 1862–1650 BC.

Trussed duck in calcite, and three figs (*Ficus carica*) modelled in Egyptian 'faience'. The duck's eyes were originally inlaid. The figs have been roughly shaped with the fingers into miniature elongated replicas of the fruit.

Duck: Royal Museum of Scotland 1911.338. L: 10.6 cm. W: 4.1 cm. Figs: From Gurob, Old Kingdom Cemetery C2. One, gift of R. G. Gayer-Anderson. Fitzwilliam EGA.2478.1943, E53A,B.1921 Average H: 2.4 cm. Average W: 1.5 cm.

Miniaturised replicas of the food offerings depicted in relief on offering tables and elsewhere sometimes appear in Middle Kingdom tombs. They may be made of painted wood, 'faience' or stone. They appear first in large tomb models, particularly those in which the deceased is shown on a bier with offerings beside him, but they continue to be placed among the grave goods after the habit of providing the larger models has disappeared; this has happened, it seems, by the middle of Dynasty XII. A grave in which model figs occur is discussed under Cat. no. 112. The duck is shown, not as it normally appears on the table of offerings, freshly slaughtered with its head hanging down (see Cat. no. 20), but bound, plucked and ready for cooking. This would have been done on a spit over an open fire (de Garis Davies, *Antefoker*, pl. VIII). Among the fruit and vegetables commonly reproduced, in addition to figs, are cucumbers, bunches of grapes, sycamore figs and lubia beans. This compares well with the botanical remains found at the Middle Kingdom town of Kahun and identified by Percy Newberry in 1890. The figs were found, according to the excavators' marks which they still carry, in cemetery C2 at Gurob. They were presumably found on the surface, since they are not mentioned in the publication.

87b–d

Cf. L. Keimer in *BIFAO* 28 (1929), pp. 75–7, pl. III, 4–5, pl. VIII; Kemp and Merrillees, *Minoan Pottery*, pp. 163–6, pl. 26b; Newberry in Petrie, *Kahun*, pp. 49–50.

88 PIGEON AND CALF

Late Dynasty XII, 1862–1787 BC.

Funerary models in Egyptian faience of (a) a pigeon and (b) a young, possibly newly born calf lying with its legs folded underneath its body. The pigeon is deep blue in colour, with a thick, glassy surface. The base on which it stands is black and the feathers and eyes are picked out in the same colour; the beak is chipped. The calf is turquoise, with some unevenness of colour caused in firing. The base is again black and the black markings on head and flanks have been applied with the fingers before firing. The eyes have been carefully painted in black, and bumps for the incipient horns have been represented.

(a) From Hawara, tomb 58. University College 27975. H: 2.8 cm. W: 3.5 cm. (b) From Haraga, tomb 353. University College 18744. H: 3.3 cm. W: 5.9 cm.

The pigeon figurine was identified by its excavator as a dove, but since we know ancient Egyptians ate pigeon, this seems a more likely choice for a tomb model. Furthermore, it was found in a box with a wooden miniature of a large

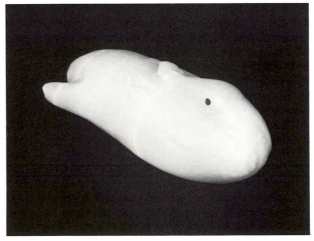

87a

88a

102

88b

storage jar and this association suggests food offerings. It is the only example of a dove/pigeon model known to me, but it can be closely dated because it comes from the intact burial of a young girl. The pottery suggests the late XIIth Dynasty, from the end of the reign of Amenemhat III.

The model of a recumbent calf comes from a tomb of similar date, to judge by the associated pottery and jewellery, but we are assuming that all the objects come from the same burial only because there was a single chamber leading off the shaft and fragments of cartonnage from only one mask or coffin were found. Models similar to this one have also been found at Lisht, Heliopolis (the tomb containing Cat. no. 112) and Abydos.

(a) Petrie *et al.*, *Labyrinth*, p. 36, pl. xxx, 6; for pigeon pie, W. B. Emery, *Archaic Egypt* (London, 1961), pp. 243–6; for pottery, cf. Do. Arnold in *MDAIK* 38 (1982) fig. 17, nos. 4–5. (b) Engelbach, *Harageh*, pl. xiv, 6; cf. Kemp and Merrillees, *Minoan Pottery*, p. 143.

89 MINIATURE CUPS

Late Dynasty XII to Dynasty XIII, 1862–1650 BC.

Two miniature cups (a, b) hand-made in deep turquoise blue 'faience' with lotus petal decoration in blue–black pigment, cf. Cat. no. 122.

Gift of R. G. Gayer-Anderson. Fitzwilliam EGA.3079-80.1943. (a) H: 2.6 cm. D: 2.5 cm. (b) H: 2.6 cm. D: 3.3 cm.

Miniature versions of the contemporary table-ware, made in 'faience', painted wood or limestone, appear in the same contexts in which the model food offerings and animals

89a, b

occur. The two examples here cannot be more precisely dated than to the whole period in which they occur, but full-sized versions in metal, Cat. no. 184, 'faience', Cat. no. 126, or pottery, Cat. no. 135b, tend to confirm that they belong to the late, rather than the early Middle Kingdom.

Cf. Hayes, *Scepter*, I, fig. 225.

SERVANT FIGURES

90 SERVANT GIRL Illustrated in colour on pl. III,2.

Late Old Kingdom, c. 2150 BC.

Plastered and painted wooden statuette of a servant girl walking with her left leg forward, carrying on her head a small chest of offerings for the deceased, which she supports with her left hand. In her right she carries a duck by its wings, and in front of her walks a young oryx or gazelle, cf. Cat. no. 39. She stands on the original rectangular base, and her left foot has been carelessly covered with a lump of coarse plaster, probably in antiquity. The lid of the chest carries a hieroglyphic inscription in black ink, naming 'the sealer of the King, sole companion and overseer of priests, Hepikem'. Length of face: 3.2 cm. Width of face: 4.7 cm. Length of eye: 2.0 cm. She wears a white linen headcloth over her shoulder-length black hair, which is held in place by a red ribbon tied at the back. The blunt-ended brows begin straight then curve downwards slightly to end parallel with the outer corner of the eyes. The eyes themselves are enormous, and made even more emphatic by being painted black (pupil and outline) and white (eyeball) in contrast to nose and mouth which are painted reddish-brown like the rest of the face and body. Outer and inner canthi are marked, but there is no cosmetic line. The nose is short with broad nostrils and the mouth has thick straight lips with deep creases at the corners. The chin is round, and the cheeks flat with just the faintest suggestion of cheek-bone. The contours of the body are shown very clearly, emphasised rather than disguised by the clinging white linen tunic she wears. The broad shoulder straps of the tunic cross over in front, exposing the breasts; the nipples are painted black. The arms are long and rounded, without a sign of musculature or bone. She has long, thin fingers and toes with white nails. On both wrists are wide green bands representing bracelets of 'faience' beads.

A peg joins the clenched right hand to the back of the duck. The feathers, head, feet and beak of the bird are painted in considerable detail. Similar care has been taken with the figure of the young oryx or gazelle. The horns have broken off and the ears are chipped, making identification uncertain. The body has been painted white with a red band along each flank and the neck. The hooves, tip of the tail, nostrils, pupils and outline of the eyes are black and the muzzle and patches over the eyes are brown.

From Meir, tomb of Hepikem. Eton College, Myers Museum I. H: 43.2 cm. W: 20.0 cm.

This is one of the finest and best-preserved statuettes of

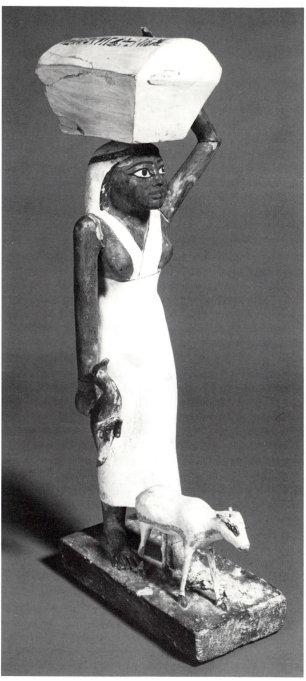

90

with the passive poses and pale skins adopted for women of higher status. Her name is not given, just the name of the tomb owner. The treatment of the eyes recalls Cat. no. 69, the funerary mask of Thay from Beni Hasan dated to Dynasty XI. Many provincial cemeteries in Middle Egypt such as Meir and Beni Hasan were in continuous use from the late Old Kingdom to the early Middle Kingdom and it is possible to observe a unity of style in their output. A companion piece to this statuette is in Copenhagen, in the Ny Carlsberg Glyptotek. The only notable differences are that the girl carries a basket on her head, containing bread and beer, instead of a casket, and that there is no inscription. It was bought in Cairo in 1894 and is known to be from Meir, but the likeness between the two pieces is so striking that they were surely made for the same burial, that of Hepikem, owner of tomb A4 at Meir.

W. M. Webb in *English Illustrated Magazine* (November, 1900), p. 171; McConnell, *Treasures of Eton*, p. 17, fig. 12; *Burlington Fine Arts Club*, 1895, p. 41, no. 58, pl. XXIV; Breasted, Jr, *Servant Statues*, p. 61, no. 5; for Copenhagen statuette, Mogensen, *Glyptothèque Ny Carlsberg*, pl. XII, A51; general discussion, H. G. Fischer in *Varia. Egyptian Studies*, I (New York, 1976), p. 41, n. 8, pp. 45–9; for the excavations at Meir and tomb A4 see Blackman, *Meir*, I, pp. 6, 10–11, 14–16.

91 MODEL GRANARY Illustrated in colour on pl. I,2, and also on p. 86.

Dynasty XI, 2023–1963 BC.

Model granary, made of Nile silt clay and painted after firing. The exterior is painted with scenes showing the measurement of grain into sacks, the procession of porters to the granary door and two men playing a board game, presumably the granary owner and a companion. Labels written in hieratic in black ink originally provided the names of almost everyone represented, but not all of these are now legible. The granary itself is composed of two storeys and is set behind high walls with access through a single narrow door. The storage area consists of ten chambers, each with a small hole in the roof where the grain was poured in and a square door at the base through which it was extracted. Access to the top five chambers was by an open staircase which rose from the narrow corridor leading to the entrance. The interior walls, stair and floor are painted yellow (representing white wash?) and the domed roofs of the upper chambers are painted grey, representing sun-dried mud brick.

Three of the scenes on the outside were intended to be read in sequence, as follows. Left side: the scribe Intef sits on a heap of grain making notes on his writing board while the serf Khunes fills the corn measure and behind Khunes, waiting to have their sacks filled, stand two more serfs, Gerhi and Khu; front: the procession to the granary consists of five men and three women, all originally identified but in hastily scribbled hieratic signs which are now almost entirely lost or illegible, the tiny figures of the women carrying correspondingly smaller sacks, the last of them being called simply 'her daughter'; right side: the head of the procession, at the door

an offering-bringer to have come from Egypt. It was purchased there by Major Myers, probably during his visit of 1893–4, see Cat. no. 23. The tomb from which it came belonged to a member of one of the great provincial families of Middle Egypt who became so powerful between the late Old Kingdom and the early Middle Kingdom.

The pose of the figure is the conventional one, but the subtlety of the carving and the freshness of the painting give it an extraordinary liveliness. The vigorous stance, with the left foot forward and the reddish-brown skin colour, contrasts

91

of the granary, consists of two men, one carrying baskets (?) on a yoke and the other a rolled-up reed mat. Their names have also disappeared, but one was described as 'his son' and the other 'his brother'. The back wall of the granary is painted with a scene of two men called Intef and Meri playing a board game, with a maidservant between them holding a feather fan and a vase of a shape used to make the water offering in temple and funerary rituals. The pose of all three figures is unconventional. Both men sit with their legs wide apart straddling their low stools, each with an elbow resting on his knee. Their heads and torsos are in profile but their legs face the viewer. The woman stands with her arms stretched out on either side of her body, which is in profile, and her feet and ankles may be glimpsed through the slats of the table. She is dressed like all the other women in a long skirt which leaves her upper body bare, but in addition wears a bracelet and necklace. Her hair reaches her waist in a long plait. The two men are dressed in a similar manner to the scribe, in shoulder-length wigs and long kilts which knot at the waist, in contrast to the porters, who wear their hair cropped and very short kilts which will not impede their work. While everyone, porters and supervisors alike, is shown to be well built, if not plump, Intef and Meri have exceptionally full figures with heavy breasts and rounded stomachs. The observations they exchange cannot be understood, since they refer to the technicalities of the game they are playing.

Probably from Salmîya, near Tôd. Ex Colman collection. Colman, Cuzens-Hardy gift. Norwich Castle Museum 37.21(1). H: 15.2 cm. W: 21.0 cm. L: 29.2 cm.

This is a unique object. The model maker has substituted painted scenes for the wooden figures which conventionally animate tomb models. Their style echoes the tomb paintings from Gebelein just a few miles south of Salmîya, which are executed in a similar medium, painted mud-plaster, as well as painted wooden coffins from the same site. It is also a reminder of the painted scenes on the walls of the tomb of Kemsit (see Cat. nos. 3–4), executed early in the reign of Nebhepetre Montuhotep.

The freshness and liveliness of the composition make up for the occasional awkwardness of pose and gesture. There was a deep division in Egyptian society between the manual worker and his superiors exemplified here by Intef the scribe and Intef (perhaps the owner of the granary) and Meri, who sit on the shady side of the building playing draughts while the porters toil in the sun. Nevertheless the name of every person is recorded, and for a very practical purpose. One of the basic needs of the dead man, referred to over and over again in funerary spells, is to re-unite his family around him in the Next World. The whole household was in effect his family, and the relationship was one of mutual dependence. Each large household was responsible for the collection, storage and distribution of food for its own use and perhaps that of smaller householders near by. The staple of the Egyptian diet was wheat for bread and barley for beer, and payment for labour was calculated in quantities of bread and beer. Everyone received rations of these appropriate to their rank, and, as texts show us, every aspect of grain growing and distribution was tightly and elaborately controlled. Since the size of the harvest each year depended entirely on the always unpredictable inundation of the Nile, storage and organised distribution of grain was an absolute necessity, and there is some evidence to show that famine was a danger early in Dynasty XI, see Cat. no. 61. It was inconceivable to an Egyptian that this fixed pattern was not to be repeated in the Afterlife, so precautions were required to ensure its establishment and continuity. The primary need was to re-create the working units which allowed the household and its estates to function, so the names of everyone had to be recorded to enable them to pass into Eternity, for ever counting the grain, carrying the sacks, or sitting in the shade.

A. Blackman in *JEA* 6 (1920), pp. 206–8, pls. XIX–XX; W. Stevenson Smith, *A History of Egyptian Sculpture and Painting in the Old Kingdom* (Boston, 1946), p. 230; H. Schäfer, *Principles of Egyptian Art* (Oxford, 1980), pp. 205–6, fig. 208; cf. Wildung, *L'Age d'Or*, fig. 23; for pottery granary model, cf. Garstang, *Burial Customs*, pl. X, fig. 201.

92 MODEL OF SERVANTS MAKING BREAD AND BREWING

Early Dynasty XII, 1963–1862 BC.

Model made of painted wood, linen and clay showing eight men and women engaged in bread-making and brewing. Two women kneeling side by side are grinding flour; another is sifting; a man mixes dough, or grinds grain in a pestle and mortar; a woman sits in front of a pile of loaves baking in conical moulds; a man walks towards her carrying two water jars on a yoke; another man is pressing rectangular lumps of barley bread through a sieve into a wide vat where it will ferment when mixed with water, and perhaps date essence, to make beer, cf. Cat. no. 48; a man approaches him carrying two utensils, one a sieve, attached to a yoke; beside the brewer is a sealed vat and a sealed and stoppered beer jar. All the components of the model have been separately made and attached to the thin plank of wood that provides the base. The paint on the figures is well preserved: the men's bodies and faces are reddish-brown, their kilts white and hair black; the women are yellowish-white, with long black hair bound up in a red fillet, cf. Cat. no. 90. All the women and one of the men have scraps of linen tied around their waists to simulate their linen kilts.

From Beni Hasan, tomb 366. Gift of the Beni Hasan

92

Excavation Committee. Fitzwilliam E.71d.1903. H: 18.5 cm. L: 41.4 cm. W: 29.7 cm.

Baking and brewing came second only to model granaries as a subject for a tomb model. The reason is obvious: when they occurred alone in the funerary formula, bread and beer could symbolise the whole range of food offerings, and in everyday life they were the rations with which people were paid for their labour. The arrangement of the figures divides them into five groups, which are not lined up symmetrically but crowded together to fit, I suspect, the irregular shape of the base board. The groups are: the two women grinding; the woman sieving; the man pounding; the water carrier and the woman baking; the man with the yoke and the brewer. The groups can be 'read' in sequence from the women grinding the flour to the men making beer with the finished loaves, but this may be fortuitous. It is easy to see from this grouping how the elaborate models of the Middle Kingdom grew out of the single, or occasionally double, figures of the Old Kingdom. Excavation photographs show that when the model was found the objects hanging from the yokes held by the two men were missing. Presumably the string holding them had rotted and they had fallen on to the base board, but they are not visible at the angle from which the photograph was taken. It remains possible, however, that the model jars, the sieve and the unknown object were added at a later stage to complete the model.

It has been suggested that the number of figures in models in a burial was directly related to the number of servants in the deceased's household. If so, Khety was an extremely wealthy man. However, this seems to me implausible, since there are too many unknown factors. A single servant may be shown more than once – for example, carrying water and carrying grain to the granary. It is the work they do which needs to be perpetuated in the Afterlife, so that the deceased may not have to undergo the hardship of manual labour; it is not the individuals themselves who are being commemorated.

The tomb of Khety, from which this model and Cat. nos. 93–5 came, was one of the few tombs found intact by Garstang. The pottery and the simple style of the rectangular

coffin suggest a date early in the XIIth Dynasty.

Garstang, *Burial Customs*, pp. 126–8, 224, fig. 124; Bourriau, *Pottery*, p. 63, no. 113; Murray, *Splendour*, pl. XIV; cf. baking scene in de Garis Davies, *Antefoker*, pl. XI B.

93 MODEL OF SERVANTS SLAUGHTERING AN OX AND COOKING

Early Dynasty XII, 1963–1862 BC.

Model made of painted wood and linen showing three (originally four) men grouped around a bound ox. Two men lean over the beast's head, one cuts its throat with a flint knife and the other holds a bowl to catch the blood. Near the ox's hind legs, the feet of a third man survive. His task was probably to cut off the haunch which symbolised the meat offering. A fourth man, stationed behind the animal's back, leans over a three-legged cauldron in which the joints of meat will be cooked after the butchering has taken place, see Cat. no. 48. The figures are similar in style to those shown in Cat. no. 92. The bodies are reddish-brown and the kilts white. The man at the cauldron also has a scrap of linen tied around his waist.

From Beni Hasan, tomb 366. Gift of the Beni Hasan Excavation Committee. Fitzwilliam E.71c,1903. H: 16.3 cm. L: 29.0 cm. W: 23.0 cm.

For the date of tomb 366, see Cat. no. 92. The use of a flint knife to slaughter the animal in the funerary ritual was traditional, but, contrary to Garstang's comments, flint tools were still widely used in the Middle Kingdom, as recent excavations of settlement sites have shown. This model represents both an activity which may be endlessly repeated in the Next World and an actual event which took place at the funeral. The ox would have been consumed by priests and mourners after the presentation of its haunch to the deceased by the chief mourner, see Cat. no. 39.

Garstang, *Burial Customs*, pp. 105, 224, fig. 94; Breasted, Jr, *Servant Figures*, p. 37, no. 3.

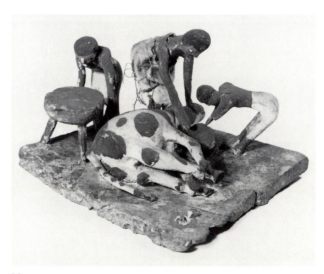

93

94 MODEL SAILING BOAT

Early Dynasty XII, 1963–1862 BC.

Model boat made of painted wood and linen, trimmed for sailing south up the Nile using the prevailing wind from the North. The pilot stands in the bows, his arm outstretched; two men lean on long quant poles, steadying themselves against the deck, pushing the boat off in shallow water from the bed of the river or a sandbank; three men work the rigging, to raise the sail and catch the wind; the steersman sits at the back manoeuvring the gigantic steering oar. The figures and the boat itself were orginally covered with a thin layer of fine plaster and painted. The boat was painted white, the figures reddish-brown with white kilts and black hair. The linen of the sail was also originally covered with a fine layer of plaster, presumably to stiffen it so that it would hold its shape. The cross-beam of the mast was made with a twig. The mast itself has had to be replaced.

From Beni Hasan, tomb 366. Gift of the Beni Hasan Excavation Committee. Fitzwilliam E.71a.1903. H: 40.5 cm. L: 62.0 cm. W: 12.4 cm.

It has been observed that if boat models are present in a tomb there are usually two of them, one rigged for sailing up river and the other for rowing downstream. Second only to the need for supplies of food and drink in the Afterlife was the desire of the dead for mobility, and in Egypt mobility meant free passage on the river. The group of two men pushing on long poles to help the boat through shallow water is an unusual feature, but one which occurs on at least two other model boats from Beni Hasan. Perhaps their stretch of river was full of sandbanks in the early XIIth Dynasty. In his outstretched hand the pilot may originally have held an object with which to test the depth of the channel (cf. Petrie and Brunton, *Sedment*, I, pl. xx). For the date of tomb 366, see Cat. no. 92.

Garstang, *Burial Customs*, p. 224; Murray, *Splendour*, pl. VIII; cf. Breasted, Jr, *Servant Statues*, pl. 76b; S. R. K. Glanville, *Wooden Model Boats. Catalogue of Egyptian Antiquities in the British Museum*, II (London, 1972), no. 12.

94

95 MODEL BOAT WITH OARSMEN

Early Dynasty XII, 1963–1862 BC.

Model boat made of painted wood and linen. There are nine crewmen: the pilot stands in the bows, behind him sit seven oarsmen, and facing them is the steersman handling the

95

large steering oar. The bodies of the crew are painted reddish-brown, their kilts white and their hair black, and they originally all wore scraps of linen tied around their waists to simulate their clothing. Two of the oarsmen no longer have them. The figures are schematically carved, so that the oarsmen's feet, for example, are completely absent.

From Beni Hasan, tomb 366. Gift of the Beni Hasan Excavation Committee. Fitzwilliam E.71b.1903. H: 25.0 cm. L: 59.0 cm. W: 12.0 cm.

For the date of tomb 366, see Cat. no. 92.

96 STATUETTE OF A HARPER

Dynasties XII–XIII, 1963–1650 BC.

Limestone statuette of a seated woman playing an upright five-string harp. Her legs are cut away below the thigh to show the harp more clearly. She wears a shoulder-length wig, or her natural hair, which is painted black and carries vertical rows of semicircular incisions to represent waves or curls. The top of the harp is also painted black, and the eyes and brows are outlined in the same colour. There are faint traces of a bracelet on her outstretched right arm, and a black line runs around the bowl of the harp. The carving of the figure and the instrument is rudimentary, recalling the style of Cat. no. 118. The nose and mouth are also a little worn. The statuette is carved in one piece with the oval base on which it sits and which is approximately 0.8 cm high.

Ex Macgregor and Beazley collections. Ashmolean 1922.212. H: 5.8 cm. W: 4.9 cm.

Statuettes of harpers, male and female, occur in tombs of the Old and Middle Kingdoms. They are also frequently represented on tomb reliefs and stelae, and on the latter not necessarily in a subordinate role. Several stelae of male harpers exist. This suggests harpers could have considerable wealth and status, presumably when attached to important households. Reisner describes a limestone statuette of a male harper from an early Middle Kingdom tomb at Sheikh Farag, and another was found in Abydos tomb 416, whose date is discussed under Cat. no. 106. The closest parallel to this example was once in the Kennard collection, and was sold at Sotheby's in 1912; this is illustrated in Reisner's article.

Garstang found the remains of a five-string harp in tomb 287 at Beni Hasan, and noted that it would have been short of resonance and would have needed frequent tuning. The tomb itself contained material from New Kingdom as well as Middle Kingdom burials.

96

Cf. G. A. Reisner in *JEA* 6 (1920), pp. 117–18, pls. XIV–XV; Garstang, *Burial Customs*, p. 153, figs. 152–3; H. Hickmann in *Bulletin de l'Institut d'Egypte* 35 (1954), pp. 309–68.

97 AN ASIATIC WOMAN AND HER CHILD
Early Dynasty XII, 1963–1862 BC.

Painted wooden statuette of a woman walking with her left foot advanced and carrying her child on her back. There is a hole in the top of the head, which is also flattened, to take a basket or tray of offerings, cf. Cat. no. 90. The woman's hair is painted black, and appears to be piled on top of the head and held in place by three concentric bands. The brows are thick and curved, painted black on top of a prominent brow-ridge. The eyes are asymmetrical, one set higher than the other; they are outlined in black with a white iris and large black pupil. There are deep pouches carved underneath the lower lids. The ears are colossal, pushed forward by the rounded masses of hair behind them. The inner ear is hollowed out. The profile of the nose is intact and shows a pronounced curve. The nostrils are extremely wide, and two deep concave creases run from them to the chin. The mouth has strongly curved, protruding lips and turns up at the corners. The chin is square, in keeping with the strong jawline which thrusts the whole face forward. The musculature and bony structure of the face are shown with unflattering realism: sunken cheeks, triangular pouches under the eyes, and lines from the nostrils. The long neck is strongly curved, suggesting the weight of the child is pushing the head forward. Only the head of the child, pegged into a hole at the base of the neck, is visible. The child's head shows no hair and its facial features are schematically reproduced. The woman supports the child inside the all-enveloping garment she wears and which she holds tightly against her body. A protrusion visible at the back may represent a harness for the child, worn underneath her dress. In contrast to the face, the modelling of the body is rudimentary. The shoulders, arms and buttocks are represented, but not the breasts or the thighs under the voluminous skirt. Garstang noted 'some traces of pattern' on the skirt, but none now remains visible. The background colour of dark red remains. The feet and legs are painted yellow and very simply suggested. The total absence of toes may have been intended to show that the woman was wearing boots, like the Asiatic woman depicted in tomb 3 at Beni Hasan (Newberry, *Beni Hasan*, i, pl. xxx). The statuette was made in four parts, with joins at the right wrist and at both ankles. The right hand and the tip of the left foot are restored and there has been some restoration of the painted features. It was found on an original rectangular wooden base which has not survived.

From Beni Hasan, tomb 181. Ex Hilton Price collection. Royal Museum of Scotland 1911.260. H: 15.3 cm. W: 4.4 cm.

The contrast between this statuette of a rugged peasant woman and the slim, girlish ideal of womanhood more commonly encountered in Middle Kingdom art, Cat. no. 90, is astonishing. Two reasons for the realism of this piece suggest themselves. Firstly the statuette represents an offering-bringer, which means that the offerings (originally carried in a basket on the head) were more important than the figure itself. There is a long tradition, going back to the Old Kingdom, which allows such subordinate figures to be depicted outside the conventions applied to figures of persons of higher status such as the tomb owner. If it was the function, rather than the person carrying it out, which was destined for immortality, then a youthful, idealised form was not essential. Secondly, it seems likely that the statuette represents a non-Egyptian, a Bedouin woman from the Eastern desert; the interest lay in her exoticism, which was therefore lovingly reproduced, almost to the point of caricature. It has invariably been assumed that this statuette represents a three-dimensional version of the painted scene in tomb 3 at Beni Hasan, the tomb of the nomarch Khnumhotep, which shows a caravan of Asiatics bringing a consignment of black eye paint, which we call *kohl*. The Asiatics include men, women and children, and a caption to the scene explains that thirty-seven of them under their chieftain arrived in Year Six of Senusret II. Among Khnumhotep's titles was 'administrator of the Eastern desert' so the appearance of Eastern desert bedouin at Beni Hasan in his time is a likely event. However, unlike the paintings, which are in their own way idealised so that none of the figures shows individuality of feature, although there are variations of pose and dress, this statuette appears to have been copied from life. If so, it may explain the considerable differences between it and the painting of the Bedouin women. The hairstyle, the enveloping garment and the baby on the back – none of these appears in the painting. It is not certain that carrying the baby in this way was a specifically non-Egyptian custom – it occurs often enough in the New Kingdom. For this reason, and because there is hardly any other point of similarity between them, it seems unwise to associate the statuette with another scene in tomb

97

14 at Beni Hasan, showing Libyans (Newberry, *Beni Hasan*, I, pl. XLV, XLVII). It is clear from other sources that Asiatics, a general term used by Egyptians for the inhabitants of the Eastern desert, Arabia, and the whole of the region of Syria–Palestine, came into Egypt in numbers during the XIIth Dynasty, see Cat. no. 39. Perhaps this woman represents a member of a tribe with different customs of dress from the group shown in tomb 3, who became part of the local scene at Beni Hasan and so became included among the types of offering bringer made in the local funerary workshops.

There is an interesting parallel in an ivory statuette in the Museum of Fine Arts in Boston, unfortunately without provenance. It is published by Wildung (*L'Age d'Or*, fig. 159) as from Kerma, but this is incorrect. The ivory shows a woman with a similar hairstyle and costume, which appears more clearly there as a fringed cloak, and with a child on her back. In this example the hands are also made as separate pieces.

Garstang, *Burial Customs*, fig. 138; Smith, *Art and Architecture*, pl. 78 (A); Aldred, *Middle Kingdom Art*, no. 30.

ART AND MAGIC

The objects prepared for the funeral, the careful wrapping of the body and the opening-of-the-mouth ceremony were all designed to ensure for the dead the basic necessities of life: a healthy body, shelter, food and servants. However, something more was needed – protection against the malignant forces of the natural and supernatural world, which infested earth and air, the night, the desert, water and the tombs of the unquiet dead. The living and the dead were equally vulnerable to them, and the same magical means were used to protect both. Nothing illustrates more vividly the parity between the two worlds of the living and the dead, or contrasts more sharply with the scenes of daily life (Cat. no. 48: Liverpool stela). Such scenes have nothing to tell us of this side of Egyptian life, for they set out to present endless scenes of busy activity all channelled towards the satisfaction of the deceased's material needs. No-one is shown idle or diseased, and very rarely old or deformed. The other side of the picture we can only infer from magical and medical texts and objects found in houses and tombs. What these evoke is the world of the Egyptian peasant captured by Winifred Blackman in the 1920s, just before it was irrevocably changed by improved education, health and communications (W. Blackman, *The Fellahin of Upper Egypt*, London, 1927). Four out of the eighteen chapters in her book are devoted wholly to magical practices: magicians and magic; the village medicine man and medicine woman; the evil eye and other superstitions; and *afarit* (ghosts). The rest of the book teems with descriptions of oral and manual rites used to avert, prophesy or cure life's misfortunes. The rituals themselves find only occasional parallels in antiquity, but the atmosphere of thought and feeling which they conjure up is overwhelmingly familiar. In 1896 Quibell, excavating on the west bank at Thebes, discovered a few Middle Kingdom shaft tombs under the storerooms at the back of the Ramesseum, the mortuary temple of Ramesses II (1290–1224 BC). At the bottom of the shaft of one tomb he found a box containing decomposed papyri, now recognised as the most important single find of Middle Kingdom papyri ever made. The find has been dated to Dynasty XIII on the basis of the handwriting of the latest texts. The documents were primarily incantations for magico-medical purposes, but also included literary texts: parts of two of the most popular stories of the time, *Sinuhe* and the *Eloquent Peasant*, a hymn to the crocodile god Sobek, and fragments of a religious drama. There was also an onomasticon listing the names of birds, plants, animals and towns in Upper Egypt and Nubia, and on the

back of three texts were fragments of reports of the royal administration surviving from an earlier use of the papyrus sheets (see Cat. no. 62: Semna despatch). All these texts, with the exception of the administrative documents, were part of the equipment of a practising magician and doctor. They show us that such a man, unlike the village magician of Egypt in the 1920s, was a member of the educated elite. He was sage, storyteller, priest and doctor, and could command the resources to ensure that his own burial was a fine one, as the coffin fragments of the master physician Wepwawetemhat illustrate, Cat. no. 67.

Close to the box of papyri, Quibell found the statuette shown in fig. 1, a young female wearing a lion mask and holding snake wands, playing the role of a beneficent lion demon, the female counterpart of Aha, later called Bes (see Cat. nos. 98–9). The statuette is now in the Manchester Museum, though sadly it is too fragile to be lent to the exhibition. The other objects from the group were fragments of magic knives, cf. Cat. nos. 102–3; a large bronze uraeus-snake, approximately twice the size of those held in the woman's hands, Cat. no. 100, found entangled in a mass of hair (probably a wig); an ivory clapper, cf. Cat. no. 101; a segment of magic rod, cf. Cat. no. 104; 'faience' statuettes of baboons and a lion, cf. Cat. no. 106; female fertility figurines, cf. Cat. nos. 118–21; 'faience' miniature drinking cups, cf. Cat. no. 89; beads; amulets; and a 'faience' model cucumber. Apart from the last four items, which are conventional grave goods of the time, and an ivory statuette of a boy carrying a calf, which may be of a later date, all are instruments of magic. They were necessary for the performance of the manual rites which invariably accompanied the oral recitations set out in the papyri. Moreover the objects can almost all be paralleled from settlement sites, showing that these rites were carried out impartially, for the living as for the dead.

The most frequently depicted protagonist in the struggle against evil forces was the lion or lion demon – part beast, part human. The lion, most powerful of the animals known to the Egyptians, was most clearly identified with the King in the visual form of the sphinx (see Cat. no. 138), but occurs from earliest times as an image of irresistible but benign power. In the Middle Kingdom lions appear in many different contexts but convey the same idea. They may be shown standing on their hind legs (sometimes holding a captive), as a support for furniture or decoration for a hairpin; their heads serve as water spouts in royal mortuary temples at

Lisht; and they occur in desert hunting scenes in tombs. The iconography of the lion demon, identified by inscriptions as Aha, may have evolved from the use of lion masks, one of which was found in a house at Kahun. There is no standard image in the Middle Kingdom. There are male and female forms, which may be youthful or old; the body may be upright or dwarfish and the head may be more or less lion-like. It used to be thought that the iconography evolved under foreign influences, from South, East or West, but recent studies by Romano and Altenmüller place them firmly within the context of Egyptian religious imagery. The association with snakes is present from the beginning but snakes have a double nature: on the one hand they symbolise all the dangers against which protection is sought and on the other they are themselves strong magic, thus emblems of power in the hands of a magician, see Cat. no. 100.

It is only a restricted menagerie of beasts which recurs,

Fig. 1

over and over again, on magic knives and rods or as separate statuettes or amulets. Most of them represent potentially antagonistic powers which may be controlled by the manipulation of an image which embodies them. It is an age-old magical device and one which we still practise, albeit sub-consciously. The animals belong, not to the Black Land, the cultivated land of Egypt, the world dominated by man, but to the wild places, the marshes and swamps of the river, or to the desert. Even the cat, Cat. no. 108, is no docile pet but a hunter, at home in the desert landscape.

If the beasts represent the defensive rituals of magic, the human female figurines represent the productive ones. Again Winifred Blackman provides us with a picture of an analogous society, where fertility is the preoccupation of everyone and the bearing and rearing of children is hazardous and fear-ful. The number of baby burials on any ancient site bears this out. Early Egyptologists had some difficulty in fitting the overt sexuality of these figurines into their view of ancient Egyptian society, conditioned as it was by the elegant, fully clothed, passive image of woman presented in tomb and tem-ple paintings and sculpture. The figurines were explained as depictions of prostitutes, foreign harem women and dancing girls, that is women outside the normal bounds of society at the time they were writing. The evidence they adduced in support of this view is not standing up to recent research or to new finds from excavations in Middle Kingdom settle-ments and shrines of the goddess Hathor. The fertility figurines are, perhaps like the lions and hippopotami, repositories of power, in this case the power of human sexu-ality and fertility. They do not represent an image of an indi-vidual destined for eternity, and so they can dispense with the rigid conventions such images demanded.

DEMONS AND MAGICIANS

98 LION DEMON
Late Dynasty XII to Dynasty XIII, 1862–1650 BC.

Ivory figurine of a boy demon with the tail and mane of a lion, standing with left foot forward. The lion mane and ruff are completely stylised, but shown in great detail. The hair of the mane at front and back, where it reaches below the shoulders, is represented by diamonds hatched with verti-cal lines. The squared-off ears project at right angles. The mane has a pronounced peak in the centre of the forehead and at the back forms a wide angle at its bottom edge. The sides of the mane fall diagonally away from the face, just tip-ping the shoulders. The ruff covers the neck and consists of a rounded band with vertical striations. The face, like fig. 1, is non-human. It is extremely broad and flat, the brows are curved and incised, emphasised by a second line above them, and there is a horizontal line across the forehead. The eyes are wide and bulbous, with elongated outer canthi. The nose is short and extremely broad; the lips are straight and the bottom one is very full. Both nose and mouth have been smoothed down a little by wear. The cheek furrow, so notice-able on fig. 1, is present here, running from the wing of the

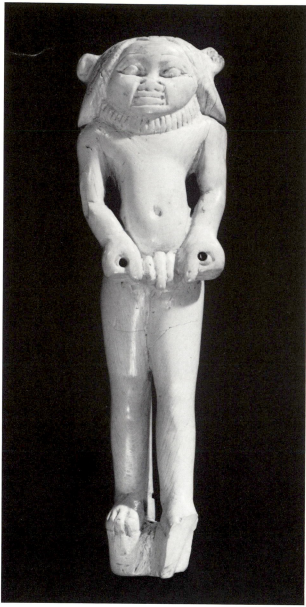

98

Archaeology in Egypt. University College 16069. H: 10.5 cm. W: 2.8 cm.

This finely carved ivory figurine adds another type to the range of Middle Kingdom lion demons. A pot belly becomes an invariable attribute of the New Kingdom Bes-image, but here occurs without the dwarfish limbs that usually accompany it. The pose, with elbows crooked, hands resting on hips (see Cat. no. 99) also becomes very common later. The head is over-large and heavy for the body, so that the figure cannot stand unsupported on its present base. It must originally have been attached to a much larger, heavier one.

The locus 1300, in which the figurine was found, contained no remains of a burial, but a large and heterogeneous collection of objects, pottery, scarabs, jewellery, stone vases, and a mummiform statuette, dating from the late XIIth Dynasty to the Second Intermediate period. Amongst them was a lump of greenish glass of Roman date (Dan Barag, personal communication), indicative of the extent to which the objects had been turned over by plunderers. Brunton, the excavator, thought they represented a dump of objects looted from the nearby tombs which cover the same period.

Petrie and Brunton, *Sedment*, I, p. 18, pl. XL; 27, pl. XLII, 7; cf. Mogensen, *Glyptothèque Ny Carlsberg*, pl. XXXIV, A.186 (where it is dated to the Saite period).

99 DANCING LION DEMON
Late Dynasty XII to Dynasty XIII, 1862–1650 BC.

Deep turquoise–blue moulded 'faience' figurine of a dwarfish lion demon, with details added in black under the glaze. The mane and ears are more simply shown than in Cat. no. 98. There is no ruff and the sides of the mane terminate in triangular points, reminiscent of the wigs of the period, Cat. no. 42. The brow projects, and both eyes, brows and pupils are emphasised in thick lines of black pigment. Nose and mouth are not touched up with paint; consequently their shape is indistinct under the thick glaze, but the nose appears extremely broad and flat. There is little detailed modelling of body and limbs. The figure is pot bellied, with protruding buttocks; both arms and legs are chubby and appear abnormally short, and there is no sign of genitalia. The hands are clenched and rest on the hips, cf. Cat. no. 98. Toe and finger nails, nipples and navel, the tip of the tail and the underside of the rectangular base are all painted black. The legs are bent to suggest movement, possibly dancing.

From Esna, tomb 275. Ex Danson collection. Liverpool Museum 1977.110.2. H: 8.6 cm. W: 4.8 cm.

Except for the dwarfism this figurine conforms closely to the appearance of the male lion demon shown on one of the wands found with the statuette of a female magician, fig. no. 1. It also comes close to the image of Aha/Bes as it appears in the early New Kingdom. The body has become distinctly dwarfish in the limbs and buttocks. The moulded technique and the soft paste of which it is manufactured made it impossible to reproduce the holes in the hands for holding snakes, but the pose is retained.

The cemetery from which it comes was excavated by John Garstang between 1905 and 1906, on the heroic scale com-

nostril through the corners of the mouth to the chin. The chin is square, the cheeks extremely wide and flat below high cheek-bones. The body, despite the prominent genitalia, is boyish. There are few indications of musculature or bone; the torso is smooth and fleshy with a pot belly and prominent navel. The limbs are rounded and youthful. The arms are abnormally short in relation to the legs, which increases the childlike appearance. The arms are held so that the clenched hands appear to present the genitalia. The hands are drilled through, like those of fig. 1, so may have been intended to hold snake wands, although no trace of them now remains. The figure stands on a 1.0 cm high kidney-shaped support, tall in relation to its own height. The tail is cut out, and runs from the base of the spine to the feet

From Sidmant, locus 1300. Gift of the British School of

99

mon at the time, with a hundred workmen to one archaeologist, or occasionally two. The results were not published by Garstang, but nearly seventy years later in 1974 by Dorothy Downes from the records which survive in Liverpool and the objects now scattered in public and private collections far and wide. Most of the tombs were shafts with four to six small chambers opening off them, each originally containing a single burial. However, due to robbery, re-use and over-hasty excavation – which only rarely recorded the exact find-spot of an object – no single burial deposit can be reconstructed. As a result the context provides only a date range between the earliest and latest object in the group which can be independently dated. This group appears to contain pottery and beads of the late Middle Kingdom, but also amulets certainly of New Kingdom type.

Downes, *Esna*, p. 52, 275 and p. 106, fig. 90; cf. Wallis, *Ceramic Art 1900*, pl. II.

100 A MAGICIAN'S WAND

Dynasty XIII, 1786–1650 BC.

Bronze cobra, in two pieces but almost complete. The cobra rears upwards, and the body (0.5 cm wide) twists in an elaborate series of coils, the tail eventually turning back over it. The coils seem to be original and not due to the crushing of the metal during burial. The markings of the hood are represented by a simple pattern of incised lines.

From tomb 5, under the Ramesseum at Thebes. Gift of the

Egyptian Research Account. Fitzwilliam E.63.1896. H: 7.0 cm. L: 16.0 cm.

This unique object was found 'entangled in a mass of hair', possibly a wig, with the statuette of a female magician holding cobras, fig. no. 1. This cobra is a larger version of the snake wands held by the statuette, and if we are right in treating the group as the equipment of a professional magician we may suppose it to be the actual wand used in the recitation of magic spells. The cobra displayed itself on the brow of Pharaoh, where it bore the title 'Great of Magic'. It was considered a potent force for both good and evil, and its depiction on magic knives shows that this power provided an important weapon in the magician's hands.

The bronze, we presume, was grasped in the middle where the body flattens out. The workmanship is simple, the metal being beaten, incised and rolled, and there are no obvious signs of wear.

Quibell, *Ramesseum*, p. 3, pl. III; cf. for workmanship, gold uraeus of King Nubkheperre Inyotef of Dynasty XVII, Aldred, *Jewels of the Pharaohs*, fig. 82.

101 CLAPPERS

Late Dynasty XII to Dynasty XIII, 1862–1650 BC.

Pair of inlaid ivory clappers with terminals in the form of cow and duck heads. The inlays have disappeared except in the cavities, which held the horns of the cow. The cow's ears were also made separately and attached, and only part of one remains. The clappers were made of a single hippopotamus horn split in two, and the rounded outer surface has been deftly worked to suggest the features of the cow's head, snout, nostril, chin, ear, and eye outlined with an incised line and a hole drilled for the inlaid pupil. The ducks' heads are more summarily treated, and the bill of one of them has broken off. There is a small hole drilled in each clapper behind the head of the duck, and through this passed a tie which originally joined them together.

Gift of G. D. Hornblower. Fitzwilliam E.151a–b.1939. H: 18.8 cm. W: 6.5 cm.

The accompaniment to singing and dancing was often rhythmic hand clapping unaccompanied by other instruments. Clappers such as these, knocked against each other like castanets, supplemented and eventually replaced the human hand. Music was the sphere of Hathor, goddess of beauty and fecundity, special protectress of women, children

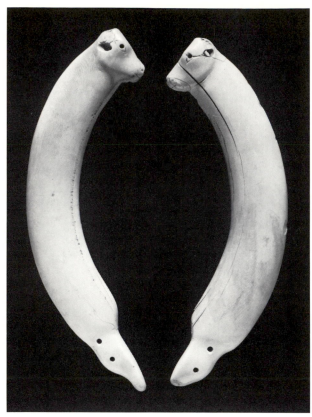

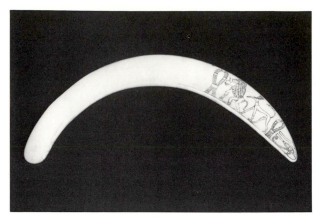

102

and the dead. The cow was her sacred animal, so is an appropriate decoration for a clapper. Rhythmic chanting was an important element in magic rituals, so it is not surprising to find the best parallel for these clappers in a pair from Kahun found with a statuette of a female lion demon like the one being impersonated by the magician from the Ramesseum tomb, fig. no. 1. They were part of the everyday lives of Egyptians, and as such have been found as often in houses as in tombs. A puzzling feature of all clappers made of ivory is their fragility and the fact that although they are often found broken, they rarely show signs of wear on the inside.

Cf. Petrie, *Kahun*, p. 30, pl. VII; for clappers in general, *Egypt's Golden Age*, pp. 261–2 and bibliography there cited.

MAGIC KNIVES AND RODS

102 MAGIC KNIFE

Late Dynasty XII, 1862–1787 BC.

Magic knife made of hippopotamus ivory showing a procession of apotropaic animals, deities and hieroglyphs moving from left to right. There are modern repairs and minor restorations. The design is incomplete but begins with the *sa* hieroglyph, which means 'protection', and takes its shape from a shelter made of reeds; next a baboon (see Cat. no. 106)

carrying a lamp and another *sa* sign; the animal of the god Seth (see Cat. no. 156); another *sa* sign; and the *wedjat* eye, the eye of the god Horus, see Cat. nos. 69–70, 172. The procession lies between two parallel lines and the draughtsman has shown great skill in enlarging the figures to take account of the increasing width of the ivory.

From Thebes. Gift of D. C. Robertson. Royal Museum of Scotland 1921.893. H: 5.5 cm. L: 33.5 cm.

The quality of the drawing, probably incised on the ivory with a flint tool, is outstanding. Many of the one hundred or so magic knives which survive are engraved in a summary, negligent style and, unlike this one, are clearly not the work of a draughtsman of the highest skill. The line is supremely assured and smooth and the composition elegant and well balanced. These qualities in particular have attracted artists past and present to the art of Egypt. Henry Moore and Eric Gill are examples from our own century.

The purpose of the knives was to confer protection by warding off evil forces, especially those threatening the most vulnerable – women, especially pregnant or nursing women, and children. The very few which are inscribed make their purpose clear. A knife divided between New York and the Louvre, whose fine engraving and subject matter also make it a good parallel for the Edinburgh knife, is inscribed 'Words spoken by the multitude of amuletic figures: We have come in order to protect the lady Meriseneb' (Steindorff, *Magical Knives*, p. 46, figs. 6, 7). The lady Meriseneb is a living person, like the other women and children to whom the inscribed wands are dedicated. This knife may be placed in Altenmüller's group V, which he dates to the late XIIth Dynasty. If further confirmation were needed, there is a scene on the wall of the XIIIth Dynasty tomb of Bebi at El Kab which shows a procession of nurses carrying objects almost certainly knives, with one distinct rounded and one pointed end. It has been suggested that the incantation of spells may have been accompanied by the rubbing of some magic substance against the flat unincised surface of the knives.

Aldred, *Middle Kingdom Art*, no. 54; scene from the tomb of Bebi, Wildung, *L'Age d'Or*, fig. 85 (incorrectly identified as the tomb of Sobeknakht); generally, Steindorff, *Magical Knives*, passim; H. Altenmüller in *Welt des Orients* 14 (1983), pp. 30–45; *id* in *SAK* 13 (1986), 1–27.

103 FRAGMENT OF A MAGIC KNIFE

Late Dynasty XIII, 1750–1650 BC.

Half of a magic knife made of hippopotamus ivory, showing a procession moving from left to right, consisting of apotropaic animals and mythical beasts, each one holding a knife. The cortège begins with a frog (see Cat. no. 112b) representing the goddess Heket, followed by a seated lion with its tongue extended; a serpent-necked feline; a crocodile representing the god Sobek (see Cat. no. 109); and a striding lion. The knife has been repaired in two places.

Gift of G. D. Hornblower. Fitzwilliam E.40.1926. H: 2.5 cm. L: 16.2 cm.

103

Another magic knife is known which carries the words 'cut off the head of the enemy when he enters the chamber of the children whom the lady has borne' (Steindorff, *Magical Knives*, p. 50). The beasts therefore commonly carry knives. No two magic knives duplicate each other exactly, but there is a common repertoire and all the beings shown here are favourites. Heket was a goddess thought to protect children in the womb and during birth and its aftermath; lions were the ubiquitous symbol of ferocity and strength, whether royal (Cat. no. 138) or divine, and crocodiles represented the god Sobek, whose cult was particularly popular from late Dynasty XII to the end of the Middle Kingdom, see Cat. no. 109. Serpent-necked felines occur in Middle Kingdom iconography in only two contexts: as here, on magic knives, and in a few tombs at el Bersha and Beni Hasan, where they appear in scenes of hunting, alongside the natural flora and fauna of the desert. The desert was, in antiquity as now, greatly feared, especially at night, as the abode of the dead, of spirits and of monsters. At the same time the division between the natural and supernatural world, which we cling to so firmly, hardly existed for the ancient Egyptian, so there would be no incongruity to them in placing a wholly mythical beast between the familiar lion and crocodile. In his unpublished study of the iconography of magic knives, Altenmüller places this one in his group VIII, which he dates to the late XIIIth Dynasty.

H. Altenmüller in *SAK* 13 (1986), pp. 17, 19.

104 SEGMENTS FROM TWO MAGIC RODS

Late Dynasty XII to Dynasty XIII, 1862–1650 BC.

Rectangular pieces of steatite, possibly originally glazed, each with a large hole 0.9 cm wide drilled through from end to end. Four segments, held together by a pin passing through the hole, made up a complete rod. Each of these segments comes from a different rod. The long side of each one is carved in relief. (a) has on each side a crouched lion followed by a crocodile, but on one side the crocodile's jaw gapes open ready to bite. It is the first or last segment of a rod so carries the head of a leopard in relief on the end. (b) has on one side a crocodile and a *sa* sign, the hieroglyph meaning protection (Cat. no. 102), and on the other a cat, Cat. no. 108. The top of each segment has a hole approximately 0.6 cm wide to take the tenon of one of the tiny figurines (see Cat. no. 105) which reproduced in the round the figures carved in relief on the sides. They would have been placed at regular intervals (3.8 cm apart, as shown by the remains of a second hole in a), seven to a complete rod.

104a, b

(a) Gift of the Trustees of the Wellcome collection (b) gift of Jack Ogden. Fitzwilliam (a) E.426.1982. H: 2.0 cm. L: 5.8 cm. (b) E.2.1986. H: 1.5 cm. L: 4.6 cm.

A magic rod in four sections, complete with seven small figurines, is in the Metropolitan Museum of Art in New York. It was acquired as part of the collection of Lord Carnarvon, and was found in the same tomb near Heliopolis as Cat. nos. 112 and 119, which the Fitzwilliam acquired from G. D. Hornblower. This is the only complete example known, but

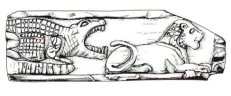

104a, b

individual segments or the accompanying figurines are not uncommon and others may exist unrecognised in collections and excavation reports. Segments of rods have been found at Thebes (with fig. no. 1), Kahun, Lisht (unpublished), Heliopolis and Byblos, all in late Middle Kingdom cemeteries and settlements but in contexts not more precisely datable. Further unprovenanced examples exist in the British Museum, and are known to have existed in 1898 in the Macgregor collection. A fragment of a glazed steatite rectangular bar EGA.1146.1943 exists in the Fitzwilliam Museum from the Gayer-Anderson collection, inscribed with the personal name and throne name of Senusret III. It is only half the width of the magic rod segments, and just over a centimetre in length, but it is pierced through in exactly the same way. The top and bottom are too narrow to bear small figurines, but each is incised instead with the figure of a crocodile. The bar must have served a similar purpose to the magic rods and the royal name provides a *terminus post quem* for their occurrence.

The iconography as well as the date range of the magic rods is simliar to that of magic knives and they are sometimes found together, see above p. 110. All the examples known to me are made of steatite, often with traces of glaze remaining.

Fischer, *Turtles*, no. 92, fig. 21, pl. 19; Kemp and Merrillees, *Minoan Pottery*, pp. 163–4; Wallis, *Ceramic Art 1898*, p. 15, figs. 22–3; Petrie, *Kahun*, pl. VIII, 11; Quibell, *Ramesseum*, pl. III.

APOTROPAIC STATUETTES

105 TURTLE FROM A MAGIC ROD
Late Dynasty XII to Dynasty XIII, 1862–1650 BC.

Wooden figurine of a water turtle, *trionyx triunguis*, with a small hole in the underside for a tenon which would have fitted into one of the holes in the top of a magic rod, cf. Cat. no. 104. The figurine has been repaired and the four feet have become worn down; the carapace is represented realistically by a carefully executed, incised criss-cross pattern.

Gift of G. D. Hornblower. Fitzwillliam E.166.1939. L: 4.8 cm. W: 3.7 cm.

A glazed steatite turtle was among the figurines found with the magic rod now in the Metropolitan Museum (26.7.1275), see Cat. no. 104, and although smaller it provides an extremely close parallel to this one.

Turtles are among the recurring representations on magic rods and knives offering protection against the malign forces of death, disease and night. Henry Fischer has suggested that the turtle was identified with the dark powers because of his hidden existence under the waters of the Nile. His flesh, although very good to eat, was proscribed, but the shell was used for various purposes and the internal organs were used in medicine.

Cf. Fischer, *Turtles*, Frontispiece (top, right), pp. 30–1, pl. 19.

106 LION AND BABOON
Late Dynasty XII to Dynasty XIII, 1862–1650 BC.

Figurines of (a) a lion and (b) a baboon standing upright, modelled by hand in Egyptian faience. Details of face, mane and paws painted in dark brown. The rectangular bases upon which both figures stand are also dark brown. The heads are disproportionately large, like those of the incised figures on magic knives and rods which they closely resemble. The lion (a) has been restored from fragments.

From Abydos, Garstang excavations of 1907, tomb 416. Ashmolean E.3275, E.3299 respectively. (a) H: 8.3 cm. W: 2.8 cm. (b) H: 7.2 cm. W: 3.4 cm.

These figurines, like Cat. nos. 105, 107–110, are clearly three-dimensional versions of the protective demons which appear on magic rods and knives, Cat. nos. 102–4. Their function may have been the same as that of the small figurines attached to magic rods. It may have been a necessary adjunct to the ritual involving magic knives to have

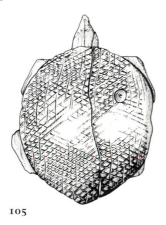

105

106a, b

three-dimensional images of the individual demons which were depicted on them.

Tomb 416 contained a Minoan vase, and for that reason, and because it was never fully published by Garstang, it has been the subject of an exhaustive study by Barry Kemp and Robert Merrillees. The cat, Cat. no. 108, is also from the tomb. The poor record of the excavation, coupled with the fact that the original number and sequence of the burials in the tomb will never be known, make the results of their study, as they admit, inconclusive. Stephen Snape has reconstructed the whole excavation of which 416 was a part and we will understand the context better, even if we cannot date it more precisely, when his work is published.

Garstang in *LAAA* 5 (1913), pp. 107–11; Kemp and Merrillees, *Minoan Pottery*, pp. 105–75.

107 HEAD OF A SNAKE
Late Dynasty XII to Dynasty XIII, 1862–1650 BC.

Egyptian faience figurine of a snake, broken off behind the head. The 'faience' is deep turquoise in colour with details painted black. The snake was modelled by hand; the wrinkles under the neck, the mouth and the eyes were incised in the paste before firing. The markings of the skin are represented by a pattern of black dots.

Bequest of Sir Robert Greg. Fitzwilliam E.377.1954. H: 2.0 cm. L: 3.7 cm.

This is another representation of the figures which appear on magic knives, but figurines of snakes are rare – the only other example known to me is from the North Pyramid cemetery at Lisht. The beneficent demons on the knives are usually shown biting or crushing snakes and it is often argued from this that the particular role of the knives was to provide protection against snakebite. Snakes, however, symbolised a multitude of evil forces, and in the New Kingdom *Book of the Dead* the great serpent Apophis was their chief embodiment. Nevertheless, there were also benign serpent demons, guardians of fertility (whose image appears on beds) and protectors of the dead. This head surely belonged to one of these.

It was bought by Robert Greg from a Cairo dealer, so its attribution to the Middle Kingdom depends entirely on its style.

Cf. Hayes, *Scepter*, I, p. 227.

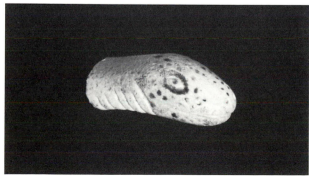

107

108 CAT
Late Dynasty XII to Dynasty XIII, 1862–1650 BC.

Egyptian faience figurine of a cat, poised to jump. Its back is arched, its front legs outstretched, the back ones bent. The tail is curled around the right leg. It has been modelled by hand and set on a rectangular base, edged with deep purple. The fur (represented by horizontal dashes), nose, eyes and brows have been picked out in deep purple. There is some unevenness of colour, which ranges from pale turquoise to deep blue, due to uneven firing and fading of the glaze, and both ears are broken off.

108

From Abydos, Garstang excavations of 1907, tomb 416. Department of Egyptology, University of Liverpool E.160. H: 4.2 cm. L: 7.1 cm.

This figurine represents no cosy domestic pet but a half-feral predator. Dogs had been part of the domestic scene since the Old Kingdom, appearing in scenes of hunting but also in a more intimate setting under the tomb owner's chair, and accompanying him on walks. Many of them have pet names. Cats, on the other hand, only appear in such scenes from Dynasty XII onwards and are not at this time given names, but just called 'the Cat'. They are shown hunting game in the desert or the marshy stretches of the river, and it is their aggressive hunting skills which probably originally led to their domestication. They would have provided efficient protection against rats and possibly snakes. Perhaps it was this role which led them to be included in the repertoire of images and figurines on, and associated with, magic knives and rods, see Cat. nos. 102–4. A 'faience' head of a cat from Kahun town emphasises that the magical protection such figures offered applied equally to the living and the dead.

For the date of tomb 416, see Cat. no. 106. Kemp and Merrillees, *Minoan Pottery*, pp. 143–4, pls. 10, 11, 15, 16; *ILN* (27 July 1907), p. 137; cf. H. G. Fischer in *MMJ* 12 (1977), p. 178, n. 32; for cats hunting in the desert, Newberry, *Beni Hasan*, I, pl. xxx.

109 CROCODILE
Late Dynasty XII to Dynasty XIII, 1862–1650 BC.

Wooden crocodile figurine. Carved naturalistically in the soft wood, with some wear on the snout. The bulbous nose, heavy brow-ridge, hump of skin and muscle at the back of

the neck, contracted legs, markings of the skin and tail-ridge are reproduced with care, indicating considerable familiarity with the reptile's appearance. The crocodile is shown with its mouth shut, in contrast to Cat. no. 104a.

From Kahun. University College 16741. H: 1.4 cm. L: 9.4 cm.

This figurine comes from the town of Kahun but could equally well have been found in a tomb. Crocodiles were greatly feared (but see also Cat. no. 172), and as a consequence they are, with lions, the most commonly represented animal on the instruments of protective magic, see Cat. nos 103–4. In the mid-second millennium they were still common in the marshes of the Faiyum, the fertile depression fed by a tributary of the Nile, about forty miles south of Memphis, where Kahun was situated. Nowadays crocodiles in Egypt are confined to the extreme south of the country, but stories still circulate of sudden and ferocious attacks on unlucky fishermen or bathers.

The Faiyum was a centre of royal irrigation and building projects from the reign of Senusret I onwards. The cultivable land was increased and royal funerary complexes, palaces and temples were built there. The principal god of the region was Sobek, the crocodile god, and this royal favouritism is reflected in the number of personal names containing the name and of references to his cult in inscriptions which survive, see Cat. no. 172. The Faiyum, a favourite resort for hunting and shooting until the Second World War, is still a pleasant place, full of gardens, orchards and groves of pine trees.

Petrie, *Illahun*, p. 11, pl. VIII, 2; cf. Wildung, *L'Age d'Or*, fig. 145.

are very much alike. Their charm has always made them attractive to collectors, so ensuring their survival, but as a consequence most of them have no details of provenance or associated objects. Their attribution to Dynasties XII–XIII is undoubted, but more precise dates or distribution can be deduced only from the few published examples from excavations. This particular example can be more closely dated than most on the basis of the associated objects in tomb 655 at Beni Hasan.

The purpose of these figurines is not certain. They are not part of the usual repertoire of protective animals found on magic knives and rods, but hedgehogs occur in tomb reliefs at Beni Hasan and elsewhere, in scenes of hunting in the desert, where many of the protective beasts, lions and cats for example, also occur. The hedgehogs appear there as part of the 'backdrop' for the hunting scenes, set in a desert landscape. The 'faience' figurines which occur in burials are from shaft tombs with small rock-cut burial chambers. These tombs contain no limestone reliefs, since they belonged to people without the resources to command such expensive funerary monuments. Perhaps the hedgehog is provided to suggest the ambiance of the hunt and the desert of the Afterlife, where the excitement of the chase exists without fear or danger.

Garstang, *Beni Hasan*, pp. 142, 234, fig. 140; *ILN* (2 April 1955), p. 605; for hedgehogs, V. von Droste zu Hülshoff, *Der Igel im alten Ägypten* (Hildesheim, 1980), passim.

110 HEDGEHOG

Early Dynasty XII, 1963–1862 BC.

Egyptian faience figurine of a hedgehog, standing on an oval base. The colour is a deep turquoise blue, slightly darker on the underside. Only the head and feet are modelled, and details are emphasised in blue–black paint under the glaze. The ears, eyes, brows, claws and spines are marked, and the edge of the base is also painted blue–black. The tip of the nose has been restored.

From Beni Hasan, tomb 655. Ex Macgregor collection. Bequest of Sir Robert Greg. Fitzwilliam E.345.1954. H: 3.8 cm. L: 6.3 cm.

Small 'faience' figurines of hedgehogs turn up sporadically in most large cemeteries of the Middle Kingdom. They differ from each other in small details – the spines may be shown in relief or the feet shown free of the base – but in essentials, in style of representation, in material, colour and size, they

110

111 HIPPOPOTAMUS

Dynasties XII–XIII, 1963–1650 BC.

Large Egyptian faience turquoise–green statuette of a hippopotamus, covered with water-lilies. The feet have been restored and the paint is a little faded. The water-lilies are outlined in blue–black pigment under the glaze, and the facial features, eyes, snout and ears have been realistically modelled by hand, and then outlined in the same blue–black pigment. The decoration is not applied haphazardly, but arranged so as to exploit the contours of the hippopotamus's body. The stem of one of the blue lotus flowers runs up the beast's face and the flower itself spreads between its ears; tiny leaf pads lie on its bulging cheeks, their stems curving around the nostrils. Each flank bears an enormous lotus flower, and another lies on the rump. On its back is a circular floral design, which may represent the fully extended water-lily seen from above.

From Thebes. Ex Reverend Greville Chester collection. British Museum EA. 35004. H: 9.2 cm. L: 18.8 cm.

The naturalism of this statuette suggests that Egyptians were familiar with the sight of these gigantic beasts rising from the waters of the Nile covered with river weeds and flowers. Their image appears on countless amulets and small figurines of wood, stone, pottery and 'faience', both fine and crudely made, found in houses as well as tombs. The hippopotamus clearly had as important a place in popular belief as the crocodile or the lion, but what exactly was it? We can see some strands of it, but certainly not all. Cults of a bull hippopotamus were established in a few places, and there is evidence that the animal was in some situations to be identified with the evil god Seth, opponent of Horus and slayer of Osiris. The frequency with which they are represented suggests that they themselves were greatly feared, despite the placid expression on the face of this fine example. Free passage on the great river was an essential to daily life in Egypt, and crossing the river was an image for the passage through death to the next life. Hippopotami are known to be a considerable hazard to boats, so for both kinds of journey it was essential at least to avoid coming into conflict with them, if not to seek their active protection. Fear of them may have inspired the scene of the weighing of the heart at the Judgement of the Dead in later New Kingdom papyri, where a monstrous, ravening hippopotamus waits to devour the hearts of the damned. In burials the 'faience' statuettes were placed inside the coffin close to the body, under the feet or in the small of the back, token of their great protective power.

Scenes of hunting hippopotami occur conventionally in Old Kingdom tombs, but it is unlikely that they were still hun-

III

119

ted in the Middle Kingdom. We cannot even be sure, in the absence of physical evidence of their bones, that they were still to be found in Egypt in the Middle Kingdom. Their ivory was plentiful, however, and the images made of them suggest they were often to be observed. The hippopotami which occur in hunting scenes in Middle Kingdom tombs are part of the flora and fauna of the Nilotic landscape, not the object of the hunt. These Nilotic scenes always form the bottom of a hunting scene, the desert scene providing the top. The blue–green 'faience' hippopotami seem to embody the most important elements of the scene: the blue–green water, the plants, birds and insects (also occasionally incorporated into the body decoration), in addition to the great River Horse itself. Since the statuettes have been found only in burials in small chambers or graves without relief decoration, it may be that they are in effect substitutes for the full scene.

Despite the numerous examples of 'faience' hippopotami, in a variety of poses, which survive in public collections, many do not come from excavated contexts. They have been collected as enthusiastically as the 'faience' hedgehogs, Cat. no. 110, and as a result only a handful are independently datable from objects found with them. These suggest that they were placed in tombs throughout the XIIth and XIIIth Dynasties, but perhaps became more popular during the latter Dynasty. While many examples have come from the west bank at Thebes, especially the Middle Kingdom cemeteries at Dra Abû el-Naga, they have turned up at other sites from the Delta (Kom el-Hisn) to Kerma in the Sudan.

H. R. Hall in *JEA* 13 (1927), pp. 57–8, pl. XXIIIb; in general, see L. Keimer in *Revue de L'Egypte Ancienne* 2 (1929), pp. 210–53; Kemp and Merrillees, *Minoan Pottery*, pp. 144–5; B. Bothmer in *Boston Bulletin* 49 (1951), pp 99–102; H. W. Müller in *Pantheon* 23 (1975), pp. 287–92; for dating in early Dynasty XII, see Beni Hasan tomb 51, Garstang, *Beni Hasan*, p. 213, and in Dynasty XIII, tomb 25 in the Asâsîf at Thebes, Carnarvon and Carter, *Five Years*, pp. 54–5, pl. LI.

112 HIPPOPOTAMUS, FROG AND JERBOA

Late Dynasty XII to Dynasty XIII, 1862–1650 BC.

(a) Head of a hippopotamus in green Egyptian 'faience'; (b) frog, also in green 'faience' with detail in brown pigment under the glaze and traces of probably modern blue pigment between front legs; (c) jerboa (desert rat) in white 'faience' with details picked out in brown pigment. The hippopotamus is of an unusually homogeneous pale green colour, and there is no trace of any painted decoration. The modelling of snout, ears, eyes and nostrils is strong and realistic and these features were originally picked out in a pigment which has almost completely faded away. The head has been broken from a statuette of a standing hippopotamus, to judge from the angle of the head. The frog, also naturalistically modelled by hand, sits on an oval base (a water-lily pad?) and has a small hole, 0.4 cm wide, in the base, pierced before firing. The eyes and the stripes down the back, like the markings on the front and back legs, are emphasised in brown pigment.

The jerboa sits with its front paws up to its mouth and its tail curled around its body almost reaching the mouth. Eyes, tip of tail, claws, fur and nose are all picked out in brown pigment.

From a tomb at el-Matarîya. Gift of G. D. Hornblower. Fitzwilliam E.277–9.1939. (a) H: 7.5 cm. W: 5.0 cm. (b) H: 3.6 cm. W: 4.2 cm. (c) H: 4.1 cm. W: 2.7 cm.

These objects came from a vaulted brick tomb discovered by Bedouin about 1913 at el-Matarîya near Heliopolis, in the desert just north of Cairo. They were first recorded in 1928 by Ludwig Keimer when they formed part of the stock of Maurice Nahman, a well-known Cairo antiquities dealer. There were many other objects in the find: stone vases, numerous animal figurines, a complete magic rod (see Cat. no. 104), the female figurine, Cat. no. 119, and models of food. They were bought by several private collectors, and most have by now found their way into public museums – the British Museum, the Metropolitan Museum, New York and the Brooklyn Museum in addition to the Fitzwilliam. The four figurines in Cambridge were brought from Nahman by G. D. Hornblower and presented by him to the Fitzwilliam in 1939.

The problems presented in trying to date the group illustrate well the difficulties encountered over and over again in examining objects obtained in Egypt during the early years of this century. Many come like these from illicit excavations or from excavations which were never published or too succinctly published to satisfy the demands of modern scholarship. Hornblower's own publication of the female figurine, Cat. no. 119, is instructive. Like most collectors, he is interested in the object itself, and the figure's context and its relationship to the other objects in the group seem hardly important at all. But we need to investigate these thoroughly if we want to know the figure's purpose and precise date.

It seems unlikely that the objects, judging by the list reconstructed by Kemp and Merrillees, represent the contents of a single burial. There were, for example, at least six figurines of hippopotami in 'faience' and one of terracotta. In this case we cannot assume that the objects form a single deposit, each dating the others by their association. The group as it survives is woefully incomplete, the stone vessels having been lost, while the pottery, which would have been the most sensitive indicator of date, was not even collected by the robbers. Perhaps we could not expect desert Bedouin in 1913 to be aware of the potential of ceramic studies.

When Keimer described the group in 1928 it seems the head of the hippopotamus had not broken away from its body, since he describes 'un petit hippopotame en faience verte, sans décoration'. Undecorated hippopotami are rare, and ones of this quality even rarer, so one cannot but lament the carelessness which has separated the head from the body. The frog is pierced in the base like the small frogs or toads associated with magic rods and knives, and like them probably represents Heket, one of the goddesses associated with childbirth. The jerboa, like the hedgehog, Cat. no. 110, may be present merely to suggest the desert landscape in which the real and mythical creatures generating protective magic dwelt.

112c, b, a

Hippopotamus head, W. M. Compton in *Ancient Egypt* (March 1931), p. 26, fig. 6; whole group, Kemp and Merrillees, *Minoan Pottery*, pp. 163–4; L. Keimer in *BIFAO* 28 (1929), pp. 49–50.

113 PAIR OF WRESTLERS

Late Dynasty XII to Dynasty XIII, 1862–1650 BC.

Painted limestone statuette of two men wrestling. One man stands with his feet apart, grasping his opponent by his upper arms, and the other kneels, trying to throw him off balance. It is a trial of strength and both men thrust their chins forward with the effort. The pose is accurately depicted but the figures are very schematically carved, the facial features, apart from the large painted eyes, hardly present at all. The two figures are not fully carved out, but reach for each other over a central block. This makes them virtually two-dimensional, but solves the sculptor's problem of finding support for figures in active motion. Most of the original paint remains. The bodies are reddish-brown, eyes are black and white, hair is black; their short kilts are white with blue stripes and, unrealistically, each wears a necklace, repre-

113

sented as a white stripe with alternate blue and black spots, and a bracelet.

From Abydos, Garstang excavations of 1907, tomb 416. Ashmolean E.3297. H: 7.8 cm. W: 10.4 cm.

Taken at face value, this modest statuette represents two men taking part in a popular sport and entertainment. Depictions of men wrestling occur in private tombs in both the Old Kingdom and Middle Kingdom, and among scenes of battle as well as scenes of sport and leisure activities. The upper part of one large wall in a tomb at Beni Hasan is entirely given over to a sequence of pairs of wrestlers demonstrating over 200 different holds. The statuette is an almost three-dimensional version of one stance in the series. However, nothing in ancient Egypt is ever simply what it appears to be, and the precise reason for this statuette's presence in the tomb escapes us. Such statuettes were not simply funerary, since similar ones appear in the houses at Kahun. It may be significant that the two men dressed exactly alike are engaged in combat, since so many Egyptian magical practices involved a struggle between opposing forces. For the date see Cat. no. 106.

Kemp and Merrillees, *Minoan Pottery*, pp. 145–6, pls. 10–11, 13, 17; cf. Klebs, *Reliefs*, pp. 151–2; Newberry, *Beni Hasan*, II, pl. V; J. Cooney in *JNES* 12 (1953) p. 5, pl. IX B; *Burlington Fine Arts Club*, 1895, p. 10, no. 53, pl. XXIII, 187.

114 DWARF

Late Dynasty XII to Dynasty XIII, 1862–1650 BC.

Egyptian faience male dwarf figurine, broken off below the knees. There is some restoration of neck and chest which includes the painted necklace. The figure is a bright turquoise blue with details emphasised or added in blue-black paint under the glaze. The head is enormous in proportion to the body, the skull elongated and flat-topped, with the (presumably) shaven hair represented by black spots. The forehead bulges and the eyes are wide open and disproportionately large. The nose is short but very broad, and the mouth very wide with straight lips. The ears stick out from the head at right angles but are not noticeably large. The body, compared

114

Leyden 348, recto 12.6, quoted by Gardiner in *Hastings Encyclopaedia of Religion and Ethics* under Magic (Egyptian) p. 266.

FEMALE FIGURINES

115 FEMALE DWARF AND HER CHILD

Late Dynasty XII to Dynasty XIII, 1862–1650 BC.

Wooden statuette, gessoed and painted, of a naked female dwarf walking with right leg forward and holding a child in her left arm. Part of the left foot and the back of the head, including the left ear, are missing. The statuette is carved out of a single piece of wood; rectangular tangs have been attached to the feet and drilled with two, possibly three, holes. The woman's hair has been drawn back from the front of her head into three bunches, each of which is made up of small plaits. The bunches, one of which has almost completely disappeared, are painted black and hang down to the middle of her back. The whole body, including the face, was once covered in reddish-brown pigment over a thin layer of fine plaster. The features of the face are outlined in black. The brows are represented in paint only. The eyes are huge, wide open, with black pupils; inner and outer canthi are marked as red dots on the white gessoed surface of the iris. The right ear is large and oval with a prominent outer rim and lobe. The nose is short and broad with strongly marked nostrils. The philtrum is present and there is a corresponding notch in the upper lip. The lower lip is straight and full. The chin is square and the cheeks flat. In curious contrast to the

with the naturalism of Cat. no. 115, is grotesque, its deformity apparently deliberately exaggerated. The arms are short and stubby, the fingers merely suggested by painted lines, and the stomach and buttocks project sharply. The genitalia are not shown, although the dwarf wears a girdle with a round pendant in the middle around his hips.

Fitzwilliam E.60.1984. H: 7.2 cm. W: 4.2 cm.

This figurine almost certainly came from a grave, since numerous examples, in a variety of poses, have been found in cemeteries in the Faiyum area (Haraga and Lisht) and at Abydos. The figurine is naked, without attributes of any kind, so that its function in the context of the grave goods remains open to different interpretations. Dwarfs appear relatively frequently in tomb scenes, on stelae and as statuettes in the round, as servants or companions of the tomb owner, and sometimes as the owner of a tomb himself. In the latter case, their deformity may not be shown at all, or it may be disguised by the skill of the artist.

Another context in which dwarfs occur is that of fertility and particularly childbirth. A magical papyrus recommends that a woman wears a 'dwarf of clay' during childbirth, and the demon Aha, later called Bes, is often shown with a dwarfish body, see Cat. no. 98. There is some evidence to show that ritual dances, perhaps associated with funeral celebrations, were also commonly performed by dwarfs.

As in the case of the female fertility figures, those physical aspects of the figure which were of particular magical significance are exaggerated to the point of caricature: the large head, the prominent stomach and buttocks, the short arms and legs. It is not the dwarf's survival into eternity which is at stake here, but the service he performed in the life of the tomb owner.

Cf. Engelbach, *Harageh*, pl. XIV, 9; Kemp and Merrillees, *Minoan Pottery*, pp. 138–9, 162–3, pls. 14, 23; D. Silverman in *Serapis*, 1 (1969), pp. 53–61; 'dwarf of clay' from Pap.

115

plump curves of the buttocks and thighs, the breasts are pendulous and almost flat. The stomach is gently rounded, with a deep, round navel, and the vulva, unusually, is marked. The modelling of buttocks, legs and arms is very skilled, the artist lovingly reproducing every curve and wrinkle of flesh in his pliant medium. The arms and legs are abnormally short, but there is no trace of caricature in the naturalistic treatment. The child, held in its mother's arm, sprawls realistically with one leg on her thigh and another against her back. Its features reproduce hers in miniature, but the proportions of the body appear to be normal. The skull is shaved, and appears elongated. The woman originally held an object in her clenched right hand and her fist has been drilled to take it.

From Abydos, Garstang excavations of 1907, locus 352. Department of Egyptology, University of Liverpool E.7081. H: 18.4 cm. W: 6.5 cm.

This is one of the finest of the servant figures to survive from the Middle Kingdom. We may presume that it was placed in the tomb so that it might carry out in the Next World whatever duties such a servant had performed in the household. Dwarfs occur frequently enough in the scenes of daily life in larger tombs to show that they were present as servants, possibly as entertainers, and here as maids or perhaps nurses. The fact that she is naked and carrying a child suggests she also functioned as an image of fertility and sexuality, see Cat. nos. 116–21.

This object was found with a statuette of a lion, possibly similar to Cat. no. 106a (Stephen Snape, personal communication), and examples have been recorded from other cemeteries. Lisht North Pyramid Cemetery produced the lower part of a statuette of a female dwarf of comparable quality. The woman wears yet another version of the tripartite hairstyle (cf. Cat. no. 118) worn by young girls and women of subordinate status.

The holes in the tangs attached to the feet suggest that a rod or pin was passed through them, perhaps to strengthen the base into which the tangs fitted. The large head with its long hair made the statuette top heavy so that extra support would be needed.

ILN (27 July 1907), p. 137; for wooden female dwarfs and dancing ivory dwarfs from Lisht, see Hayes, *Scepter*, I, p. 222, fig. 139.

116 TORSO OF A GIRL

Late Dynasty XII to Dynasty XIII, 1862–1650 BC.

Limestone torso of a girl, arms broken off at the shoulders, head at the neck and legs above the knee. She is shown naked with her legs apart, and her body was originally covered in a pink wash, except for the pubic area which was painted black. Around the waist, dipping down over the thighs and across the genitalia, are faint traces of a cowrie bead girdle (see Cat. no. 154) painted in red and black. The statue has quite a different appearance from the front and the back. The front shows traces of a painted necklace, now no more than alternate blobs of red and black at the base of the neck. There is a long, unevenly incised vertical line from neck to navel,

116

the breasts are small, high and pointed, the stomach flat and featureless and the navel round and deep. The pubic triangle is exceptionally large and outlined by roughly incised lines, and the thighs are roughly shaped. In contrast to the flat, asymmetrical carving of the front, the back, buttocks and back of the thighs express considerable sensuality through the sensitivity of the modelling, cf. Cat. no. 115. The line of the backbone deepens realistically at the small of the back. The buttocks are very broad, rounded and prominent. The wrinkles and the rolls of fat under them are carefully shown. The position of the arms is not certain, but the curve of the body suggests they were held outstretched, perhaps supporting an object above the head. Just below the neck, made as a separate piece and plastered into place in antiquity, is the bottom of a single plait of hair. This suggests a hairstyle like Cat. no. 140.

From Kahun. Manchester 268. H: 27.3 cm. W: 12.0 cm.

This is an extraordinary sculpture, and suggests that further surprises await us as town sites of the Middle Kingdom are excavated instead of the tombs and temples upon which attention has concentrated so far. In style and appearance it relates to the fertility figures, Cat. nos. 115, 118–120, although the (presumably) outstretched arms are unparalleled. However it is much larger, originally about half life-size. Could it be from a house or village shrine? Petrie does not illustrate it in his publication, and contents himself with a three-line description in the text. He does show a smaller male figure, also naked, carrying a basket on its head, which is somewhat similar in style though the simple sketch in the publication may be misleading. This statuette might offer a parallel for the position of the arms. Most unfortunately we have no evidence concerning the precise context and associations of the statue at Kahun. Was it a statue in its own right or a support for a tray of offerings or incense? We do not know, but its ritual purpose is certain, and so is its association with the eternal preoccupations of fertility and sexuality.

Petrie, *Illahun*, p. 11; (see generally) David, *Pyramid Builders*, p. 134.

117 FEMALE STATUETTE

Dynasties XII–XIII, 1963–1650 BC.

Ivory statuette of a young naked girl. She stands with her arms at her sides and her legs close together. The arms are made separately and attached to the shoulders by dowels. They move freely, but there is a pair of tiny holes in each thigh and the inside of the left wrist (the lower right arm is missing) which originally held small pegs to fix the arms in place against the body. The legs are broken off just below the knee, but the ivory base survives with a rectangular hole in it to take the tang which supported the feet. The head is beautifully shaped, and covered with tiny pin pricks (representing the shaved areas of the skull). There is a pattern of pairs of holes with a triple row on the forehead. Bronze rings, of which one remains, were threaded through the holes and held miniature plaits in place in an elaborate hairstyle. The face has suffered damage to nose and mouth, but was carved with considerable skill. The brows are a thin, curved, incised line, the eyes large and oval with sculpted iris and inlaid pupil, the chin round, the ears large with only the outer rim shown. The lobes are pierced to take double loop earrings made of silver wire 0.03 cm wide. The girl's body is slim, but attractively rounded and with no trace of exaggeration. The arms are stained black from the silver bangles wound around

them and the surviving hand shows long tapering fingers with nails marked.

From Hu, tomb w72. Gift of the Egypt Exploration Fund. Fitzwilliam E.16.1899. H: 12.5 cm. W: 4.0 cm.

This charming statuette may be the earliest representation from Egypt of a woman wearing earrings. It comes, unfortunately, from a plundered shaft tomb which originally contained at least six burials. The unpublished records of its excavation show that the precise disposition of objects within the chambers was not noted, and now the only items which can be confidently associated with the figure are the lower part of a pottery fertility figure, cf. Cat. no. 120, and a string of spheroid beads of 'faience', cf. Cat. no. 161. The whole range of finds from the tomb, most of which are now in the Fitzwilliam Museum, indicate the shaft was in use from the XIIth Dynasty (beads and stone vases) to the XIIIth Dynasty (pottery). In macabre contrast to the elegance of this figure, a skull from a nearby tomb (Hu Y354), probably of the same date though no other finds survive to confirm it, shows an earring still in place on the ear, and plaits still wound around the head. At Dendera a few miles south of Hu, in 1898, Petrie found an intact burial of a young woman wearing a 'spiral of silver and two beads in the left ear'. He dated the burial to the XIIth Dynasty, but illustrated only the mirror disk, scarabs and a red jasper shell (cf. Cat. no. 165b) from the group. They confirm his dating, the scarabs being suggestive of the late rather than the early XIIth Dynasty. The present statuette has parallels in Cairo and New York, but without the earrings. The Cairo example shows clearly how the plaits were attached to the metal rings, and in this case looped around the head.

Petrie, *Diospolis Parva*, pp. 43–4, pl. XXVI; Murray, *Splendour*, pl. XXIX, 1; Wilkinson, *Egyptian Jewellery*, p. 76, no. 6; cf. Petrie, *Dendereh*, p. 22, pl. XX, Group 751; Cairo statuette, Vandier, *La Statuaire Egyptienne*, pl. XLIX, 6.

118 FEMALE STATUETTE

Dynasties XII–XIII, 1963–1650 BC.

Limestone statuette of a girl, rounded off at the knees. She stands naked, with her legs together, her arms at her sides, and wearing an elaborate tripartite hairstyle. There are traces of black pigment on the hair and eyes. The hair is divided into two sections; the front hair frames the face, with two full side bunches reaching almost to the shoulders, and the back hair is divided into three long plaits which fall to below the shoulders. The features of the face are simply cut with the minimum of modelling, large oval eyes, broad nose, straight mouth and square chin. The figure is that of a young girl with small, high breasts, nipped-in waist and slender hips and thighs. The inside edge of the arms is not indicated.

From a private collection. H: 13.5 cm. W: 4.5 cm.

Despite the difference in material and hairstyle, this statuette belongs to the same type as Cat. no. 119, within the general category of fertility figurines. The tripartite hairstyle is common throughout the XIIth and XIIIth Dynasties, but as far as I am aware it is worn by women who have lower status by reason either of their age or of their rank.

117

118

For example, no woman given the epithet *nbt pr*, 'lady of the house', on a stela is shown wearing it (see Cat. no. 48). It may even be exclusive to girls of pre-marital age. In the New Kingdom this is not the case, and an ostracon exists which shows women wearing it while nursing babies.

Cf. Hayes, *Scepter*, I, fig. 137; for New Kingdom ostracon, see G. Pinch in *Orientalia* 52 (1983), pp. 405–6; E. Brunner-Traut in *Mitteilungen des Instituts für Orientforschung* 3 (1955), pp. 25–6.

119 FEMALE FIGURINE

Late Dynasty XII to Dynasty XIII, 1862–1650 BC.

Egyptian faience moulded figurine of a naked girl, broken and repaired in the middle. She has her arms at her sides and her legs are rounded off at the knees. She wears the Hathor wig (see Cat. no. 14) with traces of her own hair on the forehead and at the back. On her breast is a hawk amulet (cf. Cat. no. 173), and on her thighs faint traces of diamond-shaped tattoos. Her wig, facial features, breasts, navel and pubic triangle were originally picked out in blue–black pigment under the glaze, and this has to a great extent faded. The modelling of the figurine is schematic.

From a tomb at El-Matarîya. Gift of G. D. Hornblower. Fitzwilliam E.191.1939. H: 12.0 cm. W: 4.3 cm.

Figurines like this one (see also Cat. no. 118), common throughout the XIIth and XIIIth Dynasties in tombs and settlements, seem to contrast oddly with the dignified representations of women on tomb reliefs. The figurines are always naked, except for an elaborate wig or hairstyle and jewellery. They are almost invariably rounded off at the knees, and never inscribed. Some of them, like this one and Cat. no. 120, show marks of tattooing on thighs, buttocks and stomach. It is clear that they represent not individuals but, like the servant figures, a function – but what function? They were first described by scholars, perhaps reluctant to accept their overt sexuality, as 'dolls'; later the term 'concubine of the

dead' was coined for them. Recent work, especially that by Geraldine Pinch, has shown that they are concerned with the whole area of man's and woman's fertility, with sexuality, but also with the conception, bearing and rearing of children. Our society makes such a deep separation between sexual pleasure and the desire for children that it may be difficult to appreciate how naturally they were combined, as they still are, in Egypt. It was her fertility which made a woman sexually attractive, hence the emphasis in these figurines on the hips and genitalia. Many of them are actually shown carrying babies, and in these cases the woman's body is rendered in exactly the same way.

Their place among the grave goods, and their occurrence in the graves of men, women and children, can be explained in two ways. They, along with all the other magical devices of everyday life, were empowered to protect the newly dead, as vulnerable as the newly born, against the dangers of the transition from death to rebirth. Once reborn, the deceased required magical help to regain their sexual potency and their fertility in order to enjoy the Afterlife to the full. The myth of Isis reviving the dead Osiris, so enabling him to father Horus, provides a parallel. Everything we know of these figures shows that they are not exceptional items – a particular man choosing to take a replica of a favourite slave girl into the Next World for example, a scenario which owes more to the Arabian Nights than to ancient Egypt – but that they are at the core of popular beliefs, see Cat. no. 116.

Particular details of the figurines, of which this is a typical example, are interesting. The absence of feet is a reminder of the mutilation of hieroglyphs depicting living beings in some funerary inscriptions of the XIIIth Dynasty, see Cat. no. 83. These, too, are deprived of feet, and perhaps for the same reason. If the figures, like the hieroglyphs, could be animated by magic, then their freedom of movement had to be controlled, otherwise they might harm the deceased, at the very least by running away and so destroying the magic. The wigs and jewellery they wear are standard for the period. The 'Hathor' wig may be of special significance because that goddess above all was concerned with matters of love and birth. During the Middle Kingdom figurines like this one were

119

dedicated at a famous shrine of Hathor at Deir el Bahri. Love poems, stories and legends all illustrate the allure felt by men for long fragrant hair, and none of the figurines, however crude, is without this essential attribute of beauty. Tattoos, like the ones shown here, have been found on the bodies of two young girls buried at Thebes during the reign of Nebhepetre Montuhotep, and it has been deduced, from the tattoos alone, that they were professional dancing girls. None of the depictions of dancing girls on tomb reliefs shows them wearing tattoos, so the assumption remains unproven. This figurine was found with the 'faience' animal figurines, Cat. no. 112. The date and character of the group is discussed under that entry.

G. Hornblower in *JEA* 15 (1929), p. 40, pl. IX; 4; Kemp and Merrillees, *Minoan Pottery*, p. 164, xii; generally, see G. Pinch in *Orientalia* 52 (1983), pp. 405–14; P. Derchain in *SAK* 2 (1975), pp. 55–74.

120 FEMALE FIGURINE

Dynasties XII–XIII, 1963–1650 BC.

Figurine of a naked woman, handmade in a marl clay. Body modelled with the fingers, details incised, arms, necklace, hair and fillet applied. The face is represented by a 'beak' pinched in the wet clay, but considerably more attention is paid to the hairstyle. This is similar to that worn by the statuette, Cat. no. 118, but the back hair, in the present case, has been pulled into a single plait. A strip of clay pricked with dots lies on the chest to represent a necklace made up of at least two strands of beads, and a line of dots on the hips represents a bead girdle. A circle of dots around the enlarged navel and on the buttocks represents tattoos. The woman is shown with her arms at her sides, her legs together ending in vestigial feet. The breasts are not marked, but the hips are enormous and project outwards in the manner of Cat. no. 116. The pubic triangle is exaggerated in size and pricked with dots to represent pubic hair.

Gift of G. D. Hornblower. Fitzwilliam E.188.1939. H: 12.2 cm. D: 4.3 cm.

This object, crude though it is, shows by its simplicity what was important about these fertility figurines to the people who made them. To shape the clay was the work of a few moments; nevertheless the maker chose to take extra time to provide an elaborate hairstyle, ornaments, and a generous physique, see Cat. no. 119. The face, breasts and feet were clearly not significant, so are hardly represented at all.

In discussing this figurine in 1981, I presented the traditional view of it as a 'concubine of the dead', though I suggested that the class generally may also have served women as emblems of fertility. I now think the significance of these figurines is much wider, and all the comments on Cat. no. 119 apply also to this figure. The obvious and gross disparity in style between this and Cat. nos. 118–19 is due partly to the difference in material and technique (the malleable clay worked by hand lends itself to exaggerated forms more readily), and (tentatively) to a difference in origin. The clay figurines of this type seem to circulate in Upper Egypt only (information supplied by Geraldine Pinch), but within that region they appear in the same contexts as the stone, 'faience' and wooden examples, that is in tombs and houses and in shrines of Hathor.

G. D. Hornblower in *JEA* 15 (1929), p. 40, pl. IX, 1–2; Bourriau, *Pottery*, no. 240, p. 119–20.

121 FERTILITY STATUETTE

Dynasty XI, 2023–1963 BC.

Wooden 'paddle doll', with an elaborate hairstyle. The plaited hair is represented by about thirty strings of black 'faience' barrel beads among which appear occasional bright

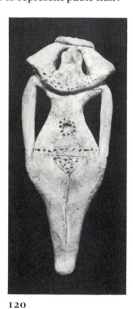

120

121

blue 'faience' ring beads. Interspersed among the beads are knots of straw representing gold hair rings, and the strings terminate in cones of unbaked clay, cf. Cat. no. 128. A face, crudely modelled and also made of unbaked mud, was probably once attached to the peg which forms the head. The body is elongated and straight-sided, only curving outwards at the hips, and terminating in an enlarged and explicit depiction of female genitalia. Around the neck and thighs are narrow black bands with white spots – representing jewellery. The body from breast to thighs appears to be covered in a brightly patterned tunic ornamented with divided diamonds of green, dark red and black. On top of this, representing beadwork perhaps, are vertical stripes in white with black spots. On the back just above the painted girdle is a twice-repeated pattern of a cross and a dot, representing tattooing.

From Thebes. Ex Hilton Price collection. Royal Museum of Scotland 1911.284. H: 22.4 cm. W: 8.0 cm.

These objects seem to be a peculiarly Upper Egyptian version of the fertility figurine and they are most plentiful in Theban cemeteries dating to Dynasty XI. However, at least two were found in tombs at Beni Hasan and one at Rifeh in Middle Egypt, but in reassuringly early deposits. One

example in the Metropolitan Museum of Art, New York, carries the painted image of Ipy, later called Thueris (see Cat. no. 176e), patron goddess of pregnant women. Another example was found in tomb 5 under the Ramesseum at Thebes, with the statuette, fig. 1, which is dated to Dynasty XIII. Not all the objects in the deposit are necessarily of the same date; nevertheless the presence of other fertility figurines, together with so many instruments of magic, suggests this item may have remained among the magician's equipment as an heirloom.

Most of the statuettes of this type, unlike the others, Cat. nos. 117–120, represent the woman clothed, and show an astonishing range of brightly and elaborately decorated garments. Not one of the hundreds which survive is exactly like another. The contrast with the plainness of women's dress shown conventionally in relief and sculpture in the round is striking.

Cf. E. Riefstahl, *Patterned Textiles in Pharaonic Egypt* (Brooklyn 1944), pp. 11–15, figs. 13–15; Hayes, *Scepter*, I, p. 219, fig. 135; Garstang, *Burial Customs*, p. 152, fig. 150; Petrie, *Objects*, p. 59, pl. LI, 379–82; Saleh and Sourouzian, *Cairo Museum*, no. 81.

DECORATIVE ART

Objects made in the Middle Kingdom differ most strikingly from those produced at earlier or later times by reason of the range and quality of materials available to the craftsman. Where the artist of the New Kingdom used coloured frit and glass, his XIIth Dynasty counterpart could call upon semi-precious stones such as amethyst, carnelian and felspar. Jewellery from quite a modest burial could include several large gold pendants and beads (see Cat. no. 159), and beads of different hard stones such as lapis lazuli, carnelian and turquoise. Some rarer stones, such as amethyst and anhydrite, appear almost exclusively in the Middle Kingdom, while others, for example obsidian and haematite, were more widely employed than in earlier or later times. This presupposes both the resources to send out expeditions to the mines in the Eastern and Western deserts, and the means to distribute the stones to workshops up and down the country.

While royal jewels such as Cat. nos. 156, 179 were undoubtedly produced only in workshops attached to the King's palace, the jewellery of private individuals, like the

156

Lady Seneb buried at Beni Hasan (Garstang, *Burial Customs*, pl. V, fig. 104), may have been made locally. If so, the dissemination of new techniques, such as granulation in gold working (see Cat. no. 157), must have been as effective as the distribution of raw materials.

127

This situation seems to obtain only in the XIIth to early XIIIth Dynasties; before and especially after that time, there are substantially fewer semi-precious stones in the burials of private persons, see Cat. no. 164. Perhaps the Egyptian habit of burying an individual's private jewels with the body was itself a factor in this rapid decline. If supplies of a particular stone were limited, as is thought to have been the case with amethyst and anhydrite, then removal from circulation of the large amounts required for deposition in tombs would have caused their rapid exhaustion. In contrast, precious metals were re-cycled by the tomb robber; gold, silver and electrum, easily melted down and always in demand, were what the robber, so often the undertaker or cemetery guardian himself, was keenest to obtain. It has been argued that it was as a result of his efforts that much of the precious metal so important to the functioning of the Egyptian economy remained in circulation. A more easily measured factor in the decline in raw material supply is the reduced number of mining expeditions in the XIIIth Dynasty. Dated inscriptions left on rocks by the leaders of such expeditions provide our evidence for this decline (Martin, *Scarabs*, p. 5, n. 2).

The motifs chosen to ornament personal possessions fall into a few well-defined categories: the natural world, and particularly the flora and fauna of the Nile; purely geometrical designs such as triangles or spirals; hieroglyphs, which may be individual signs or sign-groups conferring good luck or inscriptions naming the owner, the King or a god; finally, representations of human figures, Kings or deities. The motifs reflect a self-contained world in which nothing outside the confines of the Nile valley and the deserts flanking it has a place.

Egypt's cultural self-sufficiency is the more remarkable in that the barriers to South and North against the rest of the world were under constant threat and were finally breached during the XIIIth Dynasty. In an effort to protect the southern frontier and control immigration, the land of Nubia was colonised, yet the number of Nubian artefacts to be found in Egypt at this time is small and they enjoyed only limited circulation beyond the direct sphere of the Nubian immigrants themselves. Nubian craftsmen had virtually no impact on their Egyptian opposite numbers. A foreign community from Syria–Palestine established itself at Tell Dab'a in the Eastern Delta during the Middle Kingdom, but its impact is at present hard to assess, since so few other Delta sites of the period have been studied and Tell Dab'a itself is still being excavated. Nevertheless it is clear that the community did influence the decorative arts in Dynasty XIII by introducing a class of pottery, the so-called Tell el-Yahudiya ware, whose shapes and designs derive from the pottery of the Middle Bronze Age cultures of Syria–Palestine. It was imitated by Egyptian potters, but did not circulate widely outside Lower Egypt, except that remarkably large numbers of vessels were exported to the forts guarding the southern frontier.

We do not always understand the meaning the Egyptians attributed to the motifs they used, but we can presume that nothing is to be taken simply at face value. The water-lily, the blue lotus, appears over and over again and is here repre-

sented on cosmetic jars, Cat. nos. 122b, 125; jewellery, Cat. no. 154; and metalwork, Cat. no. 191. It was admired for its beauty, but also because it symbolised rebirth by opening its petals at sunrise and closing them at sunset, see Cat. no. 126. The scarab beetle also never lost its amuletic power even when scarabs were used for the mundane task of sealing documents or containers, see Cat. nos. 178, 180.

126

One quality which perhaps above all others characterises Egyptian design is symmetry. This shows up most clearly on a small object like a scarab, or a pectoral where the whole field is decorated, see Cat. nos. 179, 156 respectively, but is illustrated equally by the careful arrangement of a string of round beads in graduated sizes, Cat. nos. 163, 166a, b. Towards the end of the Middle Kingdom desire for symmetry gives way to *horror vacui*, a dislike of empty space, see Cat. no. 126. Designs become more crowded and individual motifs ill proportioned. The draughtsman's steady line, born of years of painstaking copying of traditional models, begins to lose its smoothness, see Cat. no. 181b. Nevertheless, this pervasive change of style, which we can observe in relief sculpture (Cat. no. 49), in the decoration of coffins (Cat. no. 70), as well as in the minor arts (Cat. no. 126), provided in its turn a stimulus to the craftsman. We may mourn a decline in technical skill, but the artist's vigour and inventiveness of design remain to be admired.

EGYPTIAN FAIENCE AND GLAZED STEATITE

122 DISH AND CYLINDER JAR
Dynasty XII, 1963–1787 BC.

Dish and jar made of Egyptian faience, modelled with the fingers; decoration and glaze applied before firing. The bowl (a) is a deep blue, with a design of water-lily petals on the underside and a zigzag motif around the flat rim, both in

128

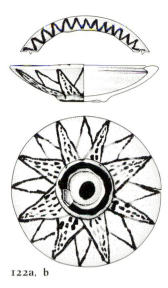

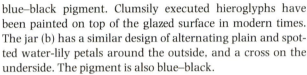

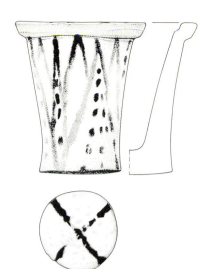

122a, b

blue–black pigment. Clumsily executed hieroglyphs have been painted on top of the glazed surface in modern times. The jar (b) has a similar design of alternating plain and spotted water-lily petals around the outside, and a cross on the underside. The pigment is also blue–black.

(a) Dish, from Beni Hasan, tomb 81. Ex Kennard collection. Bequest of E. Towry-Whyte. Fitzwilliam E.81.1932. H: 1.9 cm. W: 7.3 cm. (b) Jar, ex Kitchener collection. Gift of Sir W. P. Elderton. Fitzwilliam E.72.1955. H: 4.0 cm. W: 3.5 cm.

(a) This modest antiquity has had an interesting post-excavation history. It was found by Garstang at Beni Hasan in 1903, in a tomb containing only two burials and with objects suggesting an early XIIth Dynasty date. The dish passed to Kennard when the finds from the excavation were distributed to members of the syndicate which financed it. When his collection was sold in July 1912 this item was bought by a dealer called Lawrence, who re-sold it to E. Towry-Whyte. The dish had acquired its spurious inscription between the Kennard sale and Towry-Whyte's acquisition of it, i.e. between July 1912 and February 1913, when Towry-Whyte showed it to H. R. Hall of the British Museum asking for his reading of the inscription. H. R. Hall read it and published it as providing the name of Queen Tiy, wife of King Amenhotep III (1403–1365 BC), and her father Yuia, prince of Zahi (Syria). The dish's inscription seemed then to prove that Queen Tiy was of Syrian origin. Although he later allowed that the signs might have been touched up in 'ancient or modern times' (letter to Towry-Whyte of 22 February 1913 in Fitzwilliam Museum) Hall never doubted the inscription's authenticity. Others did, almost at once, and Aldred finally established that the signs had been painted on the surface of the glaze after the dish had been fired. We have recently confirmed this by examining the signs under high magnification and testing the pigment with acetone. It dissolves relatively easily. If Hall or Towry-Whyte had been aware of the provenance of the dish, from a Middle Kingdom tomb completed about 500 years before the birth of Queen Tiy, they would not have accepted the inscription so readily.

The material of these two vessels is described as Egyptian faience. Elsewhere in the catalogue the term 'faience' in inverted commas is also employed to differentiate this usage from the non-Egyptological use of the term to describe the glazed earthenware made in Italy during the Renaissance. Egyptologists use the term to denote a material made of granular quartz or sand (which is largely quartz) bonded by heat with sufficient alkali, from natron or plant ash, to produce a rigid, partly vitreous body. To this body, alkali glazes with a low melting point were applied, coloured with copper ores such as malachite to provide the favoured turquoise colour. In the case of these two objects the surface was decorated by painting on it before the glaze was applied, using a wash of pigment, possibly manganese, and water. The base of the dish shows how the glaze solution has run, so we can be certain it was applied to the surface.

Dish: Garstang, *Burial Customs*, p. 142, fig. 140; H. R. Hall in *PSBA* 35 (1913), pp. 63–5, pls. V–VI; *Sotheby's Sale Catalogue*, July 1912, lot no. 303; C. Aldred in *JEA* 43 (1957), p. 31, n. 3; jar: *Sotheby's Sale Catalogue*, 16 November 1938, lot no. 18; for Egyptian faience, Lucas, *Industries*, pp. 155–78; Kaczmarczyk and Hedges, *Faience*, passim but note A92–A108.

122a

123 CUP INSCRIBED FOR SOBEKHOTEP IV

Dynasty XIII, reign of Sobekhotep IV, c. 1730–1720 BC.

Cup of Egyptian faience (see Cat. no. 122), with exceptionally deep blue vitreous glaze, inscribed (in black) on the outside just below the rim with the name and throne name of King Khaneferre Sobekhotep. The signs were painted on the surface before firing. The cup may have been made by moulding it in sections over a core. It has been re-built from sherds, but the only area of restoration is a small section of the rim.

From the Asâsîf on the west bank at Thebes. Purchased by Major Myers before 1887. Eton College, Myers Museum 2199. H: 9.1 cm. D: 9.6 cm.

The provenance of this cup, which is recorded in Myers's list of his acquisitions held at Eton, seems convincing in view of the rich tombs of the XIIIth Dynasty found in the Asâsîf, notably by Carnarvon and Carter.

123

The name which follows the King's throne name, Khaneferre, in the second cartouche of the inscription begins curiously with a *rˁ* sign (Gardiner, *Grammar*, Signlist N5), but the next sign could be the head of the crocodile (Sobek) as one would expect, not the *hˁ* sign (Gardiner, *Grammar*, Signlist N28) as Newberry has it. Sobekhotep IV was one of the most powerful Kings of the XIIIth Dynasty; several colossal statues of him survive, in addition to blocks from his buildings and references to him on the monuments and records of his officials. He certainly still controlled Memphis as well as Upper Egypt, though the centre of royal power may already have begun to shift southwards.

A small number of 'faience' cups, potstands and stone vessels inscribed for XIIIth Dynasty Kings exists. This particular cup copies the ordinary pottery drinking cup of the day (see Cat. nos. 135, 136), in a more expensive material; we may presume it was not functional, but that it was a gift to a royal servant for his burial or dedicated by the King in a shrine or temple. The proportions of the cup, the ratio of breadth to height (105), would be sufficient evidence to date it to the middle of the XIIIth Dynasty even if the inscription were not

present. It is such an exact copy of the pottery prototype that I suggest tentatively that a pottery cup served as a core over which the sections of the 'faience' cup were moulded. This technique of 'faience' manufacture, moulding over a core, is known to have been practised in the Middle Kingdom, but visual examination with a hand lens provides insufficient magnification to prove the use of the technique in this case.

Burlington Fine Arts Club, 1895, p. 94, no. 15, pl. XVIII, 126; *Burlington Fine Arts Club*, 1922, p. 92, no. 48; P. Newberry in *PSBA* 25 (1903), pp. 134–5; von Beckerath, *Zweiten Zwischenzeit*, p. 249, pl. XIII (24).

124 POTSTAND OF HEKEKU

Dynasty XII, 1963–1787 BC.

Potstand of Egyptian faience (see Cat. no. 122), with a bright turquoise glaze and a painted hieroglyphic inscription around the middle, under the glaze. The inscription is the conventional funerary formula invoking Ptah, South of his Wall, Lord of Ankhtawy, and naming a man called Hekeku.

From Saqqara (?). Ex Bomford collection. Ashmolean 1971.950. H: 5.2 cm. D: 9.9 cm.

Like the cup, Cat. no. 123, this 'faience' potstand exactly copies its pottery prototype, but in this case the shape is not distinctive enough to allow it to be closely dated. Potstands vary little in shape between one epoch and the next, but if made of pottery, clay fabric or technology of manufacture may be of use in refining the dating.

The inscription invokes Ptah of Memphis, and for this reason it is suggested that this potstand came from the Middle Kingdom cemeteries at Saqqara, the necropolis of Memphis. However, the god Ptah with the same epithet is also invoked on stelae found at Abydos and elsewhere, so the evidence is not conclusive.

Cf. P. Newberry in *PSBA* 25 (1903), pp. 134–5.

124

125 COSMETIC JAR

Late Dynasty XII to Dynasty XIII, 1862–1650 BC.

Jar of Egyptian faience with a deep blue glaze fading to turquoise at the base due to uneven firing. There are deep cracks in the glaze and a slice is missing from the base of the jar. The exterior surface is completely covered with bands of decoration in dark blue under the glaze. There is a solid band of dark blue inside the rim, and pairs of short vertical lines occur at regular intervals around the outside of the rim. On the shoulder of the vessel is a lozenge pattern framed by flower petals, see Cat. no. 80; at the maximum diameter is a band of criss-cross lines suggesting the nets in which pots were carried, and below that the familiar pattern of alternating plain and spotted water-lily petals, cf. Cat. no. 122. A cross inside a circle is painted onto the base, cf. Cat. no. 122b.

126 [inside shown on p. 128]

125

From Kahun. Manchester 169. H: 12.2 cm. D: 7.7 cm.

Petrie unfortunately gives no information concerning the precise find-spot of this jar or any objects associated with it. It is illustrated with the bottom half of a fertility figurine similar to Cat. no. 119, but Petrie may have grouped the objects together because of the similarity of their material. The jar was probably used for cosmetics, and there are versions of its shape in stone, Cat. no. 150. The latter, where their context can be dated, appear to belong to the late Middle Kingdom.

Petrie, *Illahun*, pl. XIII, 19.

126 BOWL WITH BIRDS, FISH AND WATER PLANTS

Dynasty XIII, 1786–1650 BC.

Carinated, ring-footed bowl in Egyptian faience covered with deep blue glaze and with black painted decoration inside and outside. Three-quarters of the bowl has been reconstruc-

ted from sherds, and there is a small area of plaster restoration near the base. The broken section shows the body material to be light brown with a thin (0.1 cm wide) white layer of fine particles intervening between the glaze and the core. The decoration on the exterior consists of a narrow, solid black band around the rim, a band of pendant triangles filled with diagonal, parallel lines, and a Nilotic scene containing buds, leaf pads and flowers of the blue lotus, the pond weed *potamogeton lucens* L., and a bird. The base carries a linear design based on parallel lines radiating from a central point. The decoration on the interior consists of a row of regularly spaced groups of four short vertical lines, a band of alternating pendant and upright triangles filled with diagonal, parallel lines, and a counterpart to the Nilotic scene on the exterior consisting of a papyrus plant, pond weed and four *tilapia* fish.

From Hu. University College 18758. H: 7.0 cm. D: 13.0 cm.

It is interesting to note that the drawing on the inside is of higher quality than that on the outside of the bowl. The interior carries motifs taken from the flora and fauna of the river itself; the exterior, motifs from the reed beds at the river's edge. This suggests the bowl was intended to hold the water offering for the dead, and that the fish were meant to be viewed through the water.

The design as much as the individual motifs recalls the decoration of 'faience' hippopotami (see Cat. no. 111), but the addition of the linear designs above and below the Nilotic scene ensures that, unlike the hippopotami, the bowl had all available surfaces decorated. This dislike of blank space, *horror vacui*, is a characteristic of the decorative arts of Dynasty XIII and can be recognised on scarabs and even stelae of the time, cf. Cat. nos. 181b, 49 respectively. The *tilapia* fish and the blue lotus, motifs which occur over and over again, were both powerful images of rebirth: the flower because it opened at sunrise and folded its petals at sunset, and the fish because of its habit of hatching its eggs in its mouth. The young fish issuing from its mouth suggested self-propagation.

The shape of the bowl has parallels in pottery (see Cat. no. 135b), and in metal (Cat. no. 184), which can be dated to the late XIIth to XIIIth Dynasties. The decoration, in both design and motifs, has a close parallel in a bowl from an intact

131

burial at Qau, datable by pottery and a stone vase to Dynasty XIII. Petrie obtained the bowl at Hu, during his excavations at the site, but it is not mentioned in his publication and he may have purchased it. The site contains a large cemetery with graves ranging from Middle Kingdom to New Kingdom date.

The intermediate layer of fine white material laid over the core of the vessel has been noticed on other Egyptian faience objects of the Middle Kingdom. It has been suggested that it was intended to brighten the colour of the glaze by reflection and to prevent the migration of salts from the core into the glaze. The glaze is smudged on the outside, indicating that it was placed too close to another vessel during the drying or firing process.

Cf. for shape, Carnarvon and Carter, *Five Years*, pl. XLIV, 4; for decoration, A. Milward in *Egypt's Golden Age*, no. 138; G. Brunton, *Qau and Badari*, III (London, 1930), pl. XXXIII, 2; *The Macgregor Collection. Sotheby's Sale Catalogue*, 26 June – 6 July 1922, lot no. 248; material, Vandiver in Kaczmarczyk and Hedges, *Faience*, A13–14, A98–100.

127

127 HEAD OF HATHOR

Reign of Senusret I, 1943–1899 BC.

Head of the goddess Hathor in green glazed steatite with eyes inlaid in copper, calcite and obsidian. The ears have broken away. The head originally formed part of the handle of a sistrum, and is represented twice on both front and back. On one side the personal name of King Senusret I is inscribed, and on the other his throne name, Kheperkare, which means, 'The *ka* of Re comes into being.' Slots remain in the top into which the two hoops of the sistrum, which were probably made of metal, once fitted. There is also a hole just above each ear for pins which would have secured the ends of the hoops in place. Below the chin is a much larger hole for the handle proper, which may have been made in another material. The glaze is thick and shows up as black where it has penetrated cracks in the soft steatite. The large, slanting eyes have been framed in bronze, but the eyes themselves are of calcite and the pupils obsidian. The narrow cosmetic line and the brow are carved in relief. The nose is short and very broad, with deep grooves defining the nostrils, in which the glaze has collected. The philtrum is marked and the mouth is straight, with a full, pouting lower lip. The cheeks are prominent and the contours of the face are generally strongly marked.

From Thebes, purchased by Major Myers before 1887. Eton College, Myers Museum 634. H: 5.4 cm. W: 6.7 cm.

The sistrum was a musical rattle, composed of disks of metal strung on metal rods or wires which were shaken rhythmically to accompany chanting, singing and dancing. They appear often in scenes of religious ceremonial, especially in rites associated with the cult of the goddess Hathor. Her image, a woman with the ears of a cow, the beast sacred to her, is frequently integrated into the form of the sistrum. This head of Hathor is of the finest quality and inscribed with the reigning King's name, so we can presume that it was dedicated by the King, or on his behalf, in an important

shrine. Remains of a destroyed temple of Senusret I at Karnak include a double statue of the King and the goddess Hathor, so we may speculate that this superb object came from there.

It is interesting to compare this frontal image with the profile image of the King on the block from Koptos, Cat. no. 11. At all periods in Egyptian art the features of the King are reproduced in representations of the gods, albeit adapted to a particular divinity's iconography. Rounded cheeks, full lower lip and shape of eye and brow are shared by both King and goddess. The strong tilt of the inner corner of the eye towards the nose and away from the line of the brow is particularly noticeable.

Burlington Fine Arts Club, 1895, p. 89, no. 1, pl. XX, 147; Wallis, *Ceramic Art 1898*, p. 15, no. 20; for sistrum in use, Blackman, *Meir*, II, pl. XV.

128 BALL BEADS

Dynasties XI–XII, 2023–1787 BC.

Large spherical beads made of Egyptian faience, pierced through for stringing. Each is painted in dark blue under the glaze with four solid sickle-shaped zones, so that light and dark segments alternate on the surface. They came to the Fitzwilliam from two different private collections, so were not originally strung together.

Gifts of (a) G. D. Hornblower and (d), (e) R. G. Gayer-Anderson. (a) Fitzwilliam E.257.1939. D: 3.8 cm; (b) Fitzwilliam E.FG.42a. D: 3.2 cm; (c) Fitzwilliam E.FG.42b. D: 2.6 cm; (d) Fitzwilliam EGA.4591a.1943 D: 3.6 cm; (e) Fitzwilliam EGA.4591b.1943. D: 3.4 cm.

Beads of comparable size to these were worn around the neck by both men and women, and in the hair by women. Sometimes a single bead was worn, otherwise they were arranged in graduated sizes as here. A fragment of relief from the tomb of Queen Neferu, wife of Nebhepetre Montuhotep (see Cat. nos. 2, 4, 8), shows women each of whom is wear-

128a–e

ing, attached to the top of her wig, a long string of large round beads alternating with short cylinder beads. The beads would have hung down like a pseudo-plait and mixed with the dark hair of their long wigs. Another scene, from a private tomb, shows dancers each wearing a large bead fastened to the bottom of a single plait, where the girl, Cat. no. 140, wears her fish amulet. In these two examples from limestone relief the beads have been coloured white, which suggests they were made of silver or electrum.

Cf. Aldred, *Jewels of the Pharaohs*, pp. 184–5, pl. 23; de Garis Davies, *Antefoker*, pl. XXIII.

129 GAMING PIECES

Middle Kingdom, 2023–1650 BC.

Nine gaming pieces made of Egyptian faience and glazed blue and turquoise green. One example has black streaks in a turquoise green matrix. They may be divided into three sets according to their shape: conical, squat and squat with a rounded top.

Gift of R. G. Gayer-Anderson. Fitzwilliam EGA. 2416. 1943, 2418.1943, 2420.1943, 2424.1943, 2431.1943, 2433.1943, 2442.1943, 2450.1943, 2452.1943. H: from 0.8–2.2 cm. W: 1.1 cm.

These pieces all come from the same private collection, but there is no evidence to indicate that they derive from a single find, or even that they were all acquired at the same time. Pieces of this shape have been found with the boards used to play the perennially popular *senet* game. Egyptians loved board games and played them at every opportunity (see Cat. no. 91), so much so that they were a significant ingredient in the happy life of the Next World. Gaming pieces and boards were often placed among the grave goods or depicted on the walls of tombs and sides of coffins.

129a–i

For the game of *senet*, T. Kendall in *Egypt's Golden Age*, pp. 263–4; for the marbelising technique, Vandiver in Kaczmarczyk and Hedges, *Faience*, A103–4.

POTTERY

130 WATER JAR FROM DENDERA

Dynasty XI, 2023–1963 BC.

Squat water jar made of a fine marl clay evenly fired to a pale yellow. It was thrown on the wheel, and the excess clay trimmed from the base with a knife.

From Dendera, tomb 271. Gift of the Egypt Exploration Fund. Fitzwilliam E251.1899. H: 14.8 cm. D: 12.2 cm.

Both its shape and the clay of which it is made proclaim this vessel's Upper Egyptian origin. Medium-sized bag-shaped jars occur in many variants in the pottery found at Thebes in the tombs of the early Kings of Dynasty XI, the predecessors of Nebhepetre Montuhotep, who controlled only a restricted area of Upper Egypt. The clay itself, mined from soft layers of limestone rock in the desert, is fine marl A, variant 3 in the fabric classification proposed by Nordström in *LÄ*, VI, 633. Common at Upper Egyptian sites such as Thebes and Dendera, it is much rarer at Kahun, Lisht and Dahshur, and, we may presume, represents there vessels imported from the South.

The smooth, pale surface of the vessel shows up the potter's finishing techniques very clearly. The upper two-thirds has

130

been smoothed on the wheel, and the base has been cut with a knife to remove the excess clay. The sharp planes created by the knife-cuts interrupt the smooth profile created by throwing, but also provide a flat (albeit unstable) base on which the pot may stand.

Petrie, *Dendereh*, pl. XVIII, 187; Bourriau, *Pottery*, no. 21 (where dated to First Intermediate period) and bibliography there cited.

131 WATER JAR FROM SIDMANT

Dynasties XI–XII, to end of reign of Amenemhat I, 2023–1934 BC.

Slender-shouldered flask made in a medium textured, straw-tempered alluvial clay and thrown on the wheel. Below the maximum diameter the surface has been scraped vertically to remove the excess clay. A thick red slip has been applied to the surface and burnished before firing.

From Sidmant, tomb 1546. University College 18232. H: 24.8 cm. D: 10.9 cm.

This jar played the same role in the early Middle Kingdom as the jar from Dendera, Cat. no. 130, but within the pottery repertoire of the Heracleopolitan region. The cemetery in which the grave was situated was excavated by Flinders Petrie in 1921. He dated it to the IXth to Xth Dynasties because he found little in it characteristic of the XIth Dynasty, whose culture he defined by referring back to his own work in the cemeteries of Thebes. The possibility that different pottery repertoires were in use in the North and the South of Egypt was not considered, but the work of Dorothea Arnold has proved it beyond doubt. Petrie, however, unable to fit his cemetery into Dynasty XI but recognising its early Middle Kingdom character, labelled it Dynasties IX–X. The cemetery may begin as early as this, but continues through the XIth and into the XIIth Dynasty.

Tomb 1546 seems to have contained a single burial, so that all the objects found may be associated together. There were traces of a coffin, but no bones are mentioned. The shape of the flask is late in the series set out by Dorothea Arnold, and the date of the group is derived from this. The clay fabric corresponds to Nile B2 in the classification proposed by Nordström.

Petrie and Brunton, *Sedment*, I, pl. XXXII, 641; cf. Do. Arnold in *MDAIK* 28 (1972), pp. 44–5; Nordström in *LÄ*, VI, 632.

132 JAR FOR THE WATER OFFERING

Dynasty XI, 2023–1963 BC.

Globular jar with four miniature vases applied to the rim, a quatrefoil mouth and a flat base. It was made in a coarse, straw tempered alluvial clay, covered with a red wash and burnished before firing. The body was thrown on the wheel, the base, rim and vases shaped with the fingers, and the surface scraped to remove excess clay. Bands of decoration consisting of alternating lines and rows of semicircles were incised in the wet clay before the surface was burnished.

Probably from Hu. Gift of the Egypt Exploration Fund. Fitzwilliam E.28.1903. H: 21.0 cm. D: 16.9 cm.

132

Water was the most important single offering to be made for the dead, and there are, at this period, several versions of vessels or stands supporting miniature *nw* pots – the shape in which water offerings were traditionally made.

The provenance of the vessel remains in doubt, since the material from Beni Hasan, Hu and Dendera, which arrived in the Fitzwilliam between 1899 and 1903, was not immediately catalogued, and it is not possible in every case to determine now from which site a vessel came. Although Beni Hasan is in Middle Egypt and the other two sites are in Upper Egypt, our new knowledge of the regional styles of early Middle Kingdom pottery does not help us to make a choice in this case. The pottery from Beni Hasan shows a mixture of both Lower Egyptian and Upper Egyptian features. Pottery from both these regions must have been imported to the site to be copied by the potters making vessels for the necropolis. The shape of this vessel, but without the miniature vases, can be paralleled at Beni Hasan (Garstang, *Burial Customs*, pl. XII, 11). The fabric of the vessel is Nile C following the classification proposed by Nordström, *LÄ*, VI, 632.

Bourriau, *Pottery*, no. 120 and bibliography there cited.

133 WATER JAR FROM RIQQA

Mid-Dynasty XII, 1869–1798 BC.

Globular jar with funnel neck, made of a fine, sandy alluvial clay. It has been thrown in two pieces and the base has been carefully smoothed with the fingers to remove excess clay. The surface is covered with a red slip. The rim is slightly warped.

133

134

From Riqqa, cemetery A, tomb 180 or 183. Gift of the British School of Archaeology in Egypt. Fitzwilliam E.17.1913. H: 22.9 cm. D: 10.2 cm.

The proportions of this jar are exceptionally pleasing to the eye, so that the slight asymmetry of the profile is hardly noticeable. The surface of the vessel is also very smooth and only a small circle on the base, about 4 cm in diameter, has been left to be finished off by hand. Vessels of this shape, used to dispense water, usually accompany drinking cups of the type of Cat. nos. 135–6, which are made of the same sandy Nile silt fabric. (Nile B1 in the classification proposed by Nordström, *LÄ*, VI, 631–2). They are especially characteristic of the cemeteries in the Faiyum region but may appear in any cemetery of late XIIth to early XIIIth Dynasty date in Egypt or Nubia, see Cat. no. 136.

Bourriau, *Pottery*, no. 96 and bibliography there cited.

134 TALL POTSTAND

Dynasties XII–XIII, 1963–1650 BC.

Tall potstand made of a medium textured, straw-tempered alluvial clay. Thrown on the wheel in two parts and joined in the middle. The exterior is covered with a thick red slip.

British Museum EA. 58240. H: 27.6 cm. D: 16.5 cm.

The stela of Montuhotep, Cat. no. 36, shows a potstand of this shape in use. It supports a round-bottomed drinking cup and brings it within the reach of a man sitting on a chair. The shape and technology of potstands change more slowly than, for example, the drinking cups themselves, so this example cannot be dated very precisely.

135 DRINKING CUPS FROM ABYDOS

Dynasties XII–XIII, 1963–1650 BC.

Small bowls, one (a) hemispherical and one (b) carinated, thrown on the wheel and made of a fine sandy alluvial clay. (a) The base has been smoothed with the fingers and a line of thin red wash applied to the rim. (b) The base has been cut with a knife and a criss-cross design, imitating the string of a carrying net, has been applied in red to the upper body.

From Abydos, Peet excavations. Gift of Egypt Exploration Fund. (a) From tomb x63. Fitzwilliam E.182.1910. H: 7.6 cm. D: 11.6 cm. (b) From tomb B13. Fitzwilliam E.45.1910. H: 5.1 cm. D: 10.0 cm.

Small hemispherical cups in a fine, sandy Nile clay are the most characteristic and often the most abundant type of pottery on a Middle Kingdom site, and every archaeologist is familiar with their distinctive rim sherds. The gradual evolution of their shape and technology between Dynasties XI and XIII has been studied by Dr Dorothea Arnold, and they can now be closely dated. (a) On the basis of its 152-vessel index (ratio of diameter to height) belongs in the late XIIth Dynasty. x63 is not mentioned in Peet's publication, but we may presume it was a shaft with chambers containing several

135b, a

burials. The only other object known to me from it is another hemispherical cup, whose vessel index is 106, indicating it dates to Dynasty XIII. It is not unusual to find burials dating from the late XIIth Dynasty and the XIIIth Dynasty in chambers leading off the same shaft.

(b) Came from B I 3, which also contained the shabti of Renseneb, Cat. no. 83. The bowl came from the plundered upper North Chamber which contained only another bowl of the same type and a large granite arm from a statue (information from excavator's records).

Bourriau, *Pottery*, nos. 128b and 7 respectively, and bibliography there cited.

136 DRINKING CUPS FROM BUHEN
Dynasties XII–XIII, 1963–1650 BC.

Two small bowls, one (a) gently carinated and the other (b) deep with a smooth profile. Both have round bases and have been thrown on the wheel. They are made of a fine sandy alluvial clay containing conspicuous amounts of mica. (a) The surface of the lower body has been trimmed with a knife and the excess clay pushed away from the base with the fingers. A line of thin red wash has been applied to the rim. (b) The base has been trimmed with a tool and a line of thin red wash applied to the rim. Smudges of carbon around the rim indicate the cup was re-used as a lamp.

From Buhen, s9–185 and s9–180. University College 21660 and 21662. (a) H: 7.3 cm. D: 11.2 cm; (b) H: 8.5 cm. D: 10.8 cm.

Drinking cups were, not suprisingly, found in great numbers at Buhen, one of the great fortresses set up to control the southern border of Egypt, see Cat. nos. 33, 62. It was excavated by W. B. Emery as part of the Unesco campaign to study the monuments of Nubia before they were flooded by the lake created by the Aswan High Dam. These cups were almost certainly made locally at Buhen, hundreds of miles from the workshops which produced Cat. nos. 135a, b. In shape there is no distinction to be made, but the micaceous clay and thick walls of the Buhen vessels, 0.4 and 0.6 cm respectively, are distinctive. The vessel indices of the Buhen cups indicate that (a) belongs in the late XIIth and (b) in the early XIIIth Dynasty, which fits the history of the fortress as it has been reconstructed by H. S. Smith. The uniformity of culture which they imply between Egypt proper and the colonies of Egyptians living in the fortresses is significant and has parallels in the way of life of some British communities in Egypt, India and elsewhere in the nineteenth century AD.

Emery, Smith and Millard, *Buhen*, I, cf. p. 166, pl. 64, type 73, type 76.

136a, b

137 STORAGE JAR
Dynasty XII, 1963–1787 BC.

Broad-shouldered storage jar, possibly used for liquids – water, beer or wine. It is made of a fine marl clay, like that of Cat. no. 130, and unevenly fired to a pale yellow with spots of pink near the base. It was thrown on the wheel, and just below the maximum diameter the exterior surface was scraped to remove the excess clay. A roughly H-shaped potmark was cut in the wet clay before firing. Just below the rim, at regular intervals, four cylindrical lumps of clay have been applied. They recall the miniature vases applied to the rim of Cat. no. 132, but are reduced in size so as to be purely decorative. On the shoulder of the jar are four incised lines, and below them groups of sickle-shaped incisions set at regular intervals around the body.

From El Kab, tomb 84. University College 18356. H: 41.0 cm. D: 24.1 cm.

The pottery from the large Middle Kingdom cemetery excavated by Quibell in 1897 shows an interesting mixture of the ubiquitous shapes of the late Middle Kingdom – the small bowls, cf. Cat. nos. 135–6, the funnel-necked jars, cf. Cat. no. 133, and the large wine jars (Quibell, *El Kab*, pl. XVI, 60) – together with pottery like this jar, which is characteristic only of Upper Egypt. The mixture of applied and incised decoration, the shape of the jar and its material, fine marl A, variant 3 in the classification proposed by Nordström, are all characteristic of Middle Kingdom pottery in Upper Egypt.

Quibell, *El Kab*, pl. XVI, 70; general, Kemp and Merrillees, *Minoan Pottery*, pp. 217–18 and bibliography there cited.

FURNITURE ATTACHMENTS

138 MINIATURE SPHINX
Early Dynasty XII, possibly reign of Senusret I, 1943–1899 BC.

Forepart of an ivory sphinx, holding the head of a prone figure of a man between its paws. Underside flat with two pegholes, the shoulders projecting, possibly in order to fit around the corner of a box or piece of furniture. Length of face: 0.9 cm. Width of face: 1.0 cm. Length of eye: 0.5 cm. Length of ear: 0.7 cm. The sphinx has the head of a King wearing the *nemes* headcloth and carrying a uraeus-snake on his brow. The *nemes* carries evenly spaced stripes in high relief across the brow and narrower, shallow stripes on the side lappets. The shape of the *nemes* is hard to reconstruct because of the position of the forward-thrusting head, but it is extremely wide, low on the brow and flat across the top of the head. Its peculiarity is the wide outward curve of the side folds, which makes each wing of the *nemes* almost as broad as the central section.

The uraeus-snake rises from the base of the frontlet and winds in five loops to the back of the head. Each brow is represented by a thin relief band which only partly follows the contour of the eye; the eyes are enormous, set aslant, with inner canthi marked, cf. Cat. no. 127. They are outlined in

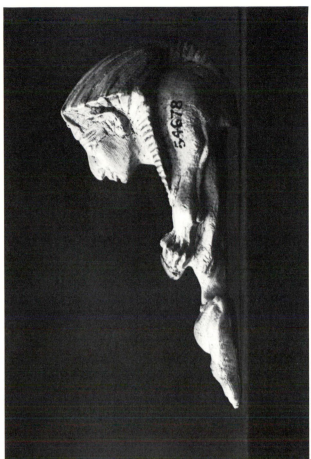

narrow bands of relief which join at the outer corners to form long fish-tailed cosmetic lines which reach the ears. These are large and set high so that they become grossly distorted by the steep angle of the wings of the *nemes*. Nevertheless, the main elements in the cartilage of the ear are shown – the outer rim, the concha, the tragus and the lobe. The nose, for once undamaged, shows a convex curve, with deep creases around the nostrils. The philtrum is marked, and the lips are thick and straight and protrude into a seeming smile. The chin is small and pointed. The cheek-bones are high and prominent in the long, narrow face overwhelmed by the gigantic *nemes*. The claws and the muscles of the arms and shoulders are shown in astonishing and realistic detail.

The prone male figure held in the sphinx's grip lies apparently pulled forward from a kneeling position. His arms are stretched out under the leonine paws, his stomach is flat on the ground and his knees are drawn up. His hair is close cropped and he wears a short kilt and belt. His tiny features – the whole figure is no larger than the sphinx's head – are merely sketched in, but the arch of his backbone and the detail of his toes are shown.

From Abydos, Garstang excavations of 1908, tomb 477. Ex Macgregor collection. Gift of Mrs Russell Rea. British Museum EA. 54678. H: 2.9 cm. L: 6.1 cm.

The only detailed account of this extraordinary object is a short note in the Journal of Egyptian Archaeology for 1928 by its excavator, John Garstang. He reported the opinion of Dr Hall of the British Museum, that the sphinx showed 'Syrian and Semitic' facial characteristics which suggested it was a portrait of one of the Hyksos Kings, who ruled, at least in Lower Egypt, after the XIIIth Dynasty. Garstang then lists the objects found in the same tomb shaft as the sphinx, together with some from two adjacent shafts, 476 and 478, which interconnected but whose deposits he thought could be distinguished from each other. They suggested, he concluded, a date close to the XIIth Dynasty.

The excavation remained unpublished, and Stephen Snape, of Liverpool University, is currently preparing part of it for publication. To him I am indebted for the information which follows. Garstang lists among the objects found with the ivory a 'scarab of lapis lazuli, inscribed, in a fine gold setting'. This is in the British Museum (BM EA 54691) but is an uninscribed cowroid set in gold. The pottery listed from the group, but not mentioned by Garstang in his note, is in my view unequivocally of the Second Intermediate period. However, the association of any object with others from the group in the three shafts 476–8 is much more doubtful than Garstang suggests. Like the other shafts in the area, which was probably west of the Shûnet-el-Zebîb, these were used several times in the period from the Middle Kingdom to the

New Kingdom, and the contents of different shafts were further mixed up by tomb robbers tunnelling underground from one to the next. The incompleteness of the excavation record delivers the 'coup de grâce' to any hope of dating the ivory from its context. The 'Pan' pottery (actually Kerma ware) from tombs in the vicinity, referred to by Garstang in support of an attribution to a Hyksos King, is irrelevant, since none was found in any of the three shafts. Nevertheless the association was repeated uncritically by Schweitzer in support of a non-Egyptian origin for the ivory.

Stylistic analysis provides the only means of refining the date further. The quality of the carving and the wealth of detail encouraged Hall to see in the sphinx a royal portrait. In my view it is an icon, a miniature version of the series of royal sphinxes of the xiith Dynasty, adapted for use as the handle of a box or perhaps to form the corner decoration of a piece of furniture. For comparison there is the image of the lion trampling and devouring prostrate enemies on an ivory wand from Lisht (Hayes, *Scepter*, I, fig. 159, top) and the wooden statuette from Thebes showing a lion standing upright, grasping the head of a kneeling captive in its claws (Hayes, *op. cit.*, fig. 141). Far from its being a portrait, the proportions of the sphinx's head and face, with the enormous eyes and heavy *nemes*, are totally unnatural, and the ears and even the nose, upon which Hall set so much store, are exaggerated to the point of caricature. Nevertheless, given that the ivory does not represent how the King actually looked, and few royal images did, can it be assigned to a particular xiith or xiiith Dynasty monarch? It is not possible to take Hall's attribution to a Hyksos King further, since there are no contemporary inscribed royal sculptures for comparison.

The soft material, common in decorative art but rare for sculptures (but see Cat. no. 98), and otherwise unknown for royal sculptures of the time, makes comparison with official hard stone sculptures difficult. The tiny scale and the unique pose also make it harder to analyse the style of the piece. Nevertheless, in my view a tentative comparison can be made with the Berlin statue of Senusret I on account of the following features: the shape of the *nemes* – short between frontlet and top of head, with a single stripe executed in relief and a pronounced outward curve of the side folds; the uraeus rising from the base of the frontlet, and the multiple windings of its body; the relief eyebrow; relief bands around the eyes, pronounced inner canthi and cosmetic line; the enormous projecting ears, set high; and the straight lips. The general shape of the face of the Berlin statue is also long and narrow with high cheek-bones. The nose on the ivory sphinx, it must be said, does not appear to suit the comparison. The nose of the Berlin statue is lost, but where representations survive, for example on one of the statues from the King's mortuary temple at Lisht now in the Cairo Museum, the profile is straight. However, on the base of the throne of these statues is a scene in relief representing the unification of Egypt, and the personification of Lower Egypt has the features of the King, including a nose with a strongly curved profile and prominent nostrils.

J. Garstang in *JEA* 14 (1928), pp. 46–7; U. Schweitzer,

Löwe und Sphinx (Glückstadt, 1948), pp. 39–40, pl. IX, 3; B. Hornemann, *Types of Ancient Egyptian Statuary*, VI, pl. 1526; Davies, *A Royal Statue Reattributed*, p. 11, n. 1; *The Macgregor Collection. Sotheby's Sale Catalogue*, 26 June–6 July 1922, lot no. 716, pl. XXI; cf. Berlin statue, Evers, *Staat aus dem Stein*, I, pls. 28, 30, 45; C. Aldred in *MMJ* 3 (1970), p. 37.

139 WOODEN FIGURINES
Late Dynasty XII to Dynasty XIII, 1862–1650 BC.

Two tiny standing figures of men (a), (b), wearing the formal dress of officials and each standing on a round base in the form of a papyrus flower. Each is carved from a single piece of wood, except that in the case of (a) a separate piece was used for the toes and the front half of the base. The figures are identical, although (b) is more worn, with a small chip missing from the nose and chipping around the bottom of the base. They wear shoulder-length wigs or wig covers, cf. Cat. no. 44, and the long kilt with a triangular pleat in the front. Despite the minuscule scale the features retain considerable character. The brows are incised; the one above the left eye of (a) has been omitted; the eyes are narrow and asymmetrical; the nose is short and pointed; the lips are straight but curving up slightly at the corners; the ears are set low and are also asymmetrical; the chin is small. There is an incised line at the base of the neck, a deeper line defining the pectoral muscles, and a faint horizontal line on the stomach, suggesting rolls of flesh. The arms hang down beside the body and the hands are held flat against the kilt. Fingers and toes are indicated. There are traces of black pigment in the incised lines of the wig.

139a, b

From Thebes (?). Gift of Jesse Haworth. British Museum EA 21578–9. (a) H: 5.8 cm. W: 1.8 cm. (b) H: 5.9 cm. W: 1.7 cm.

The pins in the supports of these tiny figures are not original. A late Middle Kingdom date for the figures is suggested by their dress and physiognomy and the treatment of their torsos. Their function is not so clear. It has been suggested that they were mechanical toys, but if so there is no remaining evidence of this. They are too heavy to stand unsupported on their present bases and these must have been fixed onto a large object. The shape of their bases suggests that they may have been gaming pieces or elaborate knobs attached to hair pins or boxes.

Cf. Petrie, *Diospolis Parva*, pl. XXVI, top right.

STONE VESSELS

140 GIRL HOLDING A *KOHL* POT

Dynasty XII, 1963–1787 BC.

Black steatite statuette on a rectangular base depicting a kneeling girl resting her buttocks on her heels and clasping a *kohl* pot. The pot has a detachable rim and is supported on a ring base, cf. Cat. no. 145c. The girl's head is smooth (presumably shaved) except for a long, wide plait of hair which falls from the top of her head down her back. The plait curls to the right (cf. Cat. no. 116), and from it hangs a fish pendant like Cat. no. 159. Her skull is elongated and flattened on top, and the facial features are roughly delineated and asymmetrical. The brows are shaped, not outlined, and so barely visible; the right eye is narrower than the left and both are outlined in bands of relief; some traces of pigment remain inside the eyes; the ears stick out at right angles to the face and are roughly chiselled, showing no internal detail; the nose is short with wide nostrils; the mouth has thick straight lips; the chin is pointed and the cheek-bones are marked. The face is broad, youthful but not noticeably feminine. The figure, on the other hand, is girlish – the breasts are small, pointed and set very high, the waist is narrow and the hips and thighs are small and rounded. She wears a short kilt from waist to calf and around her hips is a cowrie bead girdle, cf. Cat. nos. 116, 154.

From Thebes. British Museum EA 2572. H: 7.9 cm. W: 5.9 cm.

This charming object, like Cat. no. 141, is a highly ornamental container for cosmetics. The *kohl* pot which the girl offers was intended for use, shows signs of wear and probably once had a matching and close-fitting lid. Kemp and Merrillees list eight similar examples, to which may be added at least two more (unpublished) ones from Lisht.

The shape of the *kohl* pot suggests this statuette belongs in the XIIth Dynasty, although other examples, e.g. Cat. no. 141, are later.

Fischer has suggested that the figure holding the vase is a boy not a girl, but the hairstyle is, as far as I know, exclusively worn by women. Tomb scenes show acrobats (with one back and one side plait) and dancers wearing it, the statue of a naked girl from Kahun wears it, with the plait curling to the left instead of the right, and most of the figures holding jars, androgenous though they are, also wear it. Fish pendants and cowrie bead girdles are never shown worn by boys.

E. Staehelin in *ZÄS* 105 (1978), pp. 83–4, pl. IIb, c; H. Fischer in J. Assmann, E. Feucht and R. Grieshammer (eds.), *Fragen an die altägyptische Literatur. Studien zum Gedenken an Eberhard Otto* (Wiesbaden, 1977), pp. 161–5.

140

141 MAN OFFERING A BOWL

Late Dynasty XIII, 1720–1650 BC.

Limestone statuette of a man holding a bowl. The man stands with his left foot forward and his arms outstretched around the bowl, which rests on a tall support; both in turn stand on a rectangular plinth. The bowl is functional, being large enough to be used for eye paint or some other substance required in very small quantities. The statuette is schematically carved, and asymmetrical in detail. It shows a man wearing the shoulder-length wig with long triangular lappets, cf. Cat. no. 19. The brows are straight, and under them the eyes are large and bulbous. The nose is short and straight and the mouth small and clumsily carved. The man wears a long triangular beard and a high-waisted kilt with horizontal stripes.

From Haraga, tomb 162. Gift of the British School of Archaeology in Egypt. Fitzwilliam E.6.1914. H: 8.6 cm. W: 3.6 cm.

This statuette was found in the same burial as Cat. no. 57, and is dated by the associated objects to the late XIIIth Dynasty. Such a date suits the long fringed kilt and the wig which the man wears.

Engelbach, *Harageh*, p. 13, pl. XIX, 3; Vandier, *La Statuaire Egyptienne*, pp. 229, 267, pl. XCII; Kemp and Merrillees, *Minoan Pottery*, p. 149.

141

142 VULTURE FLASK Illustrated in colour on pl. IV, 4.

Dynasty XII, 1963–1787 BC.

Anhydrite flask with a flat base and a pouring lip. The flask is carved in raised relief with the figures of two vultures. Their wings are outstretched and they hold a *shen* sign between them on each side of the vessel, see Cat. nos. 11, 36, 162.

The necks and heads of the birds are carved in the round and their beaks join the lip of the flask. The eyes were originally inlaid with a strip of mother-of-pearl set into a black substance (possibly resin) which also serves to represent the pupils. The anhydrite is grey–blue in colour and covered with a thin layer of limescale. There is a small chip out of the rim which has been made up with plaster.

From Akhmîm. Gift of C. Ricketts and C. Shannon. Fitzwilliam E.54.1937. H: 9.0 cm. D: 7.5 cm.

This flask belongs to a small group of cosmetic vases in anhydrite carved with elaborate designs in relief. Ducks and monkeys (see Cat. nos. 143–4) are the most favoured motifs, but a few vases show heraldic designs, of which this is the finest example. The *shen* sign symbolises the region encircled by the sun, and so, by what seemed to the Egyptians a natural extension of the image, the land of Egypt ruled by the King. The vultures represent the goddess Nekhbet, tutelary goddess of Upper Egypt and so protectress of the King. When the King is shown in temple or tomb scenes he often appears within a frame in the top corner of which is a vulture with outspread wings holding a *shen* sign, facing him. A similar design occurs on a cosmetic vase of the early XVIIIth Dynasty from Abydos.

Anhydrite was prized for its translucency and its soft blue colour. It is close in chemical composition to gypsum, which is widely found in Egypt, and it is supposed that a particular source was discovered and mined out during the XIth to XIIIth Dynasties. The latest dated vessel in anhydrite is from the treasure of one of the minor wives of King Tuthmosis III (1479–1425 BC) of the early XVIIIth Dynasty.

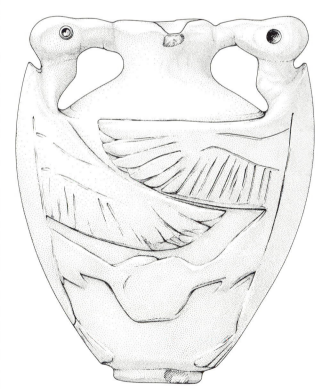

142

Attribution of the vase to an Akhmîm provenance is provided by a label adhering to the bottom and dated 26 March 1901. Ricketts and Shannon bought most of their Egyptian antiquities on the London market, so the label is almost certainly not theirs. Akhmîm has a considerable Middle Kingdom cemetery, including large rock tombs of the early xiith Dynasty; furthermore, it is situated in Upper Egypt, so would seem to be a convincing provenance for such an object.

J. Darracott (ed.) *All for Art. The Ricketts and Shannon Collection* (Cambridge, 1979), p. 21, no. 2 and bibliography there cited; cf. *kohl* pot with uraei, Downes, *Esna*, fig. 75, Wl; for design, cf. Ayrton *et al.*, *Abydos*, iii, pl. lviii, 21.

143 DUCK VASE
Dynasties xiii–xvii, 1786–1550 bc.

Anhydrite vase in the shape of a trussed duck. The vase will not stand unsupported. It is possible that a neck was originally attached to the body of the vase; if so it would have been made as a separate piece since there is no trace of a break. The detailed markings of the beak and webbed feet are reproduced with great care. A break where the duck's slender neck joins the body has been repaired. The eyes were once inlaid.

Ex Hardinge collection. Oriental Museum, University of Durham h.2259. H: 11.8 cm. D: 6.7 cm.

This is one of the finest of the small group of surviving anhydrite vases in the form of a trussed duck. Terrace lists 10 examples (excluding this one), of which four have an excavated provenance, but of these four contexts only one is published. Fortunately this excavated vase, once in the Art Institute in Chicago, offers the best parallel to the Durham vase. It comes from the north chamber of a shaft tomb at Abydos. The tomb had been robbed, and it is impossible to reconstruct any one burial deposit, but all the pottery in the tomb appears to be consistent with a date in Dynasty xvii. Anhydrite relief vases occur sporadically as late as this and even later (see Cat. no. 142), but there is no internal evidence from the vase itself to suggest it was made after the Middle Kingdom. The date depends only on the context of the close parallel from Abydos.

The motif of a trussed duck is a familiar one, since it occurs in many offering scenes, and models in wood or in stone (see Cat. no. 87a) were placed among the grave goods. Vases occur in two versions, a single one as here or a double one in which two ducks are joined together.

Cf. Peet, *Cemeteries of Abydos*, ii, pl. xiii, 14; Hayes, *Scepter*, i, fig. 157; E. Terrace in *JARCE* 5 (1966), pp. 60–1, pls. xxi–xxii.

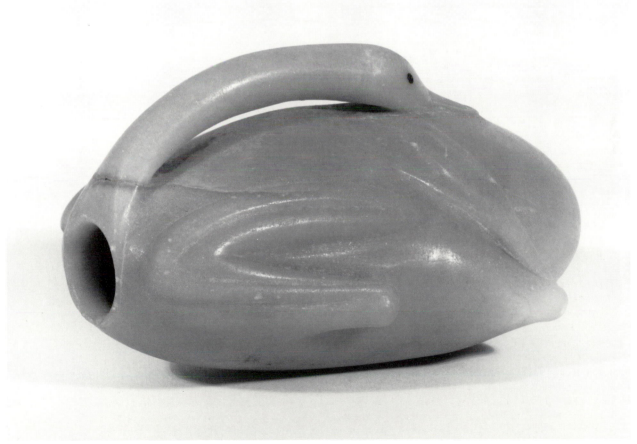

143

144 KOHL POTS WITH MONKEYS

Dynasty XII, 1963–1787 BC.

Two small anhydrite pots, (a), (b), with two monkeys depicted in relief around the outside of each. (b) Once had a separate rim like Cat. no. 145c, and both pots originally had lids. The pose of the monkeys is the same on both. They are seated upon their tails with their knees and arms bent, appearing to hold the vessel against their bodies. The carving of (a) is stiffer than that of (b), due partly to the vessel's straighter profile, and the monkeys wear collars. Unlike the trussed duck vase, Cat. no. 143, the vessels show their underlying shape; they belong to the broad, squat group of undecorated *kohl* pots, cf. Cat. nos. 145a, c.

145a–d

144b

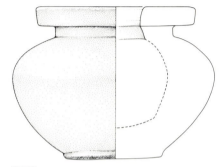

145c

144a

(a) Acquired at Thebes. Ex Mackay collection. Bristol H.4201. H: 3.0 cm. D: 4.1 cm. (b) Gift of G. D. Hornblower. Fitzwilliam E.266.1939. H: 2.2 cm. D: 3.2 cm.

The use of monkeys as a decorative device on eye-paint jars continued into the New Kingdom, when the motif was elaborated in a variety of ways. In the Middle Kingdom, monkeys are found almost exclusively as decoration on anhydrite bowls and *kohl* pots. They appear frequently in domestic scenes in tomb reliefs, showing that they were kept as pets, but they were also erotic symbols, which might explain their association with eye paint and other cosmetics. According to the evidence of excavated examples, the shape of these two *kohl* pots suggests a date in Dynasty XII.

Cf. E. Terrace in *JARCE* 5 (1966), pp. 59–60, pls. XV, XIX; see L. Manniche, *Sexual Life in Ancient Egypt* (London, 1987), pp. 43–4.

145 ANHYDRITE COSMETIC JARS

Dynasties XII–XIII, 1963–1650 BC.

(a) Broad, squat *kohl* pot with separate rim, and with body carved in one piece with the four-legged support; (b) cylinder vase; (c) broad, squat *kohl* pot with separate rim; (d) high-

shouldered *kohl* pot with originally separate rim now stuck to body. *Kohl* pot (a) now has a fitting lid of serpentine which, almost certainly, does not belong to it.

(a) Gift of C. Ricketts and C. Shannon. (b), (c) From Abydos, tombs E.251, E.182. Gift of the Egyptian Research Account. (d) Ex Benzion collection. Bequest of Sir Robert Greg. Fitzwilliam E.51.1937, E.236.1900, E.140.1900, E.272.1954. (a) H: 4.2 cm. D: 4.0 cm. (b) H: 5.4 cm. D: 4.6 cm. (c) H: 3.9 cm. D: 5.3 cm. (d) H: 3.4 cm. D: 3.5 cm.

Each of the three *kohl* pots shows the characteristically narrow opening, wide enough for the insertion of a finger or a specially designed applicator, Cat. nos. 149c, d. The substances most commonly used in antiquity for painting the eyes were malachite, a copper ore providing a green pigment, and galena, a lead ore providing a grey or black pigment. *Kohl* is a general term used for the pigments in the powdered form in which they were kept. They were mixed with water to make a paste before being applied. It was important to protect them from dust and wind, so the pots were usually sealed with a matching and tight-fitting lid, and often further protected by linen tied over this.

It is perhaps surprising that cosmetic jars of this kind, found in hundreds of graves of both men and women, can still not be dated with very great precision. It is clear that their shapes changed much less rapidly than those of most classes of pottery, and that they varied less than pottery from one region to another. Their material and technique of manufacture are also far less complex. However, they have remained neglected by scholars, and one reason for this is that the documentation of the excavated examples, which might be expected to provide a chronological framework for their study, is so poor. The excavated jar and *kohl* pot in this group, (b), (c), exemplify the problem well. Both come from cemetery E at Abydos, excavated by John Garstang in 1900. Tomb E.251, from which the cylinder vase comes, is published, but although mentioned under 'vessels of blue marble and alabaster', the jar is neither illustrated nor described. Study of the excavator's marks carried by this and the other objects from the tomb suggests that the jar was found in the same chamber as another calcite vase of the same shape (Fitzwilliam E.235.1900), a calcite *kohl* pot (Fitzwilliam E.237.1900) and a curious pottery figurine which Garstang does illustrate (*El Arábah*, pl. IV, top, middle). All these objects are compatible with a date in Dynasty XII, but we have no evidence on which to decide whether they come from the same burial or not. The *kohl* pot (c) comes from tomb E.182, which is completely unpublished. Also from this tomb, and now in the Fitzwilliam, is a scarab of late Middle Kingdom type (E.168.1900). In this case we have no further information on which to associate the objects more closely, other than the presumption that they came from the same shaft; unfortunately in cemetery E each shaft contained at least two chambers.

(a) J. Darracott (ed.), *All for Art. The Ricketts and Shannon Collection* (Cambridge, 1979), p. 21, no. 2; cf. vase in Boston from Sheikh Farag, SF 170, E. Terrace in *JARCE* 5 (1966), p. 58, n. 2; (b) Garstang, *El Arábah*, p. 45; (d) cf. Kemp and Merrillees, *Minoan Pottery*, fig. 41, no. 45.

146 GREEN LIMESTONE *KOHL* POT

Dynasty XII, 1963–1787 BC.

Green limestone *kohl* pot with separable rim and fitted lid. Smooth, highly polished outside, marks of drilling on the inside. The matrix is pale green with veins of cream and dark green running through it.

From El Kab, tomb 361. Gift of the Egyptian Research Account. Ashmolean E.2149. H: 4.9 cm. (with lid). D: 4.4 cm.

This extremely beautiful and unusual stone was used only rarely, for cosmetic vases and small statuettes. It must have

come from one of the many sources of limestone available in Egypt, but the particular quarry is unknown. Tomb 361 from El Kab is unpublished, see comments on Cat. nos. 80 and 145. The shape of the pot suggests it is later in date than the broad, squat pots of the shape of Cat. no. 145c.

For a statuette in the same material, Wildung, *L'Age d'Or*, fig. 180; cf. for similar pot in calcite from XIIIth Dynasty burial, Peet, *Cemeteries of Abydos*, II, pl. XIII, 9.

147 COSMETIC JARS OF LIMESTONE, BASALT AND SERPENTINE

Dynasty XII, 1963–1787 BC.

(a) Shouldered jar of black limestone; (b) cylinder vase of basalt; (c) tall cylinder vase of serpentine. Exterior surfaces carefully polished to remove tool marks, but horizontal drilling marks still visible on the inside of the cylinder vases.

(a), (b) Bequest of Sir Robert Greg and (b) possibly ex Benzion collection. Fitzwilliam E.115.1954, E.310.1954, E.S.11. (a) H: 9.8 cm. D: 6.7 cm. (b) H: 7.5 cm. D: 5.2 cm. (c) H: 11.0 cm. D: 8.7 cm.

Both limestone and serpentine are soft, easily worked stones and occur at many places in Egypt. Basalt is equally plentiful but very much harder. Despite this characteristic it was used from early times as a building stone and in the manufacture of stone vases. The serpentine vase, Fitzwilliam E.S.11, has no year of acquisition because we do not know when it came into the collection, only that it was before the catalogue of the Egyptian collection was begun in the 1940s. For the dating of (b) and (c) cf. Cat. no. 149.

147a, c, b

148 JAR AND *KOHL* POT OF SPECKLED LIMESTONE

Dynasty XII, 1963–1787 BC.

(a) Small cylinder jar and (b) *kohl* pot with matching lid. The speckled effect is due to a mineral growth on the surface of the stone. Drilling marks are still visible on the inside of the jar.

(a) Gift of G. D. Hornblower and (b) bequest of Sir Robert Greg. Fitzwilliam E.221.1939, E.309.1954. (a) H: 5.0 cm. D: 4.2 cm. (b) H: 3.4 cm. D: 3.8 cm.

146

148a, b

149a–d

The provenance of neither of these stone vases is known, but similar examples in well-dated deposits suggest a date in Dynasty XII.

149 COSMETIC JARS AND *KOHL* STICKS

Dynasty XII, 1963–1787 BC.

Two cylinder vases (a), (b), made of calcite with matching lids and two round-ended sticks (c), (d), made of haematite and used to apply eye paint (*kohl*). One *kohl* stick (d) has a piece of gold leaf wrapped around the end which was held in the hand.

(a)–(c) Bequest of Sir Robert Greg and (d) gift of G. D. Hornblower. Fitzwilliam E.237–8.1954, E.489.1954, E.61.1939. (a) H: 9.8 cm. D: 8.0 cm. (b) H: 11.5 cm. D: 9.5 cm. (c) H: 9.8 cm. D: 1.0 cm. (d) H: 7.3 cm. D: 1.0 cm.

'Alabaster' is still the term most commonly applied to the material of which these vases are made, although geologically it is calcite. Despite the variety of stones in use in the Middle Kingdom, calcite was still the one most frequently chosen for vases, being valued for its translucency and the contrasting bands of darker and lighter stone. There are many sources of alabaster in Egypt, the most famous quarry being at Hatnub close to Amarna. The elegant shape of these vases places them without doubt in the XIIth Dynasty. There are several parallels from closed deposits dated by royal names. Cosmetic jars usually had matching, close-fitting lids and were sometimes further sealed by a piece of cloth's being placed over the lid, pulled tight by a piece of string knotted under the rim, and perhaps sealed, see Cat. nos. 178–83. The contents were both valuable and in need of protection from dust and heat. In only a very few cases have the contents survived and been analysed, but these suggest the jars contained scented oil or fat used for cleansing or perfuming the skin.

Haematite was a favoured material for the sticks used for applying eye paint, because of its colour and its metallic lustre. It is an iron ore plentiful in Egypt, although the ancient sources remain unidentified.

Vases: cf. Hayes, *Scepter*, I, figs. 155, 157.

150 FLASK WITH RIBBED NECK

Dynasty XIII, 1786–1650 BC.

Bag-shaped flask with a ribbed neck, made of calcite, see Cat. no. 149. Tool marks smoothed away from the exterior surface but drilling marks still visible on the inside.

Bequest of Sir Robert Greg. Fitzwilliam E.30.1954. H: 17.1 cm. D: 10.2 cm.

This vase may belong to the late Middle Kingdom, since ribbing on the neck is also a characteristic of some large pottery vessels of that date from Lower Egypt.

150

Cf. Do. Arnold in *MDAIK* 38 (1982), Abb. 7, no. 10, 8, no. 10; Engelbach, *Harageh*, pl. xxxviii, 46m; for parallels in stone not so closely datable, Kemp and Merrillees, *Minoan Pottery*, p. 125, fig. 41, no. 38; Downes, *Esna*, fig. 75, Wb.

151 COSMETIC JARS OF ALABASTER (CALCITE)

Late Dynasty xii to Dynasty xiii, 1862–1650 BC.

(a) Small pear-shaped flask with flat base; (b) globular jar with flat rim; (c) small bagshaped jar; all of calcite, commonly called 'alabaster'. Chips in the rim of (a) and (c) have been restored in plaster. Exterior surfaces have been smoothed and polished but tool marks are still visible on the inside.

Bequest of Sir Robert Greg. Fitzwilliam E.249, 253, 270.1954. (a) H: 6.8 cm. D: 4.5 cm. (b) H: 6.8 cm. D: 6.5 cm. (c) H: 4.8 cm. D: 4.2 cm.

For (b) and (c), cf. Garstang, *El Arábah*, pl. iii, for date of tomb E.105, see Cat. no. 162.

152

151a, b, c

COSMETIC OBJECTS

152 PALETTE AND RUBBER

Dynasties xii–xiii, 1963–1650 BC.

Palette and rubber made of diorite. The surface of the palette and the base of the rubber have been worn by use.

Bequest of Sir Robert Greg. Fitzwilliam E.326 a, b.1954. Palette: L: 9.9 cm. W: 6.4 cm. Rubber: H: 3.7 cm. W: 2.8 cm.

The palette was used as a mortar on which to crush the pigments used to paint the face and eyes. Palettes like this occur frequently in burials throughout the xiith and xiiith Dynasties and their shape does not appear to change during that time.

Cf. Kemp and Merrillees, *Minoan Pottery*, fig. 40, no. 32.

153 IVORY COSMETIC SPOON

Dynasty xii, 1963–1787 BC.

Ivory cosmetic spoon with a terminal in the form of a duck's head. The spoon was originally made in three pieces, but the central section forming the handle is now missing. The head of the duck is carved in detail with considerable skill.

From Haraga, cemetery w2, grave 539. Gift of the British School of Archaeology in Egypt. Fitzwilliam E.11.1914. Fragment with bowl: L: 5.2 cm. W: 1.7 cm. Duck's head terminal: L: 4.3 cm. W: 1.6 cm.

None of the objects from the shallow grave from which this spoon came is illustrated in the publication. They were a pottery saucer, a copper knife, a flint flake, the cosmetic spoon and some fragments of papyrus. This was a poor burial and the poor were unable to afford specially made grave goods, so were accompanied into the Afterlife by their everyday possessions.

Engelbach, *Harageh*, pp. 2–3, pl. lxii; cf. Petrie, *Kahun*, pl. viii, 17.

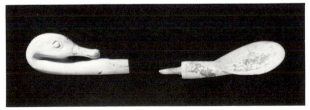

153

JEWELLERY

154 JEWELLERY

Dynasties xii–xiii, 1963–1650 BC.

Elements from several pieces of jewellery made up into a necklace. Six hollow cowrie shell beads and a clasp all made of electrum, each bead made in two halves soldered together; between them a double row of spherical beads of lapis lazuli, green felspar and amethyst. Suspended from the string are

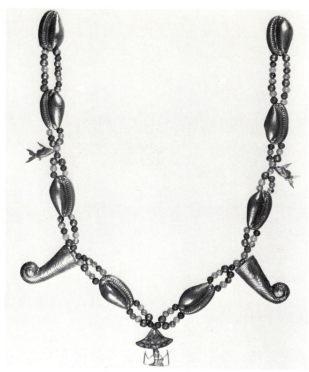

154

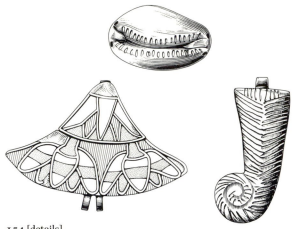

154 [details]

worn by young women, sometimes (see Cat. nos. 116, 120) with nothing else at all.

Andrews, *Jewellery*, p. 64, no. 414, pl. 32; E. Staehelin in *ZÄS* 105 (1978), p. 83, pl. IIa; British Museum, *Jewellery through 7000 Years* (London, 1976), Cat. no. 339, pp. 210–11, pl. 6.

155 SIDE-LOCK PENDANT
Dynasty XII, 1963–1787 BC.

Electrum pendant in the form of a side lock. Both this pendant and those included in Cat. no. 154 are made in the same way. The two halves of the pendant are made separately and joined down the sides with solder. They are hollow, and there is no evidence of a core. A plate has been fitted to the top to which a suspension ring has been attached. The pattern on the outside, representing the plaited hair and curl at the bottom of the side lock, is chased.

Bequest of R. G. Gayer-Anderson. Fitzwilliam EGA. 155.1947. H: 2.0 cm. W: 1.1 cm.

Examples of side-lock pendants are rare, and confined to the Middle Kingdom. The only exception is a large gilded bronze example, Fitzwilliam EGA.156.1947, which may be Roman. None of the surviving examples, eight in all, derives from an excavated context, so we can only surmise how they were worn. Their size and form suggests to me that they were hair ornaments, actually worn at the bottom of a plait of hair.

There is some uncertainty as to whether they represent a beard or a lock of hair, but both these examples seem most convincing as side locks.

Cf. Andrews, *Jewellery*, p. 94, Appendix N and bibliography there cited.

two electrum fish (see Cat. no. 160), two electrum side-lock pendants made like Cat. no. 155, an electrum *Heh* amulet (see Cat. nos. 174b, c), and a silver lotus flower pendant, inlaid with carnelian and glass, using the cloisonné technique. In the drawing the carnelian is shown by vertical hatching, the light blue glass by white, and the dark blue glass by stippling.

Said to be from Thebes. Ex Salt collection, 1835. British Museum EA. 3077. L: 47.2 cm.

The arrangement of the various elements in this necklace owes more to the taste of the nineteenth century AD than to the jewellers of the Middle Kingdom. While the components are probably all of Middle Kingdom date, they do not belong together. The cowries and spherical beads come from a girdle, such as that worn by the girl, Cat. no. 140; the side-lock and fish pendants are probably hair ornaments, and the lotus and *heh* amulets come from a necklace.

Cloisonné, a technique which becomes common in the Middle Kingdom, is used for some of the most spectacular jewels which have survived from the period, see Cat. no. 156. The inlays are usually hard stones and the presence of glass, which has been verified by the British Museum Research Laboratory, is unusual in the Middle Kingdom. Although it has been reported among the inlays in the jewellery of Princess Khnemt, probably a daughter of King Amenemhat II (1901–1867 BC), the identification is unconfirmed. Thus the presence of glass raises the possibility that the lotus pendant is of New Kingdom and not of Middle Kingdom date.

Cowrie beads used in girdles were sometimes filled with pellets so that they jingled as their owner walked. They were

155

146

156

July 1922, lot no. 1417, pl. xxxix; Aldred, *Jewels of the Pharaohs*, p. 185, pls. 25–6; Wilkinson, *Egyptian Jewellery*, p. 89, pl. xx.

157 GOLD CYLINDER

Dynasty xii, 1963–1787 bc.

Cylinder made of sheet gold over a copper core, decorated with a pattern of pendant triangles executed in granulation. The granules were attached to the sheet by a solder, possibly of electrum. The individual granules are less than 0.5 mm across and there are 1848 in all. The top and bottom of the cylinder are capped in sheet gold and a gold suspension loop has been pushed into the top.

From Haraga, tomb 211 north of Cemetery A. University College 6482. H: 5.3 cm. W: 1.1 cm.

Granulation, like cloisonné, was one of the jeweller's techniques both introduced and perfected during the xiith Dynasty. The first examples of granulation from the Near East come from Ur in Mesopotamia, and the technique may have been brought to Egypt by foreign craftsmen, since some of the earliest jewellery which uses it, from the treasure of

156 GOLD PECTORAL Illustrated in colour on pl. IV,2.

Dynasty xii, 1963–1787 bc.

Pectoral of gold with inlays of carnelian, lapis lazuli and green felspar. The pectoral is now in two sections and most of the inlays have disappeared. The back is chased and shows the design clearly. The central motif is the symbol of the goddess Bat, whose cult was centred in the seventh nome of Upper Egypt. She appears with the face of a woman and the ears and horns of a cow. Below her chin is a stylised representation of a bead collar, with five rows of cylinder beads and a row of leaf-shaped pendants. Either side of the goddess are heraldic beasts representing Upper and Lower Egypt. On the right a hawk-headed lion, a version of Horus, for Lower Egypt; on the left a lion with the head and tail of Seth, the mythological opponent of Horus, representing Upper Egypt. Framing this central image are papyrus stalks and two Sacred Eyes, see Cat. no. 68, and above it is a sun disk with uraeus-snakes.

The gold base plate for each element in the design was formed separately, possibly by beating it over a core; then the pieces were soldered together. The joins between the lions' bodies and their tails are barely visible. The strips of metal forming the cloisons for pieces of inlay (see Cat. no. 154) were then attached to the front, and the reverse was chased. Two tubes were soldered to the back to take the suspension cord.

Possibly from Dahshur. Eton College, Myers Museum 832. H: 3.8 cm. W: 5.7 cm.

Half of this pectoral, the section showing Horus, is said to have been purchased in Egypt by Major Myers at the time De Morgan was excavating the tombs of the Princesses at Dahshur. This is the visit during which Myers may also have obtained the wooden statue from the tomb of Mesehti at Asyut, Cat. no. 23, and for which his diary is missing. The other half of the pectoral came into the possession of the Rev. Macgregor, and only after the sale of his collection in 1922 were the two pieces re-united.

The quality and iconography of this pectoral suggest that it was a royal jewel, destined for a member of the royal family or a highly favoured official.

Burlington Fine Arts Club, 1922, p. 20, no. 10, A, B, pl. L; *The Macgregor Collection. Sotheby's Sale Catalogue*, 26 June–6

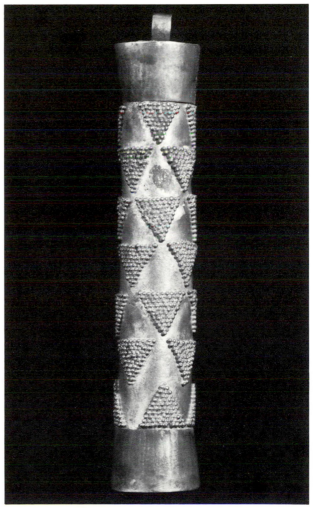

157 [over twice life size]

Princess Khnemt from Dahshur, contains non-Egyptian motifs. The granules are produced in the following way: 'small metal clippings are placed on a charcoal block and heated with a blowpipe. As they melt the surface tension of the liquid metal causes them to roll into spheres.' (J. Ogden, *Jewellery of the Ancient World*, London, 1982, p. 67.) The grains tend to cluster together, making it easier to produce 'solid' designs such as the triangles used here.

The purpose of these cylinders, like that of almost all jewellery, was to confer magic protection. Some examples, unlike this one, were hollow and contain small beads or scraps of papyrus on which charms could be written. This cylinder was found in a large tomb with a much-disturbed burial, thought to have been of a man. The burial, incidentally, also contained two golden cowrie beads (see Cat. no. 154), so perhaps cowries were not, as is often stated, exclusively worn by women. The other possibility is that the sexing of the bones in tomb 211, done on the basis of the skull, was incorrect.

It is interesting to note how quickly granulation spread from its first appearance among royal treasures to the jewels worn by private individuals. Predictably, its distribution seems limited to those cemeteries close to royal workshops. The list provided by Carol Andrews gives Saqqara, the necropolis of Memphis; Lisht, Haraga and Dahshur, all close to the capital and the royal mortuary complexes of the Faiyum; Abydos; and Thebes.

Engelbach, *Harageh*, p. 16, pl. XIV, 5; Petrie, *Objects of Daily Use*, p. 6, pl. II, 9; Ogden, *op. cit.*, p. 66; general, Andrews, *Jewellery*, p. 92, Appendix E; example (without granulation) containing papyrus, Garstang, *Beni Hasan*, p. 113

158 ELECTRUM PENDANT AND GOLD HAIR PIN Illustrated in colour on pl. IV, 3.

Dynasties XII–XIII, 1963–1650 BC.

Electrum pendant (a) in the form of an oyster shell, made of thick sheet metal beaten over a core, with a ring for attachment soldered to the top. Gold hair pin (b), its head representing the symbol of the goddess Bat, which is a woman's face

with the ears and horns of a cow, combined here with a sistrum, see Cat. no. 127. The head is soldered to the shaft of the pin.

Bequest of R. G. Gayer-Anderson. Fitzwilliam E.302a. 1947, E.158.1947. Shell: H: 3.6 cm. W: 3.0 cm. Pin: H: 11.0 cm. W: 0.5 cm.

Plain oyster-shell pendants of gold, silver or electrum were worn singly, or in a smaller version as the final row of pendants in a necklace. They are relatively common in rich burials of the XIIth to XIIIth Dynasties and occur at sites throughout Egypt. The amulets, intended to bring the wearer health, are sometimes shown in sculpture and relief, worn exclusively by women. The pin is notable for the delicacy of its workmanship and for the glowing warmth of the thick sheet gold of which it was made. Gold was prized for its malleability, which made it easy to work, and for its colour, recalling the heat and brightness of the sun. The goddess Bat was the tutelary goddess of the seventh nome of Upper Egypt and so appears among the list of divinities on the walls of the shrine of Senusret I at Karnak. However, her cult was in the process of becoming assimilated to that of Hathor, and by the New Kingdom Bat's attributes and epithets had all been adopted by Hathor. During the early XIIth Dynasty, the integration of the sistrum, associated with Hathor, with the face and horns of Bat begins. Beni Hasan tomb 2 shows priestesses of Hathor carrying such a sistrum, of which the head of the pin is a simplified version. Beauty, and specifically the beauty of women's hair, was within the realm of Hathor and her image often decorates cosmetic objects, see also Cat. no. 184.

Shell: cf. Andrews, *Jewellery*, p. 63, no. 407, p. 93, Appendix J; pin: see H. Fischer in *JARCE* I (1962), pp. 11–15; Newberry, *Beni Hasan*, I, pl. XIII; F. Ll. Griffith (ed.), *Beni Hasan*, IV (London, 1900), pl. XXV, 5.

159 GOLD CATFISH

Late Dynasty XIII to early Dynasty XIII, 1862–1750 BC.

Hair ornament in the shape of a catfish (*Synodontis batensoda*). It was made by shaping the two halves of the fish around a core, setting the tail, fins and ring for attachment into the core, and soldering the two halves together. The fish is heavy, but it is now impossible to see what the core material might be. Aldred suggests that it was fine clay. The detailed markings of the body have been reproduced by chasing.

158b

158a, b

159

From Haraga, Cemetery Λ, tomb 72. Gift of the British School of Archaeology in Egypt. Royal Museum of Scotland 1914.1079. H: 1.9 cm. L: 4.1 cm.

This is one of the largest and finest of the fish amulets, see also Cat. nos. 160, 163–4. It was found in an intact burial of a ten-year-old child, which can be dated by the shape of the *kohl* pots to the late xiith or early xiiith Dynasties. The fish was discovered inside the coffin along with other items of gold jewellery including two smaller fish and two more of the same size as the one exhibited but of lesser quality. The three large fish were hair ornaments worn suspended from the curl at the bottom of the side lock which children habitually wore. It has been suggested that these charms conferred protection against drowning. Catfish were and are common in the Nile. The charms were also worn by young girls, and among the tales of magicians written down in the Middle Kingdom and preserved in Papyrus Westcar is one which centres on the loss of such a charm. King Snefru, a Pharaoh of the Old Kingdom, was bored and to distract him his magician suggests a boating party on the lake with 'all the beautiful girls of your palace'. Twenty girls were found with shapely bodies and who had not yet given birth. They were dressed only in bead nets (see Cat. no. 80), and 'His Majesty's heart was happy to see them row' until the girl at the stroke oar touched her plaits and her fish pendant of new turquoise fell into the water. She and the rest of the rowers stopped and the magician had to be recalled to turn back the waters of the lake to reveal the pendant lying on the bottom. In addition to the evidence of the story, there are representations of women wearing such pendants, and they are shown on statuettes, see Cat. no. 140.

Engelbach, *Harageh*, pp. 14–15, pl. xxii, 5; Aldred, *Jewels of the Pharaohs*, pl. 78, p. 213; id, *Middle Kingdom Art*, p. 53, pl. 74; general, Andrews, *Jewellery*, pp. 92–3, Appendix G; H. Fischer in J. Assman, E. Feucht and R. Grieshammer (eds.), *Fragen an die altägyptische Literatur. Studien zum Gedenken an Eberhard Otto* (Wiesbaden, 1977), pp. 161–5.

160 GOLD AND ELECTRUM FISH PENDANTS
Dynasties xii–xiii, 1963–1650 BC.

Three small pendants, each in the shape of a catfish (*Synodontis batensoda*); two, (a), (c) made of gold and one, (b) made of electrum. Although they are smaller and made of thinner sheet metal, the technique of manufacture is exac-

160a, b, c

tly the same as that used to make Cat. no. 159. In this case, however, the metal has cracked sufficiently to show the core.

Bequest of R. G. Gayer-Anderson. Fitzwilliam EGA.143–5.1947. (a) L: 2.7 cm. W: 1.1 cm. (b) L: 2.2 cm. W: 0.8 cm. (c) L: 2.0 cm. W: 0.7 cm.

These pendants are perhaps too small to wear in the hair and are more likely to have been suspended from a necklace.

For general bibliography, see Cat. no. 159.

161 CARNELIAN CLAW
Dynasty xii, 1963–1787 BC.

Claw of a bird or feline carved out of carnelian and incised at the top with four lines. Pierced for stringing so that the claw hung downwards. Probably from an anklet.

Gift of R. G. Gayer-Anderson. Fitzwilliam EGA.4698.1943. H: 3.0 cm. W: 2.0 cm.

161

Several examples of claw pendants in precious metals, one of them decorated in cloisonné technique imitating feathers, were found in the royal treasures of the xiith Dynasty Queens and Princesses. This suggests that these were women's jewels and we know from other evidence that they were worn on the ankle. In an undisturbed burial of a woman at Nagᶜ el-Deir, archaeologists found such anklets still in position. Each was made up of small carnelian and amethyst beads strung with three claws made of silver and one larger one carved in bone and overlaid with bronze. At all periods natural claws were worn, for their amuletic power as much as for decoration, and we can be sure that none of this power was lost when they were reproduced in the beautiful materials available to xiith Dynasty craftsmen.

Cf. Andrews, *Jewellery*, p. 66, no. 435, p. 95, Appendix S; for Nagᶜ el-Deir burial, E. S. Eaton in *Boston Bulletin* 39 (1941), p. 97, figs. 2, 3, 5.

162 'FAIENCE' AND CARNELIAN BEADS
Early Dynasty xii, 1963–1862 BC.

String of thirty-nine spheroid beads, average dia. 1.0 cm, two small spheroid beads, average dia. 0.5 cm, thirty-one drop beads and 2 barrel beads, all of Egyptian faience. Strung with them are one large barrel bead, a small lion amulet (cf. Cat. no. 175b), and pendants in the form of uraeus-snake and a small round pot, all of carnelian. All the 'faience' beads have brown patches on top of the glazed surface.

From Beni Hasan, tomb 65. Gift of the Beni Hasan Excavation Committee. Fitzwilliam E.52.1903. L: 66.0 cm.

162

163

The beads were almost certainly re-strung by the excavator. It is probable that the spheroid beads originally made up a string on their own. Spheroid beads in Egyptian faience or in a variety of hard stones were fashionable throughout the Middle Kingdom. Like anhydrite or amethyst, they are one of the hallmarks of the period which the excavator of any Middle Kingdom site expects to find.

The coffin of Senuitef, Cat. no. 68, was also found in tomb 65 at Beni Hasan, but we cannot be sure that the beads come from the same burial. One of the pendants is in the form of a *nw* vase, a small round vessel used as a container for the water offering.

Garstang, *Beni Hasan*, fig. 100; for the *nw* vase pendant, Andrews, *Jewellery*, p. 95, Appendix T.

163 GOLD, 'FAIENCE' AND CARNELIAN BEADS AND A PENDANT
Late Dynasty XII, 1862–1787 BC.

String of forty-two graduated spheroid beads made of Egyptian faience and capped with gold. Four of the beads have lost their gold caps. The surface of the beads is remarkably smooth, except for crumbs adhering to the glazed surface of a few, and the colour is an even, pale turquoise. In the centre of the string is an amulet in the form of the *shen* sign (see Cat. no. 142), inlaid with Egyptian faience and carnelian.

From Abydos, Cemetery E.105. Gift of the Egyptian Research Account. Ashmolean E.E. 472. L: 52.5 cm.

The fashion for capping with precious metals large round beads of Egyptian faience or hard stones, such as carnelian or obsidian, is characteristic of Dynasty XII. It typifies the Egyptian jeweller's obsession with the juxtaposition of the limited colours at his disposal, and his delight in the use of gold. All the objects from E.105, with the exception of two strings of 'faience' beads, are in the Ashmolean Museum. They make a homogeneous group, which, if they can be presumed to come from a single burial, may be dated to the late XIIth Dynasty. Garstang describes E.105 only as a disturbed pit tomb, but there is evidence of the presence of only one coffin. The stone vases form a group which may be paralleled at Beni Hasan in the intact burial of the Lady of the house, Seneb. Tomb E.105 also contained the funerary figurine of the overseer of the Delta, Nakht, cf. Cat. no. 81.

Garstang, *El Arábah*, pp. 5, 32, pl. II; general, Andrews, *Jewellery*, p. 96, Appendix W; burial of Seneb, Garstang, *Burial Customs*, pp. 113–14, fig. 106.

164 BEADS AND AMULETS
Dynasties XII–XIII, 1963–1650 BC.

(a) String of tiny 'faience' ring beads with 'faience' cylinder and barrel beads, a few barrel and ring beads of Egyptian blue, small spheroid beads of carnelian and amethyst and one glass drop bead. With the string is a glazed steatite scarab and a set of very crudely made 'faience' amulets representing a lion, a baboon, a fly and the Eye of Horus. (b) String of small graduated spheroid beads of garnet with tiny ring beads of glazed steatite, small barrel beads of carnelian and 'faience', a large glazed steatite cylinder bead, two acacia seed beads of carnelian and an imitation shell bead of lapis lazuli. Hanging from the string is an electrum fish pendant made in the same way as Cat. nos. 159–60 but less well preserved.

(a) From Haraga, tomb B.244. Gift of the British School of Archaeology in Egypt. (b) From Kahun, Petrie excavations of 1899. Ex Kennard collection. Gift of Sir W. P. Elderton. Fitzwilliam E.8–9.1914, E.64.1955. (a) L: 25.6 cm. (b) L: 62.0 cm.

There were at least two burials in Haraga tomb B.244, and we do not know how the objects published from the tomb were distributed between them. If they are considered together as a single group, the scarab together with the pottery suggest a date in the XIIIth Dynasty.

It is interesting to compare these two modest strings of beads, one of the XIIth Dynasty, datable by comparison with beads from closed contexts, and one probably of the XIIIth. The fact that one comes from a town and the other from a cemetery has to be taken into account, but the personal jewellery worn by the living and the dead was not usually distinguishable. Jewellery prepared specifically for the tomb, made of 'faience' with inadequate clasps or none at all, is not represented here. The early string (b) contains many more hard stone as opposed to 'faience' beads, and fewer amulets. The range of shapes – acacia seed beads and imitation shell beads in addition to the ubiquitous spheroids and ring beads – is wider, and the quality of craftsmanship higher, in the Kahun string. This perhaps reflects changes we have noticed elsewhere (see p. 000). The XIIIth Dynasty saw a contraction of both resources and skills, and for the

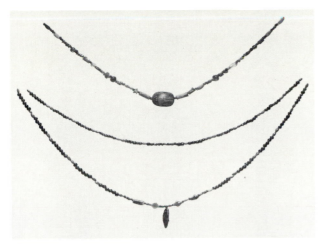

164a, b

165a, b

jeweller this meant that the hard gem stones from the deserts of Egypt and lapis lazuli from Afghanistan were harder to come by. The presence of one glass bead and several of Egyptian blue on the Haraga string is not chronologically significant, since both materials occur, albeit rarely, in the earlier period. For glass see Cat. no. 154. Egyptian blue is the principle blue pigment used by Egyptian craftsmen. Its chemical composition is similar to that of 'faience', but it is not glazed and the surface and the body are the same colour. In addition to being used as a pigment, it was made into a fine paste, shaped by hand or in moulds and fired to produce small objects: beads, amulets, rings, inlays and vases.

(a) Engelbach, *Harageh*, pls. xx, 50, L–LII; for Egyptian blue, Lucas, *Industries*, pp. 340–4; Kaczmarczyk and Hedges, *Faience*, pp. 214–18. (b) for imitation shell beads and acacia seed beads, see Andrews, *Jewellery*, pp. 91–2, 95, Appendices C, U.

165 BEADS AND AMULETS OF SEMI-PRECIOUS STONES
Dynasty XII, 1963–1787 BC.

(a) String of carnelian ring beads and amethyst and carnelian spheroid beads interspersed with a pendant, a plain scarab (see Cat. no. 166), a hippopotamus head (see Cat. no. 175c), a hawk and a lentoid bead, all of carnelian, a turtle bead of green felspar, and a fish pendant of anhydrite. (b) String of graduated spheroid beads of pale amethyst with a few spheroid beads of garnet and carnelian and barrel beads of amethyst, garnet and carnelian.

(a) From Hu, Cemetery W48. Gift of the Egypt Exploration Fund. (b) From Rifeh, tomb 68. Gift of the British School of Archaeology in Egypt. Fitzwilliam E.38.1899, E.13.1907. (a) L: 31.0 cm. (b) L: 21.6 cm.

We have no information on the precise associations of these two strings of beads, but may presume that both came from relatively modest burials, datable from other objects in the tomb to Dynasty XII. Also from W48 at Hu are two *kohl* pots in the Fitzwilliam Museum, including one comparable to Cat. no. 145c, which may be dated to the XIIth Dynasty.

Rifeh 68 contained nothing but three strings of beads, according to the excavator's notebook, and these are all in the Fitzwilliam.

(a) See Petrie, *Diospolis Parva*, pp. 42–4. (b) See Petrie, *Gizeh and Rifeh*, p. 13.

166 BEADS OF CARNELIAN, RED JASPER AND GREEN FELSPAR
Dynasty XII, 1963–1787 BC.

(a) String of graduated spheroid and barrel beads, with one drop-bead, all in carnelian. (b) String of red jasper spheroid beads with twelve oyster-shell pendants (see Cat. no. 170), two cylinder beads of red jasper, two ring beads of green felspar and five carnelian cowroid beads. (c) String of graduated spheroid beads of carnelian.

Gift of Cyril Aldred. Fitzwilliam E.5–6.1979, E.10.1979. (a) L: 46.8 cm. (b) L: 48.0 cm. (c) L: 54.3 cm.

166a, b, c

167 CARNELIAN SCARABS

Dynasties XII–XIII, 1963–1650 BC.

Five uninscribed scarabs of carnelian strung together. The details of the beetles' heads and wing cases are summarily incised on the back.

Bequest of Sir Robert Greg. Fitzwilliam E.676–80.1954. L: from 2.2 to 1.9 cm. W: from 1.6 to 1.3 cm.

These scarabs were purchased by Greg in Cairo and Luxor in 1944 and 1945, and have been restrung in the Museum. The provenance of none of them is known. Plain scarabs in hard stones such as carnelian, obsidian and amethyst are considered characteristic of Middle Kingdom jewellery, but it has been suggested that they are in fact common only in Dynasty XII, and then only up to the end of the reign of Amenemhat III (G. T. Martin, personal communication). The reason for this is that expeditions to the mines in the Eastern and Western deserts became less frequent, so the supply of the rarer stones – amethyst, jasper and felspar, for example – dwindled. Most of the hard stone scarabs have uninscribed bases, but G. T. Martin has suggested that many bases may originally have been covered in sheet gold carrying the inscription, see Cat. no. 179. Gold was the prime target for tomb robbers, so the gold would have been ripped away and the scarab, valueless to the robber, left behind.

The scarab was as much an amulet as a jewel. The scarab beetle was a symbol of regeneration and typified the transformation which the dead had to undergo to pass from this life to the Afterlife.

167

168 AMETHYST BEADS AND SCARABS

Dynasties XII–XIII, 1963–1650 BC.

(a) Five uninscribed amethyst scarabs. The backs are incised to represent the beetles' heads and wing cases. (b) String of graduated spheroid beads and three uninscribed scarabs of amethyst.

Bequest of Sir Robert Greg. Fitzwilliam E.500a–e.1954, E.498.1954. (a) L: from 2.6 to 1.6 cm. W: from 1.8 to 1.0 cm. (b) L: 60.0 cm.

Amethyst was extremely popular for beads and scarabs during the Middle Kingdom, but is rarely found thereafter. Its place may have been taken by amethyst-coloured 'faience', which began to be produced in the late XVIIIth Dynasty. Brunton suggested that amethyst beads were even more restricted in date and were popular only from the reign of Senusret II. The suggestion needs testing against a larger body of material than that available to Brunton, but individual beads of amethyst exist which are inscribed with the

168a, b

name of Senusret I. Given the amuletic power of royal names, and of that royal name in particular, the inscriptions may not be strictly contemporary with the King's reign, however.

See Andrews, *Jewellery*, pp. 95–6, Appendix V; Ward, *Scarab Seals*, I, pp. 84–6; G. Brunton, *Matmar* (London, 1948), pp. 55–6; J. R. Harris, *Lexicographical Studies in Ancient Egyptian Minerals* (Berlin, 1961), pp. 121–2.

169 HAEMATITE BEADS

Dynasty XII, 1963–1787 BC.

String of graduated barrel beads of haematite.

Bequest of Sir Robert Greg. Fitzwilliam E.501.1954. L: 44.5 cm.

Haematite was used occasionally for beads and amulets, and much more commonly for the sticks used to apply eye paint, see Cat. no. 149. This is an exceptionally fine string of beads and reflects Sir Robert Greg's particular interest in the Egyptian craftsman's skill in the cutting and polishing of hard stones.

169

170 SCARABS OF GREEN JASPER AND OBSIDIAN

Dynasty XII, 1963–1787 BC.

(a) String of seven green jasper scarabs. They are uninscribed but the backs are carved and incised to represent the beetles' heads and wing cases. (b) String of three obsidian scarabs, also uninscribed but similarly carved on the back.

Bequest of Sir Robert Greg. Fitzwilliam Museum (a) E.671–5,683–4.1954 (b) E.686–7,689.1954 (a) L: from 1.8 to 3.2 cm. W: from 0.7 to 1.3 cm. (b) L: from 1.6 to 1.9 cm. W: from 1.0 to 1.3 cm.

In the New Kingdom large scarabs of these materials were placed in the chest cavity after the body had been mummified. In this way the perishable and volatile human heart was replaced with these symbols of rebirth made in enduring stone of the propitious colours of the fertile earth, black and green. They were also inscribed with a magic spell intended to help the deceased to pass through the weighing-of-the-heart ritual in the Judgement of the Dead. The practice of placing a scarab in the chest cavity was not carried out in the funerary rituals of the Middle Kingdom, as far as we know, but the ideas behind it may well have been current. A minor official of the XIth Dynasty, Wah, whose intact burial was found at Thebes, had a large scarab of lapis lazuli placed among the wrappings of his mummy.

For the uses and sources of obsidian, see Cat. no. 15; for the scarab of Wah, Hayes, *Scepter*, I, p. 231.

170a

170b

AMULETS

171 OYSTER SHELLS WITH NAME OF KING SENUSRET I

Reign of King Senusret I, 1943–1899 BC.

Three shells (a)–(c) of the oyster *avicula (meleagrina) margaritacea*, with the outer surface removed to reveal the mother of pearl coating. Two holes have been drilled for suspension through the thickest part of each shell, and (c) also shows three tiny holes near the edge, marking the site of an

171a

ancient repair. All three shells have had their edges ground to produce a uniform circular outline. Shells (a) and (b) have been incised with the throne name of Senusret I in a cartouche, and (c) with his personal name, also in a cartouche. The cutting is of high quality, the signs being elegantly shaped and their spacing within the cartouche well judged. In (a) and (b) the *ka* sign is characterised by two tiny vertical strokes in the middle of the horizontal bar. There are traces of blue pigment within the hieroglyphs of shell (b).

(a) Bequest of Sir Robert Mond. British Museum EA.65268. (b) From Abydos. Ex Macgregor collection. Bequest of E. Towry-Whyte. Fitzwilliam E.270.1932. (c) Fitzwilliam E.203.1900. (a) H: 11.3 cm. W: 11.3 cm (b) H: 10.1 cm. W: 10.6 cm. (c) H: 9.9 cm. W: 10.4 cm.

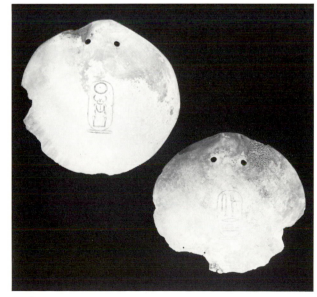

171b, c

153

Roughly fifty examples of these natural oyster-shell pendants exist world-wide in public and private collections, and most of them are inscribed with the names of Kings of Dynasty XII, the most popular name being that of Senusret I. They were probably imported into Egypt from the Red Sea Coast, where this species of oyster is still common. Winlock produced a preliminary study of the pendants in 1932, in which, while admitting the evidence was extremely slender, he suggested that they were worn as military insignia during the reign of Senusret I. One problem is that only one excavated example has been reported found in position lying on the breast of the body, and the excavation from which it comes was never fully published. The body was also accompanied by a dagger, but that hardly proves the burial to have been that of a professional soldier. Another shell was found, but out of position, on the body of a man who may have been an archer, but it came from an unpublished, illicit excavation.

Since Winlock wrote, more shells inscribed for later Kings have come to light, and Aldred has rightly linked them with the smaller shells made in precious metals (see Cat. no. 158), also often ornamented with the names of Kings. The name of a King, especially such a one as Senusret I, was a powerful amulet in itself and was worn as a protective charm by both the living and the dead. Not all shell pendants were necessarily contemporary with the King whose name they bear, but there is every reason to suppose that these three shells were contemporary, or at least belonged to the earlier XIIth Dynasty. The ka sign on two of the shells is written with two small upright strokes in the middle of the horizontal bar. These marks are not uncommon in Middle Kingdom inscriptions, both on stelae and on small objects such as scarabs. Fischer has suggested that they are particularly common in Dynasty XIII, but since they occur widely on dated stelae of early to mid Dynasty XII (reigns of Senusret I to Amenemhat II) as well as later, their appearance is not itself evidence of a late date.

Aldred describes a calcareous film which he found covering the surface and the incised signs on a similar shell bearing the name of Amenemhat II. This film convinced him of the shell's authenticity despite the unskilled cutting of the inscription. Shells (b) and (c) have been examined under magnification and show the same thin limestone deposit spreading over the surface of the incisions.

(a) I. E. S. Edwards in *BMQ* 14 (1940), no. 1, p. 4, pl. v, 1. (b) *The Macgregor Collection, Sotheby's Sale Catalogue*, 26 June–6 July 1922, lot. no. 719; for general discussion, H. E. Winlock in *Studies presented to F. Ll. Griffith* (Oxford, 1932), pp. 388–92, pls. 61–2; C. Aldred in *JEA* 38 (1952), pp. 130–2; Downes, *Esna*, p. 59, fig. 30.

172 CYLINDER BEADS INCISED WITH KINGS' NAMES

Dynasty XII, 1963–1787 BC.

Three hollow cylinder beads (a), (b) and (c), carved out of steatite and glazed. Each has been incised with the name of a King placed inside a cartouche. Bead (a) has the throne

172a, b, c

name of Senusret I, (b) the throne name of Amenemhat II and the name of Sobek, Lord of Sumenu and (c) the personal name Amenemhat, beloved of Sobek, Lord of Senet. The form of the ka sign in (a) is the same as that on the oyster shells, Cat. nos. 171a, b.

(a), (b) Gift of Sir Herbert Thompson. Fitzwilliam E.2–3.1920. (c) From Armant, Δ67. Gift of the Egypt Exploration Society. Fitzwilliam E.69.1940. (a) H: 2.3 cm. W: 0.5 cm. (b) H: 2.3 cm. W: 0.5 cm (c) H: 2.0 cm. W: 0.4 cm.

Royal names were names of power and frequently worn on amulets strung around the neck or attached to the person by some means. These cylinders may also have been used as seals. Rolled over a lump of soft mud, they would have reproduced the name, whose power would have protected the closure of the document, jar or box to which the sealing was attached. It is unlikely that (a) was ever used for this purpose, since the glaze has filled up the signs.

Two of the beads, (b) and (c), also bear the name of the crocodile god Sobek, so popular in Dynasties XII–XIII, see Cat. no. 109; they mention two different cult-places: Sumenu, which is probably to be identified with Rizeiqât near Gebelein, and Senet, which is Esna, also in Upper Egypt. It is interesting that cylinder bead (c) was found in a Middle Kingdom cemetery at Armant, not far north of Esna. Brovarski has listed fifty-two cult-places of the god Sobek throughout Egypt which occur in Middle Kingdom documents. This astonishing number may be explained by the fact that local crocodile cults were being assimilated into the single cult of Sobek at this time. The stimulus towards their assimilation may have been royal patronage, which is thought to date from the reign of Amenemhat II (see (b)), since it is his name that the earliest cylinder beads linking a royal name with that of Sobek carry. The writing of Sumenu follows the XIIth as opposed to the XIIIth Dynasty style, so all three cylinder beads were probably made in the XIIth Dynasty, even if they were not all strictly contemporary with the Kings whose names they bear. Cylinder bead (c) may refer to any of the Kings of Dynasty XII named Amenemhat, other than Amenemhat I.

See J. Yoyotte in *BIFAO* 66 (1957), pp. 81–95; E. Brovarski in *LÄ*, v, 998–1003, n. 93.

173 THE EYE OF HORUS

Dynasties XII–XIII, 1963–1650 BC.

Three amulets (a)–(c), representing the Sacred Eye of the god Horus, symbol of wholeness and wellbeing, see Cat. no. 68. Amulet (a) is made of electrum wire with two suspension rings soldered to the eyebrow; (b) is mould-made in Egyptian blue, see Cat. no. 164a; (c) is carved out of steatite and glazed turquoise green. Amulets (b) and (c) are pierced horizontally for stringing.

Bequest and gift of R. G. Gayer-Anderson. Fitzwilliam EGA.154.1947, EGA.1728–9.1943. (a) H: 2.1 cm. W: 2.4 cm.; (b) H: 1.3 cm. W: 1.6 cm.; (c) H: 1.4 cm. W: 1.6 cm.

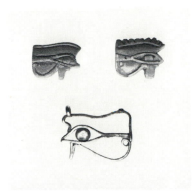 

173a, b, c

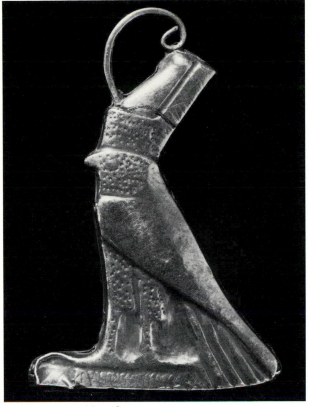

174 [almost twice life size]

174 GOLD HORUS AMULET

Dynasty XII, 1963–1787 BC.

Amulet of the god Horus as a hawk wearing the crown of Upper and Lower Egypt. It is made of thick sheet metal pressed over a positive mould. The curl and the upper part of the crown have been made separately and soldered into place. The lower part of the crown and the face and legs of the hawk have been decorated by means of a punch. The claws of the birds have been suggested by a series of vertical incised lines.

From Abydos, Frankfort excavations of 1925–6, tomb 817. University College 16229. H: 6.1 cm. W: 4.0 cm.

One of the epithets of Pharaoh was 'Horus, upon the Throne of the Living'. The King was identified with the god Horus, and in the same way his predecessor, usually his father, was identified with Osiris, the father of Horus. Horus, the archetype of the Egyptian King, is often shown wearing the royal crowns. Here he wears the crown which combines those of Upper and Lower Egypt. The amulet is flat on the underside and no visible means of attachment survives. Perhaps it was originally part of a breast ornament, the motif being a common one in pectorals, or perhaps it was always intended simply to lie within the wrappings around the body. The tomb from which it comes was never published.

For the cemetery, H. Frankfort in *JEA* 14 (1928), pp. 235–45, pls. XX–XXIII; 16 (1930), pp. 213–19, pls. XXX–XL.

175 THREE GOLD AMULETS

Dynasties XII–XIII, 1963–1650 BC.

Amulets in the form of the ibis, the bird sacred to Thoth, god of wisdom, and the hieroglyphic sign meaning 'millions of years'. The ibis, (a), has been made by joining together two pieces of sheet metal. The tip of the wing has been fitted inside along the join, like the fins of the fish, Cat. nos. 159–60, and there is no sign of a core. The figure has been soldered on to a stand, and a ring for attachment has been soldered to the back. The bodies of the hieroglyphs, (b), (c), have been modelled from sheet metal and the arms, the year-signs which they hold and the base line made out of gold wire.

(a) Bequest Sir Robert Greg. (b) Gift of Mrs M. Acworth. (c) Gift of C. Ricketts and C. Shannon. Fitzwilliam

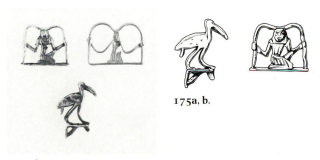

175a, b.

175a, b, c

155

E.626.1954, E.4.1954 and E.86c.1937 respectively. (a) H: 1.9 cm. W: 1.3 cm. (b) H: 1.3 cm. W: 1.5 cm. (c) H: 1.4 cm. W: 1.8 cm.

Thoth, god of wisdom, was also a master of magic, responsible for healing the eye of the god, Horus, see Cat. no. 68; his image was therefore a popular choice for amulets at all periods. The hieroglyphic signs were among those frequently used as charms for good fortune. Others were the *ankh* sign, meaning 'life', and the *nefer* sign, meaning 'good' or 'beautiful'.

176 AMULETS OF STEATITE, 'FAIENCE', CARNELIAN AND AMETHYST

Dynasties XII–XIII, 1963–1650 BC.

Amulets in the form of (a) a crocodile in glazed steatite, (b) a lion *couchant* in white Egyptian faience, (c) the head of a hippopotamus in carnelian, (d) a standing hippopotamus in calcite and (e) a figurine of Ipy, the goddess who took pregnant women under her protection, in amethyst. The lion figurine was first moulded, then the details were accentuated with a sharp tool.

(a), (d) Bequest of Sir Robert Greg. (b), (c) Gift and bequest of R. G. Gayer-Anderson. (e) Ex collection of Countess Pes di Villamarina. Gift of Sir W. P. Elderton. Fitzwilliam

E.443.1954, EGA.1945.1943, EGA.226c.1949, E.360.1954, E.36.1955, respectively. (a) L: 1.5 cm. W: 0.5 cm. (b) L: 2.8 cm. W: 1.6 cm. (c) L: 1.9 cm. W: 1.0 cm. (d) L: 3.2 cm. W: 2.0 cm. (e) H: 1.7 cm. W: 1.0 cm.

The subjects of these amulets are already familiar from their representations on magic knives and rods, and as small statuettes and figurines. For the crocodile, see Cat. nos. 104, 109, 172; for the lion, Cat. nos. 103, 104, 106; for the hippopotami, Cat. nos. 111–12. Ipy, called Thueris in the New Kingdom, was a composite of the three most powerful animals in the group: lion, hippopotamus and crocodile. She is represented as a pregnant hippopotamus standing upright, with the back of a crocodile and the paws of a lion. This fearsome-looking creature is wholly beneficent, the bringer of children to barren women, the protector of women during pregnancy and childbirth and of children during the first years of life.

For them to be effective it was important that these amulets should be worn close to the body, and most of them were worn around the neck; see Cat. no. 165b, which is a necklace incorporating a hippopotamus-head amulet. Some bracelets show how small lion amulets were fitted into them to be worn on the wrist.

(e) *Sotheby's Sale Catalogue*, 10 April 1934, lot no. 11; for the lion bracelets, cf. Aldred, *Jewels of the Pharaohs*, pls. 34, 44; for Ipy, see Ward, *Scarab Seals*, I, p. 63.

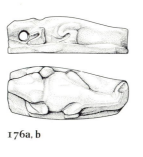

176d   177

176a, b

176e, c

176d

177 BABOON AMULET

Dynasty XII, 1963–1787 BC.

Figurine of a baboon carved from rock crystal. There is a hole drilled through the back of the head for stringing. The carving of this extremely hard material is schematic and the surface is also considerably worn.

Gift of G. D. Hornblower. Fitzwilliam E.121.1939. H: 3.6 cm. W: 1.6 cm.

As one of the dispensers of protective magic, the baboon appears frequently on magic knives, see Cat. no. 102. Like the monkey it may have suggested the force of human sexuality, and this would explain its other frequent use as decoration for cosmetic objects.

SCARABS

178 SCARABS OF STEATITE

Dynasty XI, 2023–1963 BC.

Two scarabs of glazed steatite, (a, b). Scarab (a) has a spiral pattern on its underside and (b) a stylised floral pattern. In both cases the back and legs of the beetle, *Scarabaeus sacer*, are shown in detail and the legs are cut out from the base.

(a) Gift of G. D. Hornblower; (b) from Matmar, tomb 307. Gift of the British Museum. Fitzwilliam E.439.1939, E.119.1931. (a) W: 1.9 cm. L: 2.3 cm. (b) W: 1.7 cm. L: 2.3 cm.

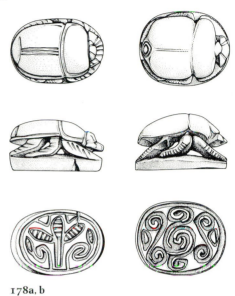

178a, b

Scarabs were potent amulets because they were made in the image of the god Khepri, 'He who came into existence by himself', and on the underside they carried mottoes or designs to bring good luck. The ability to reproduce itself which the beetle *Scarabaeus sacer* acquired for the Egyptians was based on a mistaken interpretation of a common sight. The female beetle was observed to push a ball of dung before her, from which emerged the young beetles. The fertilisation and laying of the eggs in the dung was not noticed. The analogy between the ball of dung being rolled along the ground and the sun passing across the heavens was also drawn, and this explains the role of the beetle god in assisting the dead to pass through darkness into the Next World.

The designs on early scarabs such as these occur first on seal amulets, which originate in the late Old Kingdom. Scarab (b) comes from a grave at Matmar in Middle Egypt. The grave was probably disturbed and the only other object found was a pottery vessel. The excavator, Brunton, dated the grave to the period immediately before the XIth Dynasty, but in my view this is too early. The pottery suggests an early XIth Dynasty date, as represented by the material from the el-Tarif cemetery at Thebes.

G. Brunton, *Matmar* (London, 1948), pl. XXXIII, 86.

179 SCARAB RING OF KING AMENEMHAT III 1843–1798 BC. Illustrated in colour on pl. IV,1.

Carnelian scarab mounted on a gold base plate and threaded with gold wire. The base plate is inscribed with the throne name of King Amenemhat III, followed by the phrase 'given life'. The hieroglyphic signs are elegantly cut and carefully spaced. The back of the scarab shows spots of white where the carnelian has begun to decay and the discoloration makes the style of the back hard to identify. However, the head, eyes, clypeus and division between the prothorax and the wing cases are visible, suggesting that the beetle body has been treated in a naturalistic way.

From a private collection. W: 1.1 cm L: 1.7 cm.

Finger rings, the majority with scarab bezels, first appear in Egypt during the XIIth Dynasty among the royal jewels of the Queens and Princesses buried at Dahshur and Lahun. This scarab ring in material, quality and style matches them closely. Their common characteristics are that the scarab is cut out of hard stone and the beetle back is either rendered naturalistically as here, or elaborately inlaid. They are mounted simply on gold wire, the ends twisted around the centre of the shank in imitation of the original string tie. The later rings, Cat. no. 180, show more skilled treatment of the shank. Finally, several are fixed like this example on a gold plate inscribed with a royal name.

The similarity of this ring to the group from contemporary royal burials of the late XIIth Dynasty rules out the possibility that the scarab and its plate were made after Amenemhat III's reign in commemoration of him. Moreover the inscription contains the phrase 'given life' which is usually applied to the name of the reigning Pharaoh (Gardiner, *Grammar*, paragraph 378).

The provenance of this ring is unknown but it was surely made in a royal workshop. In addition to royal examples, a few gold-plated scarab rings inscribed with the names of private persons are known. Of those listed in Martin's corpus, all belong to officials with titles linking them to the King's Residence or come from sites like Lisht, situated close to it.

For material, see comments on Cat. no. 167; cf. Aldred, *Jewels of the Pharaohs*, pl. 46; Wilkinson, *Egyptian Jewellery*, pp. 76–8; Martin, *Seals*, p. 193.

180 SCARAB RINGS

Dynasties XII–XIII, 1963–1650 BC.

Three scarabs (a–c) made of glazed steatite and set in gold bezels with gold hoops. Scarab (c) has gold wire twisted around the hoop in imitation of string. The designs on the undersides are (a) spirals and *nefer* signs, (b) a pattern using hieroglyphs and (c) interlaced coils. The backs of the beetles are much more simply reproduced than those in Cat. no. 178.

(a), (b) Bequest of R. G. Gayer-Anderson. (c) Bequest of Sir Robert Greg. Fitzwilliam E.2,7.1947, E.616.1954. (a) W: 1.4 cm. L: 2.1 cm. (b) W: 1.2 cm. L: 1.6 cm. (c) W: 1.1 cm. L: 1.6 cm.

157

180a, b, c

It is possible that these scarabs were used as seals in the same way that some cylinder beads were, see Cat. no. 172. Because sun-dried mud is surprisingly hard, many seal impressions have survived, and these show that scarabs with such designs were frequently used to seal the string ties on boxes, jars or documents, or impressed into the cones of mud used to seal large storage jars. The seal may not have been intended to function as a signature, but merely to demonstrate that the closure was intact.

Every Egyptian collection of any size has hundreds of scarabs in its possession, and they have been studied in considerable detail for at least a century. Nevertheless, they are still difficult to date precisely, partly because no single method of classification is accepted by everyone and partly because so few come from datable contexts. Classification has to be based on the style of the beetle itself, i.e. the treatment of back, legs and head, and on the design and/or inscription on the base. Where this inscription is a royal name (see Cat. nos. 179, 180), or a private name or title which can be independently dated (see Cat. nos. 182–3), a starting point for dating exists. However, scarabs are easily portable and one major complicating factor is our ignorance of how long they were in circulation before being buried, either by accident or by intentional deposition in a tomb. Scarabs provide the archaeologist with joys and frustrations similar to those presented by coins.

181 SCARABS OF TWO XIIITH DYNASTY KINGS

Neferhotep I to Merneferre Ay, c. 1730–1690 BC.

Two glazed steatite scarabs, (a) inscribed the 'Good god, Khasechemre (Neferhotep I) born of the god's father Haᶜnkhef' and (b) inscribed for Merneferre, with an *ankh* and a *nefer* sign filling up the space beside the cartouche. The design of both bases is similar, the royal name in a cartouche having been placed on the left side and the space beside it filled up, in one case with a genealogical inscription and in the other with hieroglyphs meaning 'life', and 'good'. The bodies of the scarab beetles are treated differently, and this is most evident in the profile views. The Neferhotep I scarab is larger, the head and legs are treated more naturalistically, and the back is arched, not flat as in the Merneferre example.

Gifts of (a) R. G. Gayer-Anderson and (b) Sir Herbert Thompson, Fitzwilliam EGA.607.1943, E.16.1920. (a) W: 1.7 cm. L: 2.3 cm. (b) W: 1.3 cm. L: 1.8 cm.

Scarabs inscribed with royal names are the basis of all scarab classifications. These two Kings each ruled for a comparatively short time, so it is unsurprising firstly that their scarabs show a stylistic homogeneity, and secondly that their posthumous reputation was not so great as to encourage the issue or circulation of scarabs with their names long after their deaths.

These two Kings are separated by roughly twenty-five years, according to von Beckerath's reconstruction of the chronology of Dynasty XIII. It is interesting to note that while the general design of the base had changed only slightly, significant changes had taken place in the treatment of the beetle's body, the major one being a decrease in size. That this change is a systematic one is confirmed by a study of the whole corpus of scarabs inscribed for these two Kings.

Two shared features of the base design may be noted. The delicate, controlled cutting apparent on earlier scarabs (see Cat. no. 179) has gone. The hieroglyphs are clumsy and badly spaced and the stone-cutter's line is thick and unsteady. The other characteristic is the crowding of the surface with signs and the over-elaboration of certain details, such as the double line around Neferhotep's cartouche. The same dislike of empty space is noticeable in the stelae of the period, see Cat. nos. 48, 49.

Cf. Tufnell, *Scarab Seals*, II (Part I), pp. 158–9, pls. LIV, 3116, 3127, LV, 3181–2, 3185, 3190; for (a) cf. Martin, *Seals*, nos. 919–37, pl. 26 [1–16].

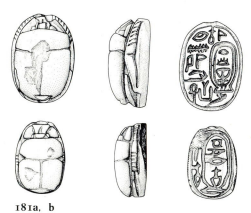

181a, b

182 SCARABS OF XIIITH DYNASTY OFFICIALS

Mid-Dynasty XIII, c. 1740–1720 BC.

Three glazed steatite scarabs, (a–c). Scarab (a) is inscribed for 'the royal seal bearer, sole companion and treasurer, Senebsuema'; (b) for 'the deceased Nebresehwy', a man with the same titles as Senebsuema; (c) for 'the royal seal bearer and high steward 'Aki'. The arrangement of the inscription is similar on all three scarabs. The most important title comes at the top, read from right to left; below it are the signs giving the name and the remaining titles or epithets. These are arranged very roughly in two columns and are to be read from top to bottom of the scarab. The signs themselves display the same clumsy cutting and poor spacing noted in Cat.

nos. 181a, b. The representation of the beetle bodies is similar to Cat. no. 181a in size as well as in details of back and profile. Scarabs (a) and (c) show a double instead of a single line separating the elytra (the wing cases), and the feathering of the back as well as the front legs is shown in scarab (c).

(a) Gift of Sir Herbert Thompson. Fitzwilliam E.94.1920, E.SC.170, E.SC.41. (a) W: 1.2 cm. L: 2.1 cm. (b) W: 1.0 cm. L: 2.3 cm. (c) W: 1.0 cm. L: 2.2 cm.

Senebsuema and Nebresehwy both held the office of treasurer, one of the most powerful in the government, and worked close to the King. They were responsible for all sealed (i.e. valuable) goods, so it is not surprising that their own seals should have been issued in considerable numbers. More than thirty scarabs of Senebsuema and eight of Nebresehwy have survived. Of the scarabs of Senebsuema only two come from excavations: one is from the town of Kahun, the other from the North cemetery at Lisht, both sites lying close to the Residence of the Kings of the XIIIth Dynasty at *Itj-Tawy*.

Senebsuema's scarabs fall into two stylistic groups distinguished both by the design of the base inscription and by the treatment of the beetle body. He is thought to have been a contemporary of the brother Kings Neferhotep I and Sobekhotep IV, although there is no direct evidence linking him to them, and it is interesting to note that both of Seneb-suema's types can be paralleled among the scarabs of these Kings. The larger of his two groups, consisting of twenty-nine scarabs, and to which scarab (a) belongs, is remarkably homogeneous, only two showing a slight variation of the base design.

Nebresehwy's eight scarabs also fall into two groups, but in this case the difference lies only in the base inscription. In one group of four scarabs, to which (b) belongs, the epithet 'true of voice', i.e. deceased, is included, and the form of the hieroglyph (022 in Gardiner's signlist) with which his name is written is different. It may or may not be significant that

the only excavated scarab of Nebresehwy is in this group and comes from the North Pyramid cemetery at Lisht. It has been suggested that these 'funerary' scarabs were worn simply as amulets, and that the identification of the scarab with the god Khepri (see Cat. no. 178) was never forgotten. It certainly seems that they were never used as seals, since no mud sealings have been found inscribed 'true of voice'. Nebresehwy's name means 'Lord of Re-sehwy', which was the temple at Lahun in the Faiyum of the crocodile god Sobek, so much favoured in the Middle Kingdom, see Cat. no. 109.

Seven scarabs and a group of five seal impressions survive of 'Aki. One scarab, (c), comes from the North Pyramid cemetery at Lisht, and the mud sealings from a townsite at Tukh, between Dendera and Luxor in Upper Egypt. The scarabs form a homogeneous group, although clearly not cut by the same hand. 'Aki held the same title as Nemtyem-weskhet (see Cat. nos. 50, 74), and although an important official, was not of the highest rank, as were the two treasurers.

(a) Martin, *Seals*, no. 1530, pl. 21 [26]; Franke, *Personendaten*, dossier 667; (b) Martin, *Seals*, no. 667, pl. 23 [4]; Budge, *Catalogue*, p. 97, no. 155; (c) Martin, *Seals*, no. 374, pl. 27 [21]; Budge, *Catalogue*, p. 97, no. 157; P. Newberry, *Scarabs* (London, 1906), p. 132, no. 10, pl. XIII, 10; Franke, *Personendaten*, dossier 192; for funerary function of scarabs, see B. Williams and J. Johnson in *Seals and Sealing in the Ancient Near East* (Malibu, 1977), pp. 137, 142.

183 SCARABS OF NEHY AND RENEFSENEB
Late Dynasty XIII, 1740–1650 BC.

Two steatite scarabs, (a) and (b), inscribed for the overseer of the interior of the inner palace, Nehy, and the scribe of the vizier, Renefseneb, respectively. The style of the hieroglyphs and their arrangement follows that of Cat. nos. 182a–c, but the treatment of the beetle body differs. Scarab (a) shows a greatly simplified representation of the back and profile, compared with Cat. no. 182a; the division between the elytra is not marked (the vertical stroke on the back is accidental) and the one between the prothorax and the elytra is marked by two horizontal notches only. The feathering on the legs is not shown at all. Scarab (b) is a simpler version of the general back and profile type of Cat.

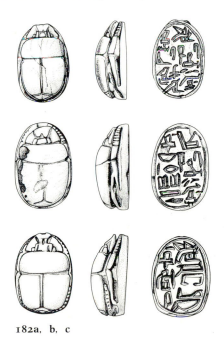

182a, b, c

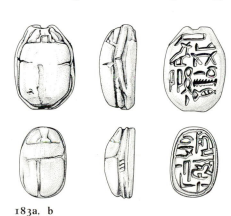

183a, b

159

nos. 181–2. The head of the beetle in particular shows a simpler outline and the legs are very shallowly cut. Scarab (b) was originally covered with a brilliant turquoise glaze.

(a) Ex Rev. Greville Chester collection, (b) Gift of Sir Herbert Thompson. Fitzwilliam E.SC.180, E.23.1920. (a) W: 1.6 cm. L: 2.2 cm. (b) W: 1.3 cm. L: 1.8 cm.

Nehy held an office in the royal palace similar to that of Shesmuhotep, whose statuette is Cat. no. 43, but he worked in the inner palace where the women and children of the royal family and the court lived. Among his duties were the ordering and collection of provisions for the people living in this secluded part of the palace. It is interesting to note that the title on the scarab is much more specific than that on the statuette of Shesmuhotep, Cat. no. 43, and this reflects the trend towards a more precise definition of officials' responsibilities that we can observe in the course of the XIIIth Dynasty. The back type belongs, I would suggest, to Martin's type 10 rather than to his type 6, and this has implications for the dating of the scarab, since Martin dates type 10 to the period following the XIIIth Dynasty, the Second Intermediate period. My own view, based on the corpus of scarabs found at Lisht, suggests a long overlap between his types 6 and 10, so that type 10 was in circulation there long before the end of Dynasty XIII.

Renefseneb was one of the large number of scribes who served the vizier, highest official in the government and the equivalent of the Prime Minister in our state. As seems clear from the drawing, I would suggest the scarab belongs to Martin's back type 8L rather than 6c, but this does not affect the dating.

(a) Martin, *Seals*, no. 764, pl. 22 [15]; Budge, *Catalogue*, p. 97, no. 154; P. Newberry, *Scarabs* (London, 1906), p. 133, pl. XIII, 11; (b) Martin, *Seals*, no. 853, pl. 30 [12]; Newberry, *op. cit.*, p. 125, pl. XI, 3.

METALWORK

184 COPPER BOWL

Late Dynasty XII to Dynasty XIII, 1862–1650 BC.

Hammered copper bowl with a carinated profile and a footed base. The thickness of the vessel wall varies considerably and where it is thinnest, at the base, a small hole has occurred. The tool marks are visible on all surfaces of the bowl.

From Kahun, found in basket no. 200. Manchester 206. H: 6.1 cm. D: 13.7 cm.

Petrie describes finding this sturdy bowl in a basket discarded in the corner of a room in the town of Kahun. With it were several copper chisels and hatchets, so we may presume the basket to have belonged to a metalworker, perhaps the man who made the bowl.

The shape is a familiar one, versions appearing in pottery, see Cat. no. 135b, and 'faience', see Cat. no. 126. The contexts in which pottery bowls of this shape occur indicate a late Middle Kingdom date, from the reign of Amenemhat III

184

onwards. The sharply carinated profile suggests that the metal version may be the prototype from which the pottery and 'faience' bowls were copied.

Petrie, *Kahun*, p. 26, pl. XVII, 7.

185 MIRROR WITH HATHOR HEAD HANDLE

Late Dynasty XII to Dynasty XIII, 1862–1650 BC.

Mirror with an elliptical copper disk and carved wooden handle. The shaft of the handle is in the shape of a thick papyrus stalk and the top is carved to represent the goddess Hathor, cf. Cat. no. 127. The same image is carved on both the front and the back of the handle. It is the face of a woman with the ears of a cow, which is the form in which Hathor is regularly depicted, but the proportions of the face are different from the usual representations. The forehead is extremely high, the face long and the ears exceptionally small. She wears the so-called 'Hathor wig', see Cat. nos. 14, 37. The two side bunches of hair terminate in fat curls which may originally have been inlaid with coloured disks. The handle of the mirror shows considerable signs of wear and is shiny through handling.

From Kahun. Manchester 189. Mirror disk: H: 11.8 cm. W: 13.3 cm. Handle: H: 14.0 cm. W: 4.1 cm.

Close dating of this mirror depends on our interpretation of the sparse information provided by Petrie about its discovery in 1889–90. He states that he found the handle in one room of a house and the mirror disk in the next room. He publishes a large group of objects found with the handle and which he clearly thought contemporary with it, but it is clear that he simply treated each room in the houses at Kahun as a single archaeological unit. We may assume that in the roughly two hundred years of the town's existence, the houses were modified many times: walls were rebuilt, pits dug and new floors laid, sealing in old rubbish. This sequence of building was not recorded by Petrie (it is hard to see how it could have been, since he cleared over two thousand rooms in the course of two seasons' work). Thus we must presume that the objects he apparently found

185

186 MIRROR INSCRIBED FOR MONTUEMHAT

Early Dynasty XII, 1963–1862 BC.

Mirror with an elliptical copper disk and a carved handle of glazed steatite. The handle imitates a papyrus stalk and flower. The inscription is incised around the slit in the top of the flower which takes the tang of the mirror, and names 'the deceased, Montuemhat son of Heqaib'. The glaze is a deep turquoise green, showing up as black where it has fallen into cracks in the steatite. The resulting marbled effect compares with Cat. no. 127, and may have been intentional, since it is copied in 'faience', see Cat. no. 129.

From Thebes. Ex Salt collection. British Museum EA. 2736. Disk (including tang): H: 14.3 cm. W: 14.1 cm. Handle: H: 11.8 cm. W: 5.0 cm.

The choice of personal names and the epithet used to express the meaning 'deceased' suggest an early XIIth Dynasty date for this mirror.

Oliver Myers carried out an experiment with an ancient Egyptian mirror to test its reflective quality. While the image was not as sharp as that given by a modern shaving mirror, it was surprisingly good and would have been further

together were not necessarily contemporary but could have been deposited at any time during the town's history. One of the objects found in the room with the handle was a copper torque which Christine Lilyquist uses as evidence to suggest that the mirror may date after Dynasty XII. Since in my view the objects do not come from a closed deposit, the torque may or may not be relevant to the date of the mirror.

The image of Hathor on the handle is explained by the close association of Hathor, goddess of Love and Beauty, with cosmetic equipment of all kinds. It has been proved that mirrors were more commonly shown being used or carried by women than by men, and this is supported by the evidence of burials, where they occur more often in women's graves. However, this evidence is sometimes vitiated by the fact that the excavator has used the presence or absence of a mirror to indicate the sex of the occupant of the grave!

Petrie, *Illahun*, pp. 12–13, pl. XIII, 8; David, *Pyramid Builders*, pl. 6, pp. 160–1; Lilyquist, *Mirrors*, pp. 35, n. 396, 63, figs. 74–5.

186

improved if all the corrosion could have been removed from the metal disk. In the course of cleaning it he also discovered that one side of the mirror was slightly concave and the other convex, and the concave side provided an enlarged image. If we could establish that this curvature is a regular feature of Middle Kingdom mirrors, we could probably be certain it was done to achieve this effect.

Lilyquist, *Mirrors*, p. 47, n. 529, figs. 42–4; Sir Robert Mond and O. H. Myers, *Cemeteries of Armant*, I (London, 1937), pp. 117–18, pl. XLIV, 1.

187 DAGGER

Dynasties XII–XIII, 1963–1650 BC.

Dagger with copper blade and wooden handle. The handle was probably attached to the blade in modern times. The drawing shows traces of the adhesive used to join the two. The crescent-shaped base of the original handle, possibly of the type shown in Cat. no. 187, is still present, as are the three copper rivets originally fixing it to the blade. The blade tapers to a rounded end, and has a central rib with three incised lines on either side.

From Thebes. Ex Macgregor collection. Bequest of E. Towry-Whyte. Fitzwilliam E.377.1932. H: 28.5 cm. W: 25.0 cm.

The crudely shaped, worn wooden handle looks out of place on this finely worked dagger blade, and certainly no excavated copper dagger has a handle of this type. The sale catalogue of the Macgregor collection simply suggests that 'the handle is probably of later date than the blade'. The handle may be contemporary but part of a model dagger fashioned entirely of wood and made solely for a funeral. Several examples of such wooden daggers have survived, and they are also depicted among the funerary offerings in tomb reliefs and painted scenes on the interior of coffins.

The Macgregor Collection. Sotheby's Sale Catalogue, 26 June–6 July 1922, lot no. 1181, pl. XXXI; cf. Hayes, *Scepter*, I, pp. 283–4, fig. 186; P. Lacau, *Sarcophages Antérieurs au Nouvel Empire*, I (Cairo, 1904), pl. XLIII.

187 and 188

188 DAGGER

Dynasties XII–XIII, 1963–1650 BC.

Dagger with copper blade, copper handle inlaid with rectangular slips of a fine grained dark wood, possibly ebony, and pommel of calcite (?). The handle is attached to the blade and the inlays to the handle by a series of copper pins. The blade tapers to a rounded end and there are six shallow grooves which converge towards the point of the blade.

Museum of Archaeology and Anthropology, Cambridge 1951.716. L: 30.6 cm. W: 5.2 cm.

Daggers of this kind are relatively common, but very few have been excavated from closely dated contexts. What evidence there is suggests the type continued in use throughout the Middle Kingdom and until the beginning of the XVIIIth Dynasty, 1550 BC. The material of which the pommel is made is frequently described on other examples as ivory, but this example appears to be a soft stone, and calcite is tentatively suggested.

The same type of dagger is imitated in wood and depicted among the funerary offerings, see Cat. no. 187.

189 BATTLE AXE

Dynasties XI–XII, 2023–1787 BC.

Copper axe blade originally lashed to a wooden handle with strips of leather. The head of the handle is sheathed in copper and a copper ring below the blade also helps to protect the handle from the impact of a blow.

Gift of the family of F. W. Green. Fitzwilliam E.14.1950. L: 77.0 cm. W: 8.0 cm.

We do not know whether F. W. Green obtained the axe in Egypt or on the art market in London. This axe blade of hemispherical shape evolved from the type in use during the Old Kingdom, and was used both as a weapon and by carpenters and boatbuilders as a tool.

Kühnert-Eggebrecht, *Die Axt*, p. 25, pl. IX [5]; cf. Hayes, *Scepter*, I, p. 283, fig. 185.

190 CEREMONIAL AXE HEAD

Dynasties XI–XII, 2023–1787 BC.

Copper axe blade with a cast openwork design showing two opposing figures of the goddess Ipy (see Cat. no. 176e),

a combination of lion, crocodile and hippopotamus. The ears of the beast have become enlarged so that they look more like horns, and a flaw in casting has resulted in the front foot of the left figure not being joined to the base line.

British Museum EA. 57375. L: 9.4 cm. W: 8.3 cm.

Highly decorated weapons, intended to be worn as indications of rank or used in rituals, appear at all periods of Egyptian history. Nevertheless the goddess Ipy, so closely

190 and 191

associated with the hazards of childbirth (see Cat. nos. 121, 176e), seems a curious choice of motif for an axe. Her sphere as a protective deity was wide, however, and she appears on the side of the throne of a statue of a King of Dynasty XVII in the British Museum (EA 871). The metal of a similarly decorated axe blade in Munich was analysed and found to be 93% copper and 6% arsenic with less than one per cent of lead, silver and nickel.

H. R. Hall in *LAAA* 16 (1929), pp. 23–4, pl. XXV, 2; cf. Kühnert-Eggebrecht, *Die Axt*, pp. 51, 67–8, pl. XX, 1, 2.

191 CEREMONIAL AXE HEAD

Dynasties XI–XII, 2023–1787 BC.

Copper axe blade with a cast openwork design showing a clump of water-lilies (lotuses). Details of the flower petals have been incised in the metal. Two rectangular holes have been cast in the bottom of the axe blade to allow it to be bound to a handle.

University College 30072. H: 7.9 cm. W: 6.6 cm.

Petrie, *Tools and Weapons*, p. 8, pl. IV, 119; Kühnert-Eggebrecht, *Die Axt*, pp. 76–7, pl. XXIII, 3.

189

INDEX OF PRIVATE NAMES AND TITLES

Asterisk indicates a female name

	Cat. no.		Cat. no.		Cat. no.
*ꜣtt-ḥtpt	68	'Intf	91	Ptḥ-šdw	39
*ꜣty-ḥtp	70	'Intf	63	bꜣkt nt ḥqꜣ	
'Iy	39	'Intf 'Iw-snb	63	*Mmi	49
'Iy	50	mty n sꜣ		nbt pr	
tꜣw n sꜣtw		?'Irsi	48	*Mmi	40
'Iy-mry	20	ꜥfty ꜥꜣm		Mnw-ḥtp	40
*?'Iit-n-ḥb	45	'I.t	10	imy-r pr	
'Iw-nfr	76	ḥmt		Mn[t]w[...]	21
imy-r st		'I.t-t	41	ḥtmty bity, smr wꜥty, imy-r mšꜥ	
'Iw-snb	see 'Intf 'Iw-snb	nbt-pr		Mntw-m-ḥꜣt	185
*'Iwrri	52	'I.t-t	41	Mntw-ḥtp	36
ḥkrt-nsw		'It.f-ib	26	wꜥb	
'Ib-iꜥ	45	imy-r mšꜥ(?)		Mntw-ḥtp	36
wꜥb n 'Imn		'I.ty	45	Mntw-ḥtp	10
'Ib-iꜥ	45	'Id	50	ḥm-ntr	
ḥry-sštꜣ n 'Imn		wꜥb		Mntw-ḥtp	40
'Ib-iꜥ	45	'Idi	10	qnbty n w	
ḥtmty bity, imy-r ḥnrt		ḥmt		Mntw-ḥtp	9
'Ib-iꜥ	45	ꜥnwy	22	Mntw-ḥtp	62
sꜣb r Nḥn		imy-r pr		*Mri	50
'Ibi	50	*ꜥnḥyt	20	nbt-pr	
'Ibi	50	ꜥnḥ-n-mr	55	Mri	91
'Ibw	45	iry-pꜥt, ḥꜣty-ꜥ, rḫ nsw, wḥmw nsw		*Mri	36
sꜣb r Nḥn		ꜥqw-m-ꜥ-Ptḥ	39	Mry Kbi	63
'Ip	19	ꜥki	181c	mty n sꜣ	
'Imn-m-ḥꜣt	52	ḥtmty bity, imy-r pr wr		*Mrtyt	40
imy-r st ꜥq n ꜥt dqrw		*ꜥtw	41	nbt pr	
'Imn-m-ḥꜣt	39	*ꜥtw	50	*Msyt	39
mniw		Wꜥ-m-kꜣw	48	*Msy[t?]	45
'Imn-m-ḥꜣt	see Rn.f-ꜥnḥ 'Imn-m-ḥꜣt	Wpwꜣwt-m-ḥꜣw	67	nbt-pr	
'Imn-m-ḥꜣt Nbwy	39	wr swnw		?Mshy	51
imy-r pr n ḥtp-ntr		Wpwꜣwt-n(.i)	48	[Ny-]sw-Mntw	45
'Imn-m-sꜣ.f	45	qfny		ḥbsw(??)	
ḥm-ntr		Wnmw	48	Nb-irwt	49
'Imn-nḫt	45	wꜥb (n 'Inḥrt)		wdpw iry iꜥḥ	
imy-r šnt n(?) ḥwt-ntr		*Wsi-rs	45	Nb-r-sḥwy	181b
'Imn-ḥtp	48	Wsi	see S-n-Wsrt Wsi	ḥtmty bity, smr wꜥty, imy-r ḥtmt	
wꜥb		Wsr-wr	20	Nb-niwt	20
'Imn-ḥtp	45	gnwty		Nb-swmnw	39
sꜣb r Nḥn		Wsr-ht	71, 72	ꜥꜣm	
'Imn-ḥtp	45	ꜥhꜣwty		Nb-swmnw	45
sꜣb r Nḥn		Bb	52	sꜣb r Nḥn	
'Imny	49	sꜣ-nswt		*Nbt-it(.f)	48
iry-ꜥt wdpw		Bbi	45	nbt-pr	
'Imny	62	imy-r pr n ꜣht(?)		*Nbt-Nn-nsw	63
šmsw		*Bbi	1	*Nbt-nḥḥ	48
*'Imny	39	ḥkrt nsw wꜥtt		*Nbt-r-?i	49
'Imny(-snb)	48	*Bb-t	9	*Nbt-t	10
mty n sꜣ n ꜣbdw		Bmbw	52	Nbwy	see 'Imn-m-ḥꜣt Nbwy
?'Inḥrt-ḥtp	81	wr mdw šmꜥ		*Nbw	49
ꜥnḥ n niwt		*Bnrn-it	10	*Nbw-m-mḥ-ib	45
'Intf	91	Ptḥ-wr	49	*Nbw-ḥw-si	48
sḥ		tꜣw n ḥft-ḥr			

164

	Cat. no.		Cat. no.		Cat. no.
*Snt	10	*Kki	50	Dwꜣ-ḥtpi	41
*Snt	61	*Kki	50	Dd-'Imn	45
S[. . .]ˁnḫ.f	45	Kkw	49	_wr mḏw smˁ_	
ḫry-sšt ꜣ n 'Imn		_sḫ n pr-ˁnḫ(?)_		Dd-'Imn	45
Šmꜣ	10	*Ktw	49	_wr mḏw šmˁ_	
Šsmw-ḥtp	43	*ʔKtti	49	Ddw-Sbk Rn-snb	40
imy-r ˁḫnwty		Grḥi	91	_imy-r pr, ḥsb ˁḥˁw_	
*Qdmt	41	_ny-ḏt_		Ddw Nwb	47
Ky	61	Titi	49	*Ddt-Nwb	36
Kbi	63	_ḫtmty bity, imy-r ḫtmtyw, šms nswt_		*Dit.n.s-n.i	45
*Kbi	see Mry Kbi	*Titi	50	_bꜣkt nt ḥqꜣ_	
Kbs	45	_nbt-pr_		NAME LOST	37
šmsw		*Titiw	48	_ḥsy [t] nsw_	
Kmmw	36	*Tti	49	NAME UNCERTAIN	52
Kms	41	*Tꜣ ny(?)	45	_sꜣ-iwn-n-ʔimy-ḫt-pr (?garbled imy-ḫt sꜣ_	
*Ksnt	41	_nbt-pr_		_pr 'Iw-n)_	
nbt-pr					

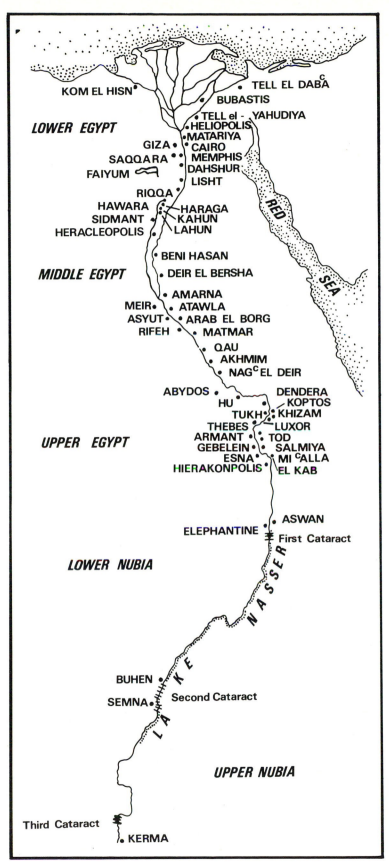